MEDIEVAL LITERATURE FOR CHILDREN

Medieval Literature for Children

Edited by
Daniel T. Kline

Routledge
New York and London

Published in 2003 by
Routledge
29 West 35th Street
New York, NY 10001
www.routledge-ny.com

Published in Great Britain by
Routledge
11 New Fetter Lane
London EC4P 4EE
www.routledge.co.uk

Routledge is an imprint of the Taylor & Francis Group.

Printed in the United States of America on acid-free paper.

Library of Congress Cataloguing-in-Publication Data

Medieval literature for children / edited by Daniel T. Kline.
    p. cm.
    Includes bibliographical references and index.
    Summary: An anthology of medieval children's literature, arranged in
various categories and interspersed with scholarly commentary.
    ISBN 0-8153-3312-9
    1. Literature, Medieval. 2. Children's literature. [1. Literature, Medieval.
2. Children's literature—Collections.] I. Kline, Daniel T.

PZ5 .M5435 2001
808.8'99282'0902—dc21

00-065294

Table of Contents

*For Sam and Jake,
and in memory of Joseph*

Acknowledgments

An anthology is a cooperative venture, and it is my pleasure to thank the individuals and institutions that have helped to bring *Medieval Literature for Children* to fruition. At the 1997 NEH Summer Institute on the Literary Traditions of Medieval Women held at Rice University, Katja Wilson (University of Georgia) initially offered me the opportunity to propose this volume for her series, Medieval Literature at the Margins, and a number of scholars from that institute have generously assisted my various inquiries. In particular, Linda McMillin, Susquehanna University, has been a continued source of encouragement and clear thinking during the project. I have also worked with several editors, but Anne Davidson, Emily Vail, and Matt Byrnie at Routledge shepherded the volume through the difficult final stages of production. Paul Levesque, an extraordinary student of mine at the University of Alaska Anchorage, saved me from many an embarrassing blunder with his thorough proofreading of the manuscript. I also want to thank the University of Alaska Anchorage for a Faculty Research and Development Travel Grant that assisted in the completion of this anthology.

I would like to thank the following institutions for allowing the contributors to *Medieval Literature for Children* to publish the following copyrighted texts and images: to the Council of the Early English Text Society for its permission to publish excerpts from the *Gesta Romanorum* in chapter 2; to the British Library, the Bodleian Library, the Cambridge University Library, the Lambeth Palace Library, the Board of Trinity College Dublin, and the Master and Fellows, Trinity College Cambridge, for permission to consult the manuscripts in chapter 4; to the Lambeth Palace Library and World Microfilms for permission to reproduce MS. 853, p. 31, as figure 1; to the Plimpton Collection, Rare Book and Manuscript Room, Columbia University, for permission to edit Plimpton MS 258 in chapter 9; to the Children's Literature Association for permission to reprint "Chaucer as Teacher," which first appeared in *Children's Literature Association Quarterly*, vol. 23, no. 1, 1998; to the Bodleian Library, University of Oxford, for permission to reproduce figures 21 and 22, images of Eng. Poet a. 1, fols. 124v detail and 125r detail, in chapter 12; to the publisher Boydell & Brewer for permission to transcribe the poems in chapter 12 from the facsimile of *The Vernon Manuscript: A Facsimile of Bodleian Library, Oxford, MS. Eng. Poet. a. I*, Introd. I. A. Doyle (Cambridge: D. S. Brewer, 1987); to the Warden and Fellows of Winchester College for permission to publish an edition of *Occupation and Idelness* from MS Winchester College 33A, ff. 65r–73v in chapter 14; and to the Trustees of the National Library of Scotland for permission to publish an edition of *Sir Gowther* from Adv MS. 19.3.1 in chapter 16.

Medieval Children's Literature: Problems, Possibilities, Parameters

DANIEL T. KLINE

Scholarly interest in the medieval family, and particularly in medieval children's lives, has burgeoned since the publication of Philippe Ariès' *Centuries of Childhood* (1962). Ariès argued that "In medieval society the idea of childhood did not exist" (129), for too many children died (39). Because of this "demographic wastage" (40), the Middle Ages were indifferent to childhood as a concept and a distinct phase of life. In what is fundamentally an extension of Ariès' thesis, many critics reason that if the medieval period had no discrete conception of children or childhood, then it follows that the Middle Ages could not have possessed anything like "children's literature." For example, in "Defining Children's Literature," the lead article in *Only Connect: Readings on Children's Literature* (1996), Peter Hunt states unequivocally, "When the mortality rate was high, and in strata of society where poverty and subsistence were the norm (that is, until the eighteenth century), the view of childhood as a protected stage was not possible. In medieval times, there was little concept of childhood" (13).

However, Ariès' thesis has been effectively put to rest by the findings of a number of contemporary historians. To name just three scholars concerned with England, Barbara Hanawalt, Sue Sheridan Walker, and Ronald C. Finucane all have established that late-medieval English families were indeed lovingly invested in, deeply committed to, and keenly aware of their children as children and not as "miniature adults."[1] Although Ariès does remind us that a vast distance separates medieval views of children and childhood from contemporary understandings, literary critics have served to advance Ariès' outmoded notion by their inattention both to current historical findings and to the variety of materials available to younger audiences in the Middle Ages. As children's literature scholar Gillian Adams writes, "Medieval and early modern scholars are unanimous in discarding the Ariès thesis. . . . [and] it is time for children's literature scholars to do the same" (3).

1

Medieval Literature for Children seeks to overcome the gap between medievalists and children's literature specialists by providing a variety of medieval texts whose audience included children and youth, with introductory essays that supply the historical framework, cultural background, and critical apparatus necessary to comprehend these older texts. In essence, the medieval specialists whose essays comprise *Medieval Literature for Children* grapple with issues that have traditionally occupied the critics of children's literature, and the volume crosses traditional disciplinary boundaries to address the question: "Since medieval persons valued their children and recognized their distinctiveness, what does medieval children's literature look like, how does it function, and what does it say about medieval culture and its view of children and childhood?" Of course, the answers vary, but more than anything else the essays in *Medieval Literature for Children* reveal the diversity, sophistication, and complexity of literature addressed to medieval children and youth.

The Problem of Definition

However, many studies of children's literature spend little or no time on the medieval period, for if the contemporary study of children's literature has a *grand recit* or foundational narrative, it usually begins with the Puritan educational program, with perhaps some mention of Caxton previously, and moves to the discipline's founding moment, John Newberry's 1744 publication of *A Little Pretty Pocket-Book*.[2] Indeed, the relative paucity of available texts and the difficulties of language make pre–printing press children's literature difficult to study, while the relatively narrow diffusion of manuscript materials makes it difficult to draw any general conclusions about medieval youths' access to literature. Furthermore, the evolutionary viewpoints, nationalist assumptions, and teleological perspectives of many nineteenth- and twentieth-century critics have tended to infantalize medieval literature generally as embryonic or incomplete, awaiting full maturity or fulfillment at a later historical moment (Couch, "Childe Hood"). These biases would seem to be the impetus behind Bennett Brockman's claim that "It appears that we can say accurately, although perhaps a bit startlingly, that all the literature of fourteenth- and fifteenth-century England is children's literature" (58). As a result, the operant definition motivating many scholars' approach to literature for children and youth in earlier historical periods tends to marginalize the kind of texts available in the Middle Ages. Illustrating the issue, the venerable Darton's *Children's Books in England* defines the "children's book" as those "printed works produced ostensibly to give children spontaneous pleasure, and not primarily to teach them, nor solely to make them *profitably* quiet" (1, emphasis Darton). What I would like to focus on briefly is the effect of excluding didactic materials from consideration of children's literature and the hazards of separating didacticism from pleasure in medieval texts.

First, definitions like Darton's not only deny the category "literature" to the pre–printing press Middle Ages, but its narrow view of didacticism excludes most medieval writings in general. Chaucer's *Canterbury Tales* is structured around a tale-telling contest to be judged according to which stories best mix *sentence* (moral sense) and *solaas* (pleasure), to use the Host's words (A.798), and it is in the interplay of these two perspectives that Chaucer's tale collection achieves much of its energy.[3] Imagine the *Canterbury Tales* without the *Parson's Prologue and Tale,* on the one hand, or the *Miller's, Pardoner's,* or *Wife of Bath's Tales,* on the other. Furthermore, the line between purpose and pleasure is neither static nor simply determined, for even in the *Retraction*—seemingly, a most moral and didactic epilogue to the *Canterbury Tales*—Chaucer disowns "the tales of Caunterbury, thilke that sownen into synne" (I.1085), without naming the offending tales and leaving the delicious ambiguity intact. Didacticism, like beauty, is in the eyes of the beholder. John Gower, Chaucer's contemporary and friend, likewise situates one of his major works, the *Confessio Amantis*, between *earnest* and *game* (8.3109).[4] What we find in many medieval works, whether sermons, school texts, saints' lives, romances, fabulae, lyrics, or plays, is a mixture of morality and mirth, teaching and delight—something, I dare say, we still value in present-day Newberry or Caldecott Award winners.

Second, it is precisely because we look to children's literature to teach social norms and positive values that we must seriously entertain the didactic tendency in medieval children's literature. For in the same way the literature of the Middle Ages expresses the social attitudes and anxieties of its era, so also modern literature for children grapples with the concerns of our own times. To take even a cursory survey of children's literature over the last forty years is to read a social history of late-twentieth-century culture.[5] For example, recent award-winning children's books have tackled such contemporary issues as death, divorce, homelessness, disability, natural disaster, racism, violence, and sexuality, addressing these issues with an eye toward facilitating a child's understanding and enriching her experience in a broadly liberal manner.[6] At the same time, popular—and very "medieval"—story collections like William J. Bennett's *The Book of Virtues: A Treasury of Great Moral Stories* and *The Moral Compass: Stories for a Life's Journey* convey generally conservative social norms and traditional standards of behavior by appending brief moral statements to stories from a variety of cultures and historical periods.[7] Although the literary modes, instructional methods, and technical artistry of modern books for children are quite different from those of older tales, contemporary children's literature shares the same goals of many a medieval text: conveying the values, attitudes, and information necessary for children and youth to survive or even advance within their cultures. Hence,

Hunt's categorical dismissal of pre-1744 texts and his artificial distinction between " 'live' books and 'dead' books" that "concern no one else except historians" (*Defining,* 14–15) both fail to recognize the significant continuity between medieval and modern children's texts and serve to enact a significant modernist bias against older literature. Such a simplistic distinction between so-called live and dead books seems to be more a characteristic of market forces than of generic attributes and begs a number of questions: "Dead" for whom, upon what basis, and to what end?

Third, denying medieval didactic texts the status of literature ignores contemporary literary theory's insistence upon recognizing the ideological dimensions of any textual product and the cultural currents it negotiates. Many critics question the notion of a "neutral" text and hold that all forms of communication—no matter how innocuous—hold a persuasive or didactic edge. In other words, no text is only and simply pleasurable, for all literary production, whether for children, adults, or both, is ideologically freighted and carries some broader point of view or specific agenda.[8] Straightforwardly didactic texts simply advertise their ideological leanings more directly than do many other forms of literature. Recognizing the ideological dimensions of texts of all sorts, even those of historically and geographically remote cultures, raises even seemingly simplistic or self-evident texts to the status of meaningful cultural artifacts. Definitions like Darton's, which artificially separate delight from dogma, or Hunt's, which disconnect dead from live literature, inadequately account for the historical and cultural dynamics of medieval culture, work against the medieval period's own sense of the wider purposes of literature, and contradict even our own evaluation of worthwhile contemporary books for children. Thus, the essays comprising *Medieval Literature for Children* challenge the traditional account of— and suggest alternative trajectories in—the development of children's literature.

The Possibility of Medieval Literature for Children

Medieval Literature for Children has been assembled with these provisions in mind, and because current scholarship of children's literature has insufficiently accounted for the literary materials available to younger audiences in the Middle Ages, I offer the following general definitions. First, "medieval" has been broadly construed to indicate the roughly one thousand–year period in Europe from the fall of Rome (476) to the Reformation in the West (1517). This includes sixteenth-century materials that are traditionally perceived as "medieval," particularly drama prior to the Elizabethan period in England. The works in *Medieval Literature for Children* are largely from the high and late medieval period (roughly from eleventh to the fifteenth centuries), with an emphasis in Middle English texts, while the manuscript and/or printing histories may extend hundreds of years both before and after the version at hand.

Second, "children" has been taken to mean the age cohorts from infancy (*infancia*) to childhood (*puericia*) through adolescence (*adholenscia*)[9] and does not exclude a mixed child-adult audience. In Nicholas Orme's reckoning, the medieval period produced "works aimed specifically at the young, works suitable for use by adults or the young, and works intended for adults that reached the young unofficially or by chance" ("Children," 218). Likewise, a broader sense of literacy is necessary and includes oral as well as aural facility in vernacular literature, for "reading" and "being read to" were equally important experiences of literature in the medieval period (Orme, "Children," 229–30) as they are now for contemporary youth. For the most part, each selection in *Medieval Literature for Children* exhibits identifiable linguistic, stylistic, codicological, or contextual traits that associate it with a youthful audience, while many of the texts also exhibit characteristics of contemporary "cross-written" texts (see Knopflmacher and Myers).

Third, in *Medieval Literature for Children* "literature" has been interpreted to include a wide variety of texts, from the self-consciously didactic and educational to the more recognizably literary and artistic, and cultural and historical writings are examined with the same attention as are traditionally defined literary texts. The contributors bring a broadly New Historicist perspective, as defined by Mitzi Myers, to the problem of medieval children's literature:

> A New Historicism of children's literature would integrate text and sociohistoric context, demonstrating on the one hand how extraliterary cultural formations shape literary discourse and on the other how literary practices are actions that make things happen—by shaping the psychic and moral consciousness of young readers but also by performing many more diverse kinds of cultural work, from satisfying authorial fantasies to legitimating or subverting dominant class and gender ideologies, from mediating social inequalities to propagandizing for causes, from popularizing new knowledges and discoveries to addressing live issues . . . It would want to know how and why a tale or poem came to say what it does, what the environing circumstances were . . . and the kinds of cultural statements and questions the work was responding to. (Quoted in Hunt, Introduction, 12)

In addition to examining questions of gender, race, and class, Myers goes on to note that this approach to children's literature would also address "a book's material production, its publishing history, its audiences and their reading practices, its initial reception, and its critical history" and how and why it fell into or out of favor (12). Readers will find just such an emphasis in the chapters that follow. The volume highlights the literature of late-medieval England in Middle English, but also includes translations from older Latin works, Old English, and medieval Welsh.[10] I hope that the current selections will stimulate further research into the literature available to youth from a variety of medieval cultures—including those of Islamic and Judaic heritage; from central, southern, and eastern Europe; as well as from the Iberian peninsula and other regions—and subcultures, like male and female monastic institutions, noble houses, schools and universities, or merchant and trade guilds.

The Generic Possibilities of Medieval Children's Literature

Once the definition of literature for medieval youth expands to include the broadly didactic, the possibilities for analysis and understanding increase dramatically. *Medieval Literature for Children* is divided somewhat artificially into five parts, based upon similarities of form and purpose, the selections varying within each chapter according to the date, place, and language of composition. Each primary source is preceded by an introductory essay with selected bibliography, and except for works in Middle English, all texts are translated.

Part 1, Didactic and Moral Literature, is made up of tale collections and fabulae, those compendia or encyclopedic sources that combine a number of related tales, stories, anecdotes, and exempla according to common themes or for pointed moral, ethical, or religious application. During the Middle Ages, stories were collected under related categories (bestiaries, encyclopedias), as part of a narrative plan (in frame tales like the *Canterbury Tales* and the *Lais* of Marie de France), for a specific purpose (saints' lives like the *South English Legendary*), or serially in the *Gesta Romanorum* and the *Alphabet of Tales*. Three chapters represent this didactic and moral literature. In chapter 1 William Hodapp introduces the fabulae of Avianus, whose work, like Aesop's, instructed students in Latin grammar and moral instruction through proverbial animal stories. Lynnea Brumbaugh-Walter follows in chapter 2 with a selection of exempla—in this case, secular stories with Christian moral application—from the *Gesta Romanorum*, a famous tale collection that eventually was copied in hundreds of manuscripts in several languages. Part 1 concludes with chapter 3 and Lauren Kiefer's selections from Gower's *Confessio Amantis*, a framed story collection composed for the instruction, edification, and amusement of a youthful English ruler, Richard II.

Part 2, Courtesy and Conduct Literature, is specifically concerned with social deportment, as well as generalized moral instruction. These texts were meant for youthful instruction in behavior, service, etiquette, and other aspects of socialization, for they transmitted the social values of the aristocracy and, increasingly, the socioeconomic aspirations of the growing moneyed and merchant classes. This literature demands examination not only for its social context but also for its generic and stylistic attributes, and a number of so-called courtesy texts are more ambitious and literary in nature. Cindy Vitto's definition in her chapter on *The Book of the Knight of the Tower* illustrates the complexity of the genre (chapter 6, as follows):

> As the term is used here, a courtesy book is a work intended to teach proper behavior, ranging from keeping decorous and regular religious observance, to following approved principles of ethical behavior, to acknowledging and accommodating differences among various categories of people (especially in terms of class and gender hierarchies), to conducting business and social activities in such a way as to invite the approbation of one's peers, to knowing and performing the minute niceties of conduct that allow one to be accepted in polite society. In short, then, a courtesy book can deal with topics ranging from the religious to the ethical to the practical. The emphasis throughout, though, is on proper behavior (in contrast to a true metaphysical understanding and acceptance), with the ultimate purpose of achieving the good opinion of others, especially one's superiors. (93–94)

Courtesy and Conduct Literature is represented in the three chapters of part 2. In chapter 4 Martha Dana Rust demonstrates convincingly that even the seemingly simplistic "ABC of Aristotle" conveys a complex ideology of conduct and behavior to the point of creating a particular youthful subjectivity. Deanna Evans discusses the fifteenth-century *Babees Book* in chapter 5 as an example of the Latin *facetus* tradition, designed to inculcate proper deportment for young men who were to serve in aristocratic houses. Rounding out part 2, Cindy Vitto's chapter 6 presents a Middle English text translated from French. Translated by Caxton, *The Book of the Knight of the Tower* is a collection of vivid stories, precepts, and anecdotes for the chevalier's daughters after the death of his wife to instruct them in honorable living and courtly values.

The selections in part 3, Educational and Instructional Literature, are distinguished by their educational settings (teacher or parent to student) and objectives (the communication of a specific body of content) for a particular purpose. Stephen Harris has translated one of the more commonly recognized pieces of medieval children's literature, Aelfric's *Colloquy*, in chapter 7. Produced to instruct young novice monks in Latin, the *Colloquy* delightfully mixes instruction and wit in a dialogue format that conveys the charming, even sometimes whimsical, give and take between teacher and students. In the mid-thirteenth century, members of the English nobility needed assistance in learning the French required by their station, and Walter of Bibbesworth's *Tretiz*, the subject of Kathleen Kennedy's chapter 8, is a French-language textbook in rhymed Anglo-Norman verse, written for the Duchess of Pembroke's children. In chapter 9, Paul Acker's edition of a school primer from the Plimpton manuscript collection at Columbia University (Plimpton MS 258) reveals the basic instruction typically given youngsters in late-medieval England. It begins with an ABC before moving into the basic prayers of the Church (Pater Noster, Ave Maria, and the Apostle's Creed) and thence to other commonplaces of Christian instruction. Chapter 10, the final section of part 3, presents a substantial excerpt of one of the most important pieces of medieval children's literature by one of the greatest writers of the Middle Ages: Chaucer's *Treatise on the Astrolabe*, addressed to his ten-year-old son, Lewis. Introduced by Sigmund Eisner's deliberations upon "Chaucer as Teacher," Marijane Osborn's contemporary translation offers a technically precise and eminently readable version of Chaucer's *Astrolabe*, also known as the earliest piece of technical writing in English.

Part 4 turns toward explicitly Religious Literature, with four generically varied and fascinating works. In chapter 11 Patrick Cook introduces and translates the *Ecloga Theoduli*, or *Eclogues of Theodulus*, a mainstay of high medieval Latin education. An important work of the Carolingian renaissance, the *Ecloga* introduced students both to Greco-Roman mythology and to Old Testament narrative, while presenting an interpretive paradigm designed to integrate the two traditions. Julie Nelson Couch's new edition of two important Marian miracle stories, "The Child Slain by Jews" and "The Jewish Boy," illuminates in chapter 12 the recognizably childlike sense of piety and playfulness of these texts. In chapter 13, the medieval debate poem is represented in Judith Deitch's edition of the Middle English *Ypotis*, which utilizes the *puer senex* (wise child) topos to startling effect in its communication of Christian doctrine.

Medieval Literature for Children concludes with three works in part 5, Entertainment and Popular Literature. Popular performance forms like the romance and drama certainly appealed to younger audiences. Romances like *King Horn, Beves of Hampton*, and *Guy of Warwick*, whose heroes progress through the life cycle from birth through death and whose elements of fantasy, daring-do, and the struggle against evil still appeal to audiences young and old, appear to have been staple entertainment in the late-medieval household. Brian S. Lee has produced a new edition of the school drama *Occupation and Idleness*, in chapter 14. A direct and delightful account of a schoolboy's temptation and eventual redemption, *Occupation and Idleness* reveals as much about the late-medieval schoolroom as it does about traditional Christian doctrine. The focus shifts in chapter 15 to the Welsh *Mabinogi* and Stephen Yandell's excerpts from *Math Son of Mathonwy*, as a cautionary tale for young Welsh noblemen. Mary Shaner's edition of the Middle English "monstrous" romance *Sir Gowther* in chapter 16 displays the fantastical elements of human shape shifting and its implications for the constituents of identity in a tale of Christian redemption. Probably the most recognizably literary works in the anthology, the selections in part 5 challenge a number of conventional assumptions about the function of romance, particularly by insisting that the question of age is as significant as that of gender, class, ethnicity, or religion.

Renegotiating the Parameters of Medieval Children's Literature

Since this essay began with a brief overview of the problems of the history and definition of medieval children's literature, I would like to return to the same issues at the end of this introduction. The careful and considerate investigation of the literary material directed toward youthful audiences in the Middle Ages has been hampered by a lack of understanding of the status of children in medieval culture and a particularly narrow definition of the place and the interconnectedness of didactic and other forms of textuality and literacy in the Middle Ages. The essays in *Medieval Literature for Children* indicate what a full reconsideration of the literature of medieval youth requires. First, this research must carefully analyze the paleology, codicology, composition, and marginalia of the manuscripts in which youthful texts are found (Acker, Rust, and Couch). Second, such study must consider the composition (including patronage), provenance (history of ownership), and reception history (lineage of interpretation and usage) of these important medieval texts (Hodapp, Kiefer, Evans, Cook, and Lewis), including their persistence into the contemporary period (Brumbaugh-Walter) or their failure to survive in the canon (Yandell). Third, such investigation must thoroughly explore the revision and alteration of well-known texts for evidence of their modification for a youthful audience (Eisner and Osborn, Shaner), because the tropes, rhetorical strategies, and content found suitable for medieval youth vary considerably from those of contemporary children's literature. Fourth, such research should include the identification and investigation of the kinds of text actually produced by children—things like rhymes, ditties, pen trials, copy books, handwriting exercises, and other potentially illuminating texts or text fragments (Orme, "Children," 219–224). Fifth, medieval children's literature should be examined in relation to the material culture of the Middle Ages, particularly the products, objects, and environments of everyday life (Rust, Harris, and Kennedy).[11] Sixth, new research should be undertaken to examine the performance modes of different literatures that include children in their audiences (Rust, Acker, Lee, Shaner, and Yandell). Finally, medieval children's literature should be understood within the wider context of civic activities (dramas, mummings, and pageants), religious celebrations (including local festivals, boy bishop ceremonies, and religious processions), and educational endeavors (from cathedral schools to secular grammar schools). Such dramatic and performance-oriented activities call into question defining medieval children's literature purely in terms of medieval children's literacy and open these texts to other avenues of investigation. Taken as a whole, in this turn toward cultural studies and away from purely text-centered formalist analyses, *Medieval Literature for Children* offers evidence for cultural construction of medieval children and childhood, not so much as a generalized grand and sweeping narrative of the development of childhood to the present day,[12] but in the focused examination of specific historical moments embodied in a variety of textual productions.

Therefore, rather than talk about "medieval children's literature" as a foundational, though hybrid, concept, I would like to adopt the phrase "the textual culture of medieval youth," which is to view literary production and reception of texts for medieval children and youth in the context of extra-literary works; nonliterary discourses and artifacts; and modes of performance like games and playthings, architecture, statuary, stained glass, illuminations, processionals, festivals, and local celebrations; as well as the more familiar touchstones of medieval culture. The essays of *Medieval Literature for Children* demonstrate that to separate the didactic from the artistic, the historical from the literary—courtesy books from Chaucerian tales—is fundamentally to misunderstand the literature of the Middle Ages and to hinder the understanding of the rich heritage of the textual culture of medieval youth.

Notes

1. Other important studies include Schultz, Shahar, and Orme, *Medieval Children,* which appeared after this introduction was composed.
2. Notable exceptions include Bingham and Scholt; Darton (chs. 1 and 2); Demers and Moyles; Field; Meigs, Eaton, Nesbitt, and Viguers; and Elva Smith.
3. All citations to Chaucer are to *The Riverside Chaucer,* gen. ed. Larry D. Benson (Boston: Houghton Mifflin, 1987) unless otherwise indicated. References to the *Canterbury Tales* will be indicated by group and line number parenthetically in the text.
4. All citations to Gower's *Confessio Amantis* are to *The English Works of John Gower* (2 vols.), EETS e.s. 81–82, ed. G. C. Macaulay (Oxford University Press, 1900–1901) unless otherwise indicated.
5. Even a glance at the Newberry, Caldecott, and Coretta Scott King award winners reveals the didactic aims of many recent award-winning children's books. The 2000 Newberry and Coretta Scott King winner, entitled *Bud, Not Buddy,* by Christopher Paul Curtis (Delacorte), is such a book: "Ten-year-old Bud Caldwell runs away from a foster home and begins an unforgettable journey in search of his father. His only clues are old flyers left by his now-deceased mother that point to a legendary jazz bandleader," according to the Association for Library Service to Children's Newberry Award website, <http://www.ala.org/alsc/newbery.html>. "This heartfelt novel resonates with both zest and tenderness as it entertains questions about racism, belonging, love, and hope," said Carolyn S. Brodie, chair of the Newberry Award Selection Committee. "Bud's fast-paced first-person

account moves with the rhythms of jazz and celebrates life, family, and a child's indomitable spirit."

6. See the lists of award-winning children's literature at the Newberry, Caldecott, and Corretta Scott King websites.

7. Compare *The Babees Book* (chapter 6, in this volume) with "Table Rules for Little Folks" (42–43) and "The Little Gentleman" (43), under "Self Discipline" in Bennett's *The Book of Virtues*.

8. Hollingdale reviews this question for children's literature.

9. I adopt here the terminology used in Seymour 1:162. See Burrow and Dove for analyses of the medieval "ages of man" literature.

10. Throughout *Medieval Literature for Children*, except in a few cases, the Middle English thorn (*þ*) has been replaced silently in the primary sources by *th*, and the yogh (*ȝ*) has been replaced with *g, gh*, or *y* as modern usage dictates. Punctuation has been regularized minimally according to contemporary usage.

11. See Orme, "Culture," for a preliminary examination of these questions. The extraordinary efforts of Iona and Peter Opie likewise are invaluable here.

12. See, for example, Demause. A different rendition of Demause's view of the evolution of child rearing is available online at <http://www.psychohistory.com/htm/10a_evolution.html>.

1

The Fables of Avianus

WILLIAM F. HODAPP

This chapter offers an introduction to and translation of selections from a late antique collection of forty-two fables, written in Latin elegiac couplets and attributed to a fourth-century poet named Avianus. This particular collection of fables served an important purpose in the Latin Middle Ages, for many medieval educators used these fables in part to instruct youths in Latin grammar. Although not the only collection so used, Avianus's *Fables* were extremely popular in European schools from the Carolingian period until the eighteenth century. In addition to the fables themselves, this introduction explores briefly the genre of fable and its history in classical and medieval cultures; the use of fables in medieval education, particularly Avianus's *Fables*; and the imitation of Avianus in the Middle Ages. It concludes with a note on the translations.

History: Classical and Medieval

In the ancient Greek poem "Works and Days," Hesiod (ca. 800 B.C.) offers to a certain Perses a compilation of rustic wisdom and prophetic statements, discussions of the seasons, advice on marriage, and suggestions on how to avoid offending the gods. Relatively early in the poem, Hesiod includes a fable. He states:

> And here's a fable for kings, who'll not need it explained:
> It's what the hawk said high in the clouds
> As he carried off a speckle-throated nightingale
> Skewered on his talons. She complained something pitiful,
> And he made this high and mighty speech to her:
> "No sense in your crying. You're in the grip of real strength now,
> And you'll go where I take you, songbird or not.

I'll make a meal of you if I want, or I might let you go.
Only a fool struggles against his superiors.
He not only gets beat, but humiliated as well."
Thus spoke the hawk, the windlord, his long wings beating. (235–45)[1]

Presumably the oldest recorded fable in European literature, Hesiod's tale of
the hawk and the nightingale, which follows a discourse on the five ages of
humankind, clearly illustrates the genre and its didactic context. Although
kings may not need the fable explained, the poet knows his audience does, so
he offers a long discourse on justice and concludes:

> Perses, you take all this to heart. Listen
> To what's right, and forget about violence.
> The Son of Kronos has laid down the law for humans.
> Fish and beasts and birds of prey feed on
> Each other, since there's no justice among them.
> But to men he gave justice, and that works out
> All to the good. . . . (316–22)

With the fable, then, Hesiod offers a view of the natural world in which the
strong control the weak; he counters that view, however, with another in
which the principle of justice, divinely inspired by Zeus, governs human
interaction. Macrobius Ambrosius Theodosius, writing some 1,200 years
later (ca. A.D. 400), seems to have had in mind just such a fable when articu-
lating his literary theory.

In his influential commentary on Cicero's *Dream of Scipio*, Macrobius
argues for the philosophical value of certain types of fables. He writes,
"Fables . . . serve two purposes: either merely to gratify the ear or to encour-
age the reader to good works" (1.2.7). Fables that serve the latter purpose, he
continues, "draw the reader's attention to certain kinds of virtue" (1.2.9).
This didactic aim most often comes to mind when we think of fable as genre.
As suggested by Hesiod's hawk and the nightingale, the fable is typically a
brief narrative in verse or prose that either implicitly or explicitly offers a
moral or pithy message. Characters are usually animals, inanimate objects, or
personifications that behave like humans, or they are human types, such as
the Old Man or the Youth.

Medieval fable collections, in both Latin and various vernaculars, are
rooted in the Greek tradition of fable stretching back at least to the eighth
century B.C. and Hesiod's fable of the hawk and the nightingale. The better-
known fabulist of early Greek culture, however, is Aesop, who as legend has
it was a freed slave from Samos living in the sixth century B.C. (Blackham,
5; Handford, xiv–xv). While Aesop, if he was indeed an actual person, probably never wrote down his stories, several later Greek writers published

fable collections that purported to be from him. In particular, Demetrius of Phalerum, writing in the fourth century B.C., composed a collection of fables in Greek prose that, according to H. J. Blackham, "seems to have been Aesop for the classical world" (7).

With their interest in things Greek, the Romans, of course, also picked up on the fable. Horace, for instance, alludes to fables in several *Satires* and *Epistles* and, like Hesiod, incorporates a fable in a poem when he tells the tale of the country mouse and the city mouse (*Satires,* 2.6.77–117). In this fable, a city mouse visits a country mouse and, after seeing its poor den and eating its simple food, invites the country mouse to dine in the city. The latter accepts and is initially impressed with a sumptuous meal at a palace; soon, however, ferocious dogs chase them from the hall. Upon barely escaping, the country mouse declares it has no use for such a life, preferring instead the simplicity of the country, free from fear. Horace uses the fable to underscore his central point in the poem; that is, the merits of country living far outweigh those of city living.

While Horace integrated this Aesopean fable into a larger poem, it was not until the first century A.D. that a poet composed a sequenced verse collection of fables based on Aesop. Phaedrus (d. ca. A.D. 50), an otherwise minor author, is, according to Gian Biagio Conté, "one of the greatest glories of Latin literature . . . [for] he is the first author in Greco-Roman culture to give us a collection of fables conceived as an independent poetic work and intended for reading" (433). Writing over ninety fables in iambic senarii (i.e., six iambs per line), Phaedrus divided his collection into five books and, in addition to the Aesopian stock of tales, invented fables with contemporary allusions (Rubin and Sells, 400). Another poet likewise composed a collection of fables. Writing in the second century A.D., the Greek-speaking poet Babrius, drawing on the same stock of Aesopian fables as Phaedrus, and developing his own emphases in favor of satire, composed the first collection of fables in Greek verse (Blackham, 13–14; Rubin and Sells).[2] Babrius's collection served as a key source for the fifth-century poet Avianus, whose collection of forty-two fables is the primary subject of this chapter.[3]

While neither Phaedrus nor Babrius directly influenced the fable tradition in the Latin west during the Middle Ages, Avianus and the Romulus collection inspired several medieval writers to use fable for both instruction and delight. Walter of England, for example, writing in the twelfth century, composed a collection of sixty fables in Latin elegiac couplets, based on the Romulus collection (A. Wright, 2–3). Also writing in the twelfth century, Marie de France, like her contemporary Walter, drew on the Romulus tradition when she wrote 102 fables in French octosyllabic couplets: a collection that was quite popular in the Middle Ages, as suggested by its manuscript tradition (Burgess, 573). Nor did the interest in fables wane in the later Middle Ages; for example, Robert Henryson, a fifteenth-century schoolmaster, composed a collection of fables in lowland Scots entitled *Moral Fabillis of Esope*, again derived in part from his predecessors (Wright, 5).

From Hesiod to Henryson, then, various authors were drawn to the fable as a vehicle for storytelling. Similarly, whether part of larger texts, as with Hesiod and Horace, or collected in anthologies, as with Romulus and Avianus, fables appealed to readers who sought both entertainment and philosophical insight. Indeed, the genre held an important position in literary culture in the West, from its origin in classical Greece until well into the early modern period of European history. In part, this position was secured through the educational system that used fables for grammar instruction.

Uses in Medieval Education

Grammarians used fable collections, among other texts, such as Cato's *Disticha* and Maximianus's *Elegiae*, to instruct students who had mastered the basic grammar in Donatus's *Ars minor* and *Ars maior* and Priscian's *Institutio grammatica* (Curtius, 42–43, 48–54), but who were not yet ready for poets such as Horace, Virgil, and Ovid. Beginning during the Carolingian era (eighth and ninth centuries), Avianus's *Fables* became a standard curriculum text used with youth for grammar instruction. When one works with the Latin poems, it becomes clear why teachers and students favored this collection of fables: for students, it offers a series of brief, entertaining narratives; for teachers, it presents engaging material for teaching vocabulary and grammar, as well as metrics and interpretation.[4] For instance, Avianus's choice of meter, the elegiac couplet, offered medieval students metrical complexity for grasping the quantitative values of Latin syllables—that is, the length of the syllable, which is either long or short. Briefly, the elegiac couplet consists of a dactylic hexameter line (six feet) followed by a dactylic pentameter line (five feet). The hexameter has six dactyls or spondees, with the fifth foot almost always being a dactyl and the sixth always containing two syllables; the pentameter has two "hemiepes," each containing two and one-half feet.[5] Scanning the first couplet of the first fable, for instance, illustrates well the poet's use of elegiac meter:

> *Rūstĭcă | dēflēn|tēm pār|vūm iū|rāvĕrăt | ōlĭm*
> *nī tăcĕ|lāt răbĭ|dō || quōd fŏrĕt | ēscă lŭ|pō.*

Careful mastery of Avianus's elegiac meter would have reinforced a student's earlier study of the quantitative value of Latin syllables, an aspect of elementary grammar instruction, and it would have provided metrical models for later imitation.[6]

In addition, Avianus incorporated complex syntax and a range of vocabulary, particularly synonyms, in an effort to meet the metrical and poetic demands of his chosen lines and the narrative demands of his fables. To illustrate, Fable 2, as follows, recounts the misfortunes of a tortoise that, after persuading an eagle to carry it, dies in flight. Glancing at the first four lines of this fable, for example, one finds enough grammatical variety and complexity to challenge but not overburden a student. Avianus writes:

> *Pennatis auibus quondam testudo locuta est,*
> *Si quis eam uolucrum constituisset humi,*
> *Protinus e rubris conchis proferret harenis,*
> *Quis precium nitido cortice bacca daret.*

[A tortoise once said to the feathered birds that / if any of the winged ones had settled her on the ground, / she would immediately offer it oyster shells from the beaches of the Red Seas / any one of which would give a reward from its glowing-shelled pearl.]

The syntactical complexity of this passage—with its mixed condition (i.e., the pluperfect subjective in the *protasis* of line two, followed by two imperfect subjunctives in the *apodosis* of line three and in the relative clause of line four, respectively)—elicits close examination. Students would have to parse the passage carefully to understand, for instance, the relationships between the relative clause (1.4) and the word it modifies (*concha*) or the mixed condition itself and the indirect statement of which it is part. In addition to the syntax, the passage illustrates a variety of vocabulary. The first couplet, for example, has two different words for "bird"—*avis* and *uolucri*—the second of which is here translated as "winged ones" to emphasize its difference from the first. Similarly, a synonymous idea is expressed in the two verbs of the second couplet—*proferre* ("to offer") and *dare* ("to give"). Such variety reinforces vocabulary and diction, and it illustrates to the student the verbal flexibility needed to write quantitative verse.

Finally, Avianus's collection lends itself to interpretation, evident in some of the *promythia* ("before the tale") and *epimythia* ("after the tale") attached to the fables. Such morals, or summaries of the *sententia* of texts, often came from school exercises, in which students were encouraged to paraphrase and summarize the text at hand (Quintillian, 1.9.2–3.69). While modern editors of Avianus's fables tend to excise most *epimythia* from the texts, leaving only those that seem genuinely to be from Avianus, several manuscripts contain a number of spurious *epimythia*; modern editors also usually retain four *promythia* in particular (attached to Fables 5, 7, 8, and 34), though most likely not the work of Avianus, because of their early date (Duff and Duff, 675).

Like other types of commentary, *promythia* and *epimythia* leave a record of medieval habits of reading and interpretation. Turning again to

Fable 2, for instance, one finds a two-line *epimythia* that reads, "Thus whoever is exalted and becomes puffed up with new glory / rightly pays the penalties when he desires better things." For medieval readers, one might assume, this sentiment would surely imply a warning against excessive ambition, perhaps even against wishing to rise above one's social station. Similarly, the four-line *promythia* attached to Fable 5 offers a warning against deception. In this fable, an ass finds a lion skin, clothes itself, and then terrorizes other animals until its master catches and punishes it. The *promythia* reads:

> It is fitting to measure oneself and be pleased with one's own merits
>> and not carry off for one's self the goods of another,
> lest the marvelous things, having been stripped away, cause harsh laughter
>> as soon as one has begun to continue with the usual faults.

Reading this *promythia* first orients the reader to a specific interpretation of the fable that follows. The lesson drawn, of course, fits the narrative; but one might also argue that once the *promythia* is read, the narrative fits the lesson. Clearly, the *promythia*'s writer desires to circumscribe the poem's meaning within its interpretive frame, and this interpretation most probably would have oriented medieval students when they read the fable.

Imitation and Translation

Avianus's text survives in some sixty-one manuscripts throughout Europe and some sixty-seven printed editions dating from 1494 to 1887 (Hervieux, 3.49–154). In addition, his work inspired medieval imitators, among whom Alexander Neckham is perhaps most well known to modern scholars. This twelfth-century scholar, teacher, and abbot composed two fable collections for his students: a *Novus Aesopus* ("New Aesop"), consisting of forty-two fables in elegiac couplets, based on the Romulus collection; and a *Novus Avianus* ("New Avianus"), a shorter collection based on Avianus (Hervieux, 3.222–26, 671–77). In the latter text, Neckham retells Avianus's first six fables, apparently to illustrate for pupils how to work with a source text to master syntax, vocabulary, and metrics. Interestingly, with the second fable in *Novus Avianus*, Neckham offers three versions—*copiose, compendiose*, and *subcincte*—again, presumably to illustrate three ways to retell a fable (Hervieux, 3.463–64).

A quick examination of Neckham's three versions demonstrates how the scholar-poet plays with the original as he expands or condenses it. With *copiose* ("at length"), for instance, Neckham doubles Avianus's original sixteen lines to thirty-two, using techniques of rhetorical amplification, and he

expands the first four lines, quoted earlier, to twelve by including a mono-
logue in which the tortoise examines why it wishes to fly.[7] Neckham retells
the first four lines as follows:

> A tortoise, wishing to be carried through space, revealed
>   its sorrow, beginning with words such as these:
> "I know that nature dislikes me, my strength falls short,
>   no hope of flight is given me; alas! what shall I do?
> If I lie low, the overgrown path reveals my hideouts;
>   If I move, my motion cannot be more sluggish.
> For protection, I bear a fragile shell, my eyes fail,
>   I can hardly be safe in my coverings.
> With aid from a high-flyer, I shall pursue what nature has
>   denied me; fate helps the daring; I shall seek the stars.
> To the queen of birds I shall give rewards: although the gods
>   are angered, the sparkling gem can influence her."[8]

Neckham presents here more than just a simple expansion of the original's
sense. While Avianus implies that the tortoise's excessive ambition is foolish,
Neckham draws the message out more sharply; his use of direct discourse
particularly emphasizes the tortoise's agency in its own folly, as it attempts to
thwart not only nature but also the gods.

  With his second version of Avianus's fable, *compendiose* ("a shorten-
ing"), on the other hand, Neckham reduces the poem to ten lines. Still using
direct discourse, however, he retells Avianus's first four lines with a similar
four, when he writes:

> A tortoise solicited some birds: "If any were to grant my wishes,"
>   it said, "she will be surprised and happy.
> I wish to be borne along on high: I shall enrich the bearer
>   with a gem; I shall refresh myself with new delights."[9]

Again promising reward for the bird, and anticipating renewal for itself, the
tortoise acts unwittingly, but foolishly, to bring about its own demise.
Immediately following his *copiose* version, the *compendiose* also carries an
ironic, if not satiric, edge, as the tortoise anticipates *"deliciis . . . nouis"*
("new delights") before taking flight. In his third version, then, Neckham
presents indeed a *subcincte* retelling of the second fable, compressing
Avianus's sixteen lines to four. Translated in its entirety here, the poem
reads as follows:

> A tortoise went to meet a bird, asking that she carry her
>   into the heights; the bird was persuaded by the offered reward.

> The tortoise was carried to celestial regions; bound by a fierce
> talon, her time of life closed: death was about to be embraced.[10]

Terse in its diction and detail, this poem obviously maintains just the bare
outline of the original; it is simply a poetic summary of Avianus's text. Still,
when read in order, the other two versions, particularly the *copiose*, serve as
key intertexts of the third: one quite easily supplies details gleaned from the
other two versions when reading the third. Moreover, Neckham seems to
have intended these three versions to be read together, for he provides only
one *promythia* to "govern," if one will, all three versions (each of the other
five fables also has a *promythia* and/or an *epimythia*). *Novus Avianus*, particularly the three versions of the second fable, illustrates a pedagogy outlined
by Quintillian, who suggested that retelling fables in various ways is useful
for developing facility with the language (1.9.2–3.69).

The following translation offers twelve fables from Avianus's text. This
translation provides an opportunity to examine elements of a standard school
text from which students learned, in Quintillian's words, "not only what is
eloquent, but, still more, what is morally good." While offering translations
of all the fables would be useful for a thorough study of Avianus, space limitations dictate a selection, which will always be a bit idiosyncratic. However,
the fables chosen are germane to the intent of this anthology, based on the
following criteria: (1) fables depicting children, offspring, or youths; (2)
fables revealing familiar literary or cultural topoi or themes; and (3) fables
presenting an interesting, perhaps atypical, situation.

The six fables depicting children (1, 3, 14, 25, 36, and 42) present a
range of situations. In three of these, Avianus presents children (or the
younger generation of animals) as more clever than adults. For instance, in
Fable 3, a crab chides its mother for critiquing its sideways walk when she
herself moves the same way; in Fable 25, a young boy outwits a greedy thief,
stealing the thief's cloak after he plunges into a well; and in Fable 42, a
young kid outwits a hungry wolf trying to secure its next meal. The remaining fables depicting children present different—at times, touching—portraits
of relationships between offspring and adults. Fable 14, for instance, reveals
the strength of a mother's love when a monkey argues in Jupiter's court that
her ugly offspring surpasses all others in beauty, at least in her own eye; and
Fable 36 recounts an exchange between an old ox and young calf, which ends
with the calf being led off as a sacrificial offering. Though these last two
fables present children as less wise than their elders, the predominant portrait
in the fables depicts them as wiser, even more tricky, than the adults they
encounter: a depiction that most likely appealed to the school children working with the poems.

The second group reveals familiar literary or cultural topoi or themes
and includes translations of three poems (2, 5, and 33), two of which have

been already discussed (2 and 5). Fable 2 depicts the tortoise and the eagle, while Fable 5 presents the ass clothed in the lion's skin. Both fables warn against sloth and gaining wealth and reputation by false pretenses, and Fable 33 tells the familiar story of the goose that laid golden eggs and its foolish, greedy master.

The third group of fables involves an interesting situation: three are presented in the present translation (10, 37, and 39). Fable 10, for instance, is a humorous story about a man who loses his toupee while riding his horse on an exercising field near Rome. While baldness might not usually be considered a "timeless" issue, the man's response to his detractors is instructive for all who chose to wear a toupee. Addressing a more serious issue, Fable 37 presents a dialogue between a lion and a dog on freedom and the cost of security. Although the dog indeed receives good care in exchange for its freedom, the lion's choice—though it might lead to his starvation—seems more appealing, even if more romantic. Similarly, Fable 39, through its insight into those who would agitate for war, offers an antiwar sentiment familiar to both advocates of peace and veterans of wars.

These groupings offer one way to categorize Avianus's collection, but Avianus himself offers yet another approach to his collection of fables. In the manuscripts and editions, a letter from Avianus to Theodosius precedes the fables (a translation of which is also included here). In this letter, the poet articulates his intention in composing the fables and quickly surveys his sources and the fable tradition. He then offers a brief instance of literary theory when he commends his book to Theodosius, saying, "You have, therefore, a work by which you might amuse your mind, exercise your character, lighten your anxiety, and safely understand the whole order of living." These four criteria suggest an approach to the fables similar to Macrobius's: For Avianus, fables can both entertain and instruct.

Notes

1. Stanley Lombardo's translation (see Hesiod) does not follow the line numbers of the original Greek; this passage corresponds to *Works and Days*, 202–12. For an accessible edition and prose translation, see Evelyn-White.
2. Nicostratus, a second Greek author also writing in the second century, composed a collection of fables that is now lost (Rubin and Sells, 400).
3. Other than his name, little is known of the poet himself. Avianus dedicated his collection to a certain Theodosius, whom most scholars consider to be Macrobius. He may also be the same Avianus whom Macrobius mentions in his *Saturnalia*, but it is impossible to know for certain (Duff and Duff, 669–70).
4. Cora Lutz describes a late-thirteenth- to early-fourteenth-century English manuscript in the Beinecke collection at Yale (MS 513), in which a copy of

Avianus's *Fabulae* appears with Theodulus's *Ecloga* and Maximianus's *Elegiae*, all standard school texts (213).

5. For useful discussions of Latin meter, see Rigg (Appendix: Metre, 313–29) or a standard Latin grammar, such as *Allen and Greenough* (401–27).

6. In Martianus Capella, Grammar discourses at length on syllables, giving an overview of the kind of instruction students received early in their Latin training (3.264–88, 76–86).

7. Strictly speaking, Neckham's text is not a translation; still, using rhetorical techniques of *inventio, amplificatio*, and *abbreviatio*, he in a sense "translates" Avianus from late-antique Latin to twelfth-century Anglo-Latin. For a near contemporary discussion of these rhetorical techniques, see Geoffrey of Vinsauf (16–18, 23–42). For recent scholarly discussions of medieval *translatio*, see Baltzell, Copeland, and Kelley.

8. Neckham opens this poem with a six-line *promythia*, hence the line numbering. The text, offered here for comparison with Avianus's Latin, is from Hervieux's edition (3.463):

> *Testudo cupiens ferri per inane, dolerem*
> *Exponit, uerbis talibus orsa, suum:*
> *Inuidisse mihi naturam sencio, uires*
> *Desunt, nulla fuge spes datur: ha! quid agam?*
> *Si lateo, latebras manifestat semita squalens;*
> *Si moueor, motus segnior esse nequit.*
> *Pro clipeo testam fragilem gero, lumina desunt,*
> *Tucior haut possum cornibus esse meis.*
> *Alitis auxilio mihi quod natura negauit*
> *Assequar; audaces sors iuuat; astra petam.*
> *Regine uolucrum dabo munera: numina quamuis*
> *Sint irata, potest flectere gemma micans. (7–18)*

9. Again, for comparison with Avinaus, the opening of Neckham's *compendiose* version reads as follows:

> *Sollicitauit aues Testudo: Mirare felixque*
> *Si qua meis uotis annuat, inquit, erit.*
> *In sublime uehi cupio: ditabo uehentem*
> *Gemma; deliciis me recreabo nouis. (Hervieux, 3.464)*

10. Briefly comparing Neckham's *subcincte* version, quoted here in its entirety, with his *compendiose* version (see n. 9) demonstrates how a student might increase vocabulary by reading the two together. The opening phrases, for instance, parallel each other grammatically, offering two different words for "bird" and two related verbs that a student could presumably master at the same time:

> *Conuenit uolucrem Testudo, rogans ut in auras*
> *Ferret eam; pretio uincitur illa dato.*

Fertur ad ethereas partes; constricta feroci
Ungue, dies uite clausit: amanda quies. (Hervieux, 3.464)

Translation

The Fables of Avianus[1]

A letter from the author to Theodosius:

When I was doubtful, excellent Theodosius,[2] about what kind of literature we should commit the memory of our name, the weaving of fables occurred to me because, in these, fiction conceived elegantly would be fitting and the necessity of truth would not burden me. For who might vie with you in oratory or who in poetry when, in these kinds of literature, you surpass both the Athenians in Greek learning and the Romans in Latin? Now, you will have known that the guide in this material is Aesop who, advised by the response of the Delphic Apollo, undertook amusing stories so that reading might be encouraged.[3] Indeed, for example, both Socrates introduced these fables in his divine works and Horace fastened them to his own poetry because, in themselves, they contain key ideas of life under the appearance of common jokes.[4] Babrius, returning to these fables in Greek iambs, abridged them in two volumes. Phaedrus also expanded to some degree a portion of these fables into fine little books.[5] From these, I have offered in one book forty-two fables, which, composed in rough Latin, I have tried to set forth in elegiac couplets. You have, therefore, a work by which you might amuse your mind, exercise your character, lighten your anxiety, and safely understand the whole order of living. We have, indeed, made trees speak, wild beasts groan with men, birds debate with words, and animals laugh so that, even by inanimate objects, a maxim might be advanced for the needs of individuals.

Group I. Fables Depicting Children
  1. The Nurse and the Child

Once, a peasant woman had sworn to her little son, who was bitterly crying,
  that if he were not still he would become a dish for a mad wolf.
A credulous wolf heard this word and remained wide awake
  before those very doors, holding onto the useless vows.
For the boy gave over his exhausted limbs to a very deep sleep;
  he also, then, took away the famished robber's hope.
When a she-wolf, his mate, perceived that he was returning
  famished to the haunts of his own woods,
she remarked, "Why do you, bringing back no prey as customary,
  thus drag your languid jaws with wasted cheeks?"
The wolf replied, "Lest you wonder, I was deceived by an evil trick

that I a wretch have hardly hidden in empty flight:
for what prey, you ask, or what can hope contain
   when the reproaches of a nurse offer only words to me?"
Let whoever believed a woman was faithful consider and know
   that these words are for him and he is marked in this poem.

3. The Crab and Its Mother

While a crab was walking backwards and pursuing crooked ways,
   it bumped its rough scales in rocky waters.
It is related that its mother, desiring to proceed by an easy course,
   had advised the crab with words such as these:
"Lest these byways please you by their crookedness, my son,
   and lest you wish to go backwards on zigzagging feet,
take pleasing ways, instead, by a direct effort, and
   set your innocent footsteps on a straightforward path."
The crab replied to her, "I shall do it if you precede me,
   and I shall follow your demonstration most certainly.
For it is extremely foolish if you, when you attempt the most crooked ways,
   act as censor and critique the faults of another."

14. The Monkey

Once Jupiter had sought through the entire world
   which creature might offer the better tribute of offspring.
Every kind of wild animal in rivalry hurried to the king,
   and the cattle domesticated by man were compelled to go;
and the scaly fish were not absent from the quarrels
   nor any of the birds borne along on purer air.
Among which creatures, trembling mothers led their offspring,
   about to be shattered by the judgment of so great a god.
Then, when a short monkey brought forth her ugly offspring,
   she compelled even Jove himself to break into laughter.
Nevertheless, the most ugly mother broke out in this speech before all,
   as she desired to abolish the reproach against her race:
"Let Jupiter discern this case, whether victory should remain for anyone;
   but in my judgment, that little one surpasses all others."

25. The Boy and the Thief

A weeping boy was seated at the water's edge of a well,
   making deceptive faces with widely gaping jaws.
When a cunning thief saw the boy with tears welling up,

he asked simply what was the cause of his sadness.
The boy, feigning that his rope had suddenly separated from him,
    complained that his jar of gold had fallen into this water.
With no delay, his wicked hand drew off his protective garment,
    and, stripped, the thief immediately sought the well's depths.
The little boy, it is related, wrapped the cloak around his small neck,
    plunged into thorny bushes, and concealed himself.
But after he had undertaken dangers on a false wish and when
    he, sad about his lost cloak, sat again on the ground,
the clever thief, it is said, burst forth in speech with these laments
    and with a groan solicited the highest gods:
"After this, let him, whoever he shall be, who thinks that an urn lies
    in clear depths, consider well my lost cloak."

36. The Calf and the Ox

A beautiful calf, frolicking around with an uninjured neck,
    had seen an ox continually plowing fields.
"Hey," it said, "is it not shameful to bear chains on your aged neck
    and, with yokes in place, not to know these pleasures,
when I am allowed to run about in nearby meadows
    and permitted again to follow the shade of the grove?"
But the old ox, tired and not compelled to anger by these words,
    turned the earth as usual with the plowshare
until, with the plow set aside, it was led into a small meadow
    to stretch out gently on a grassy mound.
Soon it again saw that the calf, tied and brought to the sacred altars,
    was led near to the knife of the priest's attendant.
"Indulgence," said the witness, "has given this death to you,
    which allows you to be free from my yoke.
Therefore, it will appear better to endure extremely heavy labors
    than, as a youth, to experience pleasures soon lost."
Such is the lot of humankind that death is more quick for the happy
    while daily life denies death for the wretched.

42. The Wolf and the Kid

It happened that a kid had duped a wolf by a better path
    when it sought fields closest to nearby cottages;
from there, aiming its flight in a straight course up to the city walls,
    it stopped still among fleecy flocks.
The unwearied robber followed the kid into the middle of the city
    and tried to tempt it with thoughtful tricks:

"Do you not see," it said, "that in all the temples the victim,
    groaning repeatedly in death, bloodies the pitiless ground?
And, unless you are able to return yourself to the safe field, ah me,
    you too will be sacrificed, wearing a fillet on your forehead."
The kid replied, "Cast aside, I beg, this new concern that you fear
    and take your worthless threats with you, you rascal;
    for it will be enough that my blood be poured out in worship to the gods
    than it glut the gullet for a raving wolf."
So, when sorrows are advanced by a double misfortune,
    it is better to have earned a distinguished death.

Group II: Fables Depicting Familiar Literary and Cultural Topoi

2. *The Tortoise and the Eagle*

A tortoise once said to the feathered birds that,
    if any of the winged ones had settled her on the ground,
she would immediately offer it oyster shells from the beaches of the Red Seas[6]
    any one of which would give a reward from its glowing-shelled pearl:
for she thought it a shame that, in her slow but diligent way, she did nothing
    and made no progress through the entire day.
But when she filled an eagle with deceptive promises,
    her dishonest tongue experienced a similar honesty;
and while she sought the stars on feathers purchased wickedly,
    the unfortunate one was slain by the high-flyer's cruel talon.
Then, too, when she was soon to die, she groaned into the breezes,
    with complaints raised on high that this had been permitted;
for since this event she has offered warnings to detested sloth that
    great things are not obtained without supreme labor.
Thus whoever is exalted, and becomes inflated with new glory,
    rightly pays the penalties when he desires better things.

5. *The Ass Clothed in the Lion's Skin*

It is fitting to measure oneself and be pleased with one's own merits
    and not carry off for one's self the goods of another,
    lest the marvelous things, having been stripped away, cause harsh laughter
    as soon as one has begun to continue with the usual faults.
By chance, an ass found the hide of a Gaetulian lion[7]
    and covered his appearance with the new spoils.
And he fitted the incongruous covering to his own limbs
    and crowned his miserable head with so much honor.
But when dread, terrifying in the imitation, enveloped him,

and its assumed vigor infused his slow-moving bones,
he trampled the pastures held in common by gentle beasts
    and disturbed the panicky cattle throughout their fields.
The farmer, after he caught him by his great ear,
    subdued the captive with chains and whippings;
and, while stripping the stolen hide from the body,
    he rebuked the wretched animal in these words:
"Perhaps you may deceive the ignorant with your imitation roar;
    but to me, as before, you will always be a little ass."

33. The Goose Laying Golden Eggs

A goose was teeming with precious offspring for a certain man,
    and it bore golden eggs, which it often produced in its nest.
Nature had fixed this law for the magnificent bird:
    that it not be permitted to bear two eggs at the same time.
But its lord, hoping his greedy desire might vanish,
    could not bear detested delays concerning his own profit;
he thought to receive a great reward from the death of the bird,
    which was so wealthy from its steady offering.
After he drove his menacing knife into the exposed heart
    and saw the bird was empty of its usual eggs,
the man groaned out, beguiled by the crime of so great an error;
    for he then attributed the punishment to his own offenses.
Thus, to those who wickedly beg the gods for all things at one time,
    the gods deny even their daily prayers.

Group III: Fables Depicting Exemplary Events

10. The Bald Horseman

A bald horseman, in the habit of binding hair to his head
    and wearing another's locks on his bare crown,
came to the Campus,[8] conspicuous in flashy armor,
    and began to wheel his nimble horse about with the bridle.
From the opposite direction, Boreas's winds blew forth
    on his ridiculous head while people were looking on;
and soon, after his wig had blown off, his bare forehead gleamed
    which, covered before by hair, was of a different color.
The horseman, because he was laughed at by so many thousands,
    wisely deferred the joke with cunning conduct;
he replied, "Why marvel that my false hair has fled
    when my true hair abandoned me first?"

37. The Dog and the Lion

It is said that a fat dog had met an exhausted lion
    and uttered words with jibes mixed in. He said:
"Do you not see that my flanks are stretched under my double back
    and my noble breast luxuriates with muscles?
After leisure, I am then guided to human tables,
    taking plenty of common food with my mouth."
"But what evil iron surrounds your thick throat?"
    "It is necessary lest I flee the house I am guarding.
But you, nearly dying, wander a long time through vast wild lands
    until your prey should meet you in the forest.
Proceed, therefore, to subdue your neck to my chains,
    until you are permitted to have merited easy banquets."
Roused into a harsh anger, the lion immediately growled
    and defiant in spirit gave a noble roar.
"Go," he said, "and bear the bond on your neck as deserved,
    and may the hard chains compensate your hunger;
but when my freedom is returned with my carefree haunts,
    though famished, I seek the fields that please me.
Remember to commend these banquets more to those
    who have set aside their freedom for gluttony."

39. The Soldier Who Burned the Weapons

Once a soldier, worn out by battles, had vowed to offer
    all his weapons to flames placed close by,
both what the dying multitude had given him, the victor,
    and whatever he could seize from the fleeing enemy.
After a while, luck assisted his prayers and, mindful of his vow,
    he began to carry weapons one-by-one to an enkindled pyre.
Then a cavalry trumpet, deflecting blame with a strident roar,
    declared that it went innocent to the pyre's flames.
"No spears," it said, "attacked your muscular arms by an act
    from my strength, which you still might confirm;
but I only gathered arms with winds and songs and this, too,
    (may the stars be witness) with a humble sound."
The soldier, adding the resounding object to the crackling flames,
    said, "Now a greater punishment and sorrow seizes you;
for although you yourself cannot try or dare anything,
    this act is more cruel because you call others to be wicked."

Notes

1. Each fable included here offers some insight into the poet who wrote it and
    into the children and schoolmasters who read it through the centuries. Two
    complete English translations are available: the dual-language edition in the
    Loeb series (Duff and Duff) and a more recent rendering by Slavitt. The former
    is a fairly literal prose translation; the latter reads more like a paraphrase, sim-
    ilar to Neckham's text, than a translation of Avianus's Latin. A useful transla-
    tion in French also accompanies François Gaide's edition. The present
    translations strive for a close rendering of the original, with the goal of provid-
    ing a readable text that remains faithful to Avianus's Latin without torturing
    the English excessively. The translations are based on Leopold Hervieux's edi-
    tion, which was also checked against the Loeb and Gaide editions.
2. Most likely, Avianus refers here to Macrobius Ambrosius Theodosius, the
    author of *Commentary on the Dream of Scipio* and *Saturnalia*.
3. Delphi, a Greek city on the southern slope of Mount Parnassus, was home in
    classical culture to the Delphic oracle belonging to Apollo in his role as god of
    prophecy (Howatson, 43–4, 174–76; Avery, 117–25). Avianus's assertion that
    Aesop received his commission to compose fables from Apollo seems unique
    (Duff and Duff, 680–81, note b).
4. Plato has Socrates incorporate fables to illustrate points into a few dialogues
    (e.g., *Phaedrus*, 259; *Symposium*, 203; *Protagoras*, 320–21), and Horace inte-
    grates them into some poems (e.g., *Satires*, 2.6).
5. On Babrius and Phaedrus, see introduction (3–4).
6. *Mare rubrum*, or "red sea," is a general term for the seas bounding modern
    Saudi Arabia, including the Arabian Gulf and the modern Red Sea; *mare Ery-
    thrum*, too, was a common name for the Arabian Gulf in classical Roman cul-
    ture (Avery, 138; see also *Murray's Atlas*, map 1).
7. Gaetulia, in ancient geography, was the land of the Gaetuli, a warlike tribe that
    appears in Vergil's *Aeneid* (4.40, 326; 5.51, 192, 351). Located in North Africa,
    Gaetulia was south of ancient Maurentania and Numidia, two coastal regions,
    in parts of modern-day Morocco and Algeria (Avery, 147; see *Murray's Atlas*,
    maps 2 and 3). Avianus refers to this geographic region when identifying the
    lion's hide as Gaetulian.
8. *Campus Martius* ("the field of Mars") at Rome was first an exercise ground for
    Roman troops and then a recreation ground for Roman citizens, like the bald
    gentleman in this poem. Taking its name from an altar dedicated to Mars, it
    was located outside Rome's boundary, to the northwest. Over time, the site was
    used for various other recreational activities, including a permanent circus, and
    even later had a theater nearby (Howatson, 114; Avery, 67; see also *Murray's
    Atlas*, map 9).

2

Selections from the *Gesta Romanorum*

LYNNEA BRUMBAUGH-WALTER

In late-thirteenth-century England, a decidedly curious collection of stories known as the *Gesta Romanorum* was compiled in Latin and then widely translated—into English, German, French, Dutch, Polish, Russian, and a host of other languages—as it circulated throughout England and Europe. Though none of the English manuscripts was ever printed, and no manuscript corresponding to the printed Latin editions exists, some 200 manuscripts and scores of printed editions do survive, housing a total of 283 tales. Around 1473 (within about twenty years of Gutenberg's invention of movable type), the first printed edition of the *Gesta*, a folio of 152 stories, came out. In fact, the *Gesta* remained popular well into the nineteenth century, by which time people embraced it not so much as a means of edifying Christian laity, but of instructing and entertaining children.

The *Gesta* is curious first because, despite its title (which translates as *Deeds of the Romans*), the stories themselves tell us absolutely nothing about ancient Rome. Instead, they detail the rich variety of sources (Eastern tales, chronicles, saints' lives, fables, folk stories, classical traditions, and more) available to the compilers—and they tell us that readers valued this collection enormously. Second, even more curious is that the *Gesta* is at once highly elastic and highly formulaic. As the collection was copied and translated, it became, as Melville said of *Moby Dick*, rather a loose fish of a book. In its journey from manuscript to storybook to scholarly tome, the *Gesta* has changed in content and has, in short, been molded according to the needs of its handlers, and yet, as Brigitte Weiske's extensive 1992 study of the manuscripts shows, "secondary additions to the *Gesta Romanorum* were consistently modified so as to bring them in line with the overall exegetical purpose of the collection" (Kalinke, 612). In fact, until the eighteenth and nineteenth centuries, when editors tended to omit the moral of each tale, the overall form remained strictly consistent: a fictive narrative that begins with a reference to a Roman emperor, and then an allegorical *moralite* or *application* that offers a one-to-one correspondence between the story elements and the personifications (e.g., Soul, Vanities, Devil, Christian) of the medieval religious worldview.

The *Gesta Romanorum*'s Critical History

Though most information on the origins of the *Gesta Romanorum* is lost to us now, for hundreds of years the collection, complete with its allegorized *moralites* (or *morals*, *applications*, or *apologues*), was one of the most widespread works in circulation. "Perhaps there is no work among those composed before the invention of printing," writes Sidney J. H. Herrtage, "of which the popularity has been so great and the history so obscure" (vii). Yet it is not the work's obscure history that might hinder our appreciation of the *Gesta*; it is rather the allegories and moralizations that accompany the tales. Modern sensibilities tend to view medieval moralizing—especially allegorized moralizing—as simplistic and artificial. Allegory in itself, however, does not automatically constrain the imagination. In fact, quite the reverse is true. Its purpose, according to Gordon Teskey, is to transform what he calls the *chaotic other* of a text into the *transcendental other* of medieval Christian theology. The very word *allegory*, which means "other speaking," "evokes a schism in consciousness"—the ancient, terrifying, intolerable schism between self and other, between me and thee—and this schism is then concealed, repaired, or transcended by "imagining a hierarchy on which we ascend toward truth" (2). Allegory (unlike, for example, fable) should "[force] us to unify the work by imposing meaning on it" (4).

The problem with the *Gesta Romanorum*, however, is that (at least, for most modern sensibilities) the transformation from *chaotic* to *transcendental* is not always successful, for the poetic—if not the spiritual—shortfalls of the collection's *moralites* challenge modern sensibilities. Most of the stories seem to us already unified and meaningful, and the *moralites* seem to add layers of meaning that twist the very stories they purport to explain. Shirley Marchalonis notes, "The application changes the original meaning, often providing a theological interpretation for a story that already has a moral or ethical meaning" (311–12). In other words, the theology of the *moralite*, in many cases, cancels out the moral of the story itself. And yet the *moralites* of the *Gesta Romanorum*, distancing as many modern readers find them, can teach us much about what was meaningful both to the compilers and, to some extent, to the storytellers who first brought the tales into Europe and compiled them.

At the turn of this new century, then, literary and cultural critics have set themselves the task of encountering the chaotic otherness of different cultures with empathy, sensitivity, and, as Shulamith Shahar advises, "a degree of humility" (5). Julian Wasserman, for example, notes that in the "tug-o-war of sensibilities between an author from one period and a reader from another, the question raised is exactly whose aesthetic yardstick should be used to calculate meaning" (219). Our own aesthetic yardstick may well find the stories of the *Gesta Romanorum* delightful—and its applications intrusive. In the *Gesta*'s "Moral Lesson Taught by the Ants," for example, we post-Puritans imagine we know what is coming—a stern exhortation for youths to work hard for the future. But what we get instead is quite different: The ants' efforts to store up provisions do not come to fruition; instead they come to nought when marauding swine descend on the colony and eat the carefully hoarded grain—just as rich men do not ultimately profit from their lives' earthly labors. Nevertheless, if we analyze the story and the moral together, we not only engage with the values of the culture that produced both in tandem, we also confront and then negotiate the terrifying schism between *our own* age and *that other*.

The *Gesta* as Children's Literature

Most scholars have agreed that the *Gesta* was probably meant to be a collection of *exempla* (short, moralized tales used to illustrate the theme of a sermon), for many such collections circulated in the thirteenth century. Weiske suggests that because the work is constructed "neither systematically nor thematically," the compilation was actually "not intended as a handbook for preachers but rather as devotional reading in nonclerical circles" (Kalinke, 613). Whether the work was intended to reach an audience from the pulpit or from the hearth, however, that audience would most certainly have included children.

Immersed in a culture of children's sports, videos, television shows, computer games, toys, books—all devoted, like our day-care and school systems, to separating children's lives from adults'—we have difficulty conceiving how substantially the worlds of children and adults used to overlap. A 1953 critical history of children's literature, for example, describes the *Gesta* as a source for Chaucer, Lydgate, Boccaccio, and Shakespeare, but concludes that "Due to their ancient origin, the frankly sexual nature of the stories makes them unfit reading for children in general" (Meigs, 109–10). This judgment, it seems likely, would have been utterly incomprehensible to the Christians who compiled the work. According to the French Dominican Vincent of Beauvais, medieval preachers "[quoted] the fables of Esop" to rouse congregations that embraced both adults and children. (qtd. in Warton, cxxxix).

Further, as Brockman notes, "The medieval work participates in the vast myth of the Christian Middle Ages, and the reality it tacitly explains to mature reader and novice alike is that reality, in all its complexity. It is educative in this larger, deeper way" (41). And so, the *Gesta* often isolates story elements to explain the Christian mythos it seeks to comprehend. For example, in the fable of the "Man and the Honey in the Tree," the exotic story elements—a unicorn, a dragon, four frogs with poison breath, and two beasts gnawing at the tree of life—must have captivated young listeners; the fantastic story also embeds an important lesson: If one is consumed with desire for sweet honey, one will succumb to the deadliest dangers that threaten the human soul. The allegory of "How a Greyhound Saved a Child from a Serpent" both represents the frightening vulnerability of medieval children to the natural environment and attempts to redeem theologically the all-too-frequent deaths of children from animal attacks.

Family, Gender, and Age in the *Gesta*

The tales in the *Gesta Romanorum* figure family relationships largely in terms of blood *kin*ship, or *kind*ness—nature itself dictating how parents and children should act toward each other. The importance of blood ties, in fact, explains the premise behind "How a Stepmother Who Wished to Favour Her Own Son Was Foiled," for in this tale, a mother's favor swings between her stepson and her birth son, depending on which one she believes was born of her own body.

Perhaps this primacy of blood ties and the importance of family lineage is why intrafamily killing, which recurs regularly in these tales, is so apparently fascinating to the text's audience and compilers, and why blood ties between parent and child are often valued above a strict application of the law. In the story "Of an Emperor Who Suffered the Loss of His Eye for the Sake of His Son," the emperor-father must uphold his own edict that anyone who rapes a virgin must lose his eyes. When his own son then commits this crime, the emperor declares that "Myn ye is the ye of my sone," and orders that one of his own eyes (as well as one of his son's eyes) be plucked out. The law is thus upheld, but the son (who is, importantly, the future king) is not completely blinded. However, in another story, "How a Son Saved the Life of His Father," the law appears arbitrary and cruel, and the clever youth who subverts it not only saves his father from death, but also weds the emperor's daughter. In both tales, the *moralite* places the rescuer in the role of a redeeming godhead who also values a blood-sealed relationship over justice. However, in "How a Father Killed His Son Rather Than See Him in Pain," a tormented father poisons his son, who is so consumed with madness that, day after day, he rips his own flesh to bits. The *moralites* may seem to force the family members' roles into conformity with the Christian mythos, but that act was not so alien then as it is to us now, for Christianity itself was pervasive in part because of its grounding in images of family and blood.

It will not surprise readers of literature from the Middle Ages that many of the stories in the *Gesta* collection are rooted in misogyny—not just sexism (which may make a boy today loath to ride a girl's bicycle)—but real misogyny: deep-seated fear and hatred of women's bodies. Female adulterers regularly receive harsh punishments, for example, but their male counterparts escape unscathed. The pervasive representation of women as either victims or temptresses, allegorized into either Mother Church or worldly flesh, is, of course, both limited and limiting (though less so, I believe, when the female principle is allegorized as the human soul). But just as disturbing is the remarkable absence of girl-children from the stories. When the plot of a tale requires a child, that child is simply male, a generic "he" to represent all children. Since these misogynistic stories are educative, then, we must suppose that girl-children who had access to them learned not only submissiveness, "since a woman, unlike a man, was destined to be obedient all her life" (Shahar, 166); they also apparently learned not to see themselves as girl-children at all, only as future women, either virtuous or wicked, imaged as either Mother Church, tempting flesh, or a sinful soul.

If power, however, operates in these tales quite narrowly as a function of gender, the range of possible roles for youths varies considerably. Children are sometimes innocent, sometimes clever; sometimes victims, sometimes rescuers. While it is true that medieval texts often represent "the obligation to honour parents as not only a scriptural injunction, . . . but also the basis for the maintenance of the social order" (Shahar, 169), the *Gesta* stories often invert the parent–child hierarchy. Furthermore, they draw on the far-reaching story motif that the youngest of three siblings is either the cleverest or the most loving (and therefore the most worthy of reward)—a motif that inverts the societal privileges tied to birth-order. In fact, in "How an Emperor Bequeathed His Empire to the Most Slothful of His Sons," the inversion is even more wonderful, for it is not the bravest or the quickest or the cleverest of the king's three sons who wins the kingdom, but the most slothful —that is, the one who swears he would not bother to move even if he were lying outdoors and the rain were beating the eyes out of his head. It is hard to imagine children listening to this tale and not being utterly delighted by the one-upmanship of each brother's claims to sloth—despite the moral's firm reminder that sloth is wicked.

In sum, these "Deeds of the Romans"—*Gesta Romanorum*—aimed at Christian children and adults in the late thirteenth century, are rich, imaginative, evocative, and provocative. Twenty-first-century readers should approach these tales with more than usual care, for by now we have insulated ourselves both from childhood and from the Middle Ages. All texts, of course, translate experience rather than reflect it; but children's texts undergo two translations, for they are not based on experience itself, but on what adults imagine or remember about childhood. And though it is tempting for us to play the part of grown-up to the "childlike" or "simple" morals and didacticism of the Middle Ages, we must remember that when we condescend to medieval morality, we impoverish only ourselves.

Fables/Adventures[1]

"The Moral Lesson Taught by the Ants"[2]

Pissemers [*ants*] in somere are besy, and rennyn [*run*] faste aboute to make an hepe stuffed with whete, with the which they mow leuyn [*may live*] in wyntere. But when they han all gadered, there comyth some tyme swyne [*swine*], and distroyen it, and wastyn it, and Eten it ofte sithes [*many times*]. Right so ofte sithes many riche men gaderyn richesse; but some tyme comyn the kynges mynysters, or of lordes, or othere rauenours [*plunderers*] that ben Eyres [*heirs*] and executores, and wastyn it, and distroyen that they han gadered. As dauid [*David*] seith in the sawter [*Psalter*], swich men leuyn [*leave*] theyre richesse to othere; and also he seithe, they tresoryn and hepyn, they wote nere to whome[3] they gaderyn hem; and therefore haue they no profite of hem, no more than the pissmers haddyn of here longe gaderynge. Amen & c.

"Pwas an Emperoure: The Man and the Honey in the Tree"[4]

Pwas [*was*] an Emperoure Reignyng in the citee of Rome, & a-mong al othere thinges he lovid wel huntinge. And as he Rode in a certen tyme by a forest, he saw a man Rynne afore him, with al the myght of his bodye, & an vnycorne [*unicorn*] Rynnynge aftir him, wher thorowe the man was gretly a-dredde, that for fer he felle in to a gret diche. neuer the les he toke holde by a tree, by the whiche he wan oute;[5] & then he lokid downe, & he saw at the fote [*foot*] of the tree an hidowse pitte, and an orible dragon there in, myning [*digging*] at the tree, and abyding with an opin movthe when he shuld falle; & beside this dragon were twoo bestes, the ton [*one*] was white, the tothere [*other*] was blak; & they gnowe [*gnawed*] at the Rote [*root*] of the tree with alle theire myght, to throwe hit downe, in so muche that the wrecchid man felte it wagge [*move*]; & abowte the sydes of the diche wer iiij. frogges sterting [*jumping*], the whiche with hir venemovse brethe envenemyd [*venoumous breath poisoned*] al the diche. He cast vp his yen [*eyes*], and he saw a passage of hony fallyng fro braunche to braunche; & he sette his herte so moche to this swete syght of hony, that he forgate that othere perell. So there happid a frend of his go by the wey, & for [*because*] he sawe him in so gret perille, he fet [*fetched*] to him a laddir, that he myght come downe Safliche [*safely*]; but he yaf him [*gave himself*] so muche to this swettnes, that he wolde not thens,[6] but yete [*ate*] hony, and made him murye [*merry*], & for-gate the perillis. And with in short tyme he felle downe in to the mowthe of the dragon; and the dragon yede [*went*] downe in to the pitte, & devourid him.

Moralite. Dere frendes, this Emperoure is to vndirstond Crist Ihesu, the whiche ouer al other lovithe huntyng of soulis; & in his hunting he be-holdith a man, *scil.* priuitees of the herte. The man that flethe is a synner; the vnycome is the dede [*death*], which that euer folowithe the man, for to kylle him, as it is I-seyde, 2 *Regum [in the Second Book of Kings]. Omnes morimur*, All we dye. this diche is the worlde; the tree in the diche is the lyfe of man in the worlde, the whiche lyf bethe the ij. [*is the two*] trees[7] blak & white, *scil.* ij. tymes nyght & day Roggyd downe[8] & consumyd the tree. The place wher comithe oute iiij. frogges is the body of man, froo the whiche comithe iiij. qualites of humours, by the whiche iiij. set to-geder inordinately, the ymage [*of*] the body is dissoluid.[9] The dragon is the devil; the pitte is helle; the swetnesse is delectacion [*delight*] in synne, by the wiche a man is I-blent [*blinded*], that he may not be-holde hye perilis; the frend that Rechithe the laddir is Criste, or a prechoure, that prechithe in the name of Criste; the ladder is penaunce. And when a man delayithe for to take that ladder, For delectacion that [*he*] hathe in the worlde ofte tyme, he Fallithe sodenlye in to the movthe [*mouth*] of the deville, *scil.* that is to sey, in to his power in hell, wher the devil devourithe him; of whiche devovringe is none hope ne truste to passe,[10] [*as*] hit is I-seyde in the salme, *Spes impiorum peribit*, this is to seye, the hope or the truste of wickid men shall perisshe. *Ideo studeamus & c.*[11]

"Cesar the Emperour: How a Greyhound Saved a Child from a Serpant"[12]
Cesar the Emperoure was wyse man Reigninge in the cete of Roome; In whose Empire was a knyght, name folliculus, the whiche knight louid ouer al thinges in the worlde Iusting and tornement. & this knyght had a litle babe to son, and no mo childerin; & he ordeynid for fostering & noreshing of this childe iij. norisis [*three nurses*], *scil.* on [*one*] to wasshe his clothis, anothere to fede or to pasture him with pappe [*breast*], & the thirde to bring him on slepe with songes & Rockynges. Also this knyght lovid passantly the gre-hounde, with the faucon [*falcon*], bycause that thei neuer faylid of theire pray comunly.[13] Hit happid, that this knyght made a tornement to be proclaymid to don [*be done*], in a greene place ny [*nigh/near*] to his castel; & many come ther to. When the day come, the knyght armid him[*self*], and yede [*went*] forthe; the lady, & al his meyne [*men*], and the norisse yede forthe also, & lefte the childe in the cradille; the grehounde lay by a walle, and the favcon sat on a perche. There was in a certein hole of the same castell a serpent I-bred & broute forthe, & had be [*been*] there longe tyme; and when this ser-pent harde so grete a noyse of peple goyng oute toward the tornement, she put oute hir hede at an hole, & sawe the chylde by him selve. She come oute,

for to sle [*slay*] the childe; and when the faucon sawe that, she made gret noyse with hir winges, and there with awoke the grehounde fro slepe, that the grehounde myght go & defende the childe. Then the grehounde awakid, by stirynge of the faucones wynges, & shoke him selve, & be-helde the serpent, and Rhan fersly [*fiercely*] to hir; & the serpent was on the on [*one*] side of the cradill, & the grehounde on the othere, for to defende the childe in the cradell. & they foute sore [*fought violently*] togeder, & the serpent boot [*bit*] the grehonde grevously, that he bled stronge [*exceedingly*]; and the gre-hounde Ran woodly [*furiously*] to the addr, & slowhe [*slew*] hir; & so with hir fiting [*their fighting*] the cradil ouertornid; but the cradill had iiij. [*four*] feet, that kepte the childes fase [*face*] fro the grounde. & when the Gre-hounde had I-slawe [*slain*] the serpent, he yede [*went*] to his kenell, biside the walle, and likkid his wounde. And by that tyme the tornement was cessid & doon The norisshis come home; & when thei sawe the cradill I-tornid vpsodoune & the flor blody, & the grehound blody, also thei trowed [*believed*] that the grehounde had slayne the childe; & therefor withoute tareynge [*tarrying*], or [*ere/before*] thei wolde goo to the chylde, thei seide, "Go we, fle awey, or we be dede!": And as thei yede [*went*], the lady met with hem, as she come fro the play; & she askid of hem whi thei fledde? & thei saide, "wo is to yow & to vs, for the grehound, that ye love so welle, hathe slayneyour sone, & lithe [*lays*] by the wall al blody!" The lady fel downe on a swoune [*swoon*], and saide, "Alas! is my sonne dede?" And as she cried, the knyght come fro the tornement, and askid the cause of hir criinge. Thenne sche saide, "Wo is to yow & tome, for your grehounde hathe slayne youre sone!" then the knight was halfe woode [*mad*] for wo [*woe*]; he Enterid into the halle; and [*when*] the grehounde sawe his lorde come, he aros, and as he myght, he made Ioye with his lorde, as he was wont [*accustomed*] to do. But the knyght anon in his woodnesse, trowing the wordes of his wyf, drowe oute his swerde, and smote of [*off*] his grehoundis hede; and tho [*then*] he yode [*went*] to the cradill, & turnid hit vp with his honde, & saw his childe Safe & sounde, and biside the cradell lay the sarpent dede; & by that he vndirstode, that the grehounde had slayn the serpent, for defens of the childe. And then he cride with an hihe voyse, "Allas! allas! for at the wordes of my wyf I have slayne my gentil grehounde, that failid neuer of his pray, and also savid the lyf of my childe; therefore I wolle take penaunce." He brake his sper in thre partijs [*parts*], & put his wyf in preson, and yede [*went*] him selfe to the holy londe; & ther he livid al his lyfe, & his son helde his eritage [*heritage/inher-itance*]; & so he made a fayre ende with the worlde.

Moralitee. Dere frendes, this Emperour is the fadir of hevin; the knight in the Empyr is eche worldly man that lovithe tornementes & Iustinges, *scil.* vanitees of the worlde. The childe in the cradil is a childe wasshe in bap-tisme; the cradil hathe iiij. feet, that the visage myght not touche the erthe; so the contryte hert most have iiij. fete, that is to sey iiij. cardinales vertutes, that hit tovche not erthely thinges, ne do no thing but that shulde be plesynge to god. The Firste norise, that is sette to wasshe the childe, is contricion, the whiche wasshithe awey synne of man; & therefor seithe Ambrose, *Lacrime lavant delictum Quod pudor est Confiteri*, This is to sey, teris wasshithe synne that is shame to be shewid. The secounde noryse is confessioun, the whiche fedithe a man in goode werkes; for as the body liuithe be [*liveth by*] kindly mete [*natural meat (bodily food)*], Right so dothe the sovle [*soul*] by gostly mete [*ghostly meat (spiritual food)*]. The thirde norise, that Rockithe the childe to slepe, is verey satisfaccion [*true atonement*] for synnis, the whiche makithe a man to Reste in euerlasting Ioye [*joy*]. The knyght yede [*goes*] to the tornement, *scil.* as ofte as a man gothe to the Iolytees [*jollities*] of worldlye speculacions, & hathe delectacion [*delight*] in hem [*them*], in that that he is I-ocupied aboute the worlde, & in vnlefull [*unlawful*] desiris. Now the childe, *scil.* the soule, is lefte by hit selfe withoute helpe; for as the A-postel seithe, *Non potestis deo seruire & mammone*, this is to seyne, ye mow [*might*] not bothe serve god and the devil, or to the worlde or to the fleshe. The serpente in the hole is the devil, the whiche euer more gothe abovte to seche[*seek*] whom he maye devoure, *scil.* to sle [*slay*] a soule by dedely synne. The Faucon seynge [*seeing*] this, makethe a flakerying [*flapping*] with his wynges,—what is that? This faucon is thi consiens, that hathe twoo wynges, to stire the grehounde of [*from*] Reste; oo [*one*] wynge is hope to have euerlasting Ioye, that othir wynge is drede of euerlastinge payne; & then the faucon, *scil.* consciens, makithe soun, as ofte as he grucchithe ayens [*grumbles/complains against*] dedely synne; & therefore the apostle seithe, *Omne quod fit contra conscienciam, Edificat ad Jehennam*, vt supra.[14] And when the grehounde, *scil.* Reson, is styrid [*stirred*] fro slepe of synne then he fitithe with the serpent, in that that it stirithe a man to goode. The serpent, *scil.* the devil, woundithe the grehounde, *scil.* Resoun, as ofte as he bryngithe a man to live wilfully, & not by Resoun; & so is the blode sperkelid aboute the cradil, when that the vertus, the whiche thow toke in baptisme, be depressid [*crushed/vanquished*] & destroyed by the devill; & so the cradil of thin herte is tornid [*turned*] vpsodowne, *scil.* to the erthe. Neuerthles for the foure fete, *scil.* iiij. cardinal vertues, whiche a man Recevithe of god, a soule dieth not, *scil.*, is not dampnid, as longe as she dwellithe in the body; & therfore seithe oure saveoure, *Noli mortem Peccato is, set vt magis convertatur et viuat*, This is to seye, I wol not the dethe of a synner, but that he be conuertid, & live. The norisshes seeth & fleethe, *scil.* contricioun, confession, & satisfaccion, *scil.* when a man lithe in synne, and wol not be conuertid to god. The grehounde sleethe [*slays*] the serpent as ofte as Resoune ouercomithe the devil, & convertithe a man to god. The lady cryde, & fel to grounde, that is when a wrecchid soule tornithe to Erthely thinges, & delicates [*delights*] of the worlde; & then it criethe so hie [*high/loudly*], that the knyght, *scil.* the

man, drawithe oute the swerde of a frowarde [*proud*] wille, as ofte as he fol-
lowithe deliciousnes of the fleshe; and then hesleethe Reson, that sauid
[*saved*] the soule ayenste the serpent, *scil.* the devil. And therefore, man, yf
thow hast don by instigacion [*urging*] of the fleshe, do as did the knyght;
turne vp the cradil of thin herte by meriotry [*meritorious*] werkes, & then-
thow shalte fynde thi soule saf, & breke thi sper, *scil.* thi lyf, in iij. partiis,
scil. in prayng, fastinge, and almes; & then go to the hooly londe, *scil.* that is
to sey, the kyngdom of hevyn, &c.

"How a Father Killed His Son Rather Than See Him in Pain"[15]
Flosculus reigned in Rome, that had a sone that was wode [*mad*], that
dyverse daies rent his membres.[16] The Fadir sawe that, and yaf [*gave*] hym
venyme [*venom/poison*], and had lever slee [*rather slay*] him softly than he
shuld so rente hym self dyverse daies. The modir sawe that, and was right
sory; She wente to the domesman [*judge*], and playned [*complained*] on her
husbond, that he had slayn his sone. The fadir before the domesman
aunswered, and said, "It was a werke of charitee, and that for this skille [*reason*]. My sone all to-rente hym self[*tore into himself viciously*], and so of
longe tyme he suffred many wrecchednesse. I, that was his Fadir, seyng that,
I chase [*chose*] rather to slee hym, than longe tyme to se [*see*] hym in sorow."

Declaracio. Frendes, this Emperour is the world. The sone, that rent hym
self, is a doer of penaunce, the whiche tameth his flessh. But oure Fadir, the
whiche is the world, by the whiche we are susteyned bodely [*sustained bodily*], yeveth [*giveth*] vs venymes of the erthe of our birthe, by the whiche ofte
sithes [*many times*] we are dede. But oure modir, that is holy chirche,
accuseth the world to god. Therefore flee we the world, that oure modir, holy
chirche, may have of vs solace, grete ioye [*joy*], and gladnesse.

"Clipodius a Wyse Emperour: How a Stepmother Who Wished to Favour
Her Own Son was Foiled"[17]
Clipodius was a wyse Emperour reignynge in the citee of Rome, and his
possession was moche; the wiche weddid the dowter of a kyng, callid kinge
assireorum, & she was faire and glorious in syght, and browte forthe a faire
sone; but she dide [*died*] in hir childebed. And aftir hir dicese, the Emperoure weddid another woman, and gate [*begat*] on hir a childe; and bothe
childerin he sent to fer [*far*] contree, for to be forsterid [*fostered*], & browte
vp. so in a certeyne tyme, the wyf of the Emperour saide to him, "Sir, my
lorde, hit is x. yere agoon sithe [*ten years ago since*] I bare a sone, & sawe
him neuer sithe I bar him; and therfor I be-seche yow, that ye sende after
him, that I may see him, & have sum Ioye [*joy*] of my birthe." Thenne saide
the Emperoure, "Dame, thou wot [*know*] welle, that I gate a-nother sone of
my first wyf, and he is with him; & therfor yf we send for the ton [*one*], the

tother [*other*] must come also." thenne saide she, "Sir, I asente." Thenne the Emperour sent for hem, and thei come bothe. And whenne thei wer I-come, they wer to syght of alle men faire and welle I-shapin [*shaped*], wel I-norsshid, & welle I-norturid; and thei wer so like, that vnnethe [*scarcely/hardly*] the on myght be knowen from the tother with [*by*] eny man, but onlye of the fadir. Thenne saide the wyf, "Gode lorde, telle me whiche is my child, for sothely [*truly*] I know not whether of hem is myn?" Thenne he leyde [*laid*] his honde vpon the childe that he hadde with the firste wyf, and saide, "Lo! this is thi sone. And whenne he hadde so tolde hir, she lovid and pikid [*chose/favored*], fedde and tawgte this childe, trowing [*believing*] that he had be the same that she bare; & hilie [*highly*] dispisid hir owne sone, trowinge that he was hir stepson. Whenne the Emperoure sawe her gret vnkyndnes [*unkindness / unnaturalness*], that she wolde not love bothe y-like, he said to hir, "Woman, I have deseyvid the [*deceived thee*]; for that child that thow norisshest so moche, is not thyne, that other is thi child, that thou lovist not." What dude [*did*] she but lefte that childe, and was a boute, in al that she mygt, to plese that other. And whenne the Emperoure saw that, he saide to hir, "Dame, I have yit [*yet/again*] deseyvid the, for he is not thi sone; and yit thow shalt not knowe more sekyrnesse [*certainty*] of me, but I wolle [*will/want*] that thow wite [*know*], that on of thes is thi sone, that thow bare." Then she knelid downe vpon hir knees, and said, "Lord, for his love that hinge vpon the crosse, do tel me in certen whiche of hem is my sone, withe oute cauillacion [*trickery*]." "For sothe," quod the Emperour, "Thou shalt not know, vnto the tyme that thei come to hir ful age, by cause that Iwolle [*will/want*] that thou love hem bothe I-lyke. For whenne I saide this was thi childe, thou lovedest al him, & nothing the other; and whenne I saide that other was thi childe, thou tendeist al to him, and dispisidist that othere; and therefor I wolle, that thow love hem bothe i-lyke welle." And so she dude indede, til tyme that thei come to hir [*their*] lawful age, and mannys degree [*man's rank/station*]; & thenne the Emperoure tolde hir in certeyne whoo was hir childe, wher thorow [*where through / whereby*] she was gladde, and ful welle a-payde in herte.

Moralite. Dere frendes, this Emperoure is oure lorde Ihesu Criste. Thes too childerin bethe [*are*] chosen creatures, & wickid creatours.The moder is holie chirche, the whiche norshithe [*nourishes*] bothe the godde & the evill; For god wolle [*wills*] not that hit be certeyne to holye chirche, who is choson, and who is not; For yf holye chirche knew it, she wolde love on, & hate the other, and thenne charite shulde be distroyed, and men shulde live in discorde. But in the day of dome [*judgment*] hit shalle be declarid, who is chose, & who is not chose; and therfor late [*let*] vs do so in this worlde, that we mowe [*might*] be choson vnto the fest [*feast*] that euer is newed [*ever is renewed*], and neuer wexithe [*grows*] olde. *ad quod nos perducat Rex viuens in secula!*[18] Amen.

"Sesar a Wise Emperoure: Of an Emperor Who Suffered the Loss of His
Eye for the Sake of His Son"[19]
Sesar was a wise Emperoure Reignynge in the cetee of Rome; & he
ordeynid for a lawe, thatyf there wer eny man that defoulid a virgine, he
shulde lese [*lose*] bothe his yen [*eyes*]. This Emperoure had a sonne, that he
louid [*loved*] moche. hit [*It*] happid on a certeyne day, as this yonge man
walkid by the citee, he mette withe a fayr mayde, the dowter of a certeyne
wedowe; & he oppresseid hir, & foulid [*fouled/defiled*] hir in flesh. And the
Emperoure come to the cetee, and þe forsayde wedowe mette withe him,
knelying vppon hir knees, and seide to him, "My lorde, do Right and lawe,
as thow haste ordeynid thi selfe. For I had but oo [*one*] dowter, and thi sone
hathe defoulid hir by oppression and strength." Thenne the Emperoure was
hilie y-mevid [*highly moved*] in mynde, & saide to his sone, "A! cursid
wrecche, whi hast thow don a-yenste my lawe? þou shalt have the law withe
outene dowte, as I have ordeynid." When worthi lordes harde [heard] this,
thei seiden alle with on [*one*] voyse, "lorde, thou hast but on [*one*] sone, and
therefore it is not for the beste, that thou do oute his yen." Then seide the
Emperoure, "Sirs, ye knowithe wel, that I made the lawe, & he hathe broken
hit; & therfor sithe [*since*] he that is my sonne wolde breke hit, he shalle
have the lawe." "A! lorde," seyde thei, "for his love that dide [*died*] on the
crosse, doth not so to youre sone; for that wer aftir your discese [*death*] a
grete shame to vs, that we shulde have a blynde man to our Emperour aftir
yowe." Thenne seide the Emperoure, "Thanne shalle I a-swage [*assuage*]
the lawe in him, and yitte [*yet*] fulfille hit, and that in this maner. Myn ye is
the ye of my sone, & his ye is myn; and therfore takithe oute on ye of myn
hede, and anothere ye out of my sones hede, and so the law shalle be kepte."
Knigtes yede to, and dude [*went and did*] in al poyntes as the Emperour
comaundid, in so muche that men dradde [*dreaded*] hili the Emperoure
after, for the hard dome [*judgment*] that he had yevin [*given*] ther, & so stret-
lye [*strictly*] I-kepte.

Moralite. Dere Frendes, this Emperoure is oure lord Ihesu Crist; that
ordeynid for a lawe, that yf eny man foulid a virgine, he shulde lese his yen,
that is, the light of hevene. But the sone of the Emperoure deflourid [*deflow-
ered*] a virgine, *scil.* [*namely*] a Cristen man, that foulithe his soule by synne;
and therfor the Emperoure Criste sorewithe [*sorroweth*], whenne that the
wedowe, *scil.* consciens, pleynithe [*complains*]; & therefore he for-soke his
light in hevene, what tyme that he come dovne from hevene, and for oure
transgression & oure trespas putte him selve out from the light of hevene,
takynge the forme of a symple sarvaunt; and not only did [*plucked*] oute one
ye, but suffrid al his body to be woundid to dethe. And so he wolle [*wills*] that
thou, synner, suffre to have out an other ye, *scil.* to do stronge penaunse [*pen-
nance*] with him for thi synne, that god may seye, "As I suffred penaunce fore

the, Right so do thou, whenne thow art in dedlye synne." And so, sir, the lawe of the Emperoure may be kepte, and thou be saf, and have the empire of hevene. *Ad quod nos perducat* &c.[20]

"Alexandir a Wise Emperoure: How a Son Saved the Life of His Father"[21]
Alexandir was a wyse Emperoure Reignynge in the citee of Roome; his possessioune was moche, and amonge al other vertues that he hadde, he was large [*generous*] of his mete. And he ordeynid a lawe, that no man shulde at his borde [*table*] Ete the blake [black] syde of the playse,[22] but al the white syde, withe outen tvrnyng [*turning*]; and yf enye man dud [*did*] the contrarie, he shulde lese [*lose*] his lyfe. But then he grauntid, that the trespassour shulde aske iij bonys [*three boons*] or [*ere/before*] he deyde, Of what thinge that he wolde aske, to save his lyfe, and hit shulde be grauntid to him. So hit happid in a tyme, that ther come an Erle to court, & his sone come withe him, and they wer of fer contrees; & happed as thei Sete [*sat*] at mete, the Erle was servid with a plays, and he had goode wille to ete, & he ete the blake syde, and also white. & anoon he was accusid to the Emperour; and the Emperour seide, he shulde be dede with outen delay, as law wolde. Thenne the Erles sonne seing this, knelid [*kneeled*] afor [*before*] the Emperoure, & seid, "Lord, for love of him that dide [*died*] on cros, graunt me that I may deye for my fadir." "I assent," quod the Emperoure, "for al is on[23] to me, so that on be dede."[24] "Sir," seyde the sone, "sithe [*since*] I shall dye, I aske the law of you, *scil.* that I may have iij peticiouns or I deye." "Yis," quod the Emperour, "Aske what thow wolte, ther may no man denye hit [*it*]." "Sir," quode he, "I aske firste to have youre dowter by me a nygt in my bed." The Emperour grauntid that peticion, for lost of observaunce[25] of the lawe; but hit was gretly ayenste his herte. So the younge man hadde hir with him al nyght, but he folid [*fouled*] hir not; and therfore on the morowe the Emperour was hilie [*highly*] plesid. Tho [*Then*] he askid the secounde peticion, and saide, "Sir, I aske al your tresoure." The Emperour grauntid hit, for he wolde not be founde contrarie to his lawe. And then whenne the yonge man had his tresoure, he delte hit anoon to por & to Riche, in so moche that he wanne [*won*] ther by the wille & the love of Eueri [*every*] man. And then he askid the thirde petucion, in this forme, "Sir," he saide, "I aske the Ien [*eyes*] of alle the men that seye my fadir turne the playse, that thei be pikid [*picked*] oute." & so thowte thei on [*one*] aftir another, yf I seye so, myn yen shul be pickd oute. So hit fel, that ther was noon that wolde seye that he sawe hit, *scil.* that he sawe the Erle turne the playse in the dishe. "Loo! sir," quod the yonge man," yife [*give*] me nowe a Iuste dome [*just judgment*]." "Now for sothe [*forsooth/for truth*]," quod the Emperoure, "Sithe [*since*] ther is non that wolle seye it, ne noon accuser is I-founde, there shalle noon [*no one*] be dede [*dead, killed*]." And so he saveid his fadris [*father's*] lyfe, and was hilie comendid, and weddid the Emperours dowter.

Moralising. Dere frendes, this Emperoure is the fadir of hevin, that made this lawe, that no man sholde turne the playse. By this plays we may vndirstonde wordly goodes, the which vs ouithe [*we ought*] not to torne by the blak part, *scil.* not to fonge hem by[26] avarice, or covetise, or falshed, but that we holde vs contente withe swich as god sent; & yf we do the contrarie, we shulle be dampned. The Erle, that comyth withe his sone, is Adam, the first fadir, that come fro the felde of damask [*Damascus*] to the contree of paradyse; the whiche soone turnede the plays, *scil.* that he ete of the apple, by the whiche he was dampnid. Thenne the sonne of Adam, *scil.*, oure lorde Ihesu Criste, profird him to the Emperour of hevene, for to deye [*die*] for his fadir Adam, *scil.*, al mankynd. Neuertheles or [*ere*] he dide, he made iij. peticiouns, *scil.* for to have the dowter of the Emperour with him, *scil.* to have the sowle with him in hevene; as is saide, Os.[27] *Desponsabo te michi*, I shall wedde the soule to me. The secounde that he askid, the tresoure of the kyngdom of hevene, vnde [*understand(?) as this:*], *Sicut disposuit mihi pater meus regum, sic dispono vobis*, As my fadir hathe ordeynid the kyngdom to me, so I dispose hit to yow. The thirdde he askid alle the yen of the accusers to be don [*done*] out, *scil.* he askyd, that alle develis, that excitithe men to synne, mygte be shut fro the lyt [*light*] of euerlastyng grace. And so he savid mankynde fro dethe, browte hem to the kyngdom of hevene. *Ad quod nos & c.*[28]

"Polemius an Emperoure: How an Emperor Bequeathed His Empire to the Most Slothful of His Sons"[29]

Polemius was an Emperoure in the cetee of Rome, the whiche hadde iij. [*three*] sonnes, that he moche lovid. So as this Emperoure laye in a certeyne nyght in his bedde, he thowte to dispose his Empir, & he thought to yeve [*give*] his kyngdome to the slowest of his sones. He callid to him his sonnes, & saide, "he that is the sloweste of yow, or [*that*] most slewthe [*sloth*] is in shall have my kyngdom aftir my discese." "Thenne shall I have hit," quod the Eldest sone; "for I am so slowe, and swiche slewthe is in me, that me hadde leuer late [*rather let*] my fote brynne in the fyr, whenne I Sitte ther by, than to withdrawe, & save hit." "Nay," quod the secounde, "yit am I mor worthi thanne thow; for yf case that my necke wer in a rope to be hongid; and yf that I hadde my two hondes at wille, and in on honde the Ende of the Rope, and in that other honde a sharpe swerde, I hadde levir dye ande be hongid, than I wolde styr myn arme, and kitte [*cut*] the Rope, whereby I myte be savid." "Hit is I," quod the thirde, "that shalle Regne aftir my syre, for I passe hem bothe in slewthe. Yf I lygge [*lay*] in my bedde wyde opyn [*outdoors*], & the Reyne Rayne vppon bothe myn yen [*eyes*], yee, me hadde leuer lete hit Reyne hem oute of the hede, than I turnid me othere to the Right syde, or to the lyfte syde."[30] Thenne the Emperoure biquathe his Empir to the thirde sone, as for the slowist.

Moralite. Dere frendes, this Emperoure is the devil, that is kynge and fadir above al childerin of pryde. By the first sone is vndir-stonde the man, that dwellithe in a wickid sitee or place, by the whiche a flavme of fire, *scil.*, of synne, is stirte to [*started in*] him; & yit it is moche I-sene [*seen*], that he hadde leuer brynne [*burn*] yn synne withe hem [*them*], thanne Remeve from the companye. By the secounde sonne is he vndirstonde, that knowithe welle him selve to be fastenid in the cordes & bondes of synne, and wolle not smyte hem [*them*] aweye with the swerde of his tonge; and hadde leuer be hongid for hem in helle, thanne to be shriven her [*here*]. bi the thirde sone, vpon whom water dropis, both of the rigt ye & of the lyfte, is vndirstonde he that hurithe [*hears*] the doctrine of the ioyes [*joys*] of paradys, and of the paynis & tormentes of helle, and wolle not for slownesse of wytte torne [*turn*] him to the Right syde, *scil.* to leve synne, for love of the Ioyes, ne to the left, *scil.* to leeve synne, for drede of peynis, but lithe [*lies*] stille in synnys vnmevabely; and swiche wolle have the kyngdom of helle, & not of hevene. *A quo nos liberet, et ad quod nos perducat imperator semper iure Regnans!*[31] Amen.

Notes

1. The titles of all selections are taken from Herrtage's edition of the *Gesta.*
2. "The Moral Lesson Taught by the Ants" (Addit. MS. 9066, LIII, p. 372).
3. *Wote nere to whome:* do not know for whom
4. "Pwas an Emperoure, The Man and the Honey in the Tree" (Harl. MS. 7333, XXX, p. 109).
5. *Wan out:* won out (came out well).
6. He would not go from there.
7. *Trees* here should be *beasts.*
8. *Roggyd downe:* made rugged (wore down). The idea here is that human life in the world is like a tree being consumed by two beasts, which represent the succession of time—days and nights wearing down the physical body.
9. By which, if the four humors are not balanced, the image of the body is dissolved.
10. *None hope ne truste to passe:* there is no hope or belief that it will pass.
11. This was apparently a well-known phrase at the time of the writing, but I have not found a more complete phrase elsewhere and can offer only an idea of how it begins: *Let us be eager . . .*"
12. "Cesar the Emperour: How a Greyhound Saved a Child from a Serpant" (Harl. MS. 7333, LXVI, p. 98).
13. *Thei neuer faylid of theire pray comunly:* they habitually never failed to capture their prey.
14. All things that are done against conscience, according to John, as above. (I can find no reference to this apparently abbreviated verse in either the gospel of John or the epistles of John.)
15. "How a Father Killed His Son Rather Than See Him in Pain" (Addit. MS. 9066, XXIII, p. 341).

16. Every day tore at his body.
17. "How a Stepmother Who Wished to Favour Her Own Son Was Foiled" (Harl. MS. 7333, LV, p. 237).
18. To which place may the King who lives through the ages bring us.
19. "Sesar a Wise Emperoure: Of an Emperor Who Suffered the Loss of His Eye for the Sake of His Son" (Harl. MS. 7333, XLI, p. 165).
20. To which [place may God] bring us.
21. "Alexandir a Wise Emperoure: How a Son Saved the Life of His Father" (Harl. MS. 7333, XXXVIII, p. 153).
22. *Plaice*, a kind of European fish.
23. All is one (it is all the same).
24. As long as one dies.
25. To prevent a loss of observance.
26. *Not to fonge hem by*: not to be seized by.
27. *Os*: in Hosea. (I can find no reference to such a verse in Hosea.)
28. To which [place may God bring] us.
29. "Polemius an Emperoure: How an Emperor Bequeathed His Empire to the Most Slothful of His Sons" (Harl. MS. 7333, LVI, p. 238).
30. I would rather let it rain the eyes out of my head than to turn myself either to the right side or to the left.
31. From which place (hell), may the master who reigns with justice forever free us; and to which place (heaven) may he bring us.

3
Selections from Gower's *Confessio Amantis*

LAUREN KIEFER

Not long before 1390, John Gower dedicated his *Confessio Amantis* to a young man with the heart of a boy: Richard II—the *puer indoctus* ("untaught boy") of Gower's contemporaneous *Vox Clamantis*—who had commanded Gower to write "some newe thing" for his instruction and amusement. Often examined by historians for its message to Richard regarding good leadership and good living, the *Confessio* is also praised by critics for its fluent, fast-paced narratives.[1] In short, Gower's ability to sweeten a moral with a good story gives the *Confessio* the feel of a children's book, and with good reason, since he originally wrote the book for a king whom he viewed as a child.

The *Confessio* fulfills several of the criteria for children's literature outlined by Gillian Adams in her recent article on medieval children's literature. It possesses a dedication to a named young person (Richard II, whom Gower describes as a boy [*Vox Clamantis*, 6.555–56]); it includes explanatory glosses directed at inexpert readers; and it is "referred to in other texts"—specifically, in Caxton's fifteenth-century *Book of Curtesye* (309–29; 32–33)—"as somehow connected with children or with education" (Adams, 11–12). At the same time, the *Confessio* resembles modern children's literature in a number of respects: It is based on "dialogue and incident rather than description and introspection"; it "develops within a clear-cut moral schematism"; and in its plot, "probability is often disregarded" (McDowell, 51; see also Tucker, 9–10). The *Confessio* shares these traits with much of medieval literature, which is often addressed to a mixed audience of adults and children. That Gower intended his work for an adult audience as well is reflected in his use of *crosswriting*, "a dialogic mix of older and younger voices" (Knoepflmacher and Myers, vii) emanating from the *Confessio*'s multiple narrators and thus evading the problem that Barbara Wall calls the "double address."[2]

If modern critics of children's literature are sometimes troubled by its dual audience—the degree to which adult writers, editors, publishers, and

purchasers influence stories purportedly meant for children—they can take
heart in the medieval belief that many adults are merely large children, captivated more by the pleasures of a good story than by the usefulness of wise
counsel (see also Darton, 24, on the *Gesta Romanorum*). Robert Mannyng of
Brunne, one of Gower's sources for the *Confessio*, expresses this notion,
expanding upon Gower's notion that reading "aldai" of wisdom "dulleth ofte
a mannes wit" (*Confessio Amantis*, Prologue, 14–15):

> For many beyn of swyche manere
> That talys & rymys wyle blethly here   *gladly*
> Yn gamys, yn festys, & at the ale,
> Loue men to lestene trotouale,   *listen to idle tale telling*
>   *   *   *   *   *
> For swyche men have y made thys ryme.
> (*Handlyng Synne,* 45–48, 51)

Gower's Life, Times, and Texts

The tenor and tone of Gower's early work suggest that he came late to Mannyng's understanding of his audience's childish love of amusement.[3] Born c.
1330 of a Kentish family, Gower seems to have been a member of the same
social class as his friend Geoffrey Chaucer, what one group of critics calls the
"rising bourgeoisie." Although his exact occupation is unclear, references
within his work suggest that he held a civil or legal office, and some critics
suggest that land speculation may have made him fairly wealthy. Such wealth
or status may have contributed to the concern for England's social stability
that appears in all of his major works.[4] Apart from the mellifluous but conventional *Cinkante Ballades*, a series of Anglo-Norman French love-ballads
Gower wrote some time between 1375 and 1399, all of Gower's work has
clear political or ethical implications.

 Gower dedicates himself to showing society its vices in the methodical
Mirour de l'Omme (*Mirror of Mankind*, which Gower later renamed *Speculum Meditantis*), an Anglo–Norman French work Gower probably wrote
between 1378 and 1381.[5] Gower's more public follow-up to the *Mirour,* the
Vox Clamantis (*Voice of One Crying*), appears in eleven manuscripts in three
versions, all of them penned by Gower at different stages of his career. The
earliest version, written before 1381, recapitulates the *Mirour's* schematized
didacticism, dividing the traditional three estates (those who work, those who
fight, and those who pray) into several subspecies (clergy, monastics,
knights, ministers of law) and detailing the vices of each at length. However,
the second and third versions of the *Vox* catch the reader's interest with a
nightmarish depiction of the 1381 Peasant's Revolt, in which all of the key
players have been transformed into animals.[6]

The various versions of the *Vox Clamantis* suggest that political events during this period bore out Gower's fears for his society and eventually showed him the futility of his didactic approach to resolving them. Gower's "Epistle to the King," which appears for the first time in the second version of the *Vox*, written sometime between 1381 and 1386, laments King Richard's misrule, but depicts him as blameless because of his youth ("Stat puer immunis culpe," *Vox*, 6.7.555) and in a hopeful tone asks him to receive the instruction Gower has composed for him as "gifts of God for your praise," since "this instruction is not so much mine but His" ("Scripta tue laudi suscipe dona dei: / Non est ista mea tantum doctrina, sed eius," *Vox*, 6.18.1194–95; Stockton, 249). In the third version of the *Vox*, written sometime between 1390 and 1399—that is, after Gower had finished his first version of the *Confessio Amantis*—Gower begins to lose hope. The king still behaves like an untaught boy ("puer indoctus," *Vox*, 6.7.555), so Gower can only conclude that he has deliberately rejected the proffered instruction: Richard "neglects the moral behavior by which a man might grow from a boy" ("morales negligit actus, / In quibus a puero crescere possit homo" 555–56; Stockton, 232).

Gower began the *Confessio Amantis*, then, as a last-ditch effort to provide good counsel to a young king who preferred amusement to instruction. The earliest version of the *Confessio* explains that Richard has commanded the author to write "Som newe thing . . . / That he himself it mihte loke" (*Confessio*, Prologue, 51–52) and that Gower will therefore try

> To make a bok after his heste,   *command*
> And write in such a maner wise,
> Which may be wisdom to the wise
> And pley to hem that lust to pleye. (82–85)

One may extrapolate from these lines either that Richard commanded Gower to include "pley" as well as "wisdom" in his new book, or simply that after the *Vox*'s failure to change the king's behavior, Gower adopted a new strategy, combining instruction with amusement to engage his childish audience.

The History and Development of the *Confessio*

But the *Confessio*, too, underwent three drafts. Although the first version, written before 1390 and dedicated to Richard, appears to have been the most popular, surviving in thirty-one manuscripts, the second version, which appears in seven manuscripts, was completed by 1393. By this time, Gower appears to have given up on Richard. The second and third versions of the *Confessio* are dedicated to Henry IV, and the phrase "A bok for king Richardes sake" has been replaced by "A bok for Engelondes sake" (Prologue, 24).[7] In revising the prologue to the *Confessio*, Gower focused his attention squarely on the social and political turmoil of his day, replacing the story of Richard's command with a new justification for the book.

The revised dedication reveals Gower's chastened sensibility. First, Gower dispenses with the authoritative tone of his earlier works, admitting that "What schal befalle hierafterward / God wot" (Prologue, 26–27). Gower then distinguishes between his serious purpose (instruction) and his light-hearted method (amusement). "This prologe is so assised / That it to wisdom al belongeth," Gower explains (66–67). However,

> Whan the prologe is so despended,
> This bok schal afterward ben ended
> Of love, which doth many a wonder
> And many a wys man hath put under. (73–76)

The body of the *Confessio*, then, deliberately undercuts the authoritative stance of its prologue and Gower's earlier works by dealing with a force that can confound even the wisest man: love, which promises "many a wonder" to entertain the childish hearts of Gower's listeners. True to his promise, at the end of the *Confessio*'s prologue, Gower abandons his pose as moral authority and recasts himself as a victim of unrequited love. In this connection, he promises to entertain his readers with "A wonder hap which me befell / That was to me bothe hard and fell / Touchende of love and his fortune" (l. 67–69).

In proclaiming himself a victim of love, a force "Which wol no reson understonde" and which "is blind and may noght se" (l. 46–47), Gower, as Amans, the Lover, reduces himself to the role of a child. "Wisshinge and wepinge" like a baby (*Confessio*, 1.115), he gains from a scowling Venus (172) a father figure, her priest Genius, to help him make sense of his overwhelming feelings and to decide what to do about them (180–202). Like a modern child reader, Amans occasionally displays his limited repertoire or interpretive skills by taking a story too literally or relating it too specifically to himself.[8] For example, when Genius tells the story of Apollo and Daphne to warn Amans against foolish haste in love, Amans objects that as long as his lady is "No tre, but halt hire oghne forme," he will continue to love and serve her (*Confessio*, 3.1730–35), and when Genius tries to teach Amans a larger lesson about Christian humility, Amans grows restive, complaining, "Mi fader, I am amorous" (1.2258) and demanding, "That ye me som ensample teche, / Which mihte in loves cause stonde" (2260–61).

The result of Gower's conscious attempt to engage the childish part of his audience is a compilation of over one hundred stories, narrated, like the Prologue, in fluent, unobtrusive octosyllabic couplets. Like a modern children's writer, Gower also appeals to the "grownups" who will be reading the tales aloud, by including a Latin synopsis of each tale in the margin, by sorting the tales into chapters and sections by moral category (based on the Seven Deadly Sins), and by heading each category with a descriptive Latin verse, so that any particular tale is easy to find and easy to evaluate. Critics have found in the *Confessio* references to an impressive array of sources.[9] However, the majority of the stories Gower tells are from sources that would have been familiar to his listeners since primary school: the Bible, Virgil's *Aeneid*, and, most frequently, the works of Ovid, especially the *Metamorphoses* and the *Heroides*.

The *Confessio* as Children's Literature

The three stories excerpted further on represent two different types of children's literature, familiar both to the Middle Ages and to our own time. First, in their emphasis on children's obedience to their parents, Gower's tales of Phaethon and Icarus (*Confessio*, 3.979–1071) diverge from their Ovidian source to resemble a medieval school text.[10] In the *Confessio*, both Phaethon and Icarus die by drowning because they disobey their parents' advice not to fly too high or too low. In fact, Gower has Phaethon's own father drown his child to save the earth (in the Latin marginal gloss to the tale, Phaethon falls off the chariot and drowns through his own negligence)—a pointed alteration of Ovid's version, where Zeus kills the child over his father's objections. This didactic, somewhat punitive take on a traditional story resembles nineteenth-century retellings of fairy tales for children, such as the Grimms' "The Virgin Mary's Child" ("Marienkind," Zipes, 8–11), "Little Red Cap" ("Rotkäppchen," 101–05), "Mother Trudy" ("Frau Trude," 159–60) and "The Stubborn Child" ("Das eigensinnige Kind," 422), all of which punish disobedient children (see also Tatar, 22–69). The moral also retains a surprising appeal today: Several modern children's writers retell the tale of Icarus with a very Gowerian emphasis on Icarus's disobedience of his father (Stephens and McCallum, 69; Evans and Millard, 26).

Second, "The Tale of Adrian and Bardus" (*Confessio*, 5.4947–5163) resembles the beast fables that were "a curriculum standard for young readers" in the Middle Ages (Adams, 12). In Gower's tale, poor Bardus rescues an ape, a serpent, and rich Adrian from a deep pit, only to find that the ape and the serpent willingly reward him, while Adrian refuses even to thank Bardus until he is compelled to do so by the emperor. Such "tales of helpful animals," in which "A mutual relationship and reciprocal exchange is established between man and animal" (Thomas, 112) resurface in a large number of the Grimms' fairy tales and in the fairy tales of Andrew Lang.[11] Gower's grateful animals may appeal especially to young children, who "will look for the clear workings of human laws of morality in everything, both animate and inanimate" (Tucker, 77). In fact, Nicholas Tucker contends that "children have always been attracted by the animal story, even when its real point may have been quite above their heads" (100–101). The point of Gower's story, that ingratitude is not only wrong but unnatural, is easy for a childish audience to grasp; here, the animals that behave like humans not only make the story entertaining, but help emphasize its moral.

Both stories feature authority figures attempting to dispense wisdom with varying degrees of success. As the "adult" in the story, each of these authority figures models a potential path for the young King Richard: overweening pride, futile assertiveness, or justice born of reflection. Nonetheless, it is the "children" (the lower-status individuals) in the stories who capture our attention as they manage to get their way in spite of their lowly status. Through rebellious Icarus and Phaethon and humble but triumphant Bardus, Gower shows Richard that his subjects, while nominally powerless, cannot be ignored or forgotten. A wise king does not grab at power like a childish toy, but considers the needs and desires of all of the people in his charge.

Like many writers and critics of children's literature,[12] Gower saw children and young people as easily molded, for good or ill. In his early work, for example, he worries about young children's susceptibility to the blandishments of friars (*Mirour*, 21553–64; *Vox*, 4.21.981–1014). Of the young Richard II, Gower worries that "Sin springs up on every side of the boy, and he, who is quite easily led, takes to every evil" ("Error ad omne latus pueri consurgit, et ille,/Qui satis est docilis, concipit omne malum," *Vox*, 6.7.569–70; Stockton, 232). But as later readers acknowledge, the *Confessio* offers young readers more than just moral guidelines. In Caxton's fifteenth-century *Book of Curtesye*, for example, the author of *Lytill Johan* enjoins the child to read Gower's *Confessio* for both its meaning and its style:

Redeth gower in his wrytynge moralle	*moral writing*
That auncyent fader of memorye	*memory*
Redeth his bookes/callede confessionalle	*confessional*
With many another vertuous traytte	*trait*
Ful of sentence/set ful fructuosly	*meaning; fruitfully*
That hym to rede/shal gyue you corage	*heart*
He is so ful of fruyt, sentence and langage.	*value, meaning, and*
(47; 33)	*eloquence*

It is not just the *Confessio's* "sentence"—its meaning—that renders it appropriate for children, but its "langage" and the way it is deployed, "set ful fructuously." As little John's father-figure shows in his exhortation, the *Confessio* transcends its origins as an example to the childish Richard, to offer "corage"—heart and solace—to children of any generation.

Notes

1. See, for example, Gaylord, 281; Fisher et al., 2205–6; Yeager, *John Gower,* 313; and C. S. Lewis, 206–8.
2. Wall, 20–36. For further discussion of the *Confessio*'s multiple narrators, see Wetherbee, "John Gower," 598–99; Farnham, 144–46; and Echard, 1–8. On the negative aspects of the dual audience of children's literature, see Hunt, *Defining,* 4; Nodelman, 92–94; Lesnik-Oberstein, 3; and Wall, 13.
3. In terms of the current controversy regarding the nature and function of children's literature—should it be, or indeed, can it be, written purely to amuse? Or is didacticism one of its inescapable features? (Adams, 6–7; Nodelman, 64–73; Lesnik-Oberstein, 38–40; Tucker, 115)—Gower seems prescient. In his admission that "who al of wisdom writ / It dulleth ofte a mannes wit / To him that schal it aldai rede" (*Confessio,* Prologue, 13–15) and his avowed plan therefore to "go the middel weie / And wryte a bok betwen the tweie, / Somwhat of lust, somwhat of lore" (16–18), Gower anticipates John Newbery's motto, "Delectando monemus, Instruction with Delight" (Darton, 1–2); the overt tendencies of a number of nineteenth-century writers for children (Wall, 42–61; Shavit, 166–77) and of famous compilers of fairy tales such as the Brothers Grimm (Tatar, 3–69; Nodelman, 247–50; Thomas, 111–14; Shavit, 22); and the covert tendencies of children's literature in our own time (Briggs, 21; Nodelman, 155–62; May, 18; Sutherland, 143–57; Tucker, 193–97).
4. For further discussion and debate concerning Gower's possible social, occupational, and financial status, see Fisher et al., 2199; "John Gower," Wetherbee, 589; Fisher, 55–56; Burrow, "Chaucer and Gower," 48; Strohm, 31; Diller, 51; and Macaulay, 134. For the possible impact of these factors on Gower's message, see Fisher, 97–99, and Richard Firth Green, 182.
5. For fuller descriptions of the *Cinkante Ballades* and the *Mirour de l'Omme,* see Calin, 372–85, and Wetherbee, "John Gower," 590–94. For additional discussion of their manuscript history, see Wetherbee, "John Gower," 592; Bestul, 307–8; and Fisher et al., 2198.
6. For fuller descriptions of the *Vox Clamantis,* see Wetherbee, "John Gower," 594–97, and Wickert, 27–67, and see Fisher, 306, 308, for a list of individual manuscripts. For a fuller discussion of the *Vox*'s Epistle to the King, see Wickert, 131–69, and Stow, 13–14.
7. Fisher et al. explain that the third recension of the *Confessio Amantis,* which appears in eleven manuscripts, was "evidently compiled at the time of Henry's accession by conflating the texts of recensions one and two" (2203; see Fisher, 304–5, 309, for a list of individual manuscripts of the *Confessio*). Gower's later works confirm this shift of focus. A number of his minor Latin works implicitly criticize Richard (see Coffman, 955–64; Fisher, 127–32), while the English *In Praise of Peace* (1399) and the Latin *Cronica Tripertita* (1399–1400) both praise Henry, the latter at Richard's expense (see also Fisher, 109–15; Grady, 558–72; and Wetherbee, "John Gower," 608–9). Finally, the Anglo–Norman French *Traitié pour essampler les amantz mariez* positions itself as a postscript to the final version of the *Confessio Amantis* that is addressed to the people of England rather than to her king.

8. On the ramifications of repertoire—the background and skills a child brings to a
    text—see Nodelman, 19; Tucker, 128–32; and Wall, 15. For further discussion of
    Amans's childishness and limitations as a reader, see Peck, xxi; Wetherbee,
    "John Gower," 601; Axton, 29; Allen, 635; Calin, 394; and Nicholson, 195–99.
9. Gower's sources include, from the classical tradition, Horace, Livy, Hyginus,
    Valerius Maximus, Josephus Flavius, the *Historia Alexandri*, the pseudo-
    Aristotelian *Secretum secretorum*, and *Servius's Commentary on the Aeneid*;
    Christian sources Methodius, Isidore of Seville, Gregory, Peter Comestor,
    Giles of Rome, and Augustine; French sources Godfrey of Viterbo, Benoît de
    Sainte-Maure, the *Roman de Sept Sages*, the *Roman de la Rose*, and the
    Ovide moralisé; Italian sources Boccaccio, Guido delle Colonne, and
    Brunetto Latini; and English sources Nicholas Trevet, William Langland, and
    Robert Mannyng of Brunne (Fisher et al., 2206–7). For the use of Ovid in
    medieval schools, see Hexter, 18–19, and McGregor, 29–51.
10. For Ovid's tales of Phaethon and Icarus, see *Metamorphoses*, 2.1–366,
    8.183–235. Gower's versions of Ovid's tales resemble the medieval version
    of Statius's *Achilleis*, included in the schoolchild's *Liber Catonianus* "for its
    account of how Achilles obeyed his mother Thetis" (Adams, 10).
11. Relevant tales from the Brothers Grimm include "The White Snake" ("Die
    weisse Schlange," Zipes, 67–69), "The Golden Bird" ("Der goldene Vogel,"
    216–22), "The Two Brothers" ("Der zwei Brüder," 230–47), "The Queen
    Bee" ("Die Bienenkönigin," 252–53), "The Two Travelers" ("Die beiden
    Wanderer," 385–93), "Faithful Ferdinand and Unfaithful Ferdinand" ("Fer-
    anand getrü und Ferenand ungetrü," 447–51), "The Little Hamsterfrom the
    Water" ("Das Meerhäschen," 596–99), "Puss in Boots" ("Der gestiefelte
    Kater," 652–55), and "The Faithful Animals" ("Die treuen Tiere," 685–88).
    On relevant tales from Andrew Lang, see Burne, 146.
12. See, for example, Nodelman, 73–74; Harris, 126; Edger Jones, 28; and Tucker,
    190–91.

The Tale of Phaethon

The Marginal Gloss

Here the Confessor offers an exemplum against the vice of negligence and
says that when Phaethon, the Sun's son, had to drive his father's chariot
through the air, he was warned by his father to rein the horses in diligently,
with an even hand, so that they would not stray from the path, but he ignored
his father's advice due to his own negligence and allowed the horses to wander too low with the chariot, so that not only was the earth set aflame with
fire, but he caused himself to plunge to his own death by falling from the
chariot into a river.

The Tale

Phebus, which is the Sonne hote,   *named*
That schyneth upon Erthe hote   980
And causeth every lyves helthe,

He hadde a Sone in al his welthe,
Which Pheton hihte, and he
   desireth   *was named*
And with his Moder he conspireth,
The which was cleped Clemenee,   *called*
For help and conseil, so that he
His fader carte lede myhte   *father's chariot*
Upon the faire daies brihte.
And for this thing thei bothe preide
   Unto the fader, and he seide   990
He wolde wel, bot forth withal   *in addition*
Thre pointz he bad in special   *ordered, commanded*
Unto his Sone in alle wise,
That he him scholde wel avise   *consider, reflect on*
And take it as be weie of lore.   *by way of, as a type of; teaching*
Ferst was, that he his hors to sore
Ne prike, and over that he tolde   *spur*
That he the renes faste holde;
And also that he be riht war
In what manere he lede his charr,   1000   *chariot*
That he mistake noght his gate,
Bot up avisement algate   *consideration at all times*
He scholde bere a siker yhe,   *sure eye*
That he to lowe ne to hyhe   *neither too low nor too high*
His carte dryve at eny throwe,   *time*
Wherof that he mihte overthrowe.
And thus be Phebus ordinance
Tok Pheton into governance
The Sonnes carte, which he ladde:
   Bot he such veine gloire hadde   1010   *vainglory, vanity, pride*
Of that he was set upon hyh,
That he his oghne astat ne syh   *state, condition; did not see*
Thurgh negligence and tok non
   hiede;
So mihte he wel noght longe spede.   *succeed*
For he the hors withoute lawe
The carte let aboute drawe
Wher as hem liketh wantounly,   *wantonly*
That ate laste sodeinly,   *suddenly*
For he no reson wolde knowe,
This fyri carte he drof to lowe,   1020
And fyreth al the world aboute;
Wherof thei weren alle in doubte,   *fear*

And to the god for helpe criden
Of suche unhappes as betyden.   *misfortunes; happened*
Phebus, which syh the necgligence,
How Pheton ayein his defence   *against; prohibition*
His charr hath drive out of the
   weie,
Ordeigneth that he fell aweie
Out of the carte into a flod
And dreynte. Lo now, hou it stod   1030   *drowned*
With him that was so necgligent,
That fro the hyhe firmament,
For that he wolde go to lowe,
He was anon doun overthrowe.

The Tale of Icarus

The Marginal Gloss

An exemplum about the same thing, concerning Icarus, Daedalus's son, who
was living in the Minotaur's prison when Daedalus, having made wings to fly
out from there, firmly ordered him not to ascend too high on account of the
Sun's heat. Disregarding this due to his own negligence, Icarus rose very
high, then suddenly fell to earth and died.

The Tale

In hih astat it is a vice   *high standing*
To go to lowe, and in service
It grieveth forto go to hye,
Wherof a tale in poesie   *poetry, verse*
I finde, how whilom Dedalus,
Which hadde a Sone, and Icharus   1040
He hihte, and thogh hem thoghte lothe,   *hateful*
In such prison thei weren bothe
With Minotaurus, that aboute
Thei mihten nawher wenden oute;   *might nowhere; go*
So thei begonne forto schape   *contrive*
How thei the prison mihte ascape.
This Dedalus, which fro his yowthe
Was tawht and manye craftes cowthe,   *knew*
Of fetheres and of othre thinges
Hath mad to fle diverse wynges   1050   *flee*
For him and for his Sone also;
To whom he yaf in charge tho   *then*

And bad him thenke therupon,
How that his wynges ben set on
With wex, and if he toke his flyhte
To hyhe, al sodeinliche he mihte   *suddenly*
Make it to melte with the Sonne.
And thus thei have her flyht begonne
Out of the prison faire and softe;   *carefully; quietly*
    And whan thei weren bothe alofte,   1060
This Icarus began to monte,   *mount, ascend*
And of the conseil non accompte   *counsel; no account*
He sette, which his fader tawhte,   *He set*
Til that the Sonne his wynges cawhte,
Wherof it malt, and fro the heihte
Withouten help of eny sleihte
He fell to his destruccion.
And lich to that condicion
Ther fallen ofte times fele   *many*
    For lacke of governance in wele,   1070   *control; happiness*
Als wel in love as other weie.

The Tale of Adrian and Bardus

The Marginal Gloss

Here he speaks of how animals in their kindness naturally outdo the ungrateful man. And he offers an exemplum concerning Adrian, a Senator of Rome,
who went hunting in a certain Forest and fell into a deep Well, unbeknownst
to his companions, while he was pursuing his prey. When a certain pauper
named Bardus came upon him and threw down a rope, expecting to pull up a
man, he first pulled out an Ape; second, a Snake; and third, Adrian, who
despised the pauper and refused to give him anything as a reward. But both
the Snake and the Ape sufficiently repaid his gracious kindness with separate
gifts.

The Tale

To speke of an unkinde man,
I finde hou whilom Adrian,   *formerly*
Of Rome which a gret lord was,[1]
Upon a day as he per cas   4940   *by chance*
To wode in his huntinge wente,   *the woods*
It hapneth at a soudein wente,   *sudden turn*
After his chace as he poursuieth,

Thurgh happ, the which noman
    eschuieth,   *chance; no one avoids*
He fell unwar into a pet,   *pit*
Wher that it mihte noght be let.   *prevented*
The pet was dep and he fell lowe,
That of his men non myhte knowe
Wher he becam, for non was nyh,
Which of his fall the meschief syh.   4940 *saw*
And thus al one ther he lay
Clepende and criende al the day   *calling*
For socour and deliverance,   *aid*
Til ayein Eve it fell per chance,   *toward evening*
A while er it began to nyhte,
A povere man, which Bardus hihte,   *who was named Bardus*
Cam forth walkende with his asse,
And hadde gadred him a tasse   *gathered; heap*
Of grene stickes and of dreie   *dry*
To selle, who that wolde hem beie,   4960
As he which hadde no liflode,   *livelihood*
Bot whanne he myhte such a lode
To toune with his Asse carie.
And as it fell him forto tarie   *befell*
That ilke time nyh the pet,   *same*
And hath the trusse faste knet,   *bundle; tied*
He herde a vois, which cride dimme,   *faintly*
And he his Ere to the brimme   *ear; brink, edge*
Hath leid, and herde it was a man,
Which seide, "Ha, help hier Adrian,   4970
And I wol yiven half mi good."   *give half my possessions*
The povere man this understod,
As he that wolde gladly winne,
And to this lord which was withinne
He spak and seide, "If I thee save,
What sikernesse schal I have   *certainty*
Of covenant, that afterward   *promise, contract*
Thou wolt me yive such reward
As thou behihtest nou tofore?"   *promised; just now*
That other hath his othes swore   4980 *oaths*
Be hevene and be the goddes alle,
If that it myhte so befalle
That he out of the pet him broghte,
Of all the goodes whiche he oghte
He schal have evene halvendel,   *half*

This Bardus seide he wolde wel;
And with this word his Asse anon
He let untrusse, and therupon   *untie*
Doun goth the corde into the pet,
To which he hath at ende knet   4990   *fastened*
A staf, wherby, he seide, he wolde
That Adrian him scholde holde.
Bot it was tho per chance falle,
Into that pet was also falle
An Ape, which at thilke throwe,   *that same*; *time*
Whan that the corde cam doun lowe,
Al sodeinli therto he skipte   *jumped*
And it in bothe his armes clipte.   *clasped*
And Bardus with his Asse anon
Him hath updrawe, and he is gon.   5000
But whan he sih it was an Ape,
He wende al hadde ben a jape   *thought*; *trick*
Of faerie, and sore him dradde.[2]
And Adrian eftsone gradde   *immediately*; *cried out*
For help, and cride and preide faste,   *prayed earnestly*
And he eftsone his corde caste;   *soon after*
Bot whan it cam unto the grounde,
A gret Serpent it hath bewounde,
The which Bardus anon up drouh.
And thanne him thoghte wel ynouh,   5010
It was fantosme, bot yit he herde   *apparition, hallucination*
The vois, and he therto ansuerde,
"What wiht art thou in goddes
    name?"   *creature*
"I am," quod Adrian, "the same,
Whos good thou schalt have evene
    half."
Quod Bardus, "Thanne a goddes   *in God's name*
    half
The thridde time assaie I schal":   *try*
And caste his corde forth withal   *therewith*
Into the pet, and whan it cam
To him, this lord of Rome it nam,   5020   *seized*
And therupon him hath adresced,
And with his hand fulofte blessed,
And thanne he bad to Bardus hale.   *pull*
And he, which understod his tale,
Betwen him and his Asse al softe

Hath drawe and set him up alofte
Withouten harm al esely.   *gently, easily*
He seith noght ones "grant merci,"   *thank you*
Bot strauhte him forth to the cite,   *straightway, right away*
And let this povere Bardus be.   5030   *poor*
And natheles this simple man
His covenant, so as he can,
Hath axed; and that other seide,   *asked*
If so be that he him umbreide   *reproached*
Of oght that hath be speke or do,   *anything*
It schal be venged on him so,   *shall be avenged*
That him were betre to be ded.
And he can tho non other red,   *knew; advice*
But on his asse ayein he caste
His trusse, and hieth homward faste: 5040
And whan that he cam hom to bedde,
He tolde his wif hou that he spedde.   *fared*
Bot finaly to speke oght more
Unto this lord he dradde him sore,   *very much feared*
So that a word ne dorste he sein: *dared; say*
And thus upon the morwe ayein,
In the manere as I recorde,
Forth with his Asse and with his
     corde
To gadre wode, as he dede er,
He goth; and whan that he cam ner   5050
Unto the place where he wolde,
He hath his Ape anon beholde,
Which hadde gadred al aboute
Of stickes hiere and there a route,   *quantity*
And leide hem redy to his hond,
Wherof he made his trosse and bond;   *his pack and bundle*
Fro dai to dai and in this wise
This Ape profreth his servise,
So that he hadde of wode ynouh.
   Upon a time and as he drouh   5060
Toward the wode, he sih besyde
The grete gastli Serpent glyde,[3]
Til that sche cam in his presence,
And in hir kinde a reverence   *her way*
Sche hath him do, and forth withal
A Ston mor briht than a cristall
Out of hir mouth tofore his weie

Sche let doun falle, and wente aweie,
For that he schal noght ben adrad.[4]
Tho was this povere Bardus glad,   5070
Thonkende god, and to the Ston   *thanking*
He goth and takth it up anon,
And hath gret wonder in his wit
Hou that the beste him hath aquit,   *beast; repaid*
Wher that the mannes Sone hath
   failed,
For whom he hadde most travailed.   *worked*
Bot al he putte in goddes hond,
And torneth hom, and what he fond
Unto his wif he hath it schewed;   *showed*
And thei, that weren bothe lewed,   5080 *uneducated, ignorant*
Acorden that he scholde it selle.   *agreed*
And he no lengere wolde duelle,
Bot forth anon upon the tale
The Ston he profreth to the sale;
And riht as he himself it sette,
The jueler anon forth fette   *fetched*
The gold and made his paiement,
Therof was no delaiement.
Thus whan this Ston was boght
   and sold,
Homward with joie manifold   5090
This Bardus goth; and whan he cam
Hom to his hous and that he nam   *took*
His gold out of his Purs, withinne
He fond his Ston also therinne,
Wherof for joie his herte pleide,
Unto his wif and thus he seide,
"Lo, hier my gold, lo, hier mi Ston!"
His wif hath wonder therupon,
And axeth him hou that mai be.
"Nou be mi trouthe I not," quod he,   5100 *know not*
"Bot I dar swere upon a bok,
That to my Marchant I it tok,
And he it hadde whan I wente:
So knowe I noght to what entente
It is nou hier, bot it be grace.   *now here*
Forthi tomorwe in other place
I wole it fonde forto selle,   *try*
And if it wol noght with him duelle,

Bot crepe into mi purs ayein,
Than dar I saufly swere and sein,   5110   *safely*
It is the vertu of the Ston."
The morwe cam, and he is gon
To seche aboute in other stede   *seek; place*
His Ston to selle, and he so dede,   *did*
And lefte it with his chapman there.   *dealer*
Bot whan that he cam elleswhere,
In presence of his wif at hom,
Out of his Purs and that he nom   *when; took*
His gold, he fond his Ston withal: *as well*
And thus it fell him overal,   5120
Where he it solde in sondri place,
Such was the fortune and the grace.
Bot so wel may nothing ben hidd,
That it nys ate laste kidd: *is not at last known*
This fame goth aboute Rome
So ferforth, that the wordes come
To themperour Justinian;   *the emperor*
And he let sende for the man,
And axede him hou that it was.
And Bardus tolde him al the cas,   5130
Hou that the worm and ek the beste,
Althogh thei maden no beheste,   *promise*
His travail hadden wel aquit;   *Had well repaid his work*
Bot he which hadde a mannes wit,
And made his covenant be mouthe
And swor therto al that he couthe   *could*
To parte and yiven half his good,
Hath nou foryete hou that it stod,   *forgotten*
As he which wol no trouthe holde.   *promise*
This Emperour al that he tolde   5140
Hath herd, and thilke unkindenesse
He seide he wolde himself redresse.
And thus in court of juggement
This Adrian was thanne assent,   *sent for*
And the querele in audience   *quarrel, conflict*
Declared was in the presence
Of themperour and many mo;
Wherof was mochel speche tho   *much*
And gret wondringe among the press.   *crowd*
     Bot ate laste natheles   5150
For the partie which hath pleigned   *complained*

The lawe hath diemed and ordeigned	*judged; ordained*
Be hem that were avised wel,	*very learned*
That he schal have the halvendel	
Thurghout of Adrianes good.	
And thus of thilke unkinde blod	*ungrateful*
Stant the memoire into this day,	*stands, continues*
Wherof that every wysman may	
Ensamplen him, and take in mynde	*learn from*
What schame it is to ben unkinde; 5160	
Ayein the which reson debateth,	
And every creature it hateth.	

Notes

1. By setting the story in Rome in the reign of the emperor Justinian, Gower gives a false historical backdrop to a story that originates in the Sanskrit *Panchatantra* (c. 200 B.C.), where a poor Brahman pulls an ungrateful goldsmith out of a pit (Ryder, 112–17). The exemplum against ingratitude made its way to Europe via the Arab *Kalila wa Dimnah*; it also appears in the twelfth-century *Speculum stultorum* (Longchamp, 122–33); in the *Gesta Romanorum* (Swan, 257–60); and in Matthew Paris (Giles, 2.143–45); see Hiscoe, 233, for more analogues.

2. In the *Physiologus*, "the basic compendium of 'Christian zoology' " (Janson, 17), the ape is said to represent the devil (Curley, 39).

3. Yeager sees in this line a deliberate "manipulation of sound" to convey "the motion of the serpent through the accents and caesura," as well as "a reptilian hiss" and "dry scrape of scale" in the "repeating, guttural 'gr/gas/gly' " (*John Gower's Poetic*, 29; but see Gaylord, 265–66, for an opposing view).

4. This association of snake and jewels can also be found in *Confessio*, 1.463–80, where the adder is said to stop its ear with its tail to keep people from charming it out of the jewel it keeps in its head. The earliest source for the notion that snakes possess jewels is the Greek Soracus; Gower may have found the idea in Isidore of Seville's *Etymologiae* or in Brunetto Latini's *Li Livres dou Tresor* (l. 138; 109).

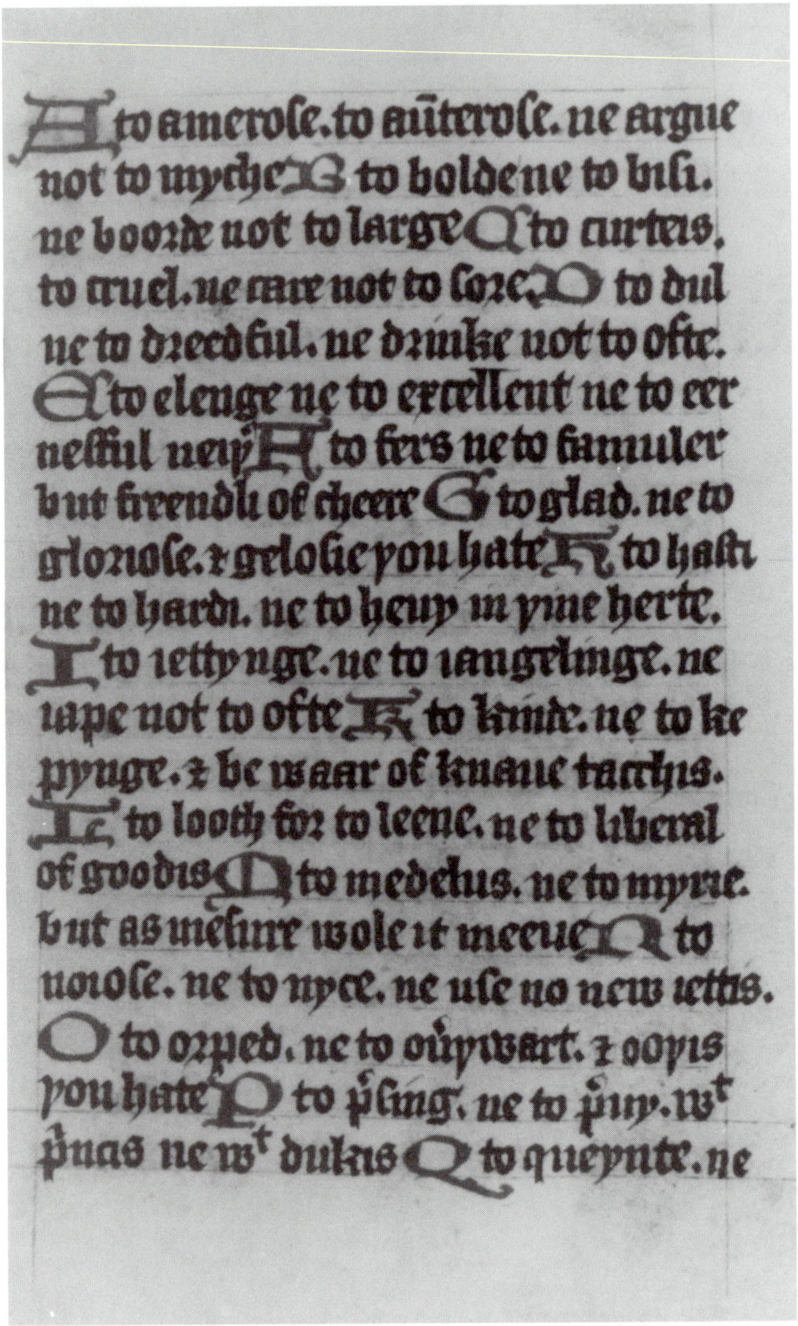

A͵ to amerose.to autterose. ne argue
not to myche B to boldene to bisi.
ne boorde not to large C to curteis,
to cruel.ne care not to sore D to dul
ne to dredful. ne drinke not to ofte.
E to elenge ne to excellent ne to eer
nessul neiȝ F to fers ne to famuler
but frendli of cheer G to glad. ne to
glorose. z gelosie you hate H to hasti
ne to hardi. ne to heuy in yine herte.
I to lettynge. ne to iangelinge. ne
iape not to ofte K to kinde. ne to ke
pynge. z be waar of knaue tacchis.
L to looth for to leene. ne to liberal
of goodis M to medelus. ne to myrie.
but as mesure wole it meeue N to
noiose. ne to nyce. ne use no new iettis.
O to orped. ne to ouyrwart. z oopis
you hate P to plsing. ne to priy. wᵗ
pnas ne wᵗ dulnis Q to queynte. ne

Figure 1. The "ABC of Aristotle."

4

The "ABC of Aristotle"

MARTHA DANA RUST

The "ABC of Aristotle" is a late Middle English alliterative *abecedarium* that counsels adherence to Aristotle's "Golden Mean": the doctrine that health and happiness in life are to be found by seeking a path of moderation in all things. (See figure 1.) The poem illustrates this wisdom by listing extremes of behavior that a child or young adult should resist, occasionally offering a balanced alternative between two forms of extravagance already enumerated. The ideal of moderation is then stated formally in the poem's last line: "a mesurable meene is eu*ere* þe beste of alle." In accordance with the formal device of an *abecedarium*, the undesirable modes of conduct are arranged in alphabetical order, each line of the poem beginning with a successive letter of the alphabet, running from A through W and excluding J and U.[1] The poem's alliterative verse form makes way for at least two additional behavioral extremes within each line, so that, all told, it lists fifty-seven peccadilloes to be avoided.

The "ABC of Aristotle" has been transmitted in two versions—one with a prologue and one without—and survives in fourteen manuscript witnesses: more than either the *Lay Folks' Catechism* or Chaucer's *Legend of Good Women*.[2] Judging from this relatively large number of surviving witnesses, Thorlac Turville-Petre concluded that this "dreary alphabetical list of admonitions" was "dispiritingly popular" (122). In the introductory essay that follows, I hope to show that the evident popularity of the "ABC of Aristotle" was well justified: not as another example of the fifteenth-century reading audience's reputed penchant for all that was "dispiritingly" didactic, but rather because it weaves into one short poem themes that were closely interwoven in late-medieval English culture—elementary education, courtesy, and affective devotion.[3] In addition, and more important, for a society in which lay literacy was increasingly the norm, even as it posed a mobile threat to the status quo, the "ABC of Aristotle" mapped on to the very elements of literacy a strategy for the production of individuals who would themselves bear a certain resemblance to alphabetical characters. Socially legible and well wrought, the "lettered" children and adults who knew Aristotle's "ABC" would know their place in the world.

Date and Authorship

The "ABC of Aristotle" has twice been attributed to Benedict Burgh (fl. 1472), clerk, translator, teacher, and friend of John Lydgate, and he is an attractive candidate for the role.[4] One manuscript witness to the poem, British Library MS Harley 1706, ascribes it to "Mayster Benett"; moreover, works known to have been written by Burgh share the didactic content and classroom affiliations that the "ABC of Aristotle" displays.[5] But popular familiarity with pseudo-Aristotelian advice on personal conduct, in addition to the vogue for alphabetic poems during this period, suggests that many a late-medieval English writer might have conceived of an "ABC" devoted to the ideal of the Golden Mean; in fact, there seems even to have been more than one "Benett" capable of such a production. Sixteenth-century bibliographer John Bale attributes an "Alphabetum Aristotelis" to one Benedict Anglus (fl. 1340), once prior of the Austin friars at Norwich and later assistant to the bishop of Norwich and Winchester (Poole and Bateson, 46).[6] With two claimants to the moniker "Mayster Benett" in Harley 1706, the poem's authorship may be forever in doubt; nevertheless, Burgh's credentials still provide a useful template with which to imagine the true author of the "ABC of Aristotle," for whoever wrote it was no doubt someone *like* Burgh: an earnest, ingenious, and experienced teacher but a poet of only modest talent at best.[7]

Probably the earliest manuscript witness to the poem is Lambeth Palace Library 853. The editors of the *Middle English Dictionary* have dated it "c. 1450," by which they designate the fifty-year span extending from 1425 to 1475 (1:18). Given the dates of the two possible authors of the poem, then, the second quarter of the fifteenth century is likely to be the latest possible date of its composition. Lambeth Palace Library 853 also includes the poem's prologue, evidence that these lines were part of the original composition and not a later accretion. Since the Lambeth witness to the "ABC of Aristotle" seems, therefore, to be both early and complete, it is the copy of the poem I have selected to transcribe for this edition.[8]

Poetic Structure: The *Abecedarium*

The term *abecedarium* may give a modern reader at least a moment's consternation, unused, as we are, to alphabet poems, but the form enjoyed a consistent popularity throughout the Middle Ages. In Middle English the form even had its own generic term: *abece*, also spelled *a.b.c.*[9] The *abeces* with the longest history in the West are those preserved in the Old Testament; among these, the most elaborate is Psalm 118.[10] Written in stanzas of 8 lines, each of which begins with the same letter, the poem's 22 stanzas use the 22 letters of the Hebrew alphabet in order. Perhaps inspired by Old Testament examples, many poets of the late-antique and early-medieval period penned alphabetical compositions, including Commodian, Augustine, Hilary of Poitiers, Fortunatus, and Caelius Sedulius. Early *abecedaria* from Britain and Ireland include a hymn on Patrick attributed to his nephew Sechnall, the "Altus Prosator" attributed to Columba, an *abece* on Æthelthryth by Bede, and several alphabetical pieces by Wulfstan. Merovingian and Carolingian poets of *abecedaria* were especially prolific, composing poems on topics as diverse as the Battle of Fontenoy, the miracles of Saint Ninian, and the preterit tense.[11]

Although late Middle English *abeces* are written on a similarly broad spectrum of topics—from the names of plants to the Passion of Christ—many of them are also both united and set apart from earlier *abecedaria* by a shared set of allusions to the customary page layout of the alphabet in devotional primers for children.[12] As Nicholas Orme has explained, the alphabet was usually set down for young scholars in primers in a standardized form: it began with a cross, was followed by a capital "A" and then by the rest of the alphabet; after the Latin characters, there often appeared the customary abbreviations for *et* and *con*, three dots, or "tittles," and the words *est amen* (*English Schools*, 61).[13] Following the alphabet, most primers then presented basic prayers—the Lord's Prayer, the Hail Mary, and the Creed—and continued with miscellaneous didactic material. A child working with a primer would first make the sign of the cross and utter the words "Christ's cross me speed" and would then go on to read—or to recite—the alphabet and ensuing prayers. We find occasional references to this practice of recitation in Middle English lyrics; for instance, the late-fourteenth-century poem "Pierce the Ploughman's Crede" begins "Cros, and Curteis Crist this begynnynge spede / ... / A. and all myn A.b.c. after haue y lerned, / And [patred] in my paternoster iche poynt after other, / And after all, myn Aue-marie almost to the ende; / But all my kare is to comen for y can nohght my Crede" (1–8). Given our knowledge of a primer's usual format, it is clear that the speaker in this poem is trying to work his way through one.

Among the Middle English *abeces* that refer to the arrangement of the alphabet in primers, the *abece* on the cross at the beginning of the "English Register of Godstow Nunnery" (*Index of Middle English Verse, IMEV* 664) is perhaps the most striking example.[14] The poem begins, as do primer alphabets, with a cross; reading the ✠ as the word *cross*, the poem's first line is "Cross of iheſu criste be euer oure spede." There follows—in the place of a primer's unadorned series of letters—a twenty-seven-line verse meditation on the cross, each line of which begins with a successive letter of the alphabet: "And . . . / Blessid . . . / Crist . . . / Dede . . . / Euer . . ." and so on. The penultimate line is given to two of the auxiliary symbols often found at the end of primer alphabets, "Titulle of þi passion Poynte us saue", and the poem concludes with another cross: "As to thy ▧ reuerence we may haue".[15] A poem that is much less obviously related to primer alphabets is Chaucer's "An ABC." Even though Chaucer's *abece* stops at the letter Z, a look at the poem's source reveals its place in a lineage of "primer *abeces*," for Chaucer's alphabetic hymn to the Virgin Mary is a translation of a prayer in Guillaume de Deguileville's *Le Pelerinage de vie humaine* (10,894–11,192)—an alphabetical prayer whose own ties to primer alphabets are marked in its final stanzas, which are for *et* and *con*, respectively.[16]

Predictably, considering the devotional content of primers, most of the Middle English *abeces* that display a structural affiliation with primer alphabets are on devotional themes. Perhaps it is a testimony, then, to an expansion of the generic requirements of the *abecedarium* in its incarnation in fifteenth-century English manuscript culture that certain fixtures of primer alphabets have also been grafted on to several copies of the "ABC of Aristotle." For instance, the copy in Additional 60577 begins with a ▧ and the words "Crystys crosse be oure spede: w^t grace m*ercye in all oure nede" and concludes with a prayerful "to Cryste pray we where soo wee bee. / That we may lerne thys .A.B.C."[17] Displaying a similar influence, the Harley 1304 witness concludes with the line "xyz xy wyth esed *and per* se Tytell Tytell Tytell than Est *and* Amen," where *esed* is possibly the French name for the letter Z—*zed*—and "Tytell Tytell Tytell than Est *and* Amen" refers to the usual conclusion of primer alphabets.

Audiences and Codicological Contexts

The books in which the "ABC of Aristotle" are preserved aptly reflect the crosscurrents among affective devotion, moral didacticism, and elementary pedagogy that traverse the history of the medieval *abecedarium* from its exemplars in the Old Testament to the "ABC of Aristotle" itself. In several volumes, the "ABC" appears in the midst of longer sequences of material that are clearly directed to young people. For instance, in Harley 5086 the "ABC" is tucked between a poetic treatment of table etiquette—the so-called *Babees Book* (*IMEV* 1576)—and a short piece in prose offering dietary advice; similarly, in Harley 541, it follows a fragment of Lydgate's "Dietary" (*IMEV* 824), which begins, much in the tone of a vigilant parent, "For helthe of body keep fro cold thyn hed," and another poem on table manners, beginning "Lytylle childrene, here ye may lere / Moche curtesy þat is wrytyne here" (*IMEV* 1920). Even in Additional MS 37049, a religious miscellany not otherwise overtly directed to youth, the "ABC" follows a collection of 104 admonitory distichs flanked by drawings of a teacher and boyish student.[18]

In other volumes, the "ABC" appears in contexts that link its teachings on moderation to works advocating judicious self-inspection and resistance to the allure of all temporal things—admonitions suitable for a relatively mature audience. In Lambeth 853, for instance, the "ABC" is bound in the manuscript several quires away from advice the volume offers to young children and their guardians, a group of poems that includes "How the Good Wijf tauʒt Hir Douʒtir" (*IMEV* 671, 1882), "How the Wise Man tauʒt His Son" (*IMEV* 1877, 1891, 1985), and Lydgate's "Stans Puer ad Mensam" (*IMEV* 2233). Instead, the "ABC" appears after a prayer beseeching aid in forbearing worldly vanity (*IMEV* 1727) and before a poem on the instability of earthly goods (*IMEV* 4160). The basic philosophical harmony between the Christian ideal of temperance and the pagan "Golden Mean" implicit in these codicological juxtapositions are further elucidated by a lengthy—and also alphabetical—addition to the "ABC of Aristotle" in Harley 1304. Inserted just after the poem's prologue, this *abece* within an *abece* begins by commending moderation—"Attemperance"—because it is pleasing to (a presumably Christian) God: "Attemperaunce in Alle thynge, Alle-myghty god loueth." Subsequent lines provide a decidedly devotional supplement to the merely courteous behavior the "ABC of Aristotle" otherwise advocates: "Better bowe þan breke . . . / Care for þⁱ Conscience . . . / Dred god," and so on through the alphabet to "V" for "Voide vices" (11–30).[19] The last seven lines of this intriguing interpolation also clearly credit the divine—and not Aristotle—for the doctrine of "mesure": "And mesur*e* he taughte us in alle his wise werk*is* / Ensample by the extremitees þat vicous Arn Eu*er*" (34–35).

In addition to the works placed before and after—or, in the case of Harley 1304, within—the "ABC of Aristotle," the titles and postscripts that frame it on the manuscript page also provide telling clues about the poem's perceived audience and usefulness. In Humphrey Newton's commonplace book (Bodleian MS Lat. Misc. C.66), the "ABC of Aristotle" is written on a narrow paper insert, giving it the appearance of a grocery list used as a bookmark. Along its cramped margin, forming a border perpendicular to the lines of the poem, Newton has remarked, "These byn gode p*r*ouerbis to set in þe bordere of þe halle," suggesting the poem's usefulness to a general audience. In contrast, the poem's *mise-en-page* in Additional MS 37049 makes its pedagogical value vivid and its youthful audience obvious: The poem is introduced with the line "þis is þe a b. c. of arystotyll of gode doctrine" and is accompanied by a painted image of a teacher (Aristotle himself, perhaps?) ensconced in an elevated chair, with book and pen in hand.

Sources and Themes: "A Mesurable Meene"

A quick glance at the entries in Bartlett Whiting's *Proverbs, Sentences, and Proverbial Phrases* for the key words *mean* and *measure* provides ample evidence of the truly proverbial quality of the sentiment expressed in the last line of the "ABC of Aristotle": "a mesurable meene is eu*ere* þe beste of alle." In fact, the collection of aphorisms in British Library Additional MS 37049, one of the manuscripts that preserves a copy of the "ABC of Aristotle," includes several statements of this ideal: "Mesure is a myry mele" (59), "Of þi sorow be noght to sadde / Ne of þi ioy be noght to gladde" (11–12), and "Clym not to hye lest at þo*u* falle" (36). Devotional works also stress the importance of "mesure": John Thoresby's *Lay Folks' Catechism*, for instance, counts it as the seventh virtue, noting that "mesur*e* ys mede to vs in al þat we do" (87). The ubiquitous nature of this theme suggests that the author of the "ABC of Aristotle" would have had many sources from which to draw for a poem about moderation, but the link to Aristotle points to specifically Aristotelian—and pseudo-Aristotelian—elaborations of this ideal as the source for the poem.

The *locus classicus* in Aristotle's work for the explication of the mean as a standard guide for conduct is Book II of the *Nicomachean Ethics*, a work that could have been available to a fifteenth-century author in the Latin translation of Robert Grosseteste produced around 1240. There Aristotle defines moral excellence as "the quality of aiming at the intermediate" (1106b) and provides detailed examples of the intermediate state with respect to numerous emotions and actions.[20] Many of the emotional states Aristotle discusses find a place in the *abece* that bears his name: Where the *Ethics* counsels "proper pride" as the mean between "undue humility" and "empty vanity" (1107b), the "ABC" at line D warns against being "to dreedful"—that is, too timorous or too solicitous—and at line G against being too vain, "to gloriose." Similarly, where the *Ethics* encourages friendliness as the desirable course between obsequiousness and flattery, on the one side, and quarrelsomeness, on the other (1107b), the "ABC" urges the reader to be "freendli of cheere" at line F, and cautions against being "to pr*e*sing"—or praising—at line P and against being "to quarelose" at line Q.

While these examples are noteworthy enough to suggest that the author of the "ABC of Aristotle" may have read the *Nichomachean Ethics*, much of Aristotle's philosophy on conduct could also have been transmitted to him through the legend of Aristotle's education of Alexander, preserved in the texts of the *Secretum Secretorum* tradition.[21] In these works, the ideal of moderation, although not treated as analytically as it is in the *Ethics*, is nevertheless a recurrent theme. On the problem of how to spend and receive money, for instance, Aristotle advises Alexander that a king should strive "Twen moche and lyte / A mene devise / Of to mekyl / And streight Coveitise" (Steele, *Secrees*, 762–63). Similarly, in a discussion of temperance, Aristotle recommends that "in ettynge and drynkynge," too little is better that too much, "but the mene alboth Surmountyth in bountee"; for good health in general, Aristotle asserts, "Mesure in al thynge helth kepyth, and therfor haue mesure in mete and drynke, in slepynge in wakynge, in trauaill in reste, in blode-lettynge and in all othyr thyngis" (Steele, *Three Prose Versions*, 187, 237).

As this handful of examples suggests, the "ABC of Aristotle" makes a just claim to passing on the lore of the ancient philosopher. However, if we compare the "ABC" and the *Secretum* tradition in terms of their intended audiences and characteristic advice, we find that the poem strays from its sources in subtle yet telling ways. First, audiences: Aristotle's advice is meant (though fictionally, to be sure) to edify a king—a single, uniquely privileged individual. The prologue of the "ABC of Aristotle," on the other hand, represents its advice as "councel for riʒt manye clerkis & knyʒtis a þousand." The codicological evidence indicates that children and average householders were drawn into its crowded audience as well. Indeed, the last line of the prologue in one manuscript exhorts "eueryman *and* child" to take heed of the advice that follows, and three witnesses specify that the poem "myght amend a *meane* man" (my emphasis)—where Lambeth 853 notes only that it might "ameende a man." Distinguished by their very ordinariness, these readers of the "ABC" would occupy positions on the ladder of social hierarchy several rungs below the singular, royal audience of the *Secretum Secretorum*, and for them, the essence of proper conduct had perhaps less to do with finding a mean between two extremes of behavior or emotion than it did with finding one's place in the "middle" of an increasingly complex and fluid social order.

It is perhaps for this reason that at the line for M in the "ABC of Aristotle," more than half of the manuscripts stress "*manner*" rather than "measure" as a guide to conduct. In this way, where Lambeth exhorts one to act "as mesure wole it meeue," Additional 36983 advises readers and listeners to behave "as gode man*er* askes." In line with its middle-class audience, the "ABC of Aristotle" also focuses on behaviors that might please or offend a superior—whether knight, clerk, or child's superior. The admonition at line P against being "to p*r*euy w*ith* p*r*incis ne w*ith* dukis" is a clear case in point, as is the advice to "queeme [please] weel ʒoure souereyns" at Q. Many other offenses on the list are implicitly against the proper decorum of socially stratified relationships and tend to be those that only an underling would be able to commit. For instance, a king might be tyrannical and ruthless, but only his servant could be "noiose"—or annoying—one of line N's featured misdemeanors.

As a remedy to these offenses, the "ABC of Aristotle" offers not only a "mesurable meene" but also the alphabet itself. By mapping a status-conscious guide to conduct onto an *abece*—onto a tool of elementary literacy—it suggests that the ordered series of graphemes itself provides an exemplum of proper conduct. In addition, it implies that along with properly modulated habits, the right use of letters may also constitute a means by which aspiring young people might insert themselves into the social hierarchy at a point slightly above their given rank. We see an example of an attempt at this kind of mobility in the famous "Pardon Scene" in *Piers Plowman*. In that scene, Piers—a "meane man" if there ever was one—employs his elementary literacy to arrive at his own interpretation of a scriptural passage, an act that causes him to become legible to the priest as one who is "lettred a litel" (VII.132). Acknowledging his literacy, Piers replies, " 'Abstynence the Abesse . . . myn a.b.c. me taughte' " (VII.133). As Josephine Koster Tarvers points out, to live according to the teachings of "Abstynence" would be to exercise self-restraint, or *mesure* (138). Personifying this first entry in an alphabetically ordered confessor's manual as his teacher, Piers's response neatly articulates the potent link between alphabetical and behavioral indoctrination, on the one hand, and a sense of textual empowerment, on the other—a link that is also implicit in the "ABC of Aristotle."

The half-century between Langland's composition of the "Pardon Scene" and the appearance of the "ABC of Aristotle" was fraught with the controversies arising from the fact that *many* a "meane man" had been taught his "a.b.c."[22] In view of this history of unrest, then, the "ABC of Aristotle"— with its instructions on conduct for those of middling social rank—may also act as a corrective for the uppity tendencies of a newly literate class, for it fashions mannerly readers after the nature of alphabetical characters: as compliant mediations of the "text" of social order. By the time another half-century had passed, the excessively decorated letters so characteristic of handwritten texts would themselves have given way to the more modest and controlled presentation afforded them by the emerging print technology—a development that provides its own poignant epilogue to the "ABC of Aristotle."

Notes

1. The dearth of words for discourteous behavior beginning with X in Middle English may be the reason the poem ends with W. Other Middle English alphabet poems do run all the way through Z—the line for X usually being given to some form of "Xristus" for Christ (see, for instance, Chaucer's "An ABC," line 161). See explanatory notes to lines I and V for brief explanations of the omission of J and U in the poem.

2. *IMEV* numbers reference the *Index of Middle English Verse* by Brown and Robbins and its *Supplement* by Robbins and Cutler. The *IMEV* indexes the "ABC of Aristotle" under three numbers: 471, 3793, and 4155. *IMEV* 4155

has a prologue, while 471 and 3793 do not; the difference between 471 and 3793 is very slight: the first line of the former begins with "Be"—"Be nen to Aventorous to Amerous"—the first line of the latter with "To": "To Amerous to Anterous." Cameron Louis lists fourteen manuscript witnesses to the poem (3356); according to Carleton Brown (311), though, the leaf now bound into Douce 384, which preserves the last eleven lines of the poem only, was originally part of the witness in Harley 1304, to which the missing lines have been added by a later hand. To Louis's list of essentially thirteen witnesses, then, a fourteenth may be added: another copy of *IMEV* 3793, which survives in the so-called Winchester Anthology, British Library Additional 60577 (f. 57v).

3. For a discussion of the received notion of fifteenth-century taste for literary didacticism, see Lerer, 3–21; for a useful overview of late-medieval English education and its related codes of courtesy and devotion, see Bennett.

4. Steele attributes the poem to Burgh (*Secrees*, xviii), as do Ward and Waller (2:238). For a biographical sketch of Burgh, see Steele, xvii–xviii.

5. These include Burgh's translation of Cato's *Distichs* (*IMEV* 854), a poem in praise of Lydgate (*IMEV* 2284), and his completion of the *Secrees of Old Philisoffres*, which was begun by Lydgate, but was yet unfinished at his death in 1467. Works doubtfully attributed to Burgh include the *Parvus Cato* (*IMEV* 3955) and "A Christmas Game" (*IMEV* 2749).

6. For a biographical sketch of Benedict Anglus, see the *Dictionary of National Biography* (s.v. "Benedict of Norwich," IV:216).

7. For additional discussion of the poem's authorship, see Förster, "Zu dem."

8. Lambeth 853 is also dubbed the "preferred" manuscript for this poem by the editors of the *Middle English Dictionary* (1:23, hereafter *MED*). The next-earliest witness would be British Library MS Additional 37049, dated to the middle of the fifteenth century; this witness does not have a prologue.

9. *MED*, s.v. "abece," definition 4a: "[a] poem whose successive lines or stanzas begin with the letters of the alphabet in order."

10. Additional Old Testament *abecedaria* include Sirach 51.13–30, Lamentations 1–4 (four complete alphabet poems), Proverbs 31:10–31, and Psalms 9–10, 25, 34, 37, 111, 112, and 145.

11. The poems on the Battle of Fontenoy and on the preterit tense are edited by Ernest Duemmler (II.138–39, I.625–28). Karl Strecker edits the poem on the miracles of Saint Ninian (961–62). For bibliographic citations for the other Christian Latin *abecedaria* listed here, see Halsall, 78, nn. 37–48. Crampton also provides a thorough bibliography of alphabet poems in her discussion of the history of the genre (193–94). For a survey of early alphabet poems in Greek and Hebrew, see Marcus.

12. The alphabet of plant names is *IMEV* 1378.5, and *IMEV* 604, 1483, 1523 are all *abeces* on the Passion. For additional Middle English alphabet poems, see the indexes to the *IMEV* and its *Supplement* (s.v. "ABC poems").

13. By the late Middle Ages, the term *title* meant many things, including "an inscription, esp. the superscription on Christ's cross," "a small mark or stroke

made with a penpoint," and the name for the abbreviation symbol for Latin *est* (*MED*, s.v. "title," 1a and b). The "tittles" in primer alphabets resemble Parkes's description of the medieval punctuation mark called a *positura*, which indicated the end of a division of text (*Pause and Effect*, 306 and plates 25 and 27). For illustrative plates of five different fourteenth- and fifteenth-century primer alphabets, see Wolpe. See also chapter 9 in this anthology.

14. This poem is preserved as one of several devotional pieces prefixed to the mid-fifteenth-century "Register of Godstow Nunnery"; together, the pieces are reminiscent of a primer as well, for the poem on the cross is followed by verse renderings of the Lord's Prayer, the Hail Mary, the Creed, a Form of Confession, and miscellaneous other prayers, including graces for before and after meals.

15. Since the poem takes the cross as its subject, "Titulle" here makes punning reference to both its sense as the superscription on Christ's cross and as a mark of punctuation. In the manuscript, "Titulle" and "Poynte" are in red ink; the initial cross is in blue with red pen flourishing.

16. In her notes to "An ABC" in the *Riverside Chaucer*, Laila Z. Gross observes that Chaucer "did not include Deguileville's two last stanzas for *et* and *c* (= *cetera*)" (1076). The tradition of primer *abeces* that I have been discussing would favor reading this terminal C stanza as standing for *con* rather than for *cetera*, and, in fact, the first word of the stanza is *contre* (11,181), which incorporates *con*.

17. The copies in Harley 1706 and Harley 541 (f. 228r) also begin with a ✠.

18. The distichs are printed by Brunner; see Hogg, 133–134, for reproductions of the illustrations accompanying them.

19. For the full text of this insertion, see Furnivall, *Queen Elizabeth's Achademy*, 65–66.

20. Grosseteste's Latin translation at this point reads, "Mediatas quaedam ergo est virtus, coniectatrix existens medii" (217).

21. For succinct treatments of the somewhat convoluted *Secretum Secretorum* tradition, see Cary, 105–10, and Bunt, 69–74.

22. Studies on this topic are numerous and beyond the scope of this essay, but two excellent starting points are Justice and Biller and Hudson.

The ABC of Aristotle

p. 30

W Ho so wilneþ to be wijs *and* wor
schip desirif leerne he oo lettir
and looke on anothir. of þe .a. b. c. of
aristotil argue not aȝen þat It is a cou*n*
5   cel for riȝt manye clerkis *and* knyȝtis
a þousand. and eek it myȝte ameende
a man ful ofte. ffor to leerne lore of

oo lettir *and* his lijf saue ffor to myche
of ony þing was neuere holsum Reede
10   ofte on þis rolle *and* rewle ʒᵘ eer aftir.
Whoso be greued in his goost, gouerne
him bettir. Blame he not þe barn þat
þis .a. b. c. made But wite he his wic
kid will *and* his werk aftir. It schal neuere
15   greue a good man þouʒ þe gilti be
meendid. Now herkeneþ *and* heeriþ
¶how y bigynne

p. 31

a   **A** to amerose. to aunterose. ne argue
b   not to myche **B** to bolde ne to bisi.
c   ne boorde not to large **C** to curteis.
d   to cruel. ne care not to sore. **D** to dul
    ne to dreedful. ne drinke not to ofte.
e   **E** to elenge ne to excellent ne to eer
f   nesful neiþer **F** to fers ne to famuler
g   but freendli of cheere **G** to glad. ne to
h   gloriose. *and* gelosie þou hate **H** to hasti
    ne to hardi. ne to heuy in þine herte.
i   **I** to iettynge. ne to iangelinge. ne
k   iape not to ofte **K** to kinde. ne to ke
    pynge. *and* be waar of knaue tacchis.
l   **L** to looth for to leene. ne to liberal
m   of goodis. **M** to medelus. ne to myrie.
n   but as mesure wole it meeue **N** to
    noiose. ne to nyce. ne use no new iettis.
o   **O** to orped ne to ouerþwart. *and* ooþis
p   þou hate **P** to presing. ne to preuy. wᵗ
q   princis ne wᵗ dukis **Q** to queynte. ne

p. 32

    to quarelose. but queeme weel ʒoure
r   souereyns **R** to riotus to reueling
s   ne rage not to rudeli **S** to straunge.
    ne to stirynge. ne straungeli to stare.
t   **T** to toilose. ne to talewijs. for
v   temperaunce is beest **V** to venemose.
    ne to veniable. *and* voide al vilonye.
w   **W** to wielde ne to wraþful neiþer
    waaste ne waade not to depe ¶ffor
    a mesurable meene is euere þe beste of alle.

Translation

p. 30

W*hoever wishes to be wise and*
admired by others, let him learn one letter
and look on another of the .a. b. c. of
Aristotle; argue not against that. It is counsel
5   *for right many clerks and knights*
a thousand. And also, learning the wisdom of
a letter quite often might improve a man and save his life.
For too much of anything was never wholesome. Read
10   *this scroll often and conduct yourself thereafter.*
Whoever is troubled in his spirit, govern
himself better. He should not blame the one who
made this .a. b. c. but instead understand his own wicked
will and his evil deeds after that. It will never
15   *offend a good man even though the guilty ones be*
reformed. Now hearken and hear
¶how I begin.

p. 31
a   *A too amorous, too adventurous, don't argue*
b   *too much. B too bold, nor too bothered,*
c   *don't banter too broadly. C too courteous,*
d   *too cruel, don't care too dearly. D too dismal,*
nor too distressed, don't drink too often.
e   *E too uncouth, nor too elegant, nor too*
f   *earnest either. F too fine, nor too familiar*
g   *but friendly in your manner. G too glad, nor too*
h   *gloating, and jealousy you should hate. H too hasty*
nor too hot-headed, nor too heavy in your heart.
i   *I too jaunty, nor too jabbering, don't*
k   *joke around too often. K too kind, nor too keeping,*
and beware of knaves' crude habits.
l   *L too loath to loan, nor too liberal*
m   *with your money. M too meddlesome, nor too merry,*
n   *but as moderation advises. N too*
annoying, nor too inane, don't take up any new fads.
o   *O too obstinate nor too overpowering, and oaths you*
p   *should hate. P too praising, nor too privy with*
q   *princes nor with dukes. Q too crafty, nor*
p. 32

too quarrelsome, but please well your
r   *betters. R too riotous too reveling,*

s   *don't be rudely rambunctious. **S** too standoffish,*
        nor too strident, don't stare strangely.
t   ***T** too cantankerous, nor too talkative, for*
v   *temperance is best. **V** too venomous,*
        nor too vindictive, and avoid all villainy.
w   ***W** too wild nor too wrathful, neither*
        waste nor wade too deep. ¶for
        a measurable mean is ever the best of all.

Notes

Manuscripts: Lambeth Palace MS 853 measures 6 2/5 by 4 3/5 inches, consists of 119 leaves, and is written in gothic script with 20 lines per page (James,
Descriptive 809). The "ABC" begins halfway down page 30 with a two-line
red W. Letters in bold in my text are in red in the manuscript. Primarily lexical
variants from the other witnesses to the "ABC of Aristotle" are recorded in the
notes to each line and are designated according to the following scheme: **A1**
BL Add. 36983, **A2** BL Add. 37049, **A3** BL Add. 60577, **C** Bodl. Lat. Misc.
C.66, **D** Bodl. Douce 384, **H1** BL Harley 541 (f. 213r–v), **H2** BL Harley 541
(f. 228r), **H3** BL Harley 1304, **H4** BL Harley 1706, **H5** BL Harley 5086, **T1**
Trinity College Cambridge O.2.53, **T2** Trinity College Dublin 509, **R** Bodl.
Rawlinson B.196, **U** Cambridge UL Ff.5.48. Definitions are from the *MED*;
head words are given in parentheses where their spelling is substantially different from that of the text. I thank the British Library, the Bodleian Library, Cambridge University Library, Lambeth Palace Library, the Board of Trinity
College Dublin, and the Master and Fellows, Trinity College Cambridge, for
permission to consult their manuscripts in order to prepare this edition.

    Superscriptions: A2 "þis is þe a b. c. of arystotyll of gode doctrine"; H4
"here begynneth Arystoles ABC. made by mayster Benett," followed by
a ⊠ ; A3 "⊠ Crystys crosse be oure spede: wᵗ grace mercye in all oure
nede"; H2 has no superscription but begins with a ⊠.

Line 10: *Rolle*: a scroll. *Rolles* were used specifically for legal records, but
the word is associated in a general sense with any kind of list: for example, of
town mayors, of God's elect, or, in the case of the devil's roll, of sins. Manuscript **H1** and **U** have *ragment* and *ragmon*, respectively, here, which also
denote a legal document and a "catalogue, list, or roster" (*rageman*). *Rageman* is also the name for a game that could conceivably have been played
with the "ABC of Aristotle." As William Hazlitt describes it:

> A series of poetical characters [was] written in stanzas on a long roll of
> parchment or paper, and a seal was fastened with a string to each descrip-
> tion. The roll was then folded up . . . and each person present selected a
> character by means of the seals. . . . no one could be sure, till the roll was
> opened, what kind of character he or she had picked. (68–69)

If the "ABC of Aristotle" was used for the game of *Rageman*, its apparent didacticism would have been turned to quite a different use!

Line 7: *ameende a man*: **H1**, **H3**, and **U** have "amend a meane man" (with variations on spelling among them).

Line 12: *barn*: a person.

Line 16: For "herkeneþ *and* heeriþ," **H1** has "herkyn and here eue*r*yman *and* child."

Line 17: Following the prologue, **H3** adds a 28-line alphabetical insertion, which is printed by Furnivall, *Queen Elizabeth's Achademy* 65–66.

A. *aunterous*: venturesome (aventurous). For "ne argue not to myche," **A3** has "avyse or ye answere."

B. *bisi*: solicitous, worried. *boorde to large*: to be too outspoken in one's wit (bourden).

C. *sore* (as adverb): in great amount. For *curteis*, **H3** has *cursed*; for *cruel*, **A3** has *cacthynge*, or getting, taking (cacching).

D. *dul*: depressed by trouble or sorrow. *dreedful*: timorous (dredeful). For *dul*, **H2** has *doolful*, or sorrowful (dolful).

E. *elenge*: unhappy. *excellent*: refined. *eernesful*: serious (ernestful). For *elenge*, **A2** has *eloquent*; for *eernesful*, **A1** repeats *cruell*, and **H4** has *curyous*. **A3** replaces the phrase "ne to eernesful neiþe*r*" with "loke vertue ye sewe," and **H4** replaces it with "ne curyous nethyr."

F. *fers*: proud. *famuler*: unduly intimate (familier). *cheere*: manner (chere). For *fers*, **A3** has *ffresshe*, and **H4** and **R** have *fferde*, or the state of being afraid. For *famuler*, **A3** has "freyle." **A3** also replaces the phrase "but freendli of cheere" with "false felowshippe eschewe."

G. *gloriose*: vainglorious. For *glad*, **A3** has grym*m*e, **C** has *gettyng*, and **H3** has *glosynge*, or engaging in smooth or deceitful talk. For *gloriose*, **A3** has *grounfulle*; **C** has *gangelyng* (for a definintion of which, see *iangelinge*, further on), and **H3** has *gelous gay*. For "gelosie þou hate," **A3** has "goode gouernau*n*ce suffyce"; **H3** has "gape not to wide," **H4** has "Ne to galaunt neuer," and **R** has "gelous to eche."

H. *hardi*: rash. For *hasti* **A3** has *homelye*; for *hardi* **C** has *hatefull*. For the phrase "ne to heuy in þine herte," **A3** has "hewe not to hyghe" and **C** has "hynder not þ[i] neghbor."

I. *iettynge*: to behave or dress ostentatiously (getten). *iangelinge*: prating, chatter (jangling). *iape*: to behave in a foolish or unruly manner (japen). For *iettynge*, **C** and **H4** have *joconde*; for *iangelinge*, **C** has *joly*; for *iape*, **H4** has *joye*. After *iangelinge*, **A3** adds the specification "neue*r* w[t] thy mayste*r*" in place of "ne iape not to ofte." The *Oxford English Dictionary* (*OED*) explains that until the seventeenth century, the letters I and J functioned as two forms of the letter I, indicating the vowel sounds of *i*, as well as the consonantal sounds of both *y* and soft *g*.

K. *kinde*: generous. *kepynge*: hoarding. *knave* (as adjective): crude (knavish). *tache*: a bad habit. For *kepynge*, **A3** has *knappysshe*, a variant spelling of *knavish*.

L. *to leene*: to lend. For "to looth for to leene" **A1, D, H1, H2, H3, H4, H5, R, T1**, and **T2** all warn against being too loving: for example, **A1** has "To lothe ner to lovyng." In place of "for to leene," **A2** has "ne to lefe," where *lefe* connotes being highly regarded personally; and **C** has "ne to leuyng," where *leuyng* refers to the collection of a duty; and **U** has "ne to low." For *goodis*, **H4** has *woordys*. **A3** replaces the whole phrase "to looth for to leene. ne to liberal of goodis" with "to lyght to liberalle looke or thou leepe."

M. For *medelus*, **A3** has *mournefulle*. For "as mesure wole it meeue," **A2, C, H1, H2, H5, R**, and **U** stress the importance of "manner" rather than "measure" as a guide for one's actions: for example, **A2** has "as gode man*er* askes." **H4**, on the other hand, warns against "besynesse vulefull," where *vulefull* connotes illegal or sinful (unlefful).

N. *noiose*: annoying. *nyce*: frivolous. *iet*: fashion (get). This warning recalls Chaucer's portrait of the Pardoner in the *General Prologue to the Canterbury Tales*: "Hym thoughte he rood al of the newe iet" (I.682). Instead of "ne use no new iettis," **A3** has "nygardshipe ys naught," and **A2, C, D, H3, H2, H1, H4, H5, T1, T2, R**, and **U** all warn against being overly *neuefangel*, or fond of novelty: for example, **T1** reads "ne to newfangell."

O. *orped*: stout-hearted. *ouerþwart*: reckless (overthwert). For *orped*, **A3** has *owterage*, or bibulous, boastful, unruly (outrage). For *hate*, **H4** has *haunte*. For "ooþis þou hate," **A3** reads "obedyente youe bee."

P. *presing*: flattering (preising). *preuy*: trusty (previ). For *presing*, **A2** has *precios*, or fastidious. For *preuy*, **A3** has *perte*, and **R** has *prowde*; for "w^t princis ne w^t dukis," **H4** reads, "Ne peerless w^t prynces," and **A3** has "prayse you at partynge."

Q. *queynte*: sly. *queem*: to please (quemen). *souereyns*: one's betters. For *queem*, **A2** reads *kepe*. Instead of "souereyns," **A1, A2, C, D, H1, H3, H5, T1, T2**, and **U** have some form of "master"; **H4** has "men all abowte." In place of the phrase "queeme weel ȝoure souereyns," **H2** reads "to quesytife of questions," and **A3** has "ne to bolde questyons to enquere"; and **R** has "but whan will thi maist*er*."

R. *rage*: to behave wildly (ragen). For *reueling*, **A3** has *rewthefulle*, and for the phrase "ne rage not to rudeli," the same manuscript has "rewle you by resone."

S. *straunge*: aloof. *stirynge*: provoking trouble (stiren). *straungeli*: in an unfriendly manner. For *straunge*, **D** and **H3** have *sadde*, or "serious." For *stirynge*, **H5** has "staryng"; **A1, H1, H4, T1**, and **T2** have some form of the word *steryng*, from *steren*, "to reproach"; **C, H2**, and **U** have variations of *sterne*, or "severe"; and **D** and **H3** have *sorie* and *sorry*, respectively. Instead of "ne straungeli to stare," **A1, A2, H1, H2, H5, T1, T2**, and **U** have some form of "stare not to brode"; **C** has "staye not to brode"; **D** and **H3** have "sight not to depe," where "sight" is a form of "to sigh" (siken); **H4** has "starte nat abowte," where "starte abowte" means "to move restlessly (sterten); and **R** has "stare not to prowde." In **A3**, this line reads "to spendynge to sparynge spende in dewe sesone."

T. *toilose*: contentious. *talewijs*: talkative. For *toilose*, **A2** has *trobylos*. For "temperau*n*ce is beest," **A1**, **A2**, **C**, **D**, **H1**, **H3**, **H5**, **R**, **T1**, **T2**, and **U** have "temperaunce hit hates" (with various spellings). In **A3**, this line reads, "to tempre welle *your* tales and kepe welle *your* tunge."

V. *veniable*: vindictive (vengeable). *vilonye*: disgraceful or shameful conduct (vileini). For *venemose*, **C** has *vastyng*, or fasting (fasting). For *veniable*, **H4** has *violent*, and **H5** has *envious*. For "voide al vilonye," **A2** has "Ne wast not þi tyme," and **A1**, **D**, **H1**, **H2**, **H3**, **H4**, **H5**, **R**, **T1**, **T2**, and **U** advise, instead, against being wasteful: for example, **H4** reads, "ne waste not to moche." In **A3**, this line reads, "to vowle or to vayre avyse you or ye wedde," where *vowle* would be "foul," and *vayre* would be "fair." The *OED* notes that in Middle English the letters **U** and **V** were both used to indicate either the vowel *u* or the consonant *v*. The author of the "ABC of Aristotle," however, has chosen words for his V line that begin with the consonant *v* and has not given a line to any vices that begin with the vowel *u*.

W. *waade not to depe*: an idiomatic reference to becoming deeply involved in love (waden); compare to George Ashby's *Dicta et Opiniones Diversorum Philosophorum*: "In love of women wade nat over depe" (1151). In place of "ne waade not to depe," **H4** has "Ne to wyse deme the."

X. **A3** has an X line instead of a W line, which reads, "to Cryste pray we where soo wee bee. / That we may lerne thys .A.B.C."

Concluding tags: **C** "These byn gode p*r*ouerbis to set in þᵉ bordere of þᵉ halle"; **H2** "Da tua du*m* tua su*n*t post mort*em* tu*n*c no*n* su*n*t / Omnia sapiencia est cotidie de morte cogitare" [Give what you have while you have it; after death it will no longer be yours. / The sum of wisdom is to think on death daily]; **H3** "xyz xy wyth esed *and* p*er* se Tytell Tytell Tytell than Est *and* Amen"; **H5** "yitte Lerne or be Lewde," where *lewede* denotes "uneducated, ignorant; unlettered" ("leued," la); **T1** "Tene mediu*m* si non vis p*er*dere modu*m*" [Hold to the middle if you do not want to lose your way]. **A2** concludes with the following diagram:

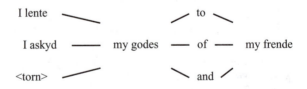

5

The Babees Book

DEANNA DELMAR EVANS

> And then I stole all courtesy from heaven,
> And dressed myself in such humility
> That I did pluck allegiance from men's hearts
> I HENRY IV(3.2.50–52)

By the time Shakespeare wrote these lines, in which King Henry IV boasts of using "courtesy" to advance his own political career, English courtesy literature had an established place in the education of young noblemen. During the Tudor period, training in courtesy was considered such an important part of a young man's education that aristocratic families sent their sons to serve in the homes of the rich and powerful. According to F. B. Millet, "The Tudor youth of noble birth often passed a number of years in the house of some courtier or ecclesiastic, and thus got much of his social and intellectual training" (2). Nor was it considered degrading for a highborn lad to assume the role of "servant," for "serving was a profession in which every rank, except royalty itself . . . might honourably wear the livery of a man of higher rank" (Rickert, xviii–xix). During this period, the famous courtesy books of Castiglione, Erasmus, and Thomas Elyot were written and studied. Indeed, it would seem that one product of the Tudor Age was the development of courtesy literature written in English. But this was not the case, for several such works written a century earlier were rooted in a tradition of Latin courtesy literature that had emerged during the twelfth century. Moreover, while the courtesy tradition had an obvious impact on court life, it probably had not originated in the great castles of Europe but "in the intellectual centers of the Middle Ages—the monastery, the school, and the university" (Brentano, 14).

    The Babees Book is one of several fifteenth-century Middle English texts on manners written for children. Edith Rickert points out that the author seems to be addressing young princes, and the poem probably was written when Edward V and Richard of York were boys (179). Found in MS. Harleian 5086, fol. 86–90, *The Babees Book* appears to have been written c. 1475. Nothing is known about its author, who claims to translate the poetic "tretys / Out of latin in-to my comvne langage" (ll. 1–2). Since the twelfth-century Latin "poems on manners were not written by the noted literary men of the day" but by "tutors of young aristocrats or by school-teachers" (Brentano, 23), it is not unlikely that the author of *The Babees Book* was an instructor of some kind, most probably a male cleric.

The poem is written in *rhyme royal* stanzas, the seven-line verse form that almost certainly was developed by Chaucer (Stevens, 62), who used it for *Troilus and Criseyde* and some of the "moral" *Canterbury Tales* in the "high style." The verse form was subsequently used by several noteworthy poets of the fifteenth and sixteenth centuries, including Lydgate, Hoccleve, Dunbar, Henryson, Hawes, and Barclay, and they all "seemed to have used it mainly because Chaucer had in his longest single-narrative poem" (Stevens, 76). Thus, the poet's decision to write *The Babees Book* in "rhyme royal" stanzas may have been determined by his belief in the seriousness of the subject matter and the literary merit of his predecessors.

It is clear that the poet took his subject seriously because the poem begins with a prayer for inspiration to God, followed by a statement of authorial intention: to teach courtesy to those of "tender age." He later prays for the help of Mary, "Modir dyngne" (l. 49), and insists that the only *mede* (reward) he desires is that his work will prove pleasing to those for whom it is intended and that they will learn from it (ll. 33–35). The poet shows concern that members of his young audience may not understand his lesson, so in the sixth stanza he encourages the children to ask (*spyrre*) the meanings of words they do not understand. He addresses his intended audience directly as "yonge Babees" blessed by being of "bloode Royalle" (l. 15) and points out that it is especially for them that he writes. To emphasize that he is writing for children, the poet states that he is not writing for the mature, who already have expertise in polite behavior, and, in a rare attempt at humor, adds that to do so would be like adding pains to hell or joy to heaven, water to the sea or heat to fire. Yet he shows some concern about the opinion of adult readers, an indication that he may hold a lower rank at court than those who will be in a position to judge the poem. This is most evident in the penultimate stanza of the poem, where he asks that he not be abused for his efforts, but invites interested readers to add to or delete from the text. However, in the final verse he turns again to his primary audience, the "swete children." He again importunes them to learn the contents of the poem and prays that almighty God will make them experts in courtesy so that they can eventually attain lasting bliss. Clearly, the poet equates polite behavior with godliness, a characteristic of medieval *facetus* literature.

The Tradition of *Facetus* Literature

The Babees Book, as a book of manners and morality, belongs to a variety of medieval courtesy literature known as *facetus* literature. The connection between the poem and *facetus* literature is made in the second stanza, which begins with an allusion to Facetus, the imaginary author of those medieval Latin books of moral behavior. Then the eighth stanza begins with an invocation to Lady Facetia, a feminine personification of the mythic Facetus. This "muse" is invoked to take pity (*Rewe*) on the poet's ignorance (*vnkunnynge*). Edith Rickert has suggested that the reason the poet feminized Facetus was because Courtesy was usually personified as a woman (180). Sister Mary Brentano provides a valuable history of this literature, indicating that the first medieval Latin poem on manners was "designated '*Doctrina Magistri Joannis Facet*' " (2). Written during the twelfth century, "*Facet*" became "the model for numerous others regulating behavior, both in the Latin and in the vernacular European languages," so that "the term *facetus* was to become the title not only for Master John's own poem but for redactions, imitations, and vernacular translations" (2). As Brentano points out, "the [*facetus*] poems were not written for the trained knight, but for the young squire, page, or school boy" (23). Since *Facett* is named in the second stanza of *The Babees Book*, its author surely envisioned the poem as belonging to this literary tradition. Brentano indicates that *Facetus* was preceded by the *Disticha Catonis* [the Distichs of Cato] (26). In this group of maxims a parental character "speaks" a miscellaneous collection of aphorisms on conduct in general; these were later translated into many of the vernacular languages of Europe and also were used in the study of elementary Latin (Mason, 6). The *Disticha Catonis* was popular in Anglo-Saxon England, where it added to "the English store of proverbs" (Brentano, 38). The original *Facetus* "inaugurated the courtesy poem in medieval European literature," but, unfortunately, "presented this new genre in the loosely constructed form of its gnomic model" (Brentano, 26). Yet even in the simplest of the aphoristic Latin courtesy poems, honor is important, and the texts "remind their readers that good or bad conduct provokes a corresponding public response" (Johnston, 33). This idea is retained in *The Babees Book*, for the poet reminds the young readers that when they refrain from chattering, it "shalle a name deserve / Of gentylnesse and of goode governaunce" (ll. 187–88).

Tracing the history of *Facetus* in England "has been complicated because the poem in both earlier and later times has been there called

Urbanus, and a Latin poem bearing this title has been attributed to Daniel Church who lived at the court of Henry II" (Brentano, 38–41). Robert Grosseteste (d. 1253), bishop of Lincoln, seemed to have a part in the development of English courtesy poetry. The bishop is believed to have authored two Latin courtesy poems: one, known by its opening words, *Liber stans puer ad mensam*, contains forty-three heroic verses (Gieben, 48). Later Middle English versions of *Stans Puer ad Mensam* and of *Urbanus*, undoubtedly the source of the children's poem called *Urbanitatis*, are included in Furnivall's collection and are closely related in content to *The Babees Book*.

The Babees Book as Courtesy Literature

Modern publication history of *The Babees Book* begins with F. J. Furnivall's 1868 edition for the Early English Text Society. (It is from Furnivall's edition that the following text is adapted.) Furnivall's *Early English Meals and Manners* includes a number of other Middle English texts on morals and manners for young people like "The A B C of Aristotle," *Vrbanitatis*, and *Stans Puer ad Mensam* (an English version of a Latin poem). The range and variety of this advisory literature indicate the widespread popularity of this genre of medieval children's literature. Early in the twentieth century Edith Rickert paraphrased the poems in Furnivall's collection in modern English to make the texts more accessible.

In spite of Rickert's attempts, *The Babees Book* has not attracted much critical attention. John Mason does refer to it as among "the most characteristic English works of civility" (292), noting, as Rickert had, that it was "designed for young children of noble, or even royal blood, and is chiefly concerned with behavior at table, though there is some advice on the general conduct of a child in the presence of his lord" (20). The "babies" addressed in the poem were, of course, children old enough to serve at table. Rickert suggested that the word *baby* at the time was "used like the Spanish *menino*" and meant "young man of good family" (179–80).

The primary lesson in *The Babees Book* for such young men concerns their duties and conduct at formal dinners. It was customary at the time for hands to be washed at table, so the child is instructed to pour out clean water into a basin and to hold the towel for his master until the latter has finished washing up. The child is not to leave the banqueting area until after grace is said. When temporarily released from his duties and seated at table with his peers, the child is to keep his knife clean and sharp, a reminder that forks were not in common use at the time. Moreover, he is advised not to hack away at his meat as if he were a field hand, a recognition of social distinction. An underlying assumption of much medieval "courtesy literature" seems to be that aristocrats are in every respect better than peasants. The child's meat was served on a "trencher," which, in the earlier Middle Ages, was a slice of whole meal bread, four days old, upon which the food was served, but by the time of the poem, was a dish made of wood (Rickert, 180). The child is advised to use his spoon for his soup, not to slurp, and not to leave his spoon in the serving dish. He is told not to stuff his mouth so full that he cannot speak and to taste every dish brought to the table. If strangers are seated with him, the child is advised to share his food because it is impolite to keep food only for himself when others are present. When he has completed his meal, the boy is to rise politely without laughing, joking, or using loud words and to proceed to his lord's table to await further instruction.

Several earlier critics have helped define the genre of courtesy literature to which *The Babees Book* belongs. Mark Johnston indicates that the term *courtesy literature* "refers generally to works, usually written in the vernacular tongues, that attempt to formalize courtly conduct: books of courtesy, guides to courtly love, manuals of chivalry, or treatises on table manners" (22). According to John Mason, "Courtesy may be tentatively defined as a code of ethics, esthetics, or peculiar information for any class-conscious group, and a courtesy book is a book which sets forth such a code" (4). Of several types of courtesy literature, it is necessary to differentiate literature that provides "rules of courtesy," defined by Mason as "the formulated standards by which the average individual of any given class acts" from "metaphysical inquiries into the divine sanctions and ultimate ends of human action, on the one hand, and into questions of 'higher' and 'lower' good on the other" (4). Or, as F. B. Millet more succinctly states, "Morals are the fundamental decencies of social conduct; manners, the ornament, in theory, of such conduct" (1). It is hardly surprising that books of manners came into being much later than treatises on behavior that emphasize morals (Rickert, xii). The necessity for such works indicates that people had enough wealth and leisure to give attention to the subject. Courtesy literature could hardly exist without some kind of implied "social relationship . . . between a class and its logical complement," such as "master and servant" or "parent and child" (Mason, 4).

The Babees Book, with its emphasis on table manners, would seem to fall into the category of the "lower good," yet its author also shows concern about morality. He equates good manners with godliness and emphasizes such moral virtues as sharing with others, not disturbing the peace of others, and not behaving in a proud, disdainful manner. Yet it must be conceded that children instructed by such a book could climb the social ladder by winning the favor of their earthly lord. Certainly, there were some who, like Shakespeare's Henry IV, used "courtesy" for political ends.

The Babees Book as Children's Literature

While it is clear that *The Babees Book* belongs to the *facetus* literary tradition, several characteristics distinguish it as children's literature. Of course, most *facetus* poems were written for the young. But in this particular poem the most obvious clue that it was written for children is the way the author addresses the intended audience: "yonge Babees" (1. 15), "swete children" (1. 36), "Bele Babees" (1. 57), and so on. While the vocabulary of the poem tends to be simple, there are some more difficult words, such as *fructuous* (1. 72) and *compendious* (1. 74). Although it can be argued that the use of rhyme would make it easier for children to listen to the directives and to memorize them, the *rhyme royal* of *The Babees Book* has little in common with nursery rhyme verse. The poet perhaps chose the stanzaic form because he believed moral works should be written in the "high style" or perhaps to show respect for the "gentle" birth of the intended audience—the "bele babies."

It is interesting to consider just how *The Babees Book* would have engaged a young audience of the late fifteenth century. Clearly, it is a didactic poem, and there is little in it to entertain or amuse children. Hence, it seems probable that children would have treated it like a school text, and it is easy to imagine its being used as an instructional reading text. It was the goal of medieval teachers to make students "sober and restrained, as adults were supposed to be" (Hanawalt, *Growing Up,* 85). Yet the author of *The Babees Book* appears to show respect for his intended audience; his gentleness in the poem seems more than deference to lineage. Moreover, the opportunity to participate at the banquet table, tasting its many and varied dishes, and the excitement of court life itself probably provided external stimulation for children to want to read and learn the text.

For a modern audience the value of *The Babees Book* is that it provides some insight into the lives of aristocratic youths during the fifteenth century. Barbara Correll, a scholar of Renaissance courtesy literature, indicates that the study of such literature provides an opportunity to "examine constructions of masculinity and their significance for gender and class at a crucial historical moment" (9). She points out that conduct literature "seeks to transform, subjugate, and produce the body it inscribes with the signs of civility. Embedded in this subjectification and cultural inscription are the issues of class and sexual differences" (14). By studying *The Babees Book* and other similar fifteenth-century texts, we will expand our knowledge of the culture that produced them. As we achieve a better understanding of what was considered "proper" behavior for young noble children, we increase our understanding of how adults attempted to shape character, particularly masculine character, at the end of the Middle Ages.

THE BABEES BOOK, OR A "LYTYL REPORTE" OF HOW YOUNG PEOPLE SHOULD BEHAVE.

In this tretys the whiche I thenke to wryte	*treatise*
Out of latyn in-to my comvne langage,	*common (vernacular)*
He me supporte (sen I kan nat endyte),	*write, compose*
The whiche only after his owne ymage	*He alone (God) who*
Fourmyd man-kynde! For alle of tendre age 5	*formed*
In curtesye Resseyve shulle document,	*receive*
And vertues knowe, by this lytil coment.	

And Facett seythe the Book of curtesye,	*Facetus*
Vertues to knowe, thaym forto haue and vse,	
Is thing moste heelfulle in this worlde trevly. 10	*health, truly*
Therfore in feythe I wole me nat excuse	
From this labour ywys, nor hit Refuse;	*surely, indeed*
For myn owne lernynge wole I say summe thing	*desire, wish*
That touchis vertues and curtesye havyng.	*touches upon, treats*

But, O yonge Babees, whome bloode Royalle 15	
Withe grace, Feture, and hyhe habylite	*high ability*
Hathe enourmyd, on yow ys that I calle	*endowed*
To knowe this Book; for it were grete pyte,	*great pity*
Syn that in yow ys sette sovereyne beaute,	*excellent beauty*
But yf vertue and nurture were withe alle; 20	
To yow therfore I speke in specyalle,	*especially*

And nouhte to hem of elde that bene experte	*not; old age*
In governaunce, nurture, and honeste.	
For what nedys to yeve helle peynes smerte,	*give; sharp*
Ioye vnto hevene, or water vnto the see, 25	*joy*
Heete to the Fyre that kan nat but hoote be?	
It nedys nouhte: therfore, O Babees yynge,	*It is not necessary*
My Book only is made for youre lernynge.	

Therfore I pray that no man Reprehende	*disapprove*
This lytyl Book, the whiche for yow I make; 30	
But where defaute ys, latte ylke man amende,	*fault is found, each*
And nouhte deme yt; [I] pray thaym for youre	*not condemn it;*
sake.	

For other mede ywys I kepe noone take   *reward*
But that god wolde this Book myhte yche
   man plese,
And in lernynge vnto yow donne somme ese.   35   *give; ease*

Eke, swete children, yf there be eny worde
That yee kenne nouhte, spyrre whils yee yt ken;   *do not know*
Whanne yee yt knowe, yee mowe holde yt   *hold it in storage*
   in horde
Thus thurhe spyrryng yee mowe lerne at   *holding yourself*
   wyse men   *back,*
Also thenke nouhte to straungely at my penne,   40
In this metre for yow lyste to procede,   *this meter, pleasure*
Men vsen yt; therfore on hit take hede.

But amonge alle that I thenke of to telle,
My purpos ys first only forto trete
How yee Babees in housholde that done duelle   45
Shulde haue youre sylf whenne yee be sette   *conduct yourself;*
   at mete,   *meal*
And how yee shulde, whenne men lyste yow   *request; merry*
   Rehete,
Haue wordes lovly, swete, bleste, and
   benyngne.
In this helpe me O Marie, Modir dyngne!   *revered*

And eke, O lady myn, Facecia!   50
My penne thow guyde, and helpe vnto me
   shewe;
For as the firste off alle lettres ys the A,
So Artow firste Modir of alle vertue.
Off myn vnkunnynge, swete lady, now Rewe;   *my ignorance; Pity*
And thouhe vntauhte I speke of governaunce,   55   *untaught, behavior*
Withe thy swete helpe supporte myn
   ygnoraunce.   *my ignorance*

A, Bele Babees, herkne now to my lore!   *instruction*
Whenne yee entre into your lordis place,
Say first, "God spede"; And alle that ben   *and all your betters*
   byfore   *that be*
Yow in this stede, salue withe humble Face;   60   *there salute*

Stert nat Rudely, komme Inne an esy pace;   *Don't stare rudely*
Holde vp youre heede, and knele but on
   oone kne
To youre sovereyne or lorde, whedir he be.

And yf they speke withe yow at youre
   komynge,
Withe stable Eye loke vpone theym Rihte.   65   *look directly*
To theyre tales and yeve yee goode herynge   *pay attention to their*
Whils they haue seyde; loke eke withe alle   *tales*
   your myhte
Yee Iangle nouhte, also caste nouhte your   *Don't chatter*
   syhte   *Don't look around*
Aboute the hovs, but take to theym entent
Withe blythe visage and spiryt diligent.   70   *a happy expression*

Whenne yee Answere or speke, yee shulle
   be purveyde   *prepared*
What yee shalle say, speke eke thing fructuous;   *profitable*
On esy wyse latte thy Resone be sayde
In wordes gentylle and also compendious,   *essential, few*
For many wordes ben rihte Tedious   75   *very tedious*
To ylke wyseman that shalle yeve audience;
Thaym to eschewe therfore doo diligence.   *to forgo*

Take eke noo seete, but to stonde be yee   *stand in readiness*
   preste;
Whils forto sytte ye haue in komaundement,   *until told to sit*
Youre heede, youre hande, your feet, holde   80
   yee in reste;
Nor thurhe clowyng, your flesshe loke yee   *don't scratch yourself*
   nat Rent;
Lene to no poste whils that ye stande present
Byfore your lorde, nor handylle ye no thyng
Als for that tyme vnto the hovs touching.   *do not handle*
                                                  household things

At euery tyme obeye vnto youre lorde   85
Whenne yee answere, ellis stonde yee styl   *otherwise stand still*
   as stone
But yf he speke; loke withe oon accorde   *one accord*

That yf yee se komme Inne eny persone
Better thanne yee, that yee goo bak anoone   *of higher station*
And gyff him place; youre bak eye in no way   90
Turne on no wihte, as ferforthe as ye may   *Turn your back on
                                                        no one*

Yiff that youre lorde also yee se drynkynge,
Looke that ye be in rihte stable sylence   *sustained silence*
Withe-oute lowde lauhtere or Iangelynge,   *laughter; chatter*
Rovnynge, Iapynge, or other Insolence.   95   *whispering; joking*
Yiff he komaunde also in his presence   *command*
Yow forto sytte, fulfille his wylle belyve,   *obey him at once*
And for youre seete, looke nat withe other stryve,

Whenne yee er sette, take noone vnhoneste tale;
Eke forto skorne eschewe with alle your myhte; 100 *do not scorn*
Latte ay youre chere be lowly, blythe, and hale,   *expression; meek*
Withe-oute chidynge as that yee wolde fyhte.
Yiff yee perceyve also that eny wihte   *any person*
Lyst yow kommende that better be thanne yee,   *commend*
Ryse vp anoone, and thanke him with herte free. 105 *immediately*

Yif that yee se youre lorde or youre lady
Touching the housholde speke of eny thinge,
Latt theym alloone, for that is curtesy,
And entremete yow nouhte of theyre doynge,   *do not interfere*
But be Ay Redy withe-oute feynynge   110   *without feigning*
At hable tyme to done your lorde service,   *appropriate time*
So shalle yee gete anoone a name of price.

Also to brynge drynke, holde lihte whanne   *hold lights*
   tyme ys,
Or to doo that whiche ouhte forto be done,
Looke yee be preste, for so yee shalle ywys   115   *ready, prompt*
In nurture gete a gentyl name ful sone;
And yif ye shulde at god aske yow a bone   *pray*
Als to the worlde, better in noo degre   *in this world*
Mihte yee desire thanne nurtred forto be.

Yif that youre lorde his owne coppe lyste   120   *is pleased to
   commende   offer his cup*
To yow to drynke, ryse vp whanne yee it take,
And resseyve it goodly withe boothe youre   *receive it
   hende;   graciously*

Of yt also to noone other profre ye make,
But vnto him that brouhte yt yee hit take
Whenne yee haue done, for yt in no kyn wyse   125
Auhte comvne be, as techis vs the wyse.   *shared, common*

Now must I telle in shorte, for I muste so,
Youre observaunce that ye shalle done at none;   *noon*
Whenne that ye se youre lorde to mete shalle goo.
Be redy to fecche him water sone;   130
Summe helle water; summe holde to he hathe   *clear*
    done
The clothe to him; And from him yee nat pace   *hold the towel*
Whils he be sette, and haue herde sayde the
    grace.

Byfore him stonde whils he komaunde yow sytte,
Withe clene handes Ay Redy him to serve;   135
Whenne yee be sette, your knyf with alle your
    wytte
Vnto youre sylf bothe clene and sharpe conserve,   *clean and sharp*
That honestly yee mowe your owne mete kerve.   *carve*
Latte curtesye and sylence with yow duelle,   *silence*
And foule tales looke noone to other telle.   140

Kutte with your knyf your brede, and breke
    yt nouhte;
A clene Trenchour byfore yow eke ye lay,   *a clean trencher*
And whenne your potage to yow shalle be   *broth*
    brouhte,
Take yow sponys, and soupe by no way,
And in youre dysshe leve nat your spone, I pray,   145
Nor on the borde lenynge be yee nat sene,   *table leaning*
But from embrowyng the clothe yeekepe clene.   *dirtying the cloth*

Oute ouere youre dysshe your heede yee
    nat hynge,
And withe fulle mouthe drynke in no wyse;
Youre nose, your teethe, your naylles, from   150
    pykynge,
Kepe At your mete, for so techis the wyse.
Eke or ye take in youre mouthe, yow avyse,   *I advise you*
So mekyl mete but that yee rihte welle mowe   *much meat*
Answere, And speke, whenne men speke to yow.   *cannot answer*

Whanne ye shalle drynke, your mouthe clence
   withe a clothe;   155
Youre handes eke that they in no manere
Imbrowe the cuppe, for thanne shulle noone   *dirty*
   be lothe
Withe yow to drynke that ben withe yow yfere.   *in your company*
The salte also touche nat in his salere
Withe nokyns mete, but lay it honestly   160   *salt cellar*
On youre Trenchoure, for that is curtesy.   *trencher*

Youre knyf withe mete to your mouthe
   nat bere,
And in youre hande nor holde yee yt no way;
Eke yf to yow be brouhte goode metys sere,   *good dishes*
Luke curteysly of ylke mete yee assay,
And yf your dysshe withe mete be tane away   165   *taste every dish*
And better brouhte, curtesye wole certeyne   *taken*
Yee late yt passe and calle it nat ageyne.

And yf straungers withe yow be sette at mete,   *visitors; at the meal*
And vnto yow goode mete be brouhte or sente,   170
Withe parte of hit goodely yee theym Rehete,   *share with them*
For yt ys nouhte ywys convenyent   *it is impolite*
Withe yow at mete, whanne other ben present,
Alle forto holde that vnto yow ys brouhte,
And as wrecches on other vouchesauf nouhte.   175   *offer nothing*

Kutte nouhte youre mete eke as it were
   Felde men,   *field hands*
That to theyre mete haue suche an appetyte
That they ne rekke in what wyse, where ne when,   *they do not care*
Nor how vngoodly they on theyre mete twyte;   *they hack away*
But, swete children, haue al-wey your delyte   180
In curtesye, and in verrey gentylnesse,
And at youre myhte eschewe boystousnesse.   *avoid rudeness*

Whanne chese ys brouhte, A Trenchoure ha   *have*
   ye clene
On whiche withe clene knyf [ye] your chese   *may carve*
   mowe kerve;
In youre fedynge luke goodly yee be sene,   185   *eating*

And from Iangelyng your tunge al-wey conserve,   *tongue, control*
For so ywys yee shalle a name deserve
Off gentylnesse and of goode governaunce,
And in vertue al-wey youre silf avaunce.   *yourself prosper*

Whanne that so ys that ende shalle kome   190   *that is, the meal is*
    of mete,   *over*
Youre knyffes clene, where they ouhte to be,
Luke yee putte vppe; and holde eke yee your
    seete
Whils yee haue wasshe, for so wole honeste.
Whenne yee haue done, looke thanne goodly
    that yee
Withe-oute lauhtere, Iapynge, or boystous   195
    worde,
Ryse vppe, and goo vnto youre lordis borde,   *table*

And stonde yee there, and passe yee him
    nat fro   *remain until*
Whils grace ys sayde and brouhte vnto an ende,   *grace is said*
Thanne somme of yow for water owe to goo,   *go for water*
Somme holde the clothe, somme poure vpon   200
    his hende
Other service thanne this I myhte comende
To yow to done, but, for the tyme is shorte,
I putte theym nouhte in this lytyl Reporte,

But ouere I passe, prayyng with spyrit   *But I skip over*
    gladde
Of this labour that no wihte me detray,   205   *abuse me*
But where to lytyl ys, latte him more adde,
And whenne to myche ys, latte him take away;
For thouhe I wolde, tyme wole that I no
    more say;
I leve therfore, And this Book I directe
To euery wihte that lyste yt to correcte.   210   *desire*

And, swete children, for whos love now
    I write,
I yow beseche withe verrey lovande herte,   *truly loving heart*
To knowe this book that yee sette your delyte;
And myhtefulle god, that suffred peynes smerte,   *God the Almighty*

In curtesye he make yow so experte,   215   *courtesy*
That thurhe your nurture and youre
   governaunce   *deportment*
In lastynge blysse yee mowe your self auaunce!   *yourself attain*

6

Selections from *The Book of the Knight of the Tower*

CINDY VITTO

This chapter deals with an important work written in French near the end of the fourteenth century and translated into Middle English: *Le Livre du Chevalier de la Tour Landry pour l'enseignement de ses filles*, or *The Book of the Knight of the Tower*. We shall examine first how this work falls within the category of courtesy or conduct book and therefore into the genre of children's literature as well. Next, we shall investigate what we know of the author, the circumstances of composition, and the reception history of the work. Finally, following an overall view of its structure and content, we shall preview how the excerpts presented here deal with a pervasive theme of conduct books, the proper obedience of female to male, as well as the dangers posed to women by the flattering attentions of would-be courtly lovers.

Generic Considerations

Courtesy books, or conduct books, constitute a distinct branch of children's literature. By their nature, courtesy books involve a dialogue between a more experienced, wiser (and therefore usually older) narrator and a less mature, less knowing (and therefore usually younger) audience. The transmission of knowledge between the narrator and audience further places the courtesy book in the larger realm of didactic literature.

Today, when we hear the term *courtesy*, our initial impression may be that a courtesy book deals with manners. During the Middle Ages and Renaissance, *courtesy* was a much more complicated term, almost impossible to define with precision. Since even the *Oxford English Dictionary* lists no definition for this phrase, most scholars who use the term are operating from an inductive knowledge of works generally recognized as falling under the rubric of "courtesy book."[1] As the term is used here, a courtesy book is a work intended to teach proper behavior, ranging from keeping decorous and regular religious observance, to following approved principles of ethical behavior, to acknowledging and accommodating differences among various categories of people (especially in terms of class and gender hierarchies), to conducting business and social activities in such a way as to invite the approbation of one's peers, to knowing and performing the minute niceties of conduct that allow one to be accepted in polite society. In short, then, a courtesy book can deal with topics ranging from the religious to the ethical to the practical. The emphasis throughout, though, is on proper behavior (in contrast to a true metaphysical understanding and acceptance), with the ultimate purpose of achieving the good opinion of others, especially one's superiors.

Because the courtesy book outlines proper behavior, the genre allows us a rare view into the cultural complexities of an era. We can glimpse the web of interrelationships among inferiors, peers, and superiors; gain a better understanding of gender relations; and, occasionally, get an intimate view of everyday life in a world very different from our own—and yet eerily similar, since basic human needs and instincts do not change to the same extent, or at the same pace, that technology and social constructs do.

The Book of the Knight of the Tower, composed near the end of the fourteenth century, serves as a book of advice for the Knight's young daughters after the death of their mother. He attempts to replace, through his words, the guidance of an older female authority figure. This work, then, qualifies as children's literature (or, more properly, adolescent literature) because it is specifically directed toward a young audience in need of an older generation's wisdom. Another characteristic that helps define this text as children's literature is its intention to instruct and entertain simultaneously. The Knight makes use of numerous short narratives to flesh out his moralizations, and he includes both personal anecdotes and dialogue to enliven the instruction.

Textual History of *The Book of the Knight of the Tower*

In his prologue, the Knight of la Tour Landry mentions that he began composing his work in 1371; we assume that he finished it in 1372 or shortly after. By the end of the fifteenth century, the book was widely known, judging from the twenty-one surviving French manuscripts. An English translation, extant in one imperfect manuscript, was made during Henry VI's reign, and then William Caxton, the man who introduced printing to England, translated the work and printed it in 1484 (Offord, xix). Apparently, Caxton's manuscript source no longer exists; the source most similar appears to be No. 9308 in the Royal Library in Brussels (Offord, xxiii). The best-known and still available complete text in French, published in 1854 by the medievalist Anatole de Courde de Montaiglon, is based primarily on two manuscripts quite different from Caxton's, one housed in the Bibliothèque Nationale and the other in the British Library (Offord, xxii). One of the first questions raised in working with *The Book of the Knight of the Tower*, then, is which version to adopt as a basis for reading. For reasons outlined further on, this chapter presents Caxton's version.

Six copies of Caxton's text are known today: two in the British Museum, one in the Bodleian Library, one in the Cambridge University Library, one in the John Rylands Library, and one in the New York Public Library. A fragment of seven leaves, in private ownership, also exists (Offord, xi). As far as we know, no second edition of Caxton's text was printed, and no part of it reproduced until 1749, although the book seems to have been well known. In 1868, Thomas Wright edited for the Early English Text Society (EETS) a version of *The Book of the Knight of the Tower*, based on a translation preserved in British Library Ms. Harley 1764. The next complete edition of *The Book of the Knight of the Tower* did not appear until 1971, when the EETS sponsored an edition by M. Y. Offord, this time based on Caxton's work. The excerpt provided in this chapter is a modernization of Offord's text.[2]

Caxton's text is used here, rather than a translation of the French text, to emphasize the significance of this work for a late-medieval audience. As a shrewd businessman, Caxton published texts from which he could be reasonably sure of securing a profit. His choice of *The Book of the Knight of the Tower* signals the work's popularity and its broad appeal. In addition, a comparison of Caxton's translation with the French manuscripts reveals that Caxton added very little, but did occasionally delete passages in order to abbreviate somewhat lengthy moralizations (Offord, xxviii). Caxton's translation, then, does no violence to the French text, but improves its readability.

Another reason for choosing Caxton's text as the basis for our excerpt is that Caxton promoted children's literature during his tenure as publisher. His publication of Aesop's *Fables* and his translation and publication of the *Roman de Reynard* tales demonstrate his affinity for children's literature that could appeal simultaneously to young and old. *The Book of the Knight of the Tower* is just one of several works of children's literature marketed by England's first printer.

Caxton's business acuity is further revealed when we consider the political context in which he chose to print this text. To begin with, he probably used the situation of the royal family to help him market this work. In his prologue, Caxton tells us that the book had come into his hands through "the request & desyre of a noble lady which hath brou3t forth many noble & fayr dou3ters" (3). N. F. Blake argues that Caxton's unnamed patron for this work was his neighbor in Westminster, Elizabeth Woodville. Blake suggests, though, that she did not actually initiate the work; rather, Caxton quite likely referred obliquely to her in the prologue as a means of magnifying the significance of his material (30–31). In addition, Caxton may have made use of the prevailing political situation to enhance the moral appeal of his work. As

Edward IV's widow, Elizabeth Woodville was at this time confronting Richard III's challenge to her oldest son's right to the throne. Although the boy and his younger brother, the "little princes," later lost their lives in the Tower, Elizabeth Woodville also had five daughters who survived infancy. The eldest, Elizabeth of York, became the next queen of England, wife not of Richard III (as he intended) but of his opponent the Earl of Richmond, known to history as Henry VII.[3] Becoming the matriarch of the House of Tudor, young Elizabeth played a crucial role, for only under the Tudors did England solidify its political position in the Renaissance world. As types of "innocence destroyed" and "savior from the next generation," then, the young princes and their sister may have exemplified for Caxton the important roles young people could play in a political context, especially if properly advised.

Authorship

Besides knowing the context in which Caxton printed this work, we know something of the author's own history as well. The first known member of the knight's family, a Landricus Dunensis, appears in a French charter between 1061 and 1063. He built the tower that gave the family its name, a tower that stands today and gives its name to the small town where it is located, La Tourlandry (Offord, xxxiv). Our author, the fourth Geoffrey de la Tour Landry, appears in the historical record several times from about the middle of the fourteenth century in connection with various campaigns of the Hundred Years War, a territorial battle between England and France over ownership of northern France (Offord, xxxv). Evidently, Geoffrey held the respectably high rank of *chevalier banneret*, meaning that he had the means to support twenty-five armed men with accompanying archers (Boisard, 137). He was married twice. With his first wife, he had at least two sons and three daughters, although relatively little is known about the children. After his first wife died, he married a rich widow, and he himself died between 1402 and 1406.

In addition to the book he wrote for his daughters, his prologue indicates that he also wrote poetry in his youth, and he intended to write a book for his sons similar to the one addressed to his daughters. We have no evidence of his poetry or the book for his sons, but we do have twenty-nine manuscripts and several printed editions of another book most likely by the same author, a work entitled *Ponthus et Sidoine* (Boisard, 152). This prose romance recounts the love of a young prince and princess (the title characters), but perhaps most interesting is the large cast of then-living individuals who appear in the book, many of them related to Geoffrey de la Tour Landry. As an additional bit of evidence for authorship, the author's own grandson was given the name Ponthus around 1390, probably the first child to be so named, although the name later became popular due to the romance's success (Bois-ard, 150).

Summary

The author's prologue to *The Book of the Knight of the Tower* gives us quite a bit of information, although some of what he says may be literary fiction rather than historical fact. The Knight begins by explaining the impetus for his work—his catching sight of his young daughters as he sat one spring day in a garden, reminiscing about his own youth and the poetry that love inspired in him then. Because the conjunction of springtime and gardens would immediately signal to a medieval audience the conventions of romance, the Knight's opening is somewhat discordant. He simultaneously speaks as a former courtly lover remembering his youth and as a father earnestly seeking to protect his daughters from men such as he once was. This ambivalence of tone can be traced throughout the work.[4]

To instruct his daughters, the Knight proposes to set before them both good and bad models of female behavior, in the form of exempla. A common tool of preachers and storytellers, the exemplum is a short narrative specifi-cally designed to point to a moral, either explicitly or implicitly stated.[5] Alto-gether, the Knight's book contains more than 140 exempla (Ho, 101). He tells us that leaving the garden, he encountered two priests and two clerks and, explaining to them his project, asked them to read to him the Bible, his-tories of kings, chronicles of France and England, and many other works in order to compile his own volume.[6]

In addition to exempla, the Knight provides a substantial comparison between the follies of Eve (62–69) and the virtues of Mary (143–48), the two women most often paired in the Middle Ages to illustrate the difference between good and bad female behavior. The book then takes an unexpected twist as the Knight recounts for his daughters a debate between himself and their mother (163–76). In this debate, he argues for the positive aspects of courtly love; however, his wife counters each of his points and declares unequivocally that indulging any man in the practice of courtly love in any way is dangerous for a woman's reputation and should be avoided at all costs. By taking the part of the courtly lover, the Knight again assumes the initial persona of the prologue, when he sat in the garden remembering his days of youthful love. His dual perspective in the prologue—as a man who had formerly courted ladies, now a father who must protect his daughters from men such as he once was—is duplicated in this domestic debate. Both scenarios remind us implicitly that although a man has little or nothing to lose by engaging in amorous play, from the woman's perspective the situa-tion is entirely different. Putting the arguments against courtly love in the voice of his wife gives them even more authority for his daughters, since their mother speaks for female experience. Indeed, she admits that she herself had been approached by a hopeful lover, but that she flatly refused him (173–74).

Finally, the Knight closes his work with an extended exemplum, in which Cato proffers three pieces of advice to his son, the last one a test of his wife to see if she can keep his secrets (183–87). Although the son ignores most of his father's advice, he does remember to test his wife and learns that she cannot be trusted. Just as the prologue introduces a level of ambivalence into the work, with the Knight acting as one-time courtly lover and now father, so this conclusion brings ambivalence at the end of the work. On one hand, the Knight's daughters are taught that they should follow their father's advice; Cato's son, who did not, came to ruin. On the other hand, the example of Cato's son indicates the likelihood that parental advice will go unheeded. Likewise, while the exemplum teaches the necessity of female discretion, it simultaneously indicates its rarity. In fact, the courtesy book genre as a whole faces this problem of a double moral: While explicitly teaching correct behavior, it implicitly expresses the likelihood that human nature will prevail and subvert the precepts being held up.

Advice on Courtly Love and on Obedience

The Knight of the Tower, writing for his unmarried daughters, is especially concerned with preserving their good reputation so that they may marry well and, once married, maintain their own and their husbands' honor. Accordingly, he returns repeatedly to the inherent danger of flattery. He warns his daughters about men who speak fairly, soliciting their love while mocking them in the company of others. In a later section of the work, though, he appears to argue the opposite while engaging in a lengthy debate on courtly love. While the Knight argues on behalf of the courtly lover, his wife forbids her daughters to entertain any conversation with such men, no matter how worthy and sincere they appear. Although she lists a few reasons for the necessity of being so stern, her initial reaction, that women must guard their reputations (164), seems most important. If such a lover approaches her, a woman must leave his company immediately or call others to her in order to prevent a private conversation (167). The Knight's wife explains that she herself has had to follow this advice on at least one occasion.

Besides avoiding the trap of courtly love, a good wife must observe strict obedience to her husband. To imprint his instruction on this point, the Knight tells a representative story of an "obedience test." Three men wagered as to whose wife would jump into a basin, without question (35–37). Although the first two wives complained and refused, the third wife was so anxious to obey that, during the meal she served the men, she misunderstood her husband's request for salt and jumped on the table. (Even in modern French the words sound similar, since the command for "jump" is *sautez* and "salt" is *saltière*.) Her alacrity led the men to excuse her from the actual test of jumping into the basin. More important, though, her eager obedience allowed her husband to win the wager. He therefore saved face before his friends, whose wives had shamed them by refusing to jump, and could now love her even more freely since she had proved her obedience. The Knight thus makes his point that a wife should obey all of her husband's requests, no matter what.

The Knight is emphatic as well about the negative consequences of a wife's disobedience. He relates, for example, one story in which the wife receives a broken nose for her disobedience (35). To further dissuade his daughters from improper behavior, he goes beyond personal reprisals to mention as well the possibility of far-reaching consequences of marital discord. For instance, one of his stories tells of a woman who left her husband after quarreling with him. That separation ultimately resulted in her rape and death, along with the death of 33,000 others (101–2).

In keeping with the social mores of the time, the Knight of the Tower clearly sets up a double standard of behavior for wives and husbands. Whereas husbands may devise obedience tests and carry them out in front of others, wives are exhorted not to engage in any guile and under no condition to question or reprove their husbands in the company of other people. He links wifely obedience to true love, although the husband apparently has no hoops to pass through in order to deserve his wife's devoted obedience. For the Knight, true love must be sought within marriage—most emphatically not within the system of courtly love—and is fostered by the wife's submission in language and deeds.

Modern readers might be appalled by the Knight's emphasis on wifely obedience. In particular, the obedience test seems effectively to reduce a wife (especially a young one) to the status of a trained animal. If she does not "perform" adequately, then the husband is entitled to be disappointed, to lose interest in her, and to place his affection elsewhere, even to punish her physically. Yet we must remember that the very existence of courtesy books such as this text indicates the existence of what Judith Fetterley has labeled the "resisting reader." If medieval women were indeed as obedient as the Knight urges them to be, there would be no need for such detailed instruction.

In this regard we might revisit and read more skeptically the Knight's story of the wife who was so eagerly obedient that she upset the meal because she thought her husband had directed her to jump onto the table (36–37). We should keep in mind the possibility that she knew he had asked her to fetch salt, not to jump. Her "obedience" may have allowed her to have her own fun at the men's expense, while simultaneously winning the wager for her husband. Thus the discerning reader need not despair; although the explicit theme is unquestioning obedience, the implicit message is that young women of the Middle Ages did enjoy some degree of agency and did manifest some measure of control, some level of disobedience, despite the concerted efforts of fathers and husbands—and authors of courtesy books—to keep them in check.[7]

Notes

1. Nicholls (12), for example, comments on the difficulty of a lack of precise definition; and Mason, one of the earliest authors on this topic, acknowledges his invention of a definition: "Courtesy . . . may be tentatively defined as a code of ethics, esthetics, or peculiar information for any class-conscious group, and a courtesy book is a book which sets forth such a code" (4).

2. Although Offord's work is readily available in most undergraduate libraries, it presents difficulties for the typical reader because it is a transcription of Caxton's book, retaining the original spelling, capitalization, and punctuation (short and long strokes rather than commas and periods). Thus these elements have here been regularized and modernized, and units of text have been separated into logical paragraphs. In addition, since Caxton worked hastily and sometimes sloppily, often retaining French vocabulary rather than searching for the English equivalent, this aspect of his work has been modernized as well. Words that would not be familiar to the reader without knowledge of French have been replaced by English words or phrases. Finally, some minor changes in word choice or position have been made silently, to enhance comprehension; however, to retain as much of the original style as possible, most words recognizable to a modern reader but possibly confusing in Caxton's context, or sentences with complicated syntax, are left unchanged, but are glossed in a note.

3. This historical situation is familiar to many through Shakespeare's play *The Tragedy of King Richard III*. For a concise overview of the actual historical situation, and the way in which Shakespeare distorted that situation for his own purposes, see Saccio (158–86).

4. See, for example, Krueger and Ho.

5. For a detailed study of the exemplum, including a discussion of its use in *Le Livre du Chevalier de la Tour Landry*, see Mosher. See also Walter.

6. What the Knight neglects to mention is that his true source, evidently, was a collection of exempla probably composed before 1300, entitled *Le Miroir des bonnes femmes* (*The Mirror of Good Women*) or *Le Miroir des preudes femmes* (*The Mirror of Wise Women*). Grigsby notes, "Not one chapter between 37 and 112 starts with a Biblical *exemplum* which is not also contained in the *Mirror*" (207); in addition, many of the nonbiblical exempla come from the same source (208).

7. The author wishes to acknowledge Ross Arthur for his assistance with both this introductory essay and the excerpts that follow.

THE BOOK OF THE KNIGHT OF THE TOWER (LE LIVRE DU CHEVALIER DE LA TOUR LANDRY POUR L'ENSEIGNEMENT DE SES FILLES)

Here begins the book which the Knight of the Tower made, and speaks of many fair examples and the instruction and teaching of his daughters.[1]

Prologue

In the year of our Lord 1371 as I was in a garden under a shadow, as it were, in the end of April, all mourning and pensive, I rejoiced just a little in the sound and song of the wild fowls, which sang in their language, as the blackbird, the redwing, the thrush, and the nightingale, which were gay and lusty.[2] This sweet song enlivened me and made my heart enjoy all, so that then I went remembering the time passed in my youth, how love had held me during that time in his service by great distress, in which I was many a year glad and joyful, and many another time sorrowful, as it does to many a lover. But all my evils have been recompensed, since the fair and good,[3] who has knowledge of all honor, all good, and fair maintaining, has been given me. And of all good she seemed to me the best and the flower in whom I so much delighted. For in that time I made songs, lays, roundels, ballads, virelays, and new songs in the best way I could. But death, which spares none, has taken her, for whom I have received many sorrows and heavinesses in such wise that I have passed my life more than twenty years heavy and sorrowful. For the heart of a true lover shall never in any time nor day forget good love but evermore shall remember it.

And thus at that time, as I was in a great pensiveness and thought, I beheld in the way and saw my daughters coming, of whom I had great desire that they should turn to honor above all other things. For they are young and little and lacking in wit and reason, wherefore they ought at the beginning to be taught and courteously corrected by good examples and doctrines, as did a queen, I suppose she was queen of Hungary, who fairly and sweetly chastised her daughters and taught them, as is contained in her book.[4] And therefore when I saw them come toward me, I remembered the time when I was young and rode with my fellowship and company in Poitou and in other places. And I remember well the deeds and sayings that they told of such things as they found with the ladies and damsels that they solicited and prayed of love. And if one would not listen to their prayer, yet another would, without abiding. And though they had good or evil answers, or they cared not at all,[5] they had neither dread nor shame, so much were they obstinate and accustomed and were very well bespoken and had fair language. For many times they would have overall delight. And thus they do nothing but deceive good ladies and damsels, and bear overall the tidings, some true and some lies, whereof there happened many times injuries and many villainous defamations without cause and without reason.

And in all the world is no greater treason than to deceive gentlewomen, or to increase villainous blame. For many are deceived by the great oaths that they use, whereof I often debate with them, and say to them, "You over-false men, how may the gods suffer you to live, that so often you perjure and foreswear yourself? For you hold no faith." But none puts it in array because they are so much and so full of disarray. And because I saw that time so led and disposed, yet I fear that some are such in this present time.

Therefore I concluded that I would cause to be made a little book wherein I would have written the good manners and good deeds of good ladies and women and of their lives, so that for their virtues and bounties they be honored, and after their death renowned and praised, and shall be to the end of the world, to take of them good example and countenance. And also by the contrary I shall cause to be written and set in a book the mishap and vices of evil women, who have used their life and now have blame, to the end that the evil may be eschewed by which they might err, who yet are blamed, shamed, and defamed.[6]

And for this cause that I have here said, I have thought on my well-loved daughters whom I see so young, to make for them a little book, to learn to read to the end that they may learn and study and understand the good and evil that is passed, to keep them from him who is yet to come. For such there be that laughs before you, who behind your back goes mocking and lying. Wherefore it is a hard thing to know the world that is now present. And for these reasons as I have said, I went out of the garden and found in my way two priests and two clerks that I had and told them that I would make a book and an exemplary for my daughters to learn to read and understand how they ought to govern themselves and keep themselves from evil. And then I made them come and read before me the book of the Bible, the gests of the kings, the chronicles of France and of England, and many other strange histories, and made them to read every book, and had them make this book, which I would not set in rhyme but all in prose, to shorten it and also make it more understandable. And also for the great love that I have to my daughters, whom I love as a father ought to love them. And then my heart shall have perfect joy, if they turn to good and to honor—that is, to serve and love God and to have the love and the grace of their neighbors and of the world. And because every father and mother after God and nature ought to teach and inform their children and to turn them from the evil way, and to show them the right way and true path, as well for the salvation of their souls as for the honor of the earthly body, I have made two books, one for my sons and the other for my daughters to learn to read.[7] And thus in learning it shall not be but that they shall retain some good example, or flee the evil and retain the good. For it may not be but in some time they shall remember some good example or some good lore after, that it shall fall and come to their mind in speaking upon this matter.

How a good woman ought not to strive with her husband (Capitulo, xvii)

A woman ought in no manner to strive against her husband nor answer him so that he takes displeasure thereby, as did the wife of a burgess who answered to her husband so noxiously and shamefully before the people that he became angry and fierce to see himself so ruled before the people that he had shame thereof. And he said to her and bade her once or twice that she should be still and leave off, but she would not. And her husband, who was wroth, smote her with his fist to the earth, and smote her with his foot on the visage so that she broke her nose, by which she was ever after disfigured. And so by her riot and annoy she got herself a crooked nose, much evil. It had been much better for her if she had held still and had suffered. Yet it is reason and right that the husband have the high words, and it is but honor to a good woman to suffer and hold herself in peace and leave the haughty language to her husband and lord. And also it is in the contrary great shame and villainy to a woman to strive against her husband, be it wrong or right, especially, I say, not before the people. But when she shall find him alone and at the right time, she may well reprehend him and advise him in showing courtesy that he had wrong and unright with him. And if he is a reasonable man, he will thank her. And if he be other, she has not yet done her part. For right so should a wise woman do by the example of the wise Queen Esther, wife of the king Ahasuerus, who was very melancholy and hasty.[8] But the good lady answered not to his ire, but after when she saw him well-tempered, in an appropriate place, and at an appropriate time, then she did what she would, and it was great wisdom of a woman. And thus ought wise women to do. According to this example, the women that are chiders and ramping are not of such obedience, as was a wife of a merchant of whom I shall say and tell you.

How a woman sprang upon the table (Capitulo, xviii)

In a time it happened that merchants of France came from certain fairs where they sought drapery, and as they came with merchandise from Rouen, one of them said, "It is a very fair thing for a man to have a wife obedient in all things to her husband. Verily," that one said, "my wife obeys me well." And the second said, "I believe that my wife obeys me better." "Yea," said the third, "let's lay a wager, that whichever wife of us three best obeys her husband and soonest does his commandment will win the wager." Thereupon they waged a jewel and all three accorded to the same, and swore that none should notify his wife of this bargain, except only to say to her, "Do that which I shall command, whatever it is."

After, when they came to the first man's house, he said to his wife, "Spring into this basin," and she answered, "Why? What need is there?" and he said, "Because it pleases me so, and I will that you do so." "Truly," she said, "I shall know first why I shall spring." And so she would not do it. And her husband waxed angry and gave her a buffet.

After this they came to the second merchant's house, and he said to his wife as the other said, that she would do his commandment. And it was not long after that he said to her, "Spring into the basin," and she demanded him why. And at the end, whatever he did, she did it not, wherefore she was beaten as that other was.

Then came they to the third man's house, and there the table was covered, with meat set thereon. And the merchant said to the other merchants in their ears that after dinner he would command her to spring into the basin. And the husband said to his wife that whatsoever he commanded her she should do it. His wife, who much loved him and heeded him, heard well the word. And so they began to eat, and there was no salt upon the table. And the good man said to his wife, "Sail sur table." And the good wife, who feared to disobey him, sprang upon the table and overthrew table, meat, wine, and platters to the ground. "How?" said the good man. "Is this the manner? Know you no other play but this? Are you mad or out of your wit?" "Sire," said she, "I have done your commandment. Have you not said that your commandment should be done whatever it was? Certainly, I have done to my power although it is your harm and hurt as much as mine. For you said to me that I should spring on the table." Said he, "I said there lacked salt upon the table." "In good faith, I understood," said she, "to spring." Then was there laughter enough and all was taken for a joke and a mockery.

Then the other two merchants said there was no need to let her spring in the basin, for she had done enough, and her husband had won the wager. And she was more praised than the other two that would not do the commandment of their husbands. For lesser people chasten their wives by buffets and strokes, but gentlewomen ought to be chastised by fair demeanor and by courtesy, for otherwise ought not to be done to them. And therefore every gentlewoman shows whether she has gentle character or not; that is, she shows by fair demeanor and by courtesy that she obeys and has every hesitation to disobey lest any harm come or might happen or fall to her. For the other two wives obeyed not their husbands as the good wife did to the third merchant, who for fear of disobedience to her husband sprang upon the table and threw down all.

And thus ought every good woman to fear and obey her lord and husband and do his commandment whether right or wrong, if the commandment be not overly outrageous. And if there be vice therein, she is not to blame, but the blame abides with her lord and husband. And also she ought not to answer to every word of every husband nor of other. And therein is peril, as in the case of the knight's daughter, who set her honor in great balance to strive and answer to the hasty squire who said to her villainy as a fool. For many be so haughty and of so evil character that they say in hastiness and heat all that they know and that comes to mouth. Therefore it is great peril to begin strife to such people, for whoever does sets his honor in great adventure, since many say in their anger more than they know, to avenge themselves.

How a woman ought not to depart nor go from her husband for any wrath or evil will that may grow or come among them (Capitulo, lxxi)

I will tell you how of a little wrath came great evil. A good man who was noble and of Mount Ephraim married a damsel of Bethlehem, who for a little incident was wroth with her husband and went again to her father's house. The good man her husband was thereof heavy and sorrowful, and went and fetched her home again. And her father blamed her and said she did not as a good wife should do. As they were going homeward, they lodged in a town named Galga, where were many worldly folk full of lechery. This folk came there where this woman and her lord were lodged. They broke the doors and by force and violence villainously took and ravished the said woman from her husband, and for nothing that their host could say or do, who would have given one of his daughters for the warrant for his hospitality, they would not leave her but had her with them.

And as the morning came, she that saw herself dishonored and so villainously shamed took in herself such shame and such a sorrow that she then died at her lord's feet, wherefore the good man was nigh dead also. And as he was come to himself again, he took and bore her body into his house, and then he made twelve pieces of her body. And upon each piece he set a leaf of paper whereon was written all the manner how it befell to her and sent these twelve pieces to twelve persons, her parents and most nigh of her kin, to the end that they should among them take vengeance of it. Whereof it befell that all her friends and her husband's friends also took thereof so great ire and wrath and had so great abomination of it that they gathered and assembled together and with great number of men and arms came to Galga and there slew 33,000 persons, men and women.

This is to you a good example how a woman ought not to leave her husband and lord for no ire nor discontent that may be between them, and a wise and good woman ought to bear and suffer the ire and wrath of her husband in the most fair and humble wise that she can, and to put herself at pains to appease him by courteous and fair words, and not leave and go from him, as did the said damsel, who left her lord and went from him, and her husband must fetch her again. By the which going she died, and so did many a one, as above is said. And if she had been in peace and still with her lord, all this great evil and sorrow had not fallen. And therefore it is sometimes good to restrain ire and subdue the heart. For this is the usage of the wise woman who tends to live peaceably and lovingly with her husband and lord.

The argument of the Knight of the Tower and of his wife[9] (Capitulo, cxxii)

My dear daughters, as for love paramours, I shall tell you all the debate and strife of me and of your mother. I would sustain against her that a lady or damsel might love paramours in certain cases, for in love is good worship unless any evil be thought in it. In this then where any evil is thought, it is not love but rather great falsehood and mischief, wherefore take you heed. And hear you the great debate and strife that was between her and me.

Thus then I said to your mother, "Lady, why shouldn't the ladies and damsels love paramours? For certainly it seems to me that in good love and true may be only wealth and honor, and also the lover is the better therefore and more gay and jolly, and also the more encouraged to exercise himself more often in arms, and takes therefore better manner in all estates to please his lady or love. And likewise does she of whom he is enamored, to please him the better as far as she loves him. And also I tell you that it is great charity when a lady or damsel makes either a good knight or a good squire. These are my reasons."

The answer which the Lady of the Tower made to her lord (Capitulo, cxxiii)

Then answered to me your mother, "Sire, I marvel not if, among yourselves, men sustain and hold this reason that all women ought to love paramours. But since this debate and strife is come before our own daughters, I will answer after my opinion and intention. For from our children we must hide nothing.

"You say, and so do all other men, that a lady or damsel is the better when she loves paramours and that she shall be the more gay and of fair manner and countenance, and how she shall do great charity to make a good knight. These words are but sport and amusement of lords and of fellows in a common language. For they that say that all the honor and worship which they get and have comes to them by their paramours, and that their love encourages them to go on voyages and to please them by state of arms, these words cost them little to say in order to get the better and sooner the grace and good will of their paramours. For many use such words and other such marvelous[10] ones, but although they say that for them and for their love they do it, in good faith they do it only to enhance themselves and to draw to them the grace and vainglory of the world.

"Therefore I charge you, fair daughters, that in this matter you believe not your father, but I pray you that you hold yourselves cleanly and without blame, and that you be not amorous for many reasons, which I shall rehearse for you. First, I say not but that every good woman of age may love well and better one than another, that is to say, folk of worship and honor, and they also that shall counsel her for her own health and worship. And thus men ought to love by this manner, the one more than the other. But as for to be so much enamored that this love be master of her and makes them to fall in some foul and shameful delight, sometimes with right and sometimes with wrong, men keep watch for this shameful deed or feat, and also such dishonor and outcry which is not soon put out. And by the false watchers and backbiters which are never ceasing to talk of some evil rather than of some good, they take away and defame the good reputation of the good women and of many a good lady. And therefore all women who are not wedded may keep and hold themselves from it, and that for many reasons.

"The first reason is because a woman who is enamored of a man may not serve God with a good heart and true as she did before. For many a one I have heard say, who have been amorous in their youth, that when they were in the church their thought and melancholy made them think more upon their delights and their paramours than they did to the service of God. And also the art of love is of such kind that when one is in the Church to hear mass and the divine service, as the priest holds the body of Our Lord between his hands, then comes most to the mind evil and foul thoughts. This is the art or craft of the goddess that men call Venus, who had the name of a planet, as I heard a good and true man say, who preached and said how once the devil entered into the body of a damned woman, who was jolly and gay and very amorous. The devil that was within her body made her do many false miracles, wherefore the pagans held her for a goddess and worshipped her as a god. And this Venus was she that gave counsel to the Trojans, that they should send Paris the son of King Priamus to Greece and that she should make him ravish and have with him the fairest lady of all Greece, whereof she said truth. For Paris did ravish the fair Helen, the wife of King Menelaus, for the which feat or deed were slain afterward more than forty kings and twelve hundred thousand[11] other persons and more. This Venus was the principal cause of all this great mischief. She was an evil goddess, full of evil temptation. She is the goddess of love which kindles and inflames amorous hearts and makes them think both day and night of the joy and foul delights of lechery. And especially when they are at the mass or hearing the divine service the devil causes this to trouble their faith and their devotion which they have toward Our Lord.

"And know you for certain, my fair daughters, that a woman who is amorous shall never set her heart on God, nor she shall not say devoutly her hours or matins nor open her heart to hear the divine service of God, whereof I shall tell you an example. Two queens were at this side of the sea, who in Lent upon Holy Thursday in the Passion Week took their foul delights and pleasure within the church during the divine service, and rested not of their folly until it was done, whereof God, who was displeased with them for their enormous and foul sin, made their foul deeds and feats to be openly known among the folk, in such a way that they were taken and put under a great and heavy vault of lead, and there they died an evil death. And the two knights their whoremongers died also, as they were flayed while still alive. Now may you see how their false love was evil and damnable, and how the temptation of Venus the goddess of love and lady of lechery tempted them so much that she made them take their foul pleasures in such holy time as upon the Thursday and Holy Friday in the Passion Week.

"By this example is well seen and known how every amorous woman is more tempted within the Church than in any other place. And the same is the first reason, how a young woman must keep herself from such foolish love and not be in any way amorous.

"The other reason is because of many gentlemen who be so false and deceitful that they solicit every gentlewoman that they may find, and to them they swear that they shall keep to them their faith and be true to them, and shall love them without falsehood or deceit, and that they would rather die than to think any villainy or dishonor, and that they shall be the better praised for the love of them, and that if they have any good and worship it shall come by them. And thus they shall show and say to them so many reasons and perversions that it is a great marvel to hear them speak. And yet more, they give out of their breasts great and feigned sighs, and make as if they were pensive and melancholy, and after they cast a false look. And then the good and goodnatured women who see them suppose that they are inflamed with true and faithful love, but all such manner of folk which make such semblance are but deceivers and beguilers of the ladies and damsels. For there is no lady or damsel that would hear them but that they should be deceived of them by their false reasons, which they should not hear.

"These are contrary to the faithful and true lovers. For he that loves with good and true love, as he comes before his paramour he is fearing and full of dread lest he do anything that might displease her. For he is not so hardy to discover or say even one word, and if he love her well I daresay that it shall be three or four years before he dares say his secret to her. But the false lovers do not do thus, for they pray all of them that they find as above is said, and are not in dread nor in fear to say all that comes upon their false tongues, and have no shame of it. And all that they may understand of them, they repeat and tell it among their fellows, and of them they hold their talking, whereof they laugh and scorn and take their disport of it. And thus by such a way they mock and scorn the ladies and damsels and make up lies of those who before were never said nor spoken of. For they to whom they tell it put it rather to some evil than some good, insomuch that from word to word and by such mocking and frivolities many ladies and damsels are often blamed."

How a woman ought not to hear the words or talking of him that prays her of love (Capitulo, cxxiiii)

"And to the end you be not deceived, keep you well from the talking of them, and if one begins to reason and talk with you of such a matter, leave him alone, or else call to you someone to hear him say what he will. And thus you shall void and break his talking. And know you for certain that if you do this once or twice he shall no more speak to you thereof, but in good faith at the last he shall praise and dread you and shall say, 'This woman is assured and firm.' And by this manner you shall not be put in their vainglory and talk and also shall not have the blame nor defamation of the world."

How the knight answered to his wife (Capitulo, cxxv)

Then I answered, "Lady, you are hard and evil in that you will not suffer that your daughters be amorous. And if it happened that some gentle knight, worshipful, mighty, and powerful enough, one of their station, had set his heart on one of them and was willing to love her and take her to his wife, why should she not love him?" "Sire," said his wife, "to this I shall answer you. It seems to me that every woman, maid, or widow may well beat herself with her own staff. For all men are not of one condition nor of one manner, for that thing which pleases one is displeasing to another, and there are some who take great pleasure of the great cheer and favor that is done to them, and that think only of the good and honest. And there are some also who are therefore more curious to demand and ask their paramours to be their wives. But there are many others who are not of such a manner, but all contrary. For when they see that their paramours pain themselves to make them cheer, they praise them less, and within their hearts are doubting of them. And as they see them so light of will and so enamored, they leave them and do not ask them to be their wives. And that many a one who shows herself too amorous and too open in beholding and in giving fair countenance loses her marriage. For certainly those who keep themselves simply and who give no fair token or favor to one more than to another be most praised, and they are therefore the sooner wedded.

"Upon this point you once told me an example, which I have not forgotten, which happened to you of a lady, to whom I give no name, whom you went once to see, willing to take her in marriage. She that knew well how it was spoken of you and her, for her marriage, made to you as great cheer as if she had loved and known your person all the days of her life.[12] You prayed her of love, but because she was not wise enough to answer you courteously and well, you asked her not. And if she had held herself more secret and covered, and more simply, you would have taken her as your wife, of whom I have since heard say that she has been blamed, but I know not for certain if it was so. And certainly, Sire, you are not the first to whom such an adventure happened. For many women have lost their marriage because of their amorous look and fair show. Therefore it is good for every unwedded woman to behave herself simply and cleanly, and especially before those whom marriage with her is spoken of. I say only that men must bear honor to every one according to what they are."[13]

How a knight loved the Lady of the Tower (Capitulo, cxxxi)

"Lady, you make me marvel how you so sore discourage them to love. Do you want me to believe you are so true in your speaking that you were never amorous? Certainly, I have well heard the complaint of some of whom you hold well your peace."

"Sire," said the Lady, "I think you would not believe me if I told you the very truth thereof, but as for saying I have not been prayed of love, I have many times perceived how some men were about to speak to me thereof, but ever I broke their words and called some other to me, whereby I broke their deed. Whereof once it befell, as many knights and ladies were playing with me, that a knight said to me how he loved me more than all the ladies in this world. And I did ask him if it was long since sickness and evil had taken him, and he answered that it was well two years gone and past, and that never he dared tell it to me. I then answered to him that it was nothing of that space of time and that he hastened himself too much and that it was but a temptation and that he should go to the church to cast holy water upon himself and say his Ave Maria, and his temptation should soon after go from him, for the love was new. And he demanded of me why, and then I said to him that no paramour or lover ought to say to his lady that he loves her until the time of seven and a half years be passed and gone, and that it was but a little temptation. Then he intended to argue and put many reasons to me, when I said all on high, 'Behold you all what this knight says, which is that it is but two years since he first loved one lady.' And then he prayed that I should keep my peace thereof and that in good faith he should never speak to me thereof. But at the last he said to me, 'Lady of the Tower, you are evil and strange, and also after your words overly proud in love. I doubt[14] that you have not always been so strange.[15] You are like the lady of the fucille,[16] who said to me that she would never hear nor understand the note and words of anyone except for one time that a knight prayed her, but she had an uncle whom she made to hide behind her to hear and understand what the knight would say, wherein she did great treason. For he thought secretly to say his reason and did not believe that anyone had heard him but herself alone, wherefore I dare almost say that both you and she are but great speakers and little piteous of those that require[17] mercy and grace. And she is of your opinion that no ladies or damsels may disport themselves with anyone other than with their lord for the reasons which you have said before.'

"But, Sire," said then the Lady of the Tower to her lord, "as for your daughters you may say to them and charge them of that which shall fall to you, but the right deed shall be done. Sire, I pray to God that they may come to worship and honor, as I desire. For my intention and will is not to ordain upon any ladies or damsels except upon my own daughters, of whom I have the chastisement and charge. For every good lady or damsel, if God be pleased, shall govern and keep herself well to her worship and honor, without me, who am of little wit and little knowing, intervening thereof."

Notes

1. From *The Book of the Knight of the Tower*, we will read the prologue, "How a good woman ought not to strive with her husband" (Capitulo, xvii), "How a woman sprang upon the table" (Capitulo, xviii), "How a woman ought not to depart from her husband for any wrath or evil will that may grow or come between them" (Capitulo, lxxi), and excerpts from the section devoted to the debate between the Knight and his wife concerning the merits of courtly love (Capitulo, cxxii through cxxxiii).

2. This initial sentence illustrates the knight's fondness for the then-fashionable rhetorical technique of doubling, in which two synonymous nouns, adjectives, or verbs appear together, not so much to add meaning as to flaunt rhetorical skill (e.g., "mourning and pensive," "sound and song," "gay and lusty"). Caxton often includes an untranslated French term rather than an English equivalent in instances of doubling. He frequently appears to have been hardpressed to come up with two different English words to express the same concept. Since the present text of *The Book of the Knight of the Tower* eliminates French vocabulary, it sacrifices some of this doubling, but the result is more pleasing to the modern rhetorical taste.

3. His lady, the woman who eventually became his wife.

4. No such book is known to us today.

5. They received indifferent answers.

6. The syntax of this sentence is rather confusing. The Knight explains that he writes the book so that his readers might avoid the evil of those women who have set a bad example and who therefore are still blamed, shamed, and defamed.

7. No copy of the knight's book for his sons survives.

8. Quick-tempered.

9. Here begins the domestic debate between the Knight and his wife. This excerpt, in dialogue format, marks a major break in the discursive nature of the preceding text and in some ways can be seen as a transition from more general to more specific instruction for the knight's daughters.

10. Incredible.

11. 120,000.

12. Because she knew that a marriage was spoken of between you and her, she treated you as if she had loved and known you her whole life.

13. Although an apparent non sequitur, this final sentence introduces the following section, not included here, on valuing others according to their social rank.

14. Suspect.

15. Remote.

16. Caxton here misreads the French, which according to Montaiglon should read, "Madame de la Jaille."

17. Solicit.

7

Ælfric's *Colloquy*

STEPHEN J. HARRIS

Ælfric's *Colloquy* was written primarily for schoolchildren. It is, first and foremost, a teaching tool, and it was used in a classroom to educate young Anglo-Saxons, aged seven and above, in spoken Latin. As a teaching tool, the *Colloquy* is engaged in a long tradition of shaping the English student. As well as suggesting something about Anglo-Saxon pedagogy, the *Colloquy* offers a glimpse of the social world of Anglo-Saxon England—if only in stereotypes. Like Chaucer in his *Canterbury Tales* almost four hundred years later, Ælfric briefly describes plowmen and huntsmen, monks and knights, cooks and merchants. His purpose is to introduce students to vocabulary specific to these crafts and, as one might expect, to introduce the nuances of Latin grammar. Students probably would have had to memorize the *Colloquy* and recite it under threat of a beating. The *Colloquy* presents a number of characters who engage a master in dialogue, each trying to outdo the other in expressing the necessity of his craft to the welfare of the community. In this stilted exuberance, each character is able to expound in some detail on the method and aim of his adopted trade. The *Colloquy* suggests something about the dynamism, if not the drama, of an early medieval classroom just after the turn of the first millennium.[1]

The Text of the *Colloquy*

The text translated here is edited by G. N. Garmonsway as *Ælfric's Colloquy* for Methuen's Old English Library. He consulted the four extant Latin manuscripts of the work, choosing to follow for his edition Cotton MS Tiberius A. iii, the only manuscript with a continuous Old English (hereafter, OE) gloss. Tiberius A. iii was at Christ's Church, Canterbury, and was written, according to Garmonsway, in the "second quarter of the eleventh century" (4) in the Carolingian minuscule of the Continent. Neil Ker is a little less precise about the date, offering instead the middle of the eleventh century for the text, and the second half of the eleventh century for the gloss.[2] Tiberius A. iii is an interesting manuscript in which to find the *Colloquy*, since it contains a number of glossed ecclesiastical texts. These include the Benedictine *Rule*, glossed continuously in OE; the *Regularis Concordia*, another monastic rule; and four additional texts concerned with the *Rule*.[3] Clearly, this manuscript was directed at the monk in his duties and intellectual responsibilities. The version of the *Colloquy* in Tiberius A. iii tends to be considered the "base text" to which later additions and interpolations are made in other versions, such as that in Oxford St. John's College 154 (Gwara and Porter, 4).[4] The Latin *Colloquy* was written by Ælfric, while the OE gloss was added later by someone else, perhaps Ælfric Bata, Ælfric's student. Bata, which means "barrel" in Latin (he was either stocky or fond of drink), may have compiled the codex, as his name is written at the front of Tiberius A. iii. Two scribes were involved in copying this entire manuscript, and the first scribe copied out the *Colloquy*. Later, three other scribes worked to gloss much of the codex in Old English, and the first of these three glossed both the *Colloquy* and the *Rule of St. Benedict* (Ker, 248). The OE gloss does not always correspond to the Latin. In line 172, for example, the Latin reads *caligas*, which are short Roman boots studded with nails, but the OE gloss is *leperhosa,* meaning "leather pants." There are not many such errors, but the fact they exist at all suggests that Ælfric did not gloss his own Latin. David Porter has pointed out a number of discrepancies between the Latin text and OE gloss and argues that the gloss probably originates later with Ælfric Bata or his school (Gwara and Porter, 44).

Translating the *Colloquy*

This translation differs in only a few regards from the one suggested by Garmonsway's glossary and a number of other extant translations. I have tried to modernize the syntax and lexicon for contemporary students only when such modernization is permitted by the sense of the original. On the whole, I stay very close to the Old English. Where the OE deviates from the Latin, I follow the version that makes most sense to the continuity of the whole. For example, at the beginning of the *Colloquy* the monk says in Latin that he is busy all day with reading and singing, "*lectionibus et cantu*" (1. 14). In the OE gloss of Tiberius A. iii, he says only that he is busy with singing, "*on sange*." But next in the OE, the monk says, "Between these I would like to learn to speak properly in Latin." Clearly, in order to make sense of the OE "between," one has to translate the Latin. Where the versions deviate, I have underlined the translation.

Intriguingly, Ælfric did not characterize his bakers and fishermen by ungrammatical speech. While such a tack would obviously contradict the purpose of the exercise, it nevertheless mitigates against considering the *Col-*

loquy a dramatic work. Consequently, I have refrained from colloquializing the speech of the students. Their speech in both Latin and Old English is free of error. Neither do we see much syntactic play in the Tiberius A. iii *Colloquy*, which further recommends its use to teachers trying to set a grammatical norm. In later versions of the *Colloquy*, Ælfric Bata has sometimes shifted words around, possibly to instruct students in Latin's variable word order. He also experiments with enclitics, ellipses, and synonyms. Porter argues that Bata's emendations suggest his text was written for students who today would be considered at the intermediate level of language proficiency (Gwara and Porter, 46–47).[5] Yet the original *Colloquy* written by Ælfric, as Garmonsway argues, was probably written for beginners (Garmonsway, "Development," 254).

The *Colloquy* describes a conversation between a master and several students. He asks them questions about their everyday duties, and they respond. It begins with a young Benedictine monk and his companions approaching the master in the afternoon after their prayers and asking to be taught proper Latin. The master agrees and asks the monk and each of his companions in turn what it is he does. The companions include a plowman, a shepherd, an ox herder, a hunter, a fisherman, a fowler (someone who catches birds), a merchant, a leatherworker, a salter, a baker, a cook, and a wise counselor. They are unlikely companions for a young monk, but the roles represent the various trades a monk may come into contact with during his years in a monastery. Each of the tradesmen describes what it is he does and how his craft is important to the community. At one point, a number of the companions get into a spirited argument about whose craft is more important. The argument is settled in favor of the plowman, who provides not only bread, but also ale. The *Colloquy* ends with the monk describing his daily schedule, including the monastic Offices he sings. The master concludes the *Colloquy* with a call to obedience and proper behavior, reminding the students not to get up to any high jinks when they leave church.

The text is clearly for beginning students and is addressed to a boy, *puer*, between seven and thirteen. The lexicon, while varied, is not eclectic. Even the Latin names of the monastic hours are translated into English. *Nocturn*, the first hour of the monastic day, becomes *uhtsang* (line 270)— literally, "day-break song." The syntax of the Latin often follows the OE, suggesting that Latin's syntactic variety was not on the menu for the *Colloquy*'s young audience. Consider line 48, which is typically a direct translation of the Latin into OE. It reads in Latin, "*Est iste ex tuis sociis?*" which translated word-for-word into OE is, "*Ys þæs of þinum geferum?*" The entire *Colloquy* is like this, suggesting that the Latin was composed according to the syntax of OE and the needs of less experienced Anglo-Saxon students. The *Colloquy* offers short, sometimes humorous portraits of craftsmen. We see the bumbling cook trying desperately to describe the necessity of his craft while the master dismissively thumbs his nose at cooking. We also see a fisherman admit he won't catch a whale because he has a cowardly soul! The fowler catches the master asking a particularly stupid question and asks in return what good it would be to keep a hawk he couldn't train (1. 131). The merchant, too, balks at a silly question when the master asks if he'll sell goods at the price he paid. "I won't," the merchant replies sharply, "what would my labor profit me, then?" At one point, the master tries to get the hunter to admit that he hunted on a Sunday, which is inappropriate, but the hunter is too quick for him. The master may rule the schoolroom, but the craftsmen show him that he doesn't have all the answers. One can imagine schoolchildren happily imagining the discomfort of the *Colloquy*'s master.

Ælfric and Education

Ælfric (c. 955–1020) began his education at Winchester under the famous Bishop Æthelwold, one of the instigators of the Benedictine reform. In his early thirties, he was sent as a teacher to Cerne Abbey in Dorset, where much of his writing was done. When he was about fifty, he was appointed archbishop of the newly established monastery of Eynsham.[6] Ælfric is perhaps the greatest prose stylist of the Old English period. His *Catholic Homilies* and *Lives of the Saints* stand today as monuments of Old English prose. His contribution to classroom education is really his Latin-English *Glossary* and *Grammar*, which David Porter has called "the most important Latin-learning text among the Anglo-Saxons" ("Anglo-Saxon," 476). Ælfric, like so many monks of his day, understood that his pastoral duty included teaching Latin to novitiates, young boys about seven years of age and older who were entering into the service of the Church. Although it was common that monks and even bishops in Ælfric's day knew little or no Latin, on the whole, a rudimentary knowledge of the language was important for a monk. Yet Ælfric faced a culture so in decline in its ability to speak and to understand Latin that he issued his homilies in English. He was also translating the Old Testament into English, although he never finished.

The Anglo-Saxon classroom was an important part of a monastery, but not all of the brothers were called upon to study. The Venerable Bede, a monk of the twin monastery of Wearmouth and Jarrow in the eighth century, speaks of brothers who were unlettered and were taught Scripture through illuminations (Riché, 393).[7] Similarly, Ælfric was presiding over a monastery in the heart of a country only recently reviving itself from the upheaval and destruction of the ninth century. Benedictine monks, especially Dunstan and his student Æthelwold, were at the forefront of a reform movement that attempted to reestablish both learning and monasteries long neglected. Æthelwold instructed a number of pupils at Winchester, including Wulfstan and Ælfric. Wulfstan later wrote that Æthelwold was very learned in grammatical arts and in the "honey-sweet system of metrics" (quoted in Lapidge, 90). Ælfric would have learned his grammar and metrics, or verse form, from Æthelwold and taught them at Eynsham.

Grammar was essential to the budding Anglo-Saxon Latinist for the simple reason that Anglo-Saxons were learning Latin as a foreign language. The Carolingians, for example, were speaking a language that, although the ancestor of French, seems to have been considered Latin.[8] Grammar included a great deal more than parsing sentences: Augustine of Hippo called it the *custos historiæ*, the guardian of history, or of cultural memory (quoted in Irvine, 4). Grammar—or, rather, *grammatica*—was the road by which one accessed the written word, especially Scripture. It included a knowledge of syntax, lexicon, and morphology, as well as of more sophisticated interpretative schema, such as the allegorical method.[9] Scripture, as Augustine had pointed out in the early fifth century, spoke to man indirectly, by means of allegories and figures. Thus, coming to an understanding of Scripture required significant training in the grammatical arts. Still, not all of Scripture was allegorical. Alcuin of York, an eighth-century English monk who was recruited by Charlemagne to undertake his educational reforms, warned that readers ought not to ignore the literal sense in plumbing for deeper mysteries (G.R. Evans, 8). Nevertheless, contemplation of the divine, whether in its material or spiritual manifestations, required Latin. While on the Continent, schools were being arranged according to the *trivium* and *quadrivium*, Anglo-Saxons focused mainly on *grammatica*. Peter Hunter Blair points out that our assumptions concerning the curriculum of English education are based primarily and probably improperly on what was happening on the Continent (*Age of Bede*, 237–52). Pierre Riché concludes, "Most of the liberal arts, then, were consciously ignored by educated Anglo-Saxon men" (388). In the *Colloquy*, we can see the master's implicit condemnation of the rhetorical arts in his diatribe against deceitful speech (1. 254 ff.).

The study of Latin that Ælfric's students undertook began with the Latin grammarians, probably Priscian and Donatus. After Ælfric wrote his *Grammar*, chances are students would have learned from it rather than from Donatus—Helmut Gneuss calls Ælfric's *Grammar* "no doubt the greatest 'publishing success' in England's early vernacular literature" (668). Ælfric himself had written a grammar to which he prefaced the sentiment, "*And ic þohte, þæt þeos boc mihte fremian iungum cildum to anginne þæs cræftes, oþþæt hi to maran andgyte becumon*" ("And I thought that this book might benefit young children undertaking this art, so that they might come to more knowledge"). To the grammar he attached a long glossary. Both the *Grammar* and the *Glossary* would have been used in concert with lessons treating of the parts of speech, declension, conjugation, and so forth. In fact, grammars represent some of the earliest Anglo-Latin manuscripts. Latin poetry, too, would have been studied, as much for its content as for its form. Anglo-Saxons seemed to have been fond of Juvencus, Sedulius, Prudentius, Virgil, Paulinus of Nola, Venatus Fortunatus, Lactantius, Statius, and Juvenal.[10] To teach spoken Latin, the colloquy form was ideal.

The *Colloquy* was used to teach unfamiliar vocabulary, often in the form of catalogues of items. Perhaps the best example of such a catalogue is Student "Fisherman's" list of fish. The terms here would be difficult for a student. For example, the Latin *lucios*, which probably refers to a pike, is a notoriously rare word. Alan of Insulis, in his late-eleventh-century *Liber de Planctu Naturæ*, pairs salmon and *lucios* (calling them both delicious), as does an early-twelfth-century anonymous continuation of Rudolfus Trudonis, *Gesta Abbatum Trudonensium*.[11] There are but a few other extant instances of the word. The jargon of the trades, trades with which the young monks would be familiar, would serve the students well in their monastic life. This use of familiar trades in colloquies is characteristic of the *Hisperica Famina*, an influential sixth-century codex written probably in Ireland or Cornwall. More than just a formal influence, Hisperic Latin, as it is called, typically flamboyant in its figures, included rare or unique terms (Garmonsway, "Development," 250). Another source, and one that seemed especially influential on Ælfric Bata, was the *Hermeneumata Pseudodositheana*, a Greek–Latin lexicon possibly introduced into England by Archbishop Theodore (Gwara, *Colloquies*, 12 ff.). At the end of the day, colloquies were used to help students master spoken Latin, which would include manners of address, some awareness of the maxims of quantity and quality, and, of course, vocabulary.

Ælfric's *Colloquy* is one of the more popular Anglo-Saxon prose texts. Virtually every generation of modern student that has studied Old English has come across the *Colloquy*. Its modern descendent is the dialogue found in so many foreign-language textbooks. Those of us who spent warm spring days in grade school trying to concentrate on foreign-language dialogues, reciting the gastronomic adventures of Pierre and Jean as they trekked through a Parisian boulangerie, can sympathize with the Anglo-Saxon student who must have timidly recited the catalogue of fish as his *magister* hovered above him, a birch rod in hand. More importantly, though, we can imagine that the practical topics and real-life characters of the *Colloquy* spoke to a pedagogical need to arrest students' attentions, which wandered as easily in the eleventh century as they do today. When we turn to the colloquies of Ælfric Bata, we see colloquies filled with drunken characters, scatological humor, and lascivious innuendo. If nothing else, such colloquies show that the medieval classroom was a place of laughter, as well as of learning.

Notes

1. G. N. Garmonsway bemoans the lack of dramatic art in any of the colloquies. They were clearly utilitarian in aim, although some of Ælfric Bata's colloquies do engage the dramatic. See Garmonsway, "Development," 248. See also Gwara.
2. Garmonsway, *Ælfric*, and Ker, item 186.
3. The contents are listed in Ker, 240.
4. Ms Oxford St. John's College 154 contains a revised version of the *Colloquy*; see Garmonsway, *Colloquy*, 2–3, and Porter, "Anglo-Saxon," 474.
5. See also Porter's discussion of Bata's grammatical emendations to one of his sources, the *De Raris Fabulis Retractata*, in "Anglo-Saxon," 470.
6. See Blair, *Anglo-Saxon*, 357–59, and Hurt.
7. See Laistner.
8. Linguists and historians disagree on whether the Carolingians were conscious of their language being categorically distinct from Latin. See Wright.
9. See Porter, "Latin Syllabus," for a discussion of how Bata's colloquies exhibit an interest in the lexicon, syntax, and morphology of Latin.
10. The list is from Gneuss, 666.
11. Alan says they are "exceptional in equal excellence." Alan of Insulis, *Liber de Planctu Naturæ* (*PL* 210:463B), translation by Moffat, 62. Rudolfus Trudonis, *Gesta Abbatum Trudonensium* (*PL* 173:188A).

Ælfric's Colloquy[1]

STUDENTS (*PUERI*):	We children bid you, Master, that you teach us to speak correctly, for we are unlearned and we speak corruptly.
TEACHER (*MAGISTER*):	What would you like to talk about?
STUDENTS:	What do we care what we talk about? As long as it's correct! Let it be useful, not worthless or base.[2]
TEACHER:	Will you be flogged in order to learn? (7)
STUDENTS:	We would rather be flogged on behalf of wisdom than not to know it. But we know you to be mild and unwilling to lash out against us unless you're compelled by us.
TEACHER:	Let me ask you, what do you say? What work do you pursue? (11)
STUDENT "MONK":	I am a professed monk, and I sing each day with my brethren, and I am busy with <u>reading and</u> singing; but between these, I would like to learn to speak properly in Latin.[3]
TEACHER:	What do these companions of yours know?[4] (17)
STUDENT "MONK":	Some are plowmen, some shepherds, some oxherders, some <u>of them</u> are also hunters, some fishermen, some fowlers, some merchants, some leatherworkers, salters, bakers.

TEACHER:	What do you say, plowman? How do you keep busy at your work? (22)[5]
STUDENT "PLOWMAN":	Oh, dear lord, I work very hard. I go out at dawn, driving oxen to the field, and yoke them to a plow. (24) Nor is there so stark a winter that I dare to lay hidden at home because of my master's ire. But the oxen having been yoked, and the shear and coulter fastened to the plow, I must plow a full acre or more each day.
TEACHER:	Do you have any companion?[6]
STUDENT "PLOWMAN":	I have a young boy driving the oxen with a goading rod, who now is hoarse because of cold and shouting.[7] (29)
TEACHER:	Do you do anything else during the day?[8]
STUDENT "PLOWMAN":	Certainly, I do more than that. I must fill the oxen's bins with hay, and water them, and carry out their dung. Oh boy, it's a lot of work. Honestly, it's a lot of work, and on account of it, I don't have any free time. (35)
TEACHER:	Shepherd! Do you have any work?
STUDENT "SHEPHERD":	Yes, lord, I have. First thing in the morning I drive my sheep to their pasture, stand over them in the heat and cold with my dogs lest wolves devour them. And I lead them to their pens, and milk them twice a day, and I maintain their pens, and that's where I make cheese and butter. And I'm faithful to my lord.
TEACHER:	Well, ox herder, what do you get up to? (43)
STUDENT "HERDER":	Well, my lord, I work a lot. When the plowman unyokes the oxen, I lead them to pasture, and all night I stand over them watching for thieves. And then, in the morning, I take them to the plowman well fed and watered.
TEACHER:	Is this one of your companions? (48)
STUDENT "HERDER":	Yes, it is.
TEACHER:	Do you know anything?
STUDENT "HUNTER":	I know one craft. (51)
TEACHER:	Which one?
STUDENT "HUNTER":	I'm a hunter. (53)
TEACHER:	Whose?
STUDENT "HUNTER":	The king's. (55)
TEACHER:	How do you keep busy at work?
STUDENT "HUNTER":	I make nets for myself and set them in a good spot, and charge my dogs so that they pursue game until they come into the net unaware, and so they get snared, and I kill them in the net.[9]

TEACHER:	Do you know how to hunt without nets? (61)
STUDENT "HUNTER":	Yeah, I can hunt without nets.
TEACHER:	How?
STUDENT "HUNTER":	I pursue game with fast dogs. (64)
TEACHER:	What game do you catch mostly?
STUDENT "HUNTER":	I catch harts, boars, roes, does, and sometimes hares.
TEACHER:	Were you hunting today? (67)
STUDENT "HUNTER":	I wasn't, since it's Sunday! But I was hunting yesterday.[10]
TEACHER:	What did you take?
STUDENT "HUNTER":	Two harts and a boar.
TEACHER:	How did you catch them? (72)
STUDENT "HUNTER":	The harts I caught in a net, the boar I killed.
TEACHER:	How did you dare to spear the boar!?!
STUDENT "HUNTER":	The hounds drove it at me, and I stood in its way and rapidly speared it. (75)
TEACHER:	You were pretty daring, then.
STUDENT "HUNTER":	A hunter can't be timid simply because erratic game live in the woods. (78)
TEACHER:	What do you do with your catch?
STUDENT "HUNTER":	I give the king whatever I get because I'm his hunter.
TEACHER:	What does he give you?
STUDENT "HUNTER":	He clothes me well, and feeds me, and sometimes he gives me a horse or money so that I'll perform my craft more gladly.[11]
TEACHER:	What craft do you know? (86)
STUDENT "FISHERMAN":	I'm a fisherman.
TEACHER:	What do you get out of your trade?
STUDENT "FISHERMAN":	Food, clothing, money.
TEACHER:	How do you catch fish? (90)
STUDENT "FISHERMAN":	I board my boat, and cast my net into a river, and I throw in a hook or bait and baskets, and whatever they trap, I take.
TEACHER:	What if they be unclean, the fish?[12]
STUDENT "FISHERMAN":	I toss the unclean ones out, and take the clean ones as food. (95)
TEACHER:	Where do you sell your fish?
STUDENT "FISHERMAN":	In town.
TEACHER:	Who buys them?
STUDENT "FISHERMAN":	Townsmen. I can't catch as many as I can sell!
TEACHER:	What fish do you land?[13] (100)
STUDENT "FISHERMAN":	Eels and pike, minnows and burbot, trout and lampreys, and whatever swims in the water. Small fish.[14]

TEACHER:	Why don't you fish in the sea?
STUDENT "FISHERMAN":	Sometimes I do, but rarely, since it's a lot of rowing for me to [get to] the sea.
TEACHER:	What do you catch in the sea? (105)
STUDENT "FISHERMAN":	Herring and salmon, porpoises[15] and sturgeon, oysters and crabs,[16] mussels, winkles, cockles, plaice and flounder and lobster, and many similar things.
TEACHER:	Would you catch a whale?
STUDENT "FISHERMAN":	No! (110)
TEACHER:	Why?
STUDENT "FISHERMAN":	Because it's a dangerous thing to catch a whale. It's safer for me to go to the river with my boat than to go with many boats a-hunting whales.
TEACHER:	Why's that? (115)
STUDENT "FISHERMAN":	Because I prefer to catch a fish that I can kill than a fish that with one blow can sink and destroy not only me but all of my companions.
TEACHER:	Still, many catch whales and avoid danger, and get good money for it. (120)
STUDENT "FISHERMAN":	That's the truth! But I don't dare because of my cowardly soul.
TEACHER:	What do you say, fowler? How do you snare birds? (124)
STUDENT "FOWLER":	I snare birds a lot of ways: sometimes with nets, with nooses, with lime, with birdcalls, with a hawk, with a trap.
TEACHER:	You have a hawk?[17]
STUDENT "FOWLER":	I have one.
TEACHER:	Can you tame them?
STUDENT "FOWLER":	Yes, I can. (130) What good would they be to me if I couldn't tame them?
TEACHER:	Give me a hawk.
STUDENT "FOWLER":	I'd be glad to, if you give me a fast dog. Which hawk would you like, a bigger one or a smaller one? (135)
TEACHER:	Give me a bigger one. How do you feed your hawks?
STUDENT "FOWLER":	They feed themselves, and me in the winter. And in the spring I let them fly to the woods; and I take young birds in the fall and tame them. (140)
TEACHER:	And why do you let the tame ones fly away from you?
STUDENT "FOWLER":	Because I don't want to feed them in the summer: They eat too much.

TEACHER:	But many fowlers feed the tame ones over the summer so they have them ready [for autumn].
STUDENT "FOWLER":	Yeah, that's what they do. But I don't want to go to so much trouble over them, since I can catch others—not one, but many more.
TEACHER:	What do you say, merchant?
STUDENT "MERCHANT":	I say that I'm useful to the king and the noblemen and the wealthy and all of the people. (150)
TEACHER:	How?
STUDENT "MERCHANT":	I board my boat with my freight, row over the high seas, sell my goods, and buy valuable goods which can't be produced here. And I transport it [all] to you here over the sea with a great deal of trouble; and sometimes I suffer shipwreck with the loss of all my goods— it's not easy to escape alive.
TEACHER:	What goods do you transport to us? (158)
STUDENT "MERCHANT":	Purples[18] and silks, valuable gems and gold, little-known[19] cloths and spices, wine and oils, ivory and bronze, copper and tin,[20] sulfur and glass, and many similar things.
TEACHER:	Will you sell your goods here for as much as you paid for them?
STUDENT "MERCHANT":	I won't. What would my labor profit me then? (165) But I want to sell them here for more money[21] than I bought them there so I can make some profit. Then I can feed myself, my wife, and my son.
TEACHER:	You, shoemaker,[22] what do you do for our general profit?
STUDENT "SHOEMAKER":	My craft truly is very useful and necessary to you.
TEACHER:	How? (169)
STUDENT "SHOEMAKER":	I buy hides and skins, and prepare them through my craft, and work them into footwear of various kinds: slippers and shoes, hobnailed boots[23] and water bottles, bridles and trappings, flasks or canteens and helmets, spurstraps and halters, purses and pokes;[24] not one of you could winter without my craft.
TEACHER:	Salter, how do we benefit from your craft? (175)
STUDENT "SALTER":	My craft is of great use to you all. None of you eats lunch or dinner[25] happily unless he be amenable to my craft.
TEACHER:	How?

STUDENT "SALTER":	Which man fully enjoys very sweet food without the taste of salt?[26] (180). Who can fill his cellar or storehouse without my craft?[27] Look, you lose butter and cheese curd unless I am present as a preservative for you; you couldn't even enjoy your herbs.[28]
TEACHER:	Baker? (185) What do you make, or can we survive without you?
STUDENT "BAKER":	You might, for a while—but not for long, or too well! Honestly, without my craft, each table would seem to be empty, and without bread, each dinner would bring heartburn. I can strengthen the heart of a man; I am the strength of men, and even the little ones won't abuse me. (191)
TEACHER:	What do we say of the cook? Do we need his craft in any way?
STUDENT "COOK":	The cook says, If you drive me out of your fellowship, you will eat your vegetables green and your meat raw—and not even rich broth may you have without my craft. (195)
TEACHER:	We don't care about your craft, and it's not necessary for us, since we ourselves can boil the things to be boiled, and roast the things to be roasted.
STUDENT "COOK":	The cook says: If you drive me thus away, if you do this, then you'll all be thralls, and none of you will be a lord.[29] (200) And without my craft you won't eat.
TEACHER:	Well, monk, you who speaks to me, I have found you to have good and extremely necessary companions. And I ask [you], who are they?[30]
STUDENT "MONK":	I have smiths, ironsmiths, goldsmiths, silversmiths, coppersmiths, woodworkers, and many other and various craft workers. (206)
TEACHER:	Have you any wise counselor?
STUDENT "MONK":	Certainly, I have. How would our gathering be guided without a counselor? (210)
TEACHER:	Wise man, which craft of these do you think to be superior?
STUDENT "COUNSELOR":	I tell you, it seems to me that the service of God holds primacy among these crafts, as one reads in the Gospel: "Firmly seek you God's kingdom and also His righteousness and all these things be given to you."[31] (216)
TEACHER:	And which do you think holds primacy among the secular crafts?

STUDENT "COUNSELOR": Tilling of the earth, since the plowman feeds us all.[32]

STUDENT "BLACKSMITH": (The smith[33] says:) Where should he get the shear or coulter or even the goad but from my craft? (221) Where the fisherman his angle, or the shoewright his awl, or the seamer[34] his needle? Is it not by my work?

STUDENT "COUNSELOR": (The counselor answers:) You speak wisely,[35] but it is preferable to all of us to live with you, plowman, than with you, [smith,] because the plowman furnishes us with bread and drink;[36] you, what do you furnish for us in your smithy but iron firesparks and the clang of beating sledgehammers and blowing bilges?[37]

STUDENT "CARPENTER": (The woodworker says:) Which of you does not use my craft? Your houses and various vessels and boats I make for you all. (230)

STUDENT "GOLDSMITH": (The goldsmith[38] answers:) Honestly, woodworker, why do you speak like that when you couldn't make a hole[39] <u>without my craft</u>.

STUDENT "COUNSELOR": (The counselor says:) Honestly, companions and good workmen, let us stop this flighting[40] quickly, and let there be kinship and agreement[41] between us and let one help the other through his craft, and to agree always with the plowman from whom we have our food and fodder for our horses. (236)

And this counsel I offer to all workers, that each one perform his craft diligently, since he who neglects his craft will be given up by the craft[42] So whether you be a masspriest, or monk, or churl, or soldier, perform or know this[43]: be what you are. Because it is much humiliation and shame for a man not to want to be that which he is, and that which he should be.[44]

TEACHER: Well, children, how do you like this speech?

STUDENTS: We like it well, but you speak very profoundly and you draw forth speech beyond our ability. (245) But speak to us according to our intellect,[45] that we may understand the things you speak about.

TEACHER: I ask you, why are you so eager to learn?

STUDENTS: Because we do not want to be like dumb animals who know nothing but grass and water. (251)

TEACHER: And what do you want?

STUDENTS:	We want to be wise.
TEACHER:	In which kind of wisdom? Will you be plastic or multifarious in your pretense,[46] deceitful in speech, illogical,[47] sneaky, speaking well and thinking evil, subjugated by charming words,[48] weakened by guile within, just as tombs are decorated on their exteriors, but full of stench within? (258)
STUDENTS:	We don't want to be wise in that way, since he is not wise who seduces himself with deception.[49]
TEACHER:	But what do you want? (261)
STUDENTS:	We would like to be sincere without hypocrisy, and wise so that we turn away from evil and do good. However, you still dispute with us more profoundly than our age can take; but speak with us concerning our habits, and not so deeply. (265)
TEACHER:	I will do just as you bid. You, boy, what did you do today?
STUDENT:	I did many things. Last night, when I heard the knell, I arose from my bed and went out to the church, and sang Nocturn with my brethren; after that we sang the "Of All Saints" and morning hymns [or Matins]. (270) After this, Prime and seven psalms with litanies and the chapter-mass; afterwards, Tierce, and did the mass of the day. After this we sang Sexte, and we ate and drank and slept and again we arose and sang None.[50] And now we are here before you, ready to hear what you have to say to us. (275)
TEACHER:	When will you sing Vespers or Compline?
STUDENT:	When it is time.
TEACHER:	Were you beaten today?
STUDENT:	I was not, since I am attentive.[51] (280)
TEACHER:	And what did your companions do?
STUDENT:	Why do you ask me about them? I don't dare give up our secrets! Each one of us knows if he was beaten or not.
TEACHER:	What do you eat during the day?
STUDENT:	I still enjoy meat, since I am a child living under the rod.[52] (285)
TEACHER:	What more do you eat?
STUDENT:	Vegetables and eggs, fish and cheese, butter and beans, and all clean things I eat—with much thankfulness.
TEACHER:	You are exceedingly greedy if you eat everything that is in front of you. (290)
STUDENT:	I am not so much of a whirlpool that I ingest every kind of food at one meal![53]
TEACHER:	But in what manner [do you eat]?
STUDENT:	I enjoy at times this food, other times that—with sobriety, as befits a monk, not with voracity, since I am not a glutton. (295)
TEACHER:	And what do you drink?
STUDENT:	Ale if I have it, or water if I don't have ale.[54]

TEACHER: You don't drink wine? (300)

STUDENT: I am not so wealthy that I might buy myself wine. And wine is not a drink for children nor for the stupid, but for the old and the wise.

TEACHER: Where do you sleep.

STUDENT: I sleep <u>in a dormitory</u> with my brethren.

TEACHER: Who wakes you to sing Nocturn? (305)

STUDENT: Sometimes I hear the knell and I get up; sometimes my teacher wakes me stiffly with a rod.

TEACHER: Well, you children and winsome students, your teacher reminds you that you be obedient to Divine Teaching and that you keep yourself noble in every place. (310) Go obediently when you hear church bells, and go into Church and bow humbly before the holy altar, and stand obediently and sing together with one voice,[55] and pray for your sins, and go out without any high jinks to the cloister or to school.

Notes

1. Speaker titles have been added to the text to facilitate reading.

2. "Base" translates the OE *fracod*, which in turn glosses the Latin (hereafter, Lat.) *turpis*. *Turpis* is often used to describe a lack of physical beauty or refinement. One might also consider the terms *ugly* or *graceless* as further possibilities.

3. Underlining signals words or phrases that are in one version (Latin or OE), but not in the other.

4. The premise of the colloquy is that a young monk has brought his lay companions to his master to learn Latin. Given that the companions are *pueri*, or children, the premise needs to be considered fictional.

5. The OE *begæst* glosses the Latin *exerces*, both of which mean to "keep busy." They all have a sense of exerting oneself, of working very hard. The master seems to be implying that the plowman doesn't work very hard, which prompts the plowman to respond as he does.

6. The master is asking if the plowman has any help in the field. But the word he uses, *geferan*, is the same as in l. 17, which describes the monk's associates. One wonders if the monk has the same relation with the workers that the plowman has with his *geferan*.

7. The translation "is hoarse" comes from the Lat. *modo raucus est*, since *has ys* seems to be a unique use of the phrase in OE.

8. The master seems skeptical about the amount of work the plowman has to do.

9. By "charging" his dogs, the hunter means he drives them at game. The Latin term is *instigare*, "to instigate." But he does not drive his dogs as the shepherd drives (*drifan*) sheep.

10. This is a very interesting moment in the *Colloquy*, since the master is trying to find out whether the hunter has been hunting on a Sunday. Clearly, the hunter is not supposed to hunt on Sundays, but then what are the master and the monk doing? If a master's job is teaching, should he be working on a Sunday, as he clearly is?

11. The term *gladly* translates as *lustlicor*, which can also be translated as "lustily." "To perform" here is actually *begancge*, or "attend to." The king wants the hunter to be better motivated in his job.

12. "Unclean" is usually thought to mean unclean according to religious dietary laws. But the fisherman catches eels. Since eels are unclean, and since the fisherman meets with no reproof from the master, what the master is implying with this question is unclear. Compare the master's attempt to trick the hunter into admitting he hunted on a Sunday.

13. "Land" translates the OE *gefehst*, "to win by fighting." It is not the same word the fisherman uses to express "to catch."

14. "*Anguillas et lucios, menas et capitones, tructas et murenas, et qualescumque in amne natant, saliu. / ælas ¬ hacodas, mynas ¬ æleputan, sceotan ¬ lampredan, ¬ swa wylce swa on wætere swymmap, sprote.*" *Anguillas* and *ælas* are certainly eels; *hacodas* is usually translated "pike" on the basis of the Latin, but pike are not always small fish, *saliu*. Some pike grow to be over twenty pounds. *Lucios* recalls a type of minnow typically called a shiner—a small, silvery mackerel—which recollects the root of *lucios, luces*, meaning "light."

15. Literally, "sea-swine"; possibly dolphins.

16. Note that shellfish is "unclean," which again raises the issue of the master's intent in l. 94.

17. Hawks were usually reserved for the ruling class, which may explain the master's apparent surprise. The master immediately assumes that the fowler means he has a wild hawk, which seems to raise the fowler's hackles. See the opening of *The Battle of Maldon* and Owens-Crocker; D'Arcussia; Landau, esp. 54.

18. The Latin, *purpura*, means purple cloth or the very expensive purple dyes used to color the cloth. Purple was the color of Roman royalty and continued to be associated with wealth and grandeur into the Anglo-Saxon Age and beyond. The Old English is *paellas*.

19. OE *selcupe* literally means "little-known," although it implies "rare" or "exotic".

20. This is a strange addition to the merchant's catalogue, since Cornwall was known all over Europe for its tin mines. Bede, in his *Ecclesiastical History of the English People* I, i, tells us that Britain is renowned for its metals. Wallace-Hadrill remarks (7), following Peter Hunter Blair, that Bede strangely does not mention tin. Perhaps Ælfric, like Bede, saw tin from Cornwall as an import from a foreign land—thus implying a rather limited referent of the master's "us" in l. 158.

21. Literally, "more dearly."

22. Literally, "shoewright." The master's demand that each participant reckon his usefulness to the community is gaining steam. The shoemaker answers the master's question in superlatives and absolutes.

23. The Latin *caligas* describes Roman boots studded with nails—a *caligarius* is a bootmaker. The OE, though, is *leperhosa*, or "leather pants," cf. Ger. *lederhosen*.

24. Lat. *marsupia*, or "pouch." The OE *fætelsas* might mean saddlebags or pouches. The term *poke*, a small sack or bag, seems to match the sense.

25. Lat. *prandio aut cena*; *prandio* was a light lunch, while *cena* was the principal Roman meal, and the second meal during the monastic day.

26. We may wonder at this assertion, but the notion here is one of balance. Sweetness is to be balanced in a meal by its opposite, saltiness.

27. The salter is referring to a salt cellar, a room or outhouse usually built into the ground in which one would keep salted fish or salted meat in order to preserve it during the winter.

28. Both the Latin and the OE suggest that the salter identifies with his salt; the same is true of the baker who identifies with his bread.

29. The cook is implying that a lord forced to do his own cooking is no better than a slave. There is a sense of social propriety and class that underlies this entire *Colloquy*; see especially ll. 240 ff. Here, the cook justifies his role by arguing that without servants, lords wouldn't be lords.

30. See Garmonsway, p. 38, n. 204, *þa* seems to be a mistake for *þu*, "you"; the Latin is *qui sunt illi*.

31. Matthew 6:33. I am translating the OE, not offering the verse.

32. The OE is *Eorptilp*, and the Lat. *Agricultura*. The OE has not adopted the Lat. terminology.

33. Lat. *ferriarius*, or "ironsmith." The OE merely has *smiþ*, or "smith."

34. As opposed to seamstress, it simply means tailor.

35. Lat, "It's true what you say" and OE, "You speak the truth wisely." The OE seems idiomatic.

36. The plowman's barley is used to make ale, thus drink: see l. 299.

37. OE *byliga*, also "bellows."

38. Lat. "ironsmith."

39. OE, idiomatic *ne furpon an þyrl*, or "not more than one hole."

40. OE *geflitu*, or "flighting"; Lat. *contentiones*, or "contentiousness."

41. OE *sibb & gepwærnyss*. *Sibb* has a sense of kinship, relations, and familial accord, while *gepwærnyss* has the sense of concord, union, agreement, and peace. The Lat. *pax et concordia* is idiomatic, "peace and concord." It is interesting that the OE uses a term of familial concord to translate *pax*: *sibb* is the source of our Modern English (hereafter ModE) *sibling*.

42. This enigmatic phrase seems to make sense in light of an identical sentiment found in Gregory the Great's *Moralia* in Job, XXVIII, x, 24: "Whosoever wants to be able to do more than has been given to him wants to exceed the measure set for him. . . . He who neglects the measure of his limits risks stepping into the abyss. And recklessly trying to snatch what is beyond him, often he will forfeit even the ability he has." Translation by Markus, 27.

43. Possibly idiomatic OE, *behwyrf þe sylfne*: "instruct yourself in this," "or change yourself to this," or "exercise yourself in this."

44. This is possibly the clearest expression of class sentiment in OE. It presumes a manner of life and station for each person exclusive of his abilities, since the OE modal *sceal*, "should," indicates future obligation—one is obliged to fulfill one's station even if otherwise inclined. The gnomic form (a gnome is a saying or proverb) indicates the pervasiveness of an Anglo-Saxon sentiment to know one's place, to do as one is bid, and not to reach beyond one's place in life.

45. OE *andgyte*, which is not the same as *lare*, or "teaching." Children are clearly seen here as intellectually incapable of understanding such profundities—it is not a matter of learning, but of development or experience.

46. Lat. *versipelles aut multiformes* and OE *prættige oþþe þusenthiwe*. *Versipelles* literally means "able to change one's skin" and is used by Pliny and Apeulius to describe a werewolf. Rhetorically, it means skilled in dissimulation. *Plastic* seems to convey *versipelles'* sense of malleability. The OE *prættige*, which is the source of ModE *pretty*, implies superficial beauty and charm. "Multifarious" translates the Lat. *milleformes*, literally, "a thousand forms," which the OE renders almost literally as *þusenthiwe*. "Pretense" translates the Lat. *mendaciis*, or "mendacity," and OE *leasungum*, or "deceit."

47. OE *onglæwlice*, an adverb meaning "without prudence, wisdom, or proof." The sense of *glæwlice*, of which this term is the negation, is a test or proof, suggesting the ordering principles of reason or common sense, logic.

48. OE *swæsum wordum*, implying "pleasant or agreeable words." My choice of *charming* is prompted by Evelyn Waugh's indictment of charm in his *Brideshead Revisited*. Charles Ryder has just returned from South America and puts up an exhibition of his new paintings. They are belittled by Anthony Blanche, a close friend, as charming, the superficial vice that kills English art and is killing Charles.

49. This gnome recalls the education programs of Bede, who did not teach the rhetorical arts as they were taught on the Continent. He anathematized philosophy as sophistic, indicting its tendency towards dissimulation in much the same manner as the master does in this section of the *Colloquy*. See Riché, esp. chapter 9.

50. Monks lived according to a monastic rule. In this case, it was the Rule of St. Benedict. Ælfric wrote an abridged version of the Winchester concord, which established the Benedictine Rule as common (with some local variation) throughout England. Most of the monk's day was sent praying. Each hour of the day had an Office, or set of sung prayers. The day began with Nocturn, today called *Matins*. The *Rule* also allowed for extra offices, one of them being the "Of All Saints," which consisted of *Matins* and *Vespers*. Then followed the seven hours of the day, *Matins* (today called *Lauds*, OE *uhtsang*); *Prime* (OE, *prim*); *Tierce* (OE, *undertid*); *Sext* (OE, *middæg*); *None* (OE, *non*); *Vespers* (OE, *æfen*), and *Compline* (OE, *nihtsangc*). See Symons, xxxi–xxxiii.

51. The master is asking whether the young novice was beaten for falling asleep during the offices. The OE phrase is *wærlice ic me heold*, "warily [or attentively] I hold myself." Older monks would walk through the choir stalls during the offices, especially *Nocturn*, which took place in the wee hours of the morning, and thwack a novice with a rod if he were found asleep instead of attentive or in prayer. This was meant not only to inculcate discipline, but, on a more symbolic level, to teach that one must always be attentive to Scripture, since inattention brings evil and sometimes pain. This young monk keeps a watchful eye.

52. OE, *under gyrda drohtniende*, is idiomatic. The young monk is saying that he can still be beaten and is therefore still under the mentorship of an older monk.

53. ModE *whirlpool* is OE *swelgere*, Lat. *vorax*, which means swallowing greed-ily or voraciously. The OE has the sense of vortex, abyss, or a whirlpool—something that swallows voraciously.

54. This recalls the necessity of the plowman to the community, since it is he who provides the hops and barley for the beer. Ale, lager, and stout were healthier than water, since, during the fermenting process, the water is boiled, thus killing germs. The young monk's aversion to wine due to its potential to ine-briate suggests that ale, a drink by implication suitable for children, may not have been as alcoholic as it is today—or it may not have contained alcohol at all.

55. OE *anmodlice*, literally the adverbial form of "with one spirit."

8

Le Tretiz of Walter of Bibbesworth

KATHLEEN KENNEDY

Prior to 1270 and most likely before 1254, Walter de Bibbesworth composed a French-language textbook in rhymed Anglo-Norman verse for the duchess of Pembroke, Lady Dionysia Mounchensey. Through his *Tretiz*, Bibbesworth assisted the duchess to teach her family the French required of medieval English nobility. John, William, and Joan, Dionysia's children, probably learned their French with the assistance of this work (Berndt, 135). Bibbesworth recognized Dionysia's familiarity with French and penned his tract in that tongue. Acknowledging that some of the more technical terms might give her difficulty, however, he glossed these words in English. Transcending its original narrow audience, the *Tretiz* attracted interest throughout the later Middle Ages as a pedagogical work.

Language Instruction in the Later Middle Ages

Early bilingual French-Latin teaching texts consisted of simple lists of nouns, called *nominalia*. Bibbesworth's tract elaborated on the *nominalia* genre by teaching both nouns and verbs and placing each in a context indicative of its definition. *Nominalia* lost favor by the fifteenth century, but the *Tretiz* continued to be copied with an ever-expanding array of glosses. Bibbesworth's employment of a rhyme scheme assisted explication of homonyms and homographs, two linguistic traps that continue to plague students today. By the late fourteenth century *nominalia* and the *Tretiz* competed with a new type of teaching tool, the *manière de langage*. The *manières* included lists of nouns, but focused on model conversations geared toward adults in activities ranging from the purchase of cloth to the propositioning of a prostitute (Kristol, *Manières*). Both the *Tretiz* and the *manières* found proponents throughout the fifteenth century until Caxton thoroughly integrated the two genres in the *Vocabulaire*, published in 1480. This fully bilingual edition added *manière*-style conversations to traditional *nominalia* lists. By offering both the *Vocabulaire* and early grammar texts, the fifteenth century marked the advent of modern language instruction, featuring textbooks inculcating an integrated program of vocabulary, grammar, and pronunciation (Merrilees, 285).

Bibbesworth's introduction, translated here, serves as a guide to the contents of the work. In it, Bibbesworth lists categories of animals, plants, and parts of the body for which he will provide a partial vocabulary, stressing French nouns typical of the *nominalia*, in the chapters making up the body of the *Tretiz*. Departing from the *nominalia* genre, Bibbesworth also details a long series of activities for which he provides both nouns and verbs within the body of the tract, thereby assisting Dionysia in teaching an entire working vocabulary. Most activities center on the household: a student learns how to weave cloth, brew ale, light the fire, and set the table. Other sections include fewer verbs, more nouns, and specialized vocabulary relating to, among other things, the parts of a cart, building a house, reaping grain, and fishing.

Bibbesworth's moral advice and word selection suggest a particular, although not exclusively female, audience. Nothing prevents the *Tretiz* from teaching both boys and girls, but the author seemingly constructs the text with a young girl's upbringing in mind. This coincides with Baugh's opinion that the childhood marriage of Dionysia's young stepdaughter, Joan, to the French nobleman William de Valence, who had yet to win his spurs, prompted the writing of the work (Baugh, 31). It seems equally possible that Joan's impending marriage to a French speaker suggested the *Tretiz*'s unique combination of full and partial vocabularies, which kept the *Tretiz* popular long after the *nominalia* genre was obsolete. The domestic focus of the chapters, which teaches a more complete vocabulary of verbs and nouns, together with passages concerning child care, and the contents of certain moralizing passages sprinkled throughout the text, suggests Bibbesworth and Dionysia had Joan's education specifically in mind.

Joan was going to require a fully functioning French vocabulary, including both nouns and verbs, for the variety of household tasks of which she would be in charge, and an even wider range of terms would also be helpful in her new life (Archer, 150). Several linguistic terms help to explain Bibbesworth's pedagogical strategy (Fasold, 40). *Code-mixing* entails using words or phrases of a second language within speech in a primary language. A student who was taught the partial vocabulary of many nouns and few verbs, characteristic of the *nominalia*, would be prepared for this level of secondary-language usage. *Code-switching* requires a higher level of education, however. An individual code-switching uses one language for most situations, but employs a secondary language under specific circumstances, a task requiring a complete vocabulary of both nouns and verbs. Children destined to move in the highest circles of the English court in the thirteenth century would require at the very least an ability to code-mix. A girl from such a social level wedded to a French native needed also to code-switch in order to manage her new household. A pedagogical work like Bibbesworth's *Tretiz*, including both nouns and verbs and taught by her stepmother, someone already familiar with the language and some of the tasks described, would allow Joan a level of fluency equal to code-switching.

Other sections explicitly teach complete vocabularies involved in certain actions Joan would have needed to discuss with fluency. The chapters "Now to Organize the House Nicely" and "Now to Light the Fire" illustrated the proper manner in which to light the fire and set the table for a meal, and focused on cleanliness and personal hygiene. The careful description of a proper table setting contrasts with the *nominalia*-style list of animals and sounds in the sections translated here. A following section, "Now the French to Arrange a Feast" lists dishes without which "no-one at the feast would be happy" (1. 1110). Bibbesworth ends his tract with this section and in the final lines reminds his readers that his text resembles the feast. Carefully prepared, the text includes all the necessary parts, both mundane and more exotic, and never remains satisfied with teaching a single option when more vocabulary could be offered.

Text and Translation of the *Tretiz*

The earliest copy of the *Tretiz* exists on a parchment roll dating to the late thirteenth century (Kristol, "Lénseignement," 323). William Rothwell's fine edition of Cambridge University Library Gg 1.1 for the Anglo-Norman Text Society serves as the source-text for the following translation, although none of the eleven remaining full-length copies has been previously translated. This copy of the *Tretiz* consists of 1,141 rhymed lines, divided into sections corresponding to different topics, plus the prose introductory letter. The following translation includes the letter and 256 lines. After the introduction, the translation continues with a section teaching the names of animals and the sounds they make. To communicate the sense of the *Tretiz* and evoke its tone, while providing a readable text, I have occasionally sacrificed strict philological and syntactical interpretations, but I have also endeavored to remain faithful to the vocabulary. For example, a modern hog in the American Corn Belt eats mash. A medieval beast, however, ate a combination of grains called dredge, and the translation retains the original term (1. 277). Onomatopoeia is difficult to translate, and I have tried to choose the Modern English equivalent of the Modern French translation of the Middle French. For example, an American bear growls, but in 1. 248 a bear *braie*, or in the

Modern French infinitive, *braire*, and the Modern English translation of *braire* is "to bray." I left the glosses in the original Middle English, as Rothwell did, but usually did not translate from them. The result allows readers to engage more closely with the Anglo-Norman text, as well as to avoid several instances where the glosses are incorrect. Seemingly odd or abrupt shifts in topic occur in each section as Bibbesworth sought to clarify a homonym or homograph. Such a leap appears between lines 265 and 273, when Bibbesworth compares *jaroile* ("quacking") and *le garoile* ("a trap"). As the translated text shows, the context of this homonym illustrates Walter's inclusion of moralizing passages throughout his work, even amidst the discussions of animal sounds and the weather.

Punning the Moral

A few examples of Bibbesworth's wordplay must suffice to illustrate a technique that he employs throughout the *Tretiz*. For example, the same enthusiasm the hen uses in laying her eggs, "*Ki geline . . . patile, E ki trop se avaunce,*" also signals the popularity of chicken cooked with egg, "*A la geline est compaignon Ki plus se avaunce pur un eof*" (ll. 282–85). Bibbesworth underlines his irony by noting that the chicken's relationship to the egg differs greatly to that of the steer with what it proudly produces, its bellow (1. 286). Bibbesworth also tells the young student directly that his or her chaperon's constant presence is required, for flatterers value not the student, but only "*tun aveir ke desire de tei aver,*" "your wealth which [the flatterer] desires to have from you" (ll. 308–9). The Middle English gloss *catel* recognizes the economic element of this swindle, but the *aveir* ("wealth or property") of a medieval woman equally included her chastity. Warnings against licentious young men also appear in the section on weather. The riddle of the wintry, frost-garden not bearing green, growing things puns on the Anglo-Norman word for orchard, *verge*, which implies the word for "green," *vet* (ll. 592–95). In lines 291–92 a man stretches, *se espreche*, and a priest preaches, *preche*. *Preche* elides with the preceding word, *eglise*, and results in a sound similar to *se espreche*, which evokes an image of the stretching gesture of a preacher (ll. 291–92). Much of the wordplay in the *Tretiz* takes on a moralizing, if humorous, tone. The spindle, *la virole*, a small shield, certainly protects the bearer against attack (1. 630). The spindle, *la virole*, also symbolized women's work, however, and an appropriately busy woman would not be open to a (probably sexual) attack by "the knife of an evil man" (1. 631).

The *Tretiz* remained useful for both boys and girls, and adults learning French might equally benefit from both the vocabulary and the moralisms. Sections including full vocabularies transcended the *nominalia* genre and allowed the *Tretiz* to remain competitive with the *manières* as styles of instruction changed. Children could learn language comprehension while performing the activities described, but adults could just as easily profit from the language instruction pertaining to these tasks with which they were already familiar. Walter's *Tretiz* provided vocabulary in a manner typical of the thirteenth century, but also taught complete vocabularies and delivered moral instruction. In so doing, the *Tretiz* of Walter of Bibbesworth demonstrated a pedagogical style that became increasingly timely as the centuries progressed.

Walter of Bibbesworth's *Tretiz*

The treatise which Monsieur Walter of Bibbesworth made for Madame Dionysia de Mounchensey in order to teach [the French] language. And this is to know about the first time when a man was born or all the language from his birth into his youth, then all the French as he progresses in age and in the estate of husbandry and household management, like [the language] for ploughing, second ploughing, fallowing land, sowing, weeding, reaping, mowing, stacking, grinding, threshing, to sell and to haul, pasturing, malting, brewing, how to arrange a high feast. Then all the French about animals and birds, each organized and taught according to its type. Then all the French concerning the woods, fields, and pastures, orchards, gardens, yards, with all the French of the flowers and fruits which are there and thus you will find everything in the correct order in which to speak and respond which all gentlemen must know. Finally, you will find everything I say first in French and then above in English.

Now About the French of Our Clothing with All Our Other Gear

Put on your clothes, good, sweet child;
Pull on your gloves, shoes, and breeches;
Put on your hood, cover your head;   185
Button your buttons and furthermore
Girdle yourself with a belt.
Do not say "you are pregnant,"
Because a woman is made pregnant by
    a man
And she is girdled with a girdle.   190
The pendant end passes through the middle
Of the belt, it passes through the tongue of   *bokel* [le mordaunt]
    the buckle;
And the tongue must also   *tongge* [li hardhiloun]
Pass through the hole from the awl.   *bore of a nalfin*

If the young child reaches his hand   195   [tru de sublioun]
Toward the bread in the morning,
Then give him a chunk,   *lompe* [une bribe]
Or a slice if you have nothing more,   *szyvere* [une lesche]
At dinner give eggs to him;
If you draw them to his eyes.   200
Remove the shell, before he swallows,   *schelle soupe* [content]
And the skin also and the white,
And give him the yolk.   *yolke* [le mouuel]
It seems a good treat for a man,
But remove the germ,   205   *sterene* [la germinoun]
A man will be sick from any of it.
I tell you likewise about the manner
And preparation of apples.
Since apples are eaten by those who
   like them
And they are claimed for small children   210
   with reason,
Remove the stem and the peel,   *stalk* [l'estiche]
If you give the bite to him.
Toss the core   *kore* [la pepinere]
And the pippins from you and plant them.

Now About the Natural Sounds of All Kinds of Animals

Now listen fittingly
About the diversity of animals,   245
Each kind in both the male and the
   female,
Each one with its nature given.
A man speaks, a bear brays   *berre* [ourse]
When he enrages himself too much;
A cow moos, a crane squawks;   250   [vache musgist,
                                                             gruue groule]

A lion roars, a coote chatters;   *romies hasil quakez*
                                                          [rougist, coudre croule]

A horse neighs, a lark sings;   *neyez larke*
A dove coos and a cock sings;   *crouke* [gerist]
A cat meows, a snake hisses;   *mewith cisses*
                                                          [mimoune, cifle]

An ass brays, a swan also hisses;   *255*   *suan cisses*
                                                          [rezane, cine recifle]

A wolf howls, a dog bays;	*wolfe yollez berkes*
And frightens man and beast often.	*Fereth* [afraye]
A polecat frightens the lamb.	[putois afraie]
A vixen barks, a badger screams;	*fox welleth brocke*
When the hound seeks [it as] prey.	260
A goose gabbles, a gander hums;	*gander* [jars]
A duck quacks in the marsh,	[ane jaroile]
But there is quacking and a trap;	[jaroil, garoile]
The difference I wish to tell you:	
The duck quacks in the river	265
If a man seeks it with a falcon,	
But before a besieged town	
Let us fix the trap in the earth	*the trappe* [le garoil]
To defend the barbicon	
From the assault which the man wishs	
to make,	270
So that the gate shall lose nothing	
Even if the soldier besieges it well.	
A toad croaks, a frog trills,	[crapaut coaule, gaille]
A snake truly also hisses.	*snake* [collure]
A pig squeals, a wild boor snorts;	275 *gris wineth boor yelleth*
A kid bleats and a bull bellows;	[Cheverau cherist
	e tor torreie]
A sow grunts when she looks for dredge;	[troye groundile, drache]
A sparrowhawk strikes the diver.	*doukere* [le plounoun]
Also say the hen cackles	*kakeles* [patile]
When she laid [eggs] in a garden or town.	280
Because I have such a formulation from	
France	
That a crested hen lays and cackles,	[poune et patile]
And that without reason urges herself	
on too much,	
For hen is the complement	
Which more recommends itself [to easily	285
go] with an egg	
Than the beef-cow does with its bellow.	
A sheep bleats, a noblewoman dances;	[berbiz baleie, bale]
A grocer takes his wares from the sack.	*bagge* [bale]
A man yawns from much age;	*gones* [baal]
He entrusts his property to his sergeant.	290

After sleeping a man stretches;	*raxes him* [se espreche]
The priest preaches in the church;	
The fisherman fishes in a river	
Now with his net, now with his hook.	
Truly he left his land fallow *295*	
To obtain fresh meat.	
When a poor woman performs the ring	
dance,	*ring* [la tresche]
[With] a spade in hand she values the	*spade* [la besche]
dance more,	
For she has nothing from which to feed	
herself,	
Neither a bit nor a slice of bread. 300	[bribe, lesche]
Her little one licks the pan.	*liketh liketh* [lesche]
Now you give to [your] young creature	
to lap	*lappen* [flater]
That licks the dew in the arbor.	*dewe* [la rosè]
Flee the flatterer who knows how to flatter	*losenge* [flater]
And to swindle people. 305	*glonden* [espeluper]
And your chaperon does not want to	
abandon [you]	
In the least, so much the chaperon holds	
dear	*a mote* [un poyton]
Not yourself only, but your wealth	*catel* [aveir]
Which [the flatterer] desires to have from you.	*have* [aver]

Now for Good Weather and for Storm

Now it rains, now it freezes;	
Now it thaws, now it refreezes.	*thaweth* [remet]
Through freezing you have ice	
And out of ice you get black ice, 575	
And although its not good to go too fast	
On the black ice [or you will] slip on the	
black ice.	
And disgusting freezing and rain	
Make the road very slippery.	*szlidinde* [lidaunt]
Now it snows, now it sleets. 580	*sletes* [cymeie]
Sleet worsens your way;	
A flake of snow passes my lips.	
So they believe that I must have been	
very thirsty.	

We will have hailstones since it hails   *haileth* [grele]
Rather a lot, not too little.   585   *smale* [grele]
I hear thunder; it thunders truly.   *thonner thondres* [toner,
                                                        toune]

For ale sours from the sound.   *toune* [toune]
Now bear with me, my foot is asleep.   *slepeth* [toune]
Not a word from you, not a sound!
The winter weather is cold;   590
I want to demonstrate an enigma:
In the winter when the weather changes
An orchard grows strangely,
An orchard grows which is without green,
  growing things,
Without leaf and without flower.   595
When fall has come,
The orchard will not then be displayed.
In winter when the weather changes
And the weather becomes strange,
Which is difficult to endure for many men, 600
On account of the discomforts of winter.
For you have chaffed your hands so much   *comeled* [estomie]
From the cold that you can in no way
Bend the two into a hook.   *hant motile* [content]
I would wish more to sit on a soft feather 605
  cushion
Close to the fire than at a ring-dance.
[My] hat garlanded with cornflowers   *bloweth* [content]
Or with a bouquet of primroses
As are hats worn by clerks in school,
Who due to boasting are not worth a   610   *keix* [frenole]
  cake,
And with a [gift of a] knife or spindle
Know how to attract a wanton woman.
Thus all who are of such a school
Are worth more in jail
Than a young woman in a lady's chamber.   615
For the hunt for women is so sweet,
When the squire or clerk embraces her,   *beclippe hure* [l'acole]
That in brief speech often
The wanton woman responds to him.
Now please God that such fools   620

Have faces full of pockmarks,   *pokes* [veroles]
And [let] all ribalds [have] measles,   [les rugeroles]
So they would then renounce embraces
And wanton women dances,
And they would avoid black places.   625
But in order to teach these innocents
About spindles I will speak more plainly:
For there are spindles and the pox.
Which are from different schools.
The spindle guards the cuff   630
From the knife of the wicked rogue,
But the pox would never destroy
The looks of a truly great lord.
But it's a true caterpillar
Which naturally grows from cabbage.   635
A worm which is colored green
In France is called a snake.

Now to Draw the Fire

*N*ow be ready to prepare [the fire],
So that we can eat soon.
One of your four valets   1000
Goes quickly to clean this hearth.
Carry the ashes to the dunghill;   *mochul* [fimer]
Make the kindling catch   *szhides* [les asteles]
With an already burning brand
Which will be brought from the kitchen.   1005
Put the kindling between
The oak logs you separate with andirons   *aundhirnes* [fers]
If you make kindling   *szhides* [asteles]
From a horse's bones, you do ill.
Put to flame the kindling cut
From oak or holly or ash   1010   *holre ayhs* [aune, freyne]
And go then to seek the fire,
Skin protected from the fire   *becche* [fust]
But due to the greenness of the kindling,   [la verdour des asteles]
I do not see sparks coming out.   *sparkes* [estenceles]
Go to look for the embers with a   1015
     potsherd;
Draw the fire, if the bishop comes.

Now be careful, good sweet brother,
Or you will quickly lose your good humor.   *glading* [bele here]
Protect your clothes from sparks;
Put stones and things into the embers.   1020

Now to Organize the House Nicely

If you think it necessary, have the house
    cleaned;
Set the table, also cover it;
The ends of the table and the sides   [les bous, les cures]
Cover with the tablecloth before the
    seigneurs.
This point at least is binding,   1025
Cover the table with a white cloth.
And also cover the second [table]
With a white cloth, if you have one.
And if the tablecloth is very dirty,   *soly* [sale]
Do not put it out in the hall;   1030   *halle* [sale]
Because a much-worn white tablecloth
Is worth more than a dirty one.   *biselet* [enboulrè, *sic*]
Wash the goblets, clean the dishes,
Cut your fingernails with scissors.   *nailes* [umbles]
Go you, scullion, with your fleshook   1035   *fleyshock* [havez]
To draw the haggis from the cooking-pot.
And put your old basket,   *hivve* [rouche]
Not the ladle, under your burden.   *ladil* [louche]
Ask Jonette who smooths your [linen] coif   *szhike* [leuche]
With a sleekstone under the ladle   1040   *ladil* [la louche]
And put the linen in the "l'ydol de lith"   *wele* [l'ydole de lith, *sic*]
Near the rose which soon withers.   *welwit* [enflestrith]
But let us return to the hive,
Where we can learn more.
The hive serves bees in truth,   1045   *bees* [ees]
Which we see flying in swarms;   *swarmes* [dees]
And one by itself in the singular
An *hony bee* is truly,
And properly a swarm of bees
In English is a *suarme of bees.*   1050
And the hive is called a honeycomb
Where bees live naturally.

Thus this sermon ends for you,   1136
For there is enough French
And a diverse number of ways of saying
    it here.
Then it ends for you, seigneurs, intending:
To commend yourselves completely to   1140
    the Son of God.
Amen.

9

A Schoolchild's Primer
(Plimpton MS 258)

PAUL ACKER

C. A. Martin, in an article discussing Middle English manuals of religious instruction, has proposed a classifying scheme for such manuals based on manuscript contexts. He outlines five types and provides instances of each, depending on whether the manual occurs (1) as the sole or predominant text; or (2) as accompanied by liturgical and homiletic texts; (3) by devotional and moral texts; (4) by meditative texts; or (5) as extracts accompanied by other texts. As an example of the first type he cites Columbia University, Plimpton MS 258, and five other manuscripts. He further characterizes examples of this subtype as didactic codices that "may have been used by priests in catechizing of the faithful"; one of these codices specifies priests' obligations to instruct the laity: "þat euerych þat vndyr hym has kepyng of sowlys, opunly on englysch vpon sundays preche and teche ham þat þey haue cure of, þe lawe and þe lore to knowe god almyzty and hys werkys" (289; Lambeth MS 408). Concerning just one of these codices, Plimpton MS 258, Martin adds: "It is possible that a slimmer version of the manual circulated, perhaps in booklet form, and was used by the laity as part of a programme of early religious instruction." In other words, the Plimpton manuscript may represent a school primer for children.[1]

Such an opinion was certainly held by the former owner of the manuscript. George Arthur Plimpton (1855–1936) was head of the Boston-based firm of Ginn and Company, a publisher of school textbooks, especially spelling books. Not surprisingly, given his occupation, Plimpton began to collect hornbooks or school primers from colonial New England, as well as medieval manuscripts illustrating the history of education, bidding at the same London auctions where other wealthy Americans such as John Pierpont Morgan were buying up treasures from private English collections.[2] His manuscripts and early printed books on mathematics were catalogued by his friend and associate David Eugene Smith, a professor at the Columbia

Teacher's College, in a book entitled *Rara Arithmetica* (1908; *Addenda*, 1939).[3] Other manuscripts from his collection were showcased in two little books entitled *The Education of Shakespeare* (1933) and *The Education of Chaucer* (1935).

The second chapter of the latter work is entitled "Elementary Education" and is divided into sections on reading and on arithmetic.[4] The section on reading provides a brief context for what is now Plimpton manuscript 258, purchased (via Quaritch) at the Sotheby's sale of Lord Amherst of Hackney manuscripts in 1909.[5] Plimpton quotes the poem with which John Trevisa prefaced his encyclopedic work *On the Properties of Things*, a manuscript of which is one of the treasures in Plimpton's collection (MS 263).[6] The poem begins: "A croys [cross] was maked al of reed [red] / In the bigynnyng of my book / That is clepid 'God me speed,' / In the first lessoun that I took. // Thanne I lernede A and B, / And other lettris by her [their] names."[7] As Plimpton notes, these lines allude to the alphabet written in the beginning of a school primer. Plimpton also quotes (18) from Chaucer's *Prioress's Tale*, referring to the schoolboy's studies: "This litel child, his litel book lernynge, / As he sat in the scole at his prymer" (B[2].516–17). After describing the contents of his manuscript, Plimpton provides a full facsimile of it,[8] as well as of a medieval French manuscript primer in his collection.

I would like to expand upon Plimpton's remarks, beginning as he does with Chaucer. The schoolboy in the *Prioress's Tale* is called "a litel clergeon, seven yeer of age, / That day by day to scole was his wone" (VII.503–4). The "litel scole of Cristen folk" (VII.495) that he walks to on a daily basis taught its pupils how "to syngen and to rede, / As smale children doon in hire childhede" (500–01). Similarly, some Middle High German tales mention urban schools that taught "singing and reading." James Schultz comments: "In the Middle Ages elementary instruction did, in fact, consist of singing, so that the pupils could assist at church services, and reading, that is Latin, the mastery of which was the paramount goal of a medieval school education" (89–90). Nicholas Orme describes the curriculum for such " 'reading' or 'song' schools" in later medieval England.[9] "Learning in an elementary school began with the alphabet, the form of which was already well established by the fourteenth century" (*English Schools,* 60–61). Orme then transcribes an alphabet from Oxford, Bodleian Library, Rawlinson MSC 209 (f. 1),[10] as typical of the medieval alphabet's sequence: "It began with a cross, followed with a capital A, and then gave the rest of the Latin alphabet in minuscule, black-letter script, with alternative forms for 'r,' 's,' and 'u.' Next came the abbreviations for *et* and *con*, then three dots or tittles and lastly the words *est amen*." This sequence accords strictly with the version in the Plimpton manuscript (f. 1), with the single exception that the Plimpton alphabet begins with a lower rather than upper case letter *a*.

Orme writes that such alphabets were written on whitewashed classroom walls, on small tablets,[11] and on the first page of "a small book of several pages called a primer . . . a religious miscellany containing the basic prayers and elements of the faith" (62). Most of the manuals of religious instruction from all of Martin's five types present the basic elements of the Christian faith in accordance with the dictates of the fourth Lateran Council in 1215 and subsequent decrees.[12] The Plimpton MS, for instance, after its opening alphabet, records the Blessing, Lord's Prayer, Hail Mary, Creed, Beatitudes, Ten Commandments, and a sampling of the many aspects of doctrine that were organized numerically: the seven deadly sins, seven principal virtues, seven works of bodily and spiritual mercy, and seven gifts of the holy ghost; the five bodily wits (or senses) and spiritual wits; the four cardinal virtues; and some perhaps less familiar numerations: the sixteen conditions of charity; the seven hindrances that prevent men from entering heaven; the five things that St. Augustine marvels at; the four tokens of salvation and the four things that are needful to every man.[13] Some manuals of religious instruction present these basic tenets as part of lengthy treatises, meditations, and explications; clearly, they are intended for more sophisticated, adult readers. The treatise on the Ten Commandments (Raymo [43]) found in several of the manuals classified by Martin and by Raymo, for example, runs to as many as twenty-three manuscript leaves.[14] But in the Plimpton MS the Ten Commandments are merely listed; indeed, throughout the Plimpton manual, religious tenets are reduced to a bare minimum, one indication that the manuscript was indeed intended for elementary education.

We note also that the texts in Plimpton MS 258 are in English, not Latin. In what sort of medieval school would basic instruction take place in English? In Chaucer's *Prioress's Tale*, after all, the only text we hear of as being learned by the eager little clergeon is a hymn to the Virgin Mary in Latin, the *Alma Redemptoris*.[15] Barbara Hanawalt writes of medieval London that in the late fourteenth and fifteenth centuries the guilds were requiring "functional literacy before an apprentice could be enrolled" (*Growing Up*, 82). The elementary educational curriculum for these budding apprentices, she suggests, "included perhaps some Latin, but certainly provided literacy in English and training in keeping accounts. . . . The presence of so many schools for elementary and commercial literacy gave rise to a considerable book trade in primers" (83). She goes on to suggest that "Girls of the better class may also have received some education. . . . They learned English and perhaps French as well as accounting, but probably not much Latin. . . . One may imagine that an educated young woman would be more desirable as a marriage partner" (83). It is perhaps among such apprentices or their eventual marriage prospects that one may seek the original owner and/or user of the Plimpton primer.[16]

Its codicological format also suggests that Plimpton MS 258 was a primer for elementary education. The manuscript is made up of a single gathering of four bifolia folded into eight leaves. It is compact in size at 5 1/4 × 3 1/2 inches, a bit smaller than a Penguin paperback. The handwriting is well spaced over the eighteen lines per page, in a carefully written bastard hand of c. 1400 that mixes anglicana a's, d's, and f's with secretary g's, r's, and w's.[17] The one indication of early ownership is unfortunately curtailed by the later cropping of the bottom margin. At the bottom of folio 8r a later (early 16c?) hand has written an anathema: "Thys boke ys yon [i.e., 'the one'] & crystes cors [Christ's curse] ys another; he that steleth the ton let hym take the tother; by the maker of . . . ," with the rest cut off. Plimpton, in *The Education of Chaucer*, does not reproduce folio 8v, no doubt because it has no text on it. But it contains the usual scribbles, in this case some attempts to write out the Ten Commandments. The hand of the anathema has written upside down on folio 8v the following: "The firste com*m*andement ys thou shallt have no oth[er] goddes; the second com*m*and[e]ment thou schallt not tak[e] the name of thy lord god yn vayne; the third com*m*[an]dement that thou kep[e] the sabat daye," and then it breaks off. These versions are not in fact copied from the manuscript's own text on folio 1v, which begins: "The first com*m*aundement is thow shalt loue thi lord god aboue all thing. The second is thow shalt not take his name in ydil. The third is thow shalt halow thi holy day." More interesting is an abortive attempt to copy out the first commandment, this time right side up at the top of folio 8v and in a more contemporary hand. The text reads: "The frist comanmend ys thow scalht . . ." I suspect that those attempts at writing *commandment* and *schalt*, while it is difficult to tell in the more fluid Middle English orthography, in fact represent genuine misspellings. Furthermore, the pen strokes [minims] are awkwardly upright and poorly inked— originally, I think, and not just due to fading. I would leave it to a paleographic expert to determine, but it seems likely to me that the line preserves a first (or "frist") attempt—a novice attempt, in any case—to copy out the most basic of texts from the beginning of the primer (or perhaps from classroom dictation or memory). The student did not reveal to us much of what he or she had learned, except perhaps that in the medieval classroom "the first commandment is thou shalt . . . learn to write out the ten commandments."[18]

Notes

1. Martin's more cautious formulation leaves open the possibility that the Plimpton primer might have been used in educative contexts other than schools and for beginning instruction to individuals other than children. Gillespie suggests that "the widespread use of such collections in schools soon expanded into a wider market" (318).

2. As noted further on, Plimpton bought his primer (via Quaritch) at the Sotheby's Lord Amherst sale in 1909; at the same sale Morgan bought (also via Quaritch) a Wycliffite New Testament (now MS M.362).

3. On Plimpton and Smith, see Acker and the references cited therein.

4. The section on arithmetic consists mainly of a partial facsimile of *The Crafte of Nombrynge*, in what is now Plimpton MS 259; see Acker.

5. March 24–27, 1909, no. 755.

6. For Trevisa's text, see Seymour. The Plimpton MS was used for copy-text by Wynkyn de Worde for his 1495 edition; see Bliss.

7. *IMEV* [*Index of Middle English Verse*] 33 (Brown). Plimpton (34–35) did not transcribe this poem from his own manuscript, but rather reproduced the text edited by H. N. MacCracken in *The Nation* 87 (1908): 92 (repr. in Perry, cxxix). Anderson gives examples of similar passages in Middle and Early Modern literature, including *Sir Gawain and the Green Knight*, ll. 757–62.

8. Plates IX.1–15, occurring on unnumbered pages 19–33. Plimpton does not reproduce folio 8v, on which see further on.

9. Moran (24) elaborates upon Orme (*English Schools*): "Song schools did not always teach reading. More often reading schools did not teach song."

10. Orme mentions that an alphabet also starts Glasgow University, Hunterian MS 472, and that in both manuscripts the alphabet is followed by "the *paternoster* and other prayers in English" (*English Schools*, 61, n.1). Hunterian MS 472 is discussed by Wolpe (under its earlier shelfmark V.6.22) and reproduced in his plate 18 (see also Tuer, 375). Martin lists Rawlinson MS C 209 under category four, but does not mention Hunterian MS 472. Gillespie (318–19) discusses the Rawlinson MS and booklets preserved in longer MSS such as the *Winchester Anthology*, which also begins with an alphabet and "may have been copied from or show the influence of a schoolbook" (337, n. 11; in this same note Gillespie mentions the Plimpton facsimile).

11. Such a tablet is called an *abece* in a Middle English poem that Moran quotes (40), the forerunner of hornbooks (which protect the text with a transparent sheet of horn) that Moran claims were in use by the end of the fifteenth century. See also Tuer, and Rust in chapter 4 of this anthology.

12. See C. A. Martin, 283–84; Gillespie, 317–18; Barratt, 413–15; Fletcher, 96–97.

13. For the manuscript titles for these works in proper sequence, see the transcription further on.

14. Paris, Bibliothèque Ste Geneviève MS 3390, fols. 1r–23v (Raymo [24] MS 52; versions of this treatise occur also in Raymo [24] MSS 2, 3, 6, 7, 15, 21, 28, 36, 38, 47, 52, and 54). Gillespie (325) describes Manchester, John Rylands University Library, MS English 85, in which brief texts "but schortli declarid" are given in a first section, then more expansive versions in a latter section. See also A. Martin, and Kellogg and Talbert.

15. Beverly Boyd in the Variorum edition of the tale emphasizes its romantic setting in "an abstract city in Asia Minor" (25) and is skeptical of attempts to align the *clergeon*'s school with specific medieval English models. However, it seems likely that Chaucer did have familiar models in mind, rather than Asian ones, of which he would have had no knowledge. Moran (60–61) interprets the *Prioress's Tale* passages to mean that the little *clergeon* is attending

a reading school in preparation for later work in grammar school, while his older friend, from whom he learns the *Alma Redemptoris*, attends a singing school: "I lerne song; I kan but smal grammeere" (VII.210). The French primer that Plimpton reproduces in facsimile in fact preserves a copy of the *Alma Redemptoris* and other Latin hymns (pl. XIII.36).

16. Moran writes that the youngest pupils in elementary reading schools "may have encountered less Latin than English by the fifteenth century" (41). While the older boys would soon be using Latin Books of Hours as their primers, manuscripts like Plimpton 258 represented "the simplest elementary English primer" (44). She suggests that the reason few of them survive may be because of the anti-Lollard distrust for religious texts in English.

17. Cf. Parkes's discussion of his plate 14(i), dated c. 1415 and characterized as an "early attempt to produce a Bastard form of Secretary, betraying considerable influence of Bastard Anglicana" (*Cursive*, 14).

18. The same hand wrote in the upper margin: Ihesus elpe me. This student may have had more reasons than usual to invoke such help.

A Schoolchild's Primer (Text from Columbia University, Plimpton MS 258)[1]

[1] [alphabet]

f. 1, line 1: _𝕏[2] a a. b. c. d. e. f. g. h. i. k. l. m. n. o. p. q. r r.[3] R s[4]. t. u. v. x. y. z. & **B**[5] □ est amen[6]

[2] [The Blessing or In Nomine Patris]

f. 1, line 3: (I)n the name of the fad‹ir› and of the sone & of the holy gost amen[7]

[3] [The Lord's Prayer or Pater Noster]

f. 1, line 5: (F)adir oure that art in heuenes ha‹lowd› be thi name. thi kyngdom come tothe [read: thi] wille be don in erthe as it is in heuen. oure eche dayes bred yeue vs today. and foryeue vs oure dettes as we forgeuen to oure detturis. and lede vs not into temptacion but deliuer vs fromyuell amen.[8]

[4] [The Hail Mary or Ave Maria]

f. 1, line 12: (H)ayle mari ffull of grace the lord is with the. blessid be thow among wemen & blessed be the frute of thi wombe ihesus amen.[9]

[5] [rubric:] the crede [the Apostles' Creed]

f. 1, line 16: (I) bileue into god fadir almyzti maker of heuen & of erthe. and into ihesu crist his oonly son oure lord. wiche was con [f. 1v] conceyued [sic] of the holy gost. boren of the virgine marie. he suffered passion vndir pounce pilate. crucified dede & beried. he went into hellis. the thrid day he rose from dethe to lijf. he stied vp to heuenes & there he sittith on the rizth side of god the fadir almyzti. from thens he is to come to deme the quicke & the dede. I beleue into the holy gost. and all holy chirche comini*n*g of seyntes forgeuenes of synnes. vprising of flessh. and liif eue*r*lasting amen.[10]

*[6] [rubric:] the x co*m*maundeme*ntis*

f. 1v, line 13: (T)he first co*m*maundeme*n*t is thow shalt loue thi lord god aboue all thing. (T)he second is thow shalt not take his name in ydil. (T)he third is thow shalt halow thi holy day. (T)he iiij*thi*s to worshippe thi fadir & moder. [f. 2] (T)he v*the* is thow shalt not sle. (T)he vj is thow shalt do no lecheri. (T)he vij is thow shalt do no thefte. (T)he v‹iij› is þ*u* shalt bere no fals witnesse. (T)he ix is thow shalt not couet thi neyzbors hous ne his lond. (T)he x is thow shalt not desire the neybors wif ne his se*r*uant ne ony thing that is his.[11]

[7] [rubric:] The vij dedly sinnes

f. 2, line 9: (P)ride wrathe & enuy ben synnes of the fend. Couetice and auarice ben synnes of the world. Gloteny slowthe & lecheri ben synnes of the flessh. & thes ben the large weyes to helle & many passen therbi to helle for thei will not bysi them to knowe god*es* co*m*maundeme*n*tes.[12]

[8] [rubric] vij principal vertues

f. 2, line 17: (M)ekenes is rote of all othir vertues & is remedie agenst the syn of p*r*ide. [f. 2v] Pacience is remedi agens the syn of wrathe. Charite is remedi agens the syn of envie. Largenes of almes dede*s* is remedi agenst the syn of couetise & auarice. Discrete abstinence is remedi agenst the syn of gloteny. Holi bisines is remedi agens the syn of slouth. Wilful chastite is remedi agens the syn of lecheri.[13]

[9] [rubric] the vij werkis of merci bodili

f. 2v, line 11: (C)ome ye blessed of my fader & take ye the kyngdome of heuen that was ordeyned for yow fro the maky*n*g of the world for whan I hongird ye fedden me. I thristed & ye gaf me to drinke. I was harborowlesse & ye harbored me. I was nakid & ye clothid me. I was in p*r*ison & ye came to me. I was [f. 3] sike & ye visitiden me. the vij werk*es* [read: vijth werke] of merci is seide in the booke of tobi biriyng of dede men that haue nede therto. & all this vij werkes of merci men doen to crist when thei doen them to his membris.[14]

[10] [rubric] the vij werkis of merci gostly

f. 3, line 7: (T)eche, cou*n*celle, chastice, comforte, fforgeff, suffre, & pray. Teche them that ben vnkunnyng. Cou*n*celle them that ben dowtyng. Chastice them that trespassen. Comforte them that sorowen. fforgeue wronges mekely. Suffur desesus paciently.[15]

[11] [rubric] the v. bodili wittes

f. 3, line 14: (H)ering, seyng, smellyng, tasting, & towching. A man synneth in hering whan he delitith him to here idell speches fablis foly & foule wordes. A man [f. 3v] synneth in seyng when is yie [i.e., his eye] is vnstabul biholding diuerse things where throw he is sterid to syn. For who that hathe a lizt yie & vnstable he shall haue a derke soule & full of syn. A man synneth in smellyng, whan he throw dilicate sauour œdelitith him to fill his bely more for lust than for nede. A man sinneth in tastyng when he tastith mete or drinke & takith it vnmesurabli where throwe he is wors disposid to serue god. A man synneth in towching when he towchit ony thing that sterith to syn wiche is forbede of god & bi his lawe.[16]

[12] [rubric] the v. gostily wittis

f. 3v, line 16: (W)ill, mynd, vndirstonding, ymaginacion, & reson. Haue ye fful will that the will of god be don [f. 4] bifore thyn owyn will[.] haue mynde of the blis of heuen & how thow mayst come therto. & also on the peynes of hell & how thow maist fle them. Vnderston what benefetes & goodnesses that god hathe don for the & how vnkynd thow art agayn. Ymagen goodnes of other men more than of thi silfe. rule thi lijf be reson aftir the forme of godes law & all tho that ben vnder thi gouernance.[17]

[13] [rubric] the iiij cardinall vertues

f. 4, line 12: (T)emporance, prudence, riztwisnes and strenkith. temporance stondithin mesurable etyng & drinkyng in sleping in wakyng in worching resting & in still beyng in clothing & so forth in all othir things to kepe thi soule & body to the plesour of god. Prudence [f. 4v] stondith in wise fleyng the wey of syn that ledith to hell & in wise goyng the wey of vertu that ledith to heuen. Ryztwisnesse stondith in rizt doyng both to god & to man. Strengeth stondith in myzti withstonding the temptacions of oureiij enymes that is the fend the world & thyn own flessh.[18]

[14] [rubric] the vij giftes of þe holi gost

f. 4v, line 9: (T)he spirit of wisdome & of vndirstonding, the spirit of councel & of strength, the spirite of connyng & of pite, the spirit of drede of the lord. The spirit of wisdom moueth a man to chese more & to charge more heuenly things than ertheli things. The spirit of vndirstonding moueth a man to vndirstond gostly things & to bisie to make his soule clene that it [f. 5] may be faire in godes sizt. The spirit of councel moueth a man to chese the good & leue the yuell & of ij good things to chese the bettur. The spirit of strength moueth a man to be strong in his soule & miztili to withstond the temptacions of oure gostily enymes. The spirit of kunnyng moueth a man to departe trouthe fro falshode & falshode from trouthe. The spirit of pite moueth a man to haue compassion of othir men*n*es dissese & for to helpe hem to his power. The spirit of drede of the lord moueth a man to do that god com*m*aundith wi*th*out ony grogyng & to forsake all prosp*er*ite that is agens god*es* will.[19]

[15] [rubric] the xvj condicions of charite that paule writith ad corinthios xiijo capitulo

f. 5v, line 1: (I)f i speke wi*th* tungis of men & of angelis & haue not charite I am made as bras sowni*n*g or as a cimbal tinking. & if I haue prophecie & know all misteries & all kun*n*yng so that I moue hilles fro*m* her places & I haue not charite I am nouzt. And if I dep*er*te al my godes into metis of pore men & I haue not charite it p*ro*fiteth to me no thing. And if I betake my bodi so that I bren*n*e & I haue not charite it p*ro*fitith to me no thing. Charite is pacient it is benigne. Charite enuieth not it dothe not wikedly it is not bolned wi*th* pride it is not couetise it sekith not tho thing*es* that ben his owne but that that is p*ro*fitable to many men. It is not stirid to wrath hit thinkith not euel it ioyeth not on [f. 6] wikidnes but it ioyeth togider to trouth[.] it sufferith all thing*es* it hop*ith* all thing*es* it susteyneth all thing*es* it beleuith all thing*es*. charite fallith neu*er* down.[20]

*[16] [rubric] the blessing*es *of god [The beatitudes, Matthew 5.1–12, plus a closing admonition]*

f. 6, line 6: (I)hesu seing the peple we*n*t vp into an hill & whan hewas sette his disciples camen to him & he opened his mowthe & tauzt hem & seyde. Blessid be pore men in spirit for the kyngdom of heue*n*nes is thers. Blessid be mild men for thei shulle wilden the erthe. Blessid be thei that mornen, for thei shal be comfortid. Blessid be thei that hungren & thurston for rithwisnes, for thei shul be fulfillid. Blessid be m*er*ciful men, for thei shul gete merci. Blessid be thei that ben of clene herte [f. 6v] ffor thei shul see god. Blessid be pecible men, for thei shull be clepid godis children. Blessed be thei that suffur p*er*secucion for rithwisnesse, for the kyngdome of heuenes is theris. ze shull be blessid when men shul curce yow & shulle repreue yow & sei all euel ayens yow lijng for me. ioye ze & be ye glad for yowre mede is plentuouse in heuenes. for so thei han p*er*sued also p*ro*phetes that were before yow [end of biblical quotation] & therfore for goddis loue that bouzt the so dere wi*th* his bittur passion eithir for drede of bittur paynes in helle either for loue of heuenen blisse forsake & dispite thi syn & kepe truly god*es* x. com*m*aundement*es*.[21]

*[17] [rubric] Seynt austyn mervelith of v. thing*es

f. 7, line 1: (T)he first is that ony man or woman dare lijf in suche a lijf that thei wold for no thing die therin. ii is that thei set so litul p*r*ice bi the sowle that god bouzt so dere[.] ii[i]e is þat thei will ley ther sowlis to wedde for ony lust or likyng. the iiij is thei will behote more in tyme of tribulacion then thei will performe in welthe. the vth is that what veniance & wondris that god sendith among the pepul that thei wil not be aknow that it is for syn.[22]

[18] [rubric] Eueri man owith to beware of vij lettingis that lette men to come to heuen

f. 7, line 15: (T)he firis is meynteyning of syn. the iidis excusing of syn. the iiid is beholding of othir mennes synnes & not of hur [f. 7v] owne. the iiijth is hiding of syn. the vth is quenching of a good purpos. the vj is multiplieng of syn. the vij is gret ocupacion about worly thinges.[23]

[19] [rubric] Also seint austyn seith bi þis iiij a man shal know if he be of the nowmer þat shall be saued

f. 7v, line 7: (T)he first is to haue a pure & a quicke deuocion in prayour to god. the ij is to haue a veri loue to god. the iij is to haue a veri contricion for syn. the iiij is to haue continuali in mynd the bittur passion of oure lord ihesu crist that he suffird for man.[24]

[20] [rubric] Here ben iiij nedeful thinges to eueri man.

f. 7v. line 15: (T)he first is to here the word of god & his law. the ij is to vndirstond it. for thouzwe here the word of god preched or red [f. 8] to vs & we haue noon vndirstonding therof it profitith not to vs. the iij is to worche therafter in dede. for thow we here the wordes of god & also vndirstond it & we do not therafter it profitith not to vs. the iiij is to continue in good werkes vnto the ende of oure lijf. for thow we do wel for a tyme & at the laste to turne ayen to syn al oure former dedis helpith vs litul or nouzt to heuenward. and therfore pray we to god of his gret merci to yeue vs grace to here his word & to vndirstond it & also to worche thereafter & so to continue in good lyuyng into the ende of oure lijf & that we may come to that lijf & ioy that euershall last Amen.[25]

Notes

1. In the transcription further on, I enclose oversize, red majuscules in parentheses. Letters that are faded on the first folio (but recoverable by ultraviolet light) are enclosed in angle brackets (as are the roman numerals added in the margin of f. 2 but partly cut off). Editorial additions and comments are enclosed in square brackets. Scribal abbreviations are expanded with italics. The curled sign for -is or -es is expanded -es, although the scribe uses both -is and -es when writing out in full the plural and genitive singular. Curled flourishes on final n's and d's are regarded as otiose. Curled final r is expanded -re since it varies with 2-shaped final r in the few places where it occurs. I render manuscript pointing as periods (or commas in some series),

but otherwise do not silently introduce punctuation or majuscules. I do, however, regularize word division according to modern practice.

Two of the items below were catalogued by Jolliffe, who provides a record of other manuscripts with the same or similar items. Although he cites (p. 106) the Plimpton facsimile, he indexes the MS as one of those for which he had incomplete information; I include a few other references from his checklist where they appear to resemble the Plimpton items. More recently, Raymo has provided a list of items in some fifty-nine "miscellaneous manuals of religious instruction," to which I refer using his numeration.

A facsimile of ff. 1–8r is found in Plimpton, *Chaucer*, pp. 19–33, and of f. 1r in Plimpton, *Shakespeare*, p. 151. An online facsimile of ff. 1–8v may be accessed at ⟨http://sunsite.berkeley.edu/Scriptorium/form_msimage.html⟩.

2. Cross inscribed in a square, in red.
3. The latter is a 2-shaped r.
4. Long s; sigma s.
5. Abbrev. for *con-*.
6. Other MSS: Oxford, Bodleian Rawlinson C. 209 (Raymo, 8), f. 1r [transcribed Orme, *English Schools,* 61]; Glasgow, Hunterian MS 472 (Raymo, 49), f. 1r [facsimile Tuer, 375: Wolpe, pl. 18 facing p. 70]; London, British Library Additional 60577, f. 120r [facsimile *Winchester Anthology*]; Manchester, John Rylands UL, MS English 85, f. 2r [transcribed Lester, 15]. For facsimiles and discussion of alphabets in Latin and German primers, see Wolpe.
7. Other MSS: Manchester, John Rylands UL English 85, f. 2v [transcribed Lester, 16].
8. Other MSS: Raymo [24] MSS 2a, 5, 8, 9, 10, 15, 16, 17, 19, 21, 23, 24, 25, 26, 28, 30, 32, 33, 35, 37, 39, 40, 41, 43, 44, 45, 46, 49, 50, 55; expositions in 4 & 52. For expositions of the Pater Noster, see Raymo [33]–[36].
9. Other MSS: Raymo [24] MSS 5, 8, 9, 10, 16, 17, 19, 21, 23, 24, 25, 28, 30, 32, 33, 37, 39, 40, 41, 44, 45, 46, 49, 50, 55; exposition in 4. For expositions of the Ave Maria, see Raymo [37].
10. Other MSS: Raymo [24] MSS 2a, 4, 5, 8, 9, 15, 16, 17, 19, 21, 23, 24, 25, 28, 30, 32, 33, 35, 37, 39, 40, 41, 44, 45, 46, 49, 50, 55. For expositions of the creed, see Raymo [40]–[41].
11. Other MSS: Raymo [24] MSS 5, 7, 8, 9, 12, 13, 14, 18, 19, 20, 23, 23a, 25, 26, 27, 31, 33, 37, 39, 40, 42, 45, 46, 48, 49, 50, 51, 53, 55; expositions in 1, 2, 3, 4, 6, 15, 21, 28, 36, 38, 47. For expositions of the Ten Commandments, see Raymo [43–47] and IPMEP [Lewis, *Index of Printed Middle English Prose*], 48, 49, and 650.
12. References: Cf. Jolliffe, p. 83, F21. Editions: Plimpton, p. 34 (modernized and inaccurate); from MS Ed 93 in Martin diss., 358. Other MSS: Raymo [24] MSS 3, 5, 6, 7, 8, 9, 11, 12, 13, 14, 18, 19, 20, 22, 22, 23a, 26, 27, 28, 31, 32, 33, 36, 38, 39, 40, 42, 45, 46, 48, 49, 50, 53.

13. Other MSS: Raymo [24] MSS 1, 2, 3, 5, 7, 12, 14, 18, 19, 20, 27, 29, 31, 32, 33, 43, 45, 46.

14. References: The first six deeds of bodily mercy were taken from Matthew 25:34–36, which this version simply quotes. The seventh deed was taken from Tobit 1:16–17. Other MSS: Raymo [24] MSS 1, 2, 3, 5, 6, 7, 8, 9, 11, 12, 14, 18, 19, 20, 21, 22, 26, 27, 28, 29, 31, 33, 36, 38, 39, 40, 42, 43, 45, 46, 48, 50, 51, 53, 54, 55, 57. See also Raymo [50]–[51].

15. Other MSS: as [9] above, except apparently not in Raymo [24] MS 46.

16. References: cf. Jolliffe, p. 75, D9? Editions: from MS Ed 93 in Martin diss., 365–66. Other MSS: Raymo [24] MSS 1, 2, 3, 5, 6, 8, 9, 11, 12, 13, 14, 18, 19, 20, 21, 22, 27, 28, 29, 31, 32, 33, 36, 38, 39, 40, 42, 43, 45, 46, 47, 48, 50, 51, 53, 55.

17. References: cf. Jolliffe, p. 75, D8? Other MSS: Raymo [24] MSS as above, except not in 22, 36, 43, and 51.

18. References: cf. Jolliffe p. 89, G22. Other MSS: Raymo [24] MSS 8, 14, 36, 39, 40, 47, 48, 50, 53.

19. Other MSS: Raymo [24] MSS 1, 3, 5, 8, 9, 12, 14, 20, 22, 23a, 25, 27, 34, 36, 38, 39, 40, 43, 47, 48, 49, 50, 57.

20. References: quoted from Cor. I 13:1–8. Listed in Jolliffe, p. 168, under incipit, but omitted p. 86, G4e. Cf. also Jolliffe, p. 87, G11. Other MSS: Raymo [24] MSS 8, 13, 14, 19, 20, 31, 32, 34, 38, 39, 43, 47. See also Raymo [58], [53], and [194].

21. Other MSS: Raymo [24] MSS 14, 20, 32, 34, 39, 40, 43, 47.

22. Other MSS: Raymo [24] MSS 14, 32, 34, 40, and Bodley, 788.

23. Other MSS: Raymo [24] MSS 14, 34; as also Raymo [96], to which add this MS.

24. References: Jolliffe, p. 106, I10. Other MSS: Raymo [24] MSS 8, 14, 32, 34, 40; see also Raymo [146], which adds two MSS (but delete Hunter, 512, which belongs under [157]).

25. References: Jolliffe pp. 105–6, I9. Editions: from MS Ed 93 in Martin diss., 384–85. Other MSS: Raymo [24] MSS 5, 14, 32, 34, 36, 47, 48, 50; see also

10
Chaucer as Teacher:
Chaucer's *Treatise on the Astrolabe*

SIGMUND EISNER AND MARIJANE OSBORN

INTRODUCTION

Sigmund Eisner

Any society must look after its young and train them to take a place in the accepted organization of the culture.[1] Although schooling was not as widespread during the fourteenth century as it is today, some children and young adults were instructed in the seven liberal arts, consisting of the *trivium*, which was grammar, logic, and rhetoric, and the *quadrivium*, which was arithmetic, geometry, astronomy, and music. When we move from the general to the specific, we see that Geoffrey Chaucer was qualified to be an instructor in at least six of the seven liberal arts—grammar, logic, rhetoric, arithmetic, geometry, and astronomy—and that he demonstrated these qualifications in his *Treatise on the Astrolabe* (a medieval astronomical instrument), which was written in or near the year 1391[2] and which was addressed at its beginning to the poet's ten-year-old son, Lewis Chaucer.

The medieval planetary astrolabe is a brass disk that hangs by a swivel from the user's thumb. Its purpose is to pinpoint the location of the celestial bodies at a particular time and thus reveal the time of day or night. It is designed like a modern circular slide rule, with all moving parts pivoting from the center of the disk. On the front of the astrolabe is a fixed plate showing the visible sky for a given latitude. Over the plate pivots a *rete*, a network that shows the moving bodies in the sky and the signs of the zodiac. The stars and the zodiac move together and are all shown on the rete. Over the rete lies a label that pivots at the center and runs from rim to rim. A cross is by the rim at the top of the disk, and letters running around the disk indicate the twenty-four hours of the day; the cross stands for noon, A for 1 P.M., B for 2 P.M., M for midnight, and so on. The back of the astrolabe contains a pivoted rule with two fins, perforated by two holes, one small and the other large. The back serves as a protractor, for with the rule, which is somewhat like a gunsight, one can learn the altitude of either the sun or another visible star.

The user of the astrolabe hangs it from his thumb and lets the sun shine through the smaller pair of holes on the label or observes a star through the larger pair of holes. Using the protractor on the rim of the back, one can determine a star's altitude. It is assumed that either the date of the day or the number of the day within the signs of the zodiac is already known. The user transfers this information to the front of the astrolabe, where nonconcentric circles of altitude are marked on the plate. This user then turns the rete until the heavenly body lies exactly on the altitude that matches the altitude just observed. Then, turning the label on the front so that it crosses the point where he or she has placed the sun or a star, the user follows the label to the rim and learns the time of day.

Chaucer's *Treatise* is divided into three parts: an introduction, a description of the parts of the astrolabe, and the conclusions or experiments possible with the instrument. In the early part of the *Treatise* Chaucer addresses a child, not only in tone but in name, but later, when the experiments become complicated, the child disappears, and Chaucer gradually adapts his language to the adult level. This shift in language and subject matter militates against Philippe Ariès' influential but largely discredited theory that the Middle Ages lacked awareness of what we today consider to be the special nature of the child and that in the fourteenth century children were both portrayed and treated as miniature adults (Ariès, 128; for one refutation of this idea, see Hanawalt, *Growing Up*, 5–6).

Some time ago I suggested that the function of Little Lewis in *A Treatise on the Astrolabe* is to serve as an audience persona, an actual person who is included in a literary work and given a character all his own (Eisner, 181). As Talbot Donaldson and others have argued, Chaucer uses his own persona as the narrator of *The Canterbury Tales* (Donaldson, 1–12; Owen, 18–24), and I believe that he creates a persona from his son to be the initial audience of the *Treatise*. Later on in the text, when Chaucer no longer needs introductory and elementary language to explain his conclusions, Lewis disappears. I suggest, therefore, that the parts directed toward the child served to ease adult readers into the more sophisticated sections of the work. In this paper I want to address only that portion of Chaucer's writing that is directed to a child.

Lewis Chaucer was certainly no mere fictional construct, although there was once a mystery about him, fed mainly by the speculations of some late-nineteenth-, early-twentieth-, and occasional late-twentieth-century scholars. No birth, baptismal, marriage, or death records survive of Lewis, and this paucity of documentation has led to much speculation. In 1380 a lady named Cecily Chaumpaigne released Chaucer from a charge of rape, *de raptu meo* (Crow and Olson, 343). Since Lewis Chaucer was ten in 1391, the dates suggest that Cecily Chaumpaigne may have been his mother. But no one has ever offered definitive proof of this hypothesis.[3] In 1917 George Lyman Kittredge suggested that Chaucer had no son named Lewis and that "Litel Lewis" was the son and namesake of Lewis Clifford, a Lollard knight. Because the younger Clifford died in October 1391, Kittredge surmised that Chaucer in his grief abandoned the *Treatise* (513–18). This theory was laid to rest by John M. Manly, who, in 1928, uncovered documents listing Lewis Chaucer as a participant in a 1403 campaign at Carmarthan Castle in Wales (430). Accompanying him were his brother, Thomas Chaucer, and four of his first cousins: John Beaufort, earl of Somerset; Henry Beaufort, bishop of Bath and Wells; Sir Thomas Beaufort; and Sir Thomas Swynford.[4] Since no further word concerning Lewis has appeared, he probably died in that engagement. In any case, there seems to be no real evidence to cause us to doubt that Chaucer had a legitimate son named Lewis and that this Lewis is addressed in the early portions of *A Treatise on the Astrolabe*.

But although Chaucer designs these passages specifically for a juvenile reader, it was not until the eighteenth century that literary critics recognized what he had done. In his *Fall of Princes*, the fifteenth-century poet and critic John Lydgate, for one, remarks merely that Chaucer wrote *A Treatise on the Astrolabe* for his son Lewis (1:7–9, Part I, ll. 246–301). Lydgate does not analyze the distinction between Chaucer's prose written for a child and that composed for adults. Lydgate's approach persisted until 1781, when Robert Henry pointedly admired Chaucer's ability to relate to a child, thus making use of the modern concept that composition designed for a juvenile audience must be unique (4:469–71). By the nineteenth century, when critics considered Chaucer's paternal relationship, they tended to sentimentalize him. William Godwin, a member of the English Romantic movement, visualized a warm and caring Chaucer sitting on a bench under some shade trees and bonding with his adoring son (2:499–501). Thomas R. Lounsbury, who really did not like the *Treatise*, saved his few words of praise for Chaucer's compassionate attitude toward his son (1:101–2).

Twentieth-century critics, on the other hand, have focused on Chaucer's pedagogical skills. Sister M. Madeleva considers Chaucer a good educator because of his sympathetic attitude toward Lewis. J. E. Cross sees the *Treatise* as a text for technically minded children and lauds Chaucer's competence in conveying information (172–75). Ralph W. V. Elliott is interested in how Chaucer alters technical language for the comprehension of a child (133–43). Thomas J. Jambeck and Karen K. Jambeck look back to the fourteenth century, when children often learned to parrot Latin without understanding its meaning, and conclude that the *Treatise* is unusual for its day in offering the child genuine learning rather than a mere ability to perform (116–22). The evolution in critical attitudes toward the *Treatise* reminds us that our own view of childhood is far from static, but Chaucer's strategy in this work indicates an understanding of the child mind that is by no means alien.

Adult-directed instructional manuals from the fourteenth century are usually sterile compendia of facts, dependent on some previous knowledge on the part of the reader. One might say that they have the incomprehensibility of some of our modern computer manuals; they are wearying to an adult and deadly to a child. But whenever Chaucer is directly addressing Lewis, the *Treatise* brings a delightful youth-oriented approach to fourteenth-century technical instruction. He opens the manual with these words: "Little Lewis, my son, I perceive well by certain evidence your ability to learn sciences touching numbers and proportions. And as well I consider your busy prayer in special to learn the treatise of the astrolabe" (Prologue, 1. 5).[5] At the end of the first paragraph he tells us that Little Lewis is at the "tendir age of ten yeer" (Prologue, 1. 25); as Hanawalt notes, fourteenth-century lawyers used phrases such as "being of tender years" to protect children's rights by pointing out their differences from adults (*Growing Up*, 6), and arguably Chaucer does the same here.

To be sure, Lewis was evidently a clever child, for by the time he was ten in 1391 he was well versed in mathematics and had an interest in astronomy. When we recall that arithmetic, geometry, and astronomy were three of the four parts of the *quadrivium*, on which was based the examination for the Master of Arts degree, we must acknowledge that Lewis had considerable erudition. Indeed, we learn later that Chaucer is teaching this material to his ten-year-old because no one else in the neighborhood knows enough about an astrolabe to teach it. But gifted as he was, Lewis was still a child. Taking Chaucer at his word, then, we see that he intends to teach a complex subject to his gifted son in a way that a ten-year-old will pay attention to and profit from; possibly, the poet's ultimate goal is to write a treatise comprehensible to everyone.[6]

What Chaucer does first is to make it clear that he is going to use language that Lewis can understand. He writes, "I will show you with very light rules and plain words in English, for you still do not know Latin very well, my little son" (Prologue, ll. 25–27).[7] Latin, of course, was the language of instruction in the fourteenth century, and *A Treatise on the Astrolabe* is almost unique among contemporary instruction manuals because it is written in English. He then explains to Lewis that information about astrolabes has been written not only in Latin but also in Greek, Arabic, and Hebrew and adds that the same information may be uttered in various languages for various peoples (Prologue, ll. 29–30).[8]

Then Chaucer offers two statements about his prose style. The first is that strange phraseology and hard sentence structure are too difficult for a child; the implication is that Chaucer will restrict himself to ordinary diction, easy sentences, and common similes that will bring to the unfamiliar an association with the familiar. And indeed he does. The azimuths of an astrolabe indicate compass directions for the user. On the astrolabe they are shown as arcs of a circle emanating from a point that represents the zenith over the user's head. Chaucer notes that "from this zenith there come curved lines like the legs of a spider or like a woman's hairnet" (1.19, ll. 1–4).[9] Later he compares the rete, or the perforated star map on the astrolabe, to a spider's web.

Chaucer's second statement is that it seems better to write a good sentence twice than have a child forget it once. That is, he promises to use repetition as a learning aid, and he does exactly that. The "mother" of the astrolabe is the main body of the instrument and is divided by various lines. Chaucer explains these divisions as follows: "This mother is divided on the back side with a line that comes descending from the ring down to the bottom border. The line from the ring to the hole in the center of the astrolabe is called the south line or else the meridional line. The rest of this line down to the border is called the north line or the midnight line" (1.4, ll. 1–9).[10] A second example of Chaucer's repetitive style in this manual is "The east side of your astrolabe is called the right side. And the west side is called the left side. Forget not this, little Lewis" (1. 6, ll. 1–3).[11] When Chaucer wants to write about a line of the astrolabe, the word *line* appears over and over again, as does the word *side* when he wants to write about what is on the two halves of the device.

Unlike other technical writers of his time, Chaucer does not assume prior knowledge on Lewis's part. For instance, when he first mentions the twelve signs of the zodiac, he names every one of them. Never one to let a bit of information or an opportunity for instruction to slip by, Chaucer later adds, "and this aforementioned heavenly zodiac is called the circle of the signs or the circle of the beasts. For *zodia* in the language of the Greeks means *beasts* in the Latin tongue" (1. 20, ll. 49–53).[12] And when he first mentions the twelve months of the year, not only does he name them, but he also explains how they got their names, how many days there are in each month, and why the months are divided as they are. The names of the signs of the zodiac and of the months appear on concentric circles inside the rim of the astrolabe. Chaucer comments:

> Next to the circle of the days follows the circle of the names of the months, that is to say January, February, March, April, May, June, July, August, September, October, November, December. The months were named, some for their characteristics, some by decrees of Arabians, and some by other lords of Rome. Also, of these months which pleased Julius Caesar and Augustus Caesar, some had days added to them. So January has 31 days, February 28. March 31, April 30, May 31, June 30, July 31, August 31, September 30, October 31, November 30, December 31. Nevertheless, although Julius Caesar took two days out of February and put them in his month of July, and Augustus Caesar called the month of August after himself and gave it 31 days, yet trust well that the sun stays no more and no less in one sign of the zodiac than in another. (1.10, ll. 1–22)[13]

Note that in this short quotation "month" or "months" appears five times, "days" appears five times,[14] and the months in their order are named twice.

The rim of the front of an astrolabe displays a cross, followed by the twenty-three capital letters of the fourteenth-century English alphabet. Each of these twenty-four digits occupies 15 of the 360 degrees of the circle on the rim, and each stands for one hour of the clock. Every 5 degrees on the border, or twenty clock minutes, contains what Chaucer calls "a mile way," possibly because a man can be expected to walk a mile in twenty minutes. Chaucer explains the border in this manner.

> The border of the front side of the astrolabe is divided from the point of the east line up to the south line under the ring in ninety degrees; and by that same proportion is every quarter divided, as is the back side. That amounts to 360 degrees. And understand well that the degrees of this border correspond with and are concentric to the degrees of the celestial equator, which is divided in the same number as every other circle in the sky. This same border is divided with twenty-three capital letters and a small cross above the south line which show the twenty-four equal hours of the clock. And, as I have said, five of these degrees make a mile way, and three mile ways make an hour. And every degree of this border contains four minutes [of the clock], and every minute sixty seconds. Now have I told you twice.[15]

Indeed he has, and the implication is "Don't you dare forget it."

Fourteenth-century technical instruction was usually written with statements of fact, coupled with conditionals and jussive subjunctives: "If one wishes to know *this*, then one must do *that*." Nicholas of Lynne, whose 1386 *Kalendarium* Chaucer read, began one typical instructional paragraph with "Now, when one may wish to know the hours of the clock and their minutes, let him take the altitude of the sun by some instrument" (188–89).[16] That is, he would start with the conditional, "when one may wish to know," and lead into the jussive subjunctive, "let him take." When writing a similar passage, Chaucer bears in mind that he is writing for a child. He moves from the third to the first person, avoids the hortatory commands to his audience, and says in a narrative manner, "For example: in the year of our Lord 1391, on the twelfth day of March, I wanted to know the time of the day. I took the altitude of my sun . . ." (2.3, ll. 15–17).[17] Nicholas of Lynn continues his explanation with a complex and prolix set of directions involving instrument, tables, and calculations. Chaucer continues his explanation with simple expository prose, depending on a visual view of an astrolabe, which presumably Lewis held in this hands.

No one style of writing directions is the best for every audience, although technical writers, from Ptolemy to the author of your computer manual, often assume that the reader can comprehend the obscure with ease. The fact is that all writers, technical or narrative, must tailor what they write to their readers. If one is going to write for children with the assumption that the child is going to acquire knowledge from reading one's words, one must recognize children's limitations of vocabulary, concepts, and experience. Chaucer is unusual not just among his contemporaries but also among technical writers through the ages in knowing how to write comprehensibly to a child. In training his son to take an adult place within fourteenth-century society, he recognizes that Lewis is not a miniature adult, but a child with a child's needs.

Notes to Introduction (Eisner)

1. This article first appeared in *Children's Literature Association Quarterly* 23, 1 (1998). It is reprinted here with the gracious permission of the Children's Literature Association.
2. In his discussion of the astrolabe, Chaucer uses examples that he dates in 1391, and most scholars have accepted 1391 as the date of composition.
3. For more about the Cecily Chaumpaigne incident, see Skeat, *Complete Works*, 1: xxxii; Cowling, 22–23; Plunkett, 33–35; Braddy, 906–11; and Delany.
4. The Beauforts were the children of John of Gaunt, duke of Lancaster and fourth son of King Edward III, and of Katherine Swynford, first John's mistress and then his wife. Katherine Swynford was also the mother of Sir Thomas Swynford by her first husband and the sister of Philippa Chaucer, Geoffrey Chaucer's wife.
5. "Lyte Lowys my sone I aperceyve wel by certeyne evydences thyn abilite to lerne sciences touching nombres and proporciouns; and as wel considre I thy besy praier in special to lerne the tretys of the Astrolabie."
6. Long ago I tried to teach my own ten-year-old how to understand an astrolabe and learned then to appreciate the skill with which Chaucer approached the same problem.
7. "Wol I shewe the under full light reules and naked wordes in Englisshe, for Latyn canst thou yit but small, my litel sone."
8. Or, as he phrases it, "Diverse pathes leden diverse folk the righte way to Rome."
9. "From this cenyth, as it semeth, there comen a maner croked strikes like to the claws of a loppe, or elles like the werk of a wommans calle."
10. "This moder is dividid on the bakhalf with a lyne that cometh descending fro the ring down to the netherist bordure. The whiche lyne, fro the forseid ring unto the centre of the large hool amidde, is clepid the south lyne, or ellis the lyne meridional. And the remenaunt of this lyne doun to the bordure is clepid the north lyne, or ellis the lyne of midnyght."
11. "The est syde of thyn Astrolabie is clepid the right syde, and the west syde is clepid the left syde. Forget not this litel Lowys."
12. "And this forseide hevenyssche zodiak is clepid the cercle of the signes, or the cercle of the bests, for 'zodia' in langage of Greke sowneth 'bestes' in Latyn tonge."
13. "Next the cercle of the daies fole with the cercle of the names of the monthes, that is to say, Januarius, Februarius, Marcius, Aprilis, Maius, Junius, Julius, Augustus, September, October, November, December. The names of these monthes were clepid, somme for her propirtees and somme by statues of Ara-

biens, somme by othre lordes of Rome. Eke of these monthes as liked to Julius Cesar and to Cesar Augustus, somme were compouned of diverse nombres of daies, as Julie and August. Than hath Januarie 31 daies, Februarie 28, Marche 31, April 30, May 31, Junius 30, Julius 31, Augustus 31, Septembre 30, Octobre 31, Novembre 30, Decembre 31. Natheles all though that Julius Cesar toke 2 daies oute of Feberer and putte hem in his month of Juyll, and Augustus Cesar clepid the month of August after his name and ordeined it of 31 daies, yit truste wel that the sonne dwellith therfore never the more ne lasse in oon signe than in another."

14. In Ms. Bodleian Library, Bodley 619, which for many reasons I believe is the best of the *Astrolabe* manuscripts, the word *daies* was used ten times in this passage. Five of them were eliminated in MS. Cambridge University Library Dd.3.53, which was the favored manuscript of Skeat. In the 1933 ancestor of the *Riverside Chaucer*, F. N. Robinson used the Bodleian manuscript most of the time, but ocasionally corrected with the Cambridge. In this paper I am following the *Riverside Chaucer*, which in this section also follows the Cambridge manuscript.

15. "The bordure of which wombe side is divided fro the point of the est lyne unto the point of the south lyne under the ring, in 90 degrees; and by that same proporcioun is every quarter divided, as is the bakside. That amountith 360 degrees. And understond wel that degres of this bordure ben aunswering and consentrike to the degrees of the equinoxiall, that is dividid in the same nombre as every othir cercle is in the highe hevene. This same bordure is divided also with 23 lettres capitals and a small cross (+) above the south lyne, that shewith the 24 hours equals of the clokke. And, as I have said, 5 of these degres maken a myle wey, and 3 mile wei maken an houre. And every degre of thys bordure contenith 4 minutes, and every minute 60 secundes. Now have I tole the twyes."

16. "Cum eciam quis scire voluerit horas de clok in earum minuta, accipiat altitudinem solis per aliquod instrumentum."

17. "Ensample as thus: the yeer of oure lord 1391, the 12 day of Marche, I wolde knowe the tyde of the day. I tok the altitude of my sonne . . ."

Marijane Osborn, translator: Chaucer's *Treatise on the Astrolabe* Addressed to His Son Lewis

As Sigmund Eisner has explained previously, Chaucer wrote his treatise on the astrolabe for his son Lewis. He addresses him by name in the introduction to the treatise and refers to him as "you" in the instructions, lending those instructions an immediacy one would hardly expect in the first treatise in English on a complex scientific instrument.

This Modern English version of Chaucer's *Treatise on the Astrolabe* is based on the edition by John Reidy in *The Riverside Chaucer* and the translation by R. T. Gunther in *The Oxford History of Science*. Unfortunately, Sigmund Eisner's Variorum Edition of the *Treatise* was not yet available at the time of this writing. What follows includes Part I of the *Treatise*, containing the description of the astrolabe, and Part II through the first four operations only. Chaucer's ten-year-old son with his newly acquired astrolabe would probably have been most interested in the first three operations that explain how to find the time of day, and the trouble Chaucer takes to make this section accessible to an intelligent child will also please any modern adult attempting to use the instrument, probably for the same purpose. Later he seems to forget about Lewis, and his prose becomes as complex as that of any other technical writer of his time. The fourth operation of Part II records Chaucer's attitude toward judicial astrology, an attitude perhaps as surprising to modern readers as the famous poet's writing of a scientific manual, and one that he may have been anxious to impress upon Lewis. Explanations not by Chaucer, most of them from Reidy's edition of his text, are inserted between brackets, and some further commentary is included in footnotes.[1]

In order to clarify his descriptions and instructions, Chaucer provides diagrams such as are found illustrating Euclid. Even when messy, these are extremely helpful, and their inscriptions in Middle English remind us that this is a medieval text. Most of the diagrams reproduced in this chapter's figures come from a single important manuscript of Chaucer's treatise.[2]

Introduction: *"Bread and Milk for Children"*[3]

Little Lewis, my son, I have observed from certain indications that you have the ability to learn the sciences concerned with numbers and proportions, and I have also taken seriously your earnest request specifically to study the *Treatise on the Astrolabe*. As a certain philosopher says, "He joins himself to his friend who agrees to the reasonable requests of his friend'; therefore, I have given you an astrolabe sufficient [adequate] for our horizon, calibrated for the latitude of Oxford. Upon it, by means of this little treatise, I propose to teach you a certain number of operations associated with this instrument.

I say *only* a certain number of operations for three reasons. The first is this. Understand that all the operations that have been found, or that might possibly be found for so noble an instrument as the astrolabe, are not known perfectly to any mortal man in this region, as I believe. A second reason is this. Truly, in every treatise on the astrolabe that I have seen there are some operations that will not completely fulfill their promise. [And finally,] some of the operations are too difficult for someone of your tender age of ten years to understand.

I will offer you this five-part treatise with very easy rules in plain English because you still do not know Latin very well, my little son. Nonetheless, these valid operations will be [comprehensible] enough for you in English, as they are in Greek for noble Greek scholars, and in Arabic for Arabians, and in Hebrew for Jews, and in Latin for the Latin people who first wrote them down out of various other languages into their own tongue, that is to say, in Latin. And God knows that in all these languages and in many more these operations have been adequately studied and taught, though by differing rules, just as different paths lead different people along the right way to Rome.

Now I humbly request every thoughtful person who reads or hears this little treatise to forgive my plain composition and my repetitions of words, for two reasons. The first is that complex prose and difficult sentences are too hard for a child to study. The second is that it truly seems to me much better to write a good sentence twice for a child rather than that he should forget it once. And Lewis, if I show you in my easy English valid explanations, and calculations not only equally valid but as many and as complex as are available in Latin in any ordinary treatise on the astrolabe, give me the more thanks, and pray that God save the king who is lord of this language, and all who are true to him and obey him, each according to his degree, the greater and the lesser. But be sure to consider this: I do not falsely claim to have discovered this system through my own labor or ingenuity. I am but an unlearned compiler of the labor of ancient astronomers.[4] I have translated their work into English only for your instruction—and with this sword shall I slay envy.

[Contents of the Treatise]

Part One. The first part of this treatise will review the markings and components of your astrolabe so that you will have a greater familiarity with your own instrument.

Part Two. The second part will teach you the practical application of the previous explanations, to such an extent and degree of precision as may be shown on so small a portable instrument. For every astronomer well knows that the smallest fractions are not shown on so small an instrument in the way that they are in complicated tables calculated for the purpose.

Part Three. The third part will contain various tables for the astrolabe: of the longitudes and latitudes of the fixed stars, of the declinations of the sun, and of the longitudes of cities and towns, and tables moreover both for the regulation of a clock and to enable you to find the meridian altitude,[5] and many another useful explanations according to the calendars of the reverend scholars Friar John Somer and Friar Nicholas of Lynn.[6]

Part Four. The fourth part will be a theoretical discussion explaining the movements of the celestial bodies along with the causes [of that motion]. In particular, the fourth part will show a table of the movements of the moon from hour to hour every day and in every sign according to your almanac.

After this table there will follow an explanation sufficient to show you in addition the way to work out this mathematical proposition so as to know, for our horizon, the degree of the zodiac with which the moon rises in any latitude [declination], and the rising of any planet according to its latitude [declination] from the line of the ecliptic.

Part Five. The fifth part will be an introductory study, based on the teachings of scholars, in which you may learn a great amount of basic astronomical theory. In this fifth part, you will find tables of the equations of "houses" according to the latitude of Oxford, and tables of the dignities of the planets, and other useful items. If God and his Mother the Virgin will allow it, [I shall include even] more than I have promised.

[Chaucer completed the treatise only to the end of Part II. The previous descriptions of Parts Three to Five document his intention, not the completed product.]

Part I

Here begins the description of your astrolabe. [See Figure 2.]

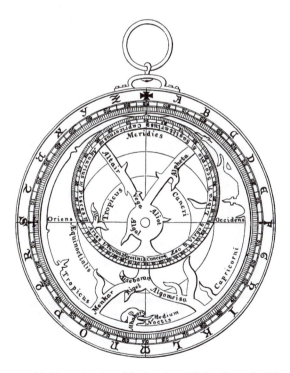

Figure 2. Diagram of the Front of an Astrolabe Based on MS. Rawlinson D. 913.

1.   Your astrolabe has a *ring* to put upon the thumb of your right hand
     for finding the height of things. Take notice that from this time for-
     ward I shall call the height of any thing that is found by the ruler [or
     alidade] "the altitude," without further discussion.

2.   This ring runs through a kind of *tower* attached to the "mother" [the
     main container plate] of your astrolabe in a hole sufficiently spacious
     not to impede the instrument from hanging plumb from its true center.

3.   The *mother* of your astrolabe is the thickest plate, hollowed out with
     a large cavity, the *womb*, that receives within it the thin *plates* [or
     "climates"] calibrated for different latitudes, and your *rete*, which is
     shaped like a sort of net or spider web.

4.   The mother is divided on the back with a *line* that descends from the
     ring down to the bottom border. This line, from the ring to the center
     of the large cavity in the middle, is called the *south line* or the *merid-
     ian line*. The remnant of this line down to the border is called the
     north line or the *midnight line*. [Whereas on a modern map north lies
     to the top, on an astrolabe the north–south directions are reversed, so
     that south is "up" and north is "down."[7]] For a fuller explanation, here
     is a figure [Figure 3].

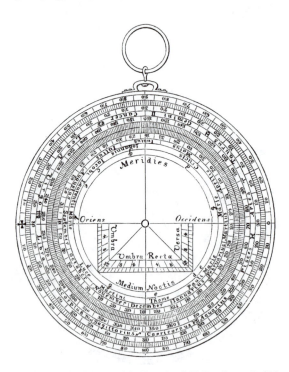

Figure 3. Diagram of the Back of an Astrolabe Based on MS. Rawlinson D. 913.

5. Crossing this long line is another line of the same length running east to west. This line, from a little cross (+) in the border to the center of the large cavity, is called the *east line* or the *oriental line*, and the remainder of this line, from the center to the border, is called the *west line* or the *occidental line*. Now you have here the four *quarters* of your astrolabe divided according to the four principle quarters [cardinal directions] of the firmament.

6. The east side of your astrolabe is called the *right side*, and the west side is called the *left side*. Do not forget this, little Lewis. Put the ring of your astrolabe upon the thumb of your right hand, and then its right side will be toward your left side, and its left side will be toward your right side. Take this for a general rule, as well for the back as for the womb side. Upon the end of this east line, as I said before, is marked a little cross (+), which is always regarded as representing the beginning of the first degree in which the sun rises.

7. From this little cross (+) up to the end of the meridian line under the ring, you will find the border divided into *90 degrees*, and every quarter of your astrolabe is divided according to that same proportion. Arabic numbers indicate every ten degrees above markers dividing the degrees into fives as shown by long markers. The spaces between these markers each contain a *mile-way* [twenty minutes, or the time it takes to walk a mile at the rate of three miles an hour], whereas every degree of the border contains four minutes, that is to say, minutes of an hour.

8. Under the circle of those degrees are written *the names of the twelve signs*: Aries, Taurus, Gemini, Cancer Leo, Virgo, Libra, Scorpio, Sagittarius, Capricorn, Aquarius, Pisces. The numbers of the degrees of those signs are written in Arabic numbers above, and with long markers dividing them into fives from the beginning of the sign up to the end. But pay attention to the fact that the degrees of the signs are each considered to be sixty minutes, and every minute is of sixty seconds, and so forth into infinitely small fractions, as says Alkabucius.[8] Therefore, understand well that one degree [of arc] on the border contains four minutes, and one degree of a sign contains sixty minutes, and keep this in mind. For a fuller explanation, here is a figure [see Figure 4, next page].

9. Next to this follows *the circle of the days*, 365 in number, that are represented in the same way as the degrees. [This circle] is also divided with long markers into fives, with Arabic numbers written beneath the circle. For a fuller explanation, here is a figure [see Figure 5, next page].

10. Next to the circle of the days follows *the circle of the names of the months*, that is to say, January, February, March, April, May, June,

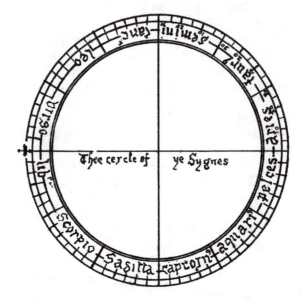

Figure 4. The Circle of the Twelve Signs.

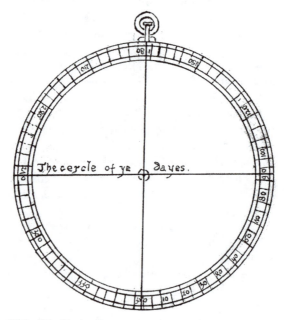

Figure 5. The Circle of the Days.

July, August, September, October, November, December. Some of
the names of these months were derived from their characteristics,
some by decrees of Arabians, and some by other lords of Rome.
Also, those months that were especially pleasing to Julius Caesar
and Augustus Caesar, such as July and August, had a different number of days. So January has 31 days, February 28, March 31, April
30, May 31, June 30, July 31, August 31, September 30, October 31,
November 30, December 31. Nevertheless, although Julius Caesar
took two days out of February and put them in his month of July, and
Augustus Caesar called the month of August after himself and gave it
31 days,[9] yet trust well that the sun stays no more and no less in one
sign of the zodiac than in another.

11.   Next follow the *names of the holy days* in the Calendar, and next to
      them the letters of the A B C on which they fall.[10]

12.   Next to the circle of the A B C, under the cross line, is marked the
      scale in the shape of two [carpenters'] squares or ladders. It is use-
      ful for many a complex calculation by means of its twelve points
      and its divisions. This scale from the cross line down to the right
      angle is called the *umbra versa*, and the bottom part is called the
      umbra recta. or *umbra extensa*. For a fuller explanation, here is a
      figure [see Figure 6].

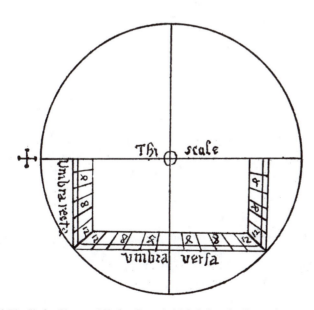

Figure 6. The **Umbra Versa** and **Umbra Recta** (mislabeled on the diagram).

13. Next you have a wide *ruler* [the sighting device usually called an *alidade*] that has on each end a square plate pierced with holes, some greater and some smaller, to receive the rays of the sun by day [so that you need not look directly at the sun itself] and to observe directly by eye the altitudes of the stars by night. [For a figure, see II.2.]

14. Next there is a large *pin* like an axle that goes through the hole. It holds the climate tables [latitude plates] and the rete in the womb of the mother. Through this pin there goes a little wedge that is called the *horse*, which holds all these parts firmly together.[11] This large pin like an axle is imagined to be the *north pole* on your astrolabe. [Figure 7 is a representation of the horse-shaped wedge redrawn from Cambridge MS. II.3.3]:

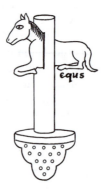

Figure 7. The Pin Called a "Horse". (Redrawn by S. Oerding from Camb. Univ. Lib. II. 3.3).

15. The womb [front] side of your astrolabe is also divided with a long cross into four *quarters* from east to west and from south to north— from the right side to the left side, as on the back. For a fuller explanation, here is a figure. [See Figure 8, next page.]

16. The border of this womb side is divided from the point of the east line up to the south line under the ring into *ninety degrees*, and every quarter is divided by the same proportion, as is the back side. That amounts to 360 degrees in all. Understand well that the degrees of this border correspond and are concentric to the degrees of the equinoctial [celestial equator], which is divided in the same number, as is every other circle in the sky. This same border is divided also with twenty-three capital letters [the number of letters in the alphabet of the time] and a small cross (+) above the south line, indicating *the twenty-four equal hours* of the clock. As I have said, five of these degrees make a "mile-way" [twenty minutes], and three mile-ways make an hour. Every degree of this border contains four minutes [of

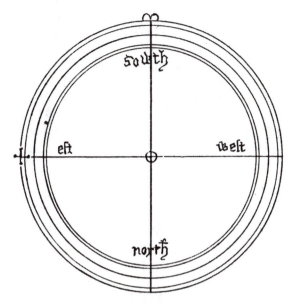

Figure 8. The Four Quarters of the Astrolabe.

the clock], and every minute sixty seconds. Now I have told you twice, and for a fuller explanation, here is a figure [see Figure 9].

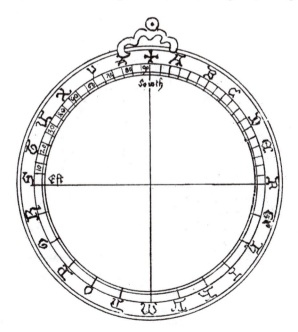

Figure 9. The Twenty-Four Hours of the Clock.

17.   The plate under the rete is inscribed with three circles. The smallest
       is called the *circle of Cancer* because the first point of Cancer turns
       always concentric upon that circle. At this first point of Cancer is the
       sun's greatest declination northward; therefore, it is called the *sum-
       mer solstice*, when according to Ptolemy the declination of the sun is
       23 degrees and 50 minutes. The sign of Cancer is called the *tropic of
       summer*—from *tropos*, which means "back again"—because then
       the sun begins to pass away from us. For a fuller explanation, here is
       a figure [see Figure 10].

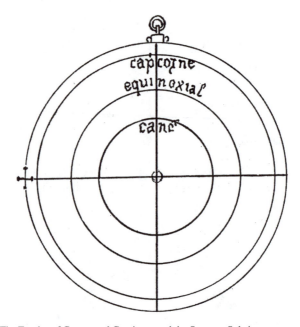

Figure 10. The Tropics of Cancer and Capricorn and the Summer Solstice.

       The middle circle of these three in terms of size is called the
equinoctial circle, upon which the first points [the beginning of the
first degrees] of Aries and Libra always turn. Understand well that
always this equinoctial circle turns exactly from due east to due west,
as I have shown you on the solid sphere [a celestial globe apparently
in Chaucer's possession]. This circle is also called the *equator* [or
"celestial equator"], that is, the "weigher [i.e., scales] of the day,"[12]
for when the sun is in the first points of Aries and Libra, then the
days and the nights are of equal length all over the world.[13] Therefore
these two signs are called the *equinoxes*. Everything that moves

within the first points of Aries and Libra is described as moving northward, and everything that moves outside these points is described as moving southward, in relation to the equinoctial. Pay attention to these latitudes [declensions] north and south, and do not forget them.

By the equinoctial circle the twenty-four equal hours of the clock are noted, for the rising of fifteen degrees of the equinoctial always makes one equal hour of the clock.[14] This equinoctial is called the girdle [belt] of the *first moving* or of the *first movable* [the *Primum Mobile*]. Note that by the first moving is meant the moving of the first movable of the eighth sphere,[15] which moves from east to west and [under the earth] back again to the east. Also it is called the *girdle* of the first moving because it divides the first movable, that is to say, the celestial sphere, into two equal parts at an equal distance from the poles of this world.

The widest of these three principle circles is called the *circle of Capricorn*, because the first degree of Capricorn turns constantly concentric upon this circle. At the first degree of Capricorn is the sun's greatest declination south, so therefore it is called the *winter solstice*. The sign of Capricorn is also called the *tropic of winter*, because then the sun begins to turn back toward us.

18. Upon this plate are certain circles called *almucantars* [which indicate celestial altitude]. Some of them seem perfect circles and some seem imperfect. The center point situated in the middle of the smallest circle is called the *zenith*. The outer circle, or the first circle, is called the *horizon*, that is to say, it is the circle that divides the [observer's] two hemispheres, the part of the sky above the earth and the part beneath. These *almucantars* are engraved by two and two [i.e., every two degrees], although on some astrolabes the *almucantars* are engraved by one degree, on others by two, and on others by three, according to the size of the astrolabe. The zenith that I mentioned is imagined to be the point straight above the crown of your head. The zenith is also the exact "pole" of the horizon in every region. For a fuller explanation, here is a figure [see Figure 11, next page].

19. From the zenith, as it seems, come arched lines like the legs of a spider, or else like the ribs of a woman's hairnet [an often ornate open-ribbed headdress], curving across the *almucantars*. These lines or divisions are called *azimuth lines*, and they divide the horizon of your astrolabe into twenty-four parts. These azimuth lines allow us to know the divisions [or bearings] of the firmament, and enable us to do other operations such as finding the position of the zenith [the place in azimuth, that is, the bearing (direction) of the highest point reached by a given star]. For a fuller explanation, here is a figure: [See Figure 12, next page]

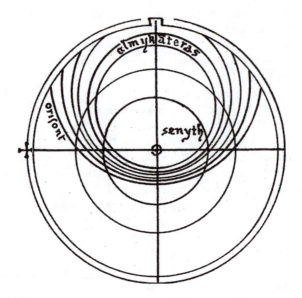

Figure 11. The *Almucantars*.

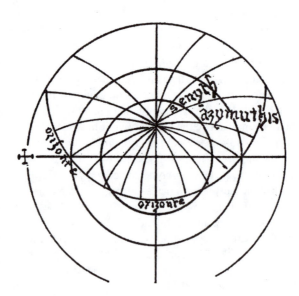

Figure 12. Azimuth Lines.

20. Next to the azimuth lines, under the circle of Cancer, there are twelve oblique divisions similar to the shape of the azimuth lines; they show the spaces of the *planetary hours.*[16] For a fuller explanation, here is a figure [Figure 13].

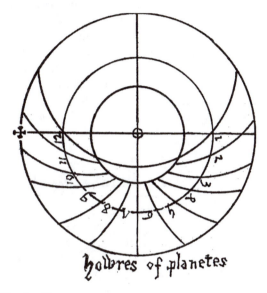

Figure 13. The Planetary Hours.

21. You can turn up and down, as you like, the *rete* of your astrolabe containing the zodiac, that is shaped like a net or a spider web, according to the classical description. It displays a certain number of fixed stars according to their longitudes and latitudes, if the maker has not erred. The *names of the stars* are engraved in the margin of the rete where they are located. [Sometimes names of the stars are engraved there, sometimes on the pointers.] The small pointer for these stars is called the *center* [or tongue]. Understand also that all the stars located inside the zodiac of your astrolabe are called stars of the north, for they rise northward of the east line, and all the rest of the stars outside of the zodiac are called the stars of the south. But I do not say that they all rise southward of the east line; witness Aldebaran and Algomaysa [Procyon]. Understand this rule in general, that those stars that are called the stars of the north rise earlier than the degree of their longitude, and all the stars of the south rise later than the degree of their longitude (I refer to the stars on your astrolabe).[17] The measure of this longitude of the stars is taken along the

line of the ecliptic in the sky. On this line, when the sun and the moon are exactly aligned, or else very close to this alignment, there is an eclipse of the sun or of the moon, as I shall explain later along with its cause.[18] The ecliptic line of your zodiac is the outside border of your zodiac, where the degrees are marked. [See Figure 14.]

The *zodiac* of your astrolabe is shaped like a circle, having a diameter according to the size of your astrolabe. It signifies that the zodiac in the sky is imagined to be a surface containing a latitude of twelve degrees, whereas all the rest of the circles in the sky are imagined to be true lines without any latitude. At the center of this celestial zodiac is imagined a line which is called the *line of the ecliptic*, along which is the continuous path of the sun.[19] Thus, there are six degrees of the zodiac on one side of the line and six degrees on the other.[20]

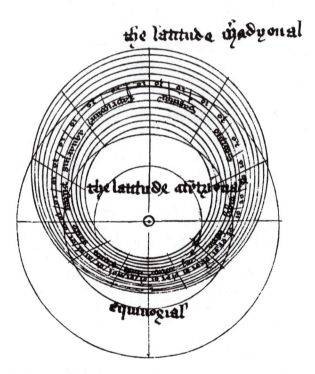

Figure 14. The Names of the Signs.

The zodiac is divided into twelve principle divisions that separate the twelve signs, and, because of the smallness of your astrolabe, [little Lewis,] every division in a sign is only divided by two degrees and two, I mean degrees containing sixty minutes. This celestial zodiac is called the circle of the signs or the circle of the animals, because *zodia* in Greek means "animals" in Latin. In the zodiac are the twelve signs that have the names of animals, either because when the sun enters in any of those signs it takes on the property of such animals, or else because the stars that are fixed there are disposed in signs of animals or shaped like animals, or else because when the planets are under those signs, they cause in us by their influence behavior and deeds like the behavior of animals.[21]

Understand also that when a hot planet comes into a hot sign, then its heat increases, whereas if a planet is cold, then its coldness diminishes because of the hot sign. And thus it follows of all the signs, whether they are moist or dry, movable or fixed, reckoning the quality of the planet as I said above. Each of these twelve signs corresponds to a particular part of one's body, and has control over it, as Aries has over your head and Taurus over your neck and throat,[22] Gemini over your shoulder joints and arms, and so forth, as shall be described more plainly in the fifth part of this treatise.[23]

The zodiac, which is part of the eighth sphere, cuts across the equinoctial [celestial equator], and cuts across it again in equal parts, of which one half declines southward and the other northward, as the *Treatise of the Sphere*[24] says clearly.

22. Next, you have a *label* that is shaped like the ruler [alidade], except that it is straight and has no pierced plates at the two ends. With the small point of this label you can calculate equations on the border of your astrolabe, as with your *almury* [the extrusion on the rete in the first degree of Capricorn]. For a fuller explanation, here is a figure [Figure 15].

Figure 15. The Label.

23. Your almury is called the *denticle* [tooth] of Capricorn, or the calculator. This almury is fixed at the first point of Capricorn [within the first degree], and it is useful for many an essential calculation in equations of various things, as shall be demonstrated. For a fuller explanation, here is a figure [see Figure 16, next page].

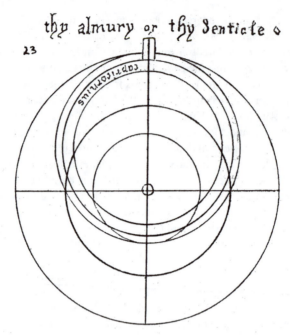

Figure 16. The Almunry.

Here ends the description of the astrolabe.

Part II

Here begin the operations of the astrolabe.

1. To find the degree where the sun is, day by day on its course. Find out
    what day of the month it is, and lay your ruler upon that day. Then the
    exact point of your ruler will be positioned in the border upon the
    degree of the sun.

    Here is an example: In the year of our Lord 1391, on the twelfth
    day of March at midday, I wanted to know the degree of the sun. I
    looked on the back of my astrolabe and found the circle of the days,
    which I recognized by the names of the months written under the cir-
    cle. Then I laid my ruler above this day, and found the point of my
    ruler in the border upon the first degree of Aries, a little within the
    degree. And thus I perform this operation. [Because of the Gregorian
    reform of the calendar in 1582, Chaucer's March 12th would be the
    equivalent of our March 21st; on the latter date we would find the sun
    near the first point of Aries.[25]]

On another day I wanted to know the degree of the sun, and this was noon on the thirteenth of December. I found the day of the month in the same manner as above, then I laid my ruler upon this thirteenth day, and found the point of my ruler in the border upon the first degree of Capricorn, a little within the degree. Then I had a clear understanding of this operation. For a fuller explanation, here is a figure [see Figure 17].

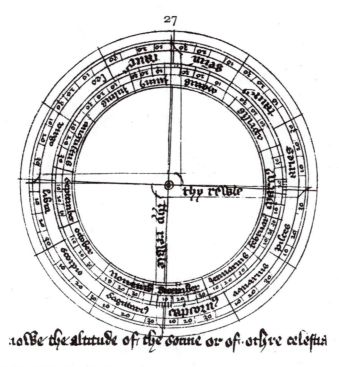

Figure 17. To Find the Calendar Date.

2. To know the altitude of the sun or of other celestial bodies. Put the ring of your astrolabe upon your right thumb, and turn your left side against the light of the sun. Move your ruler up and down until the sun's rays shine through both holes [or sights] of your ruler. See then how many degrees your ruler lays above the little cross on the east line, and take there the altitude of the sun. In this same way you can find the altitude of the moon or of bright stars at night. This chapter is so universally applicable that no more explanation is needed, but do not forget it. For a fuller explanation, here is a figure [see Figure 18, next page].

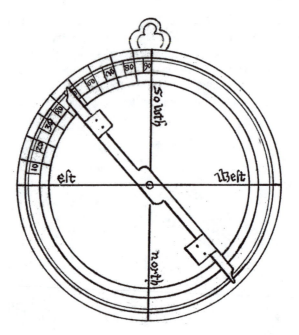

Figure 18. To Find the Altitude of the Sun.

3. To find any time of day by the light of the sun, and any hour of the
    night by the stars, and also to find by night or day the degree of any
    sign that is ascending on the eastern horizon (commonly called the
    ascendant or *horoscope*).

    Take the altitude of the sun when you like, in the way I have told
    you, and if it is before noon, set the degree of your sun among the
    almucantars on the east side of your astrolabe, and if it is after noon,
    set the degree of your sun upon the west side [as on a modern watch,
    having twelve represent south]. Take this manner of setting for a gen-
    eral rule, once and for all. When you have set the degree of the sun
    upon as many *almucantars* of height as was the altitude of the sun
    taken by your rule, lay your label upon that degree of the sun, and then
    the point of your label will be positioned in the border upon the cor-
    rect time of the day.

    Here is an example. In the year of our Lord 1391, on the twelfth
    day of March [the date of the vernal equinox in Chaucer's day, corre-
    sponding to our March 21st, as explained earlier], I wanted to know
    the time of the day. I took the altitude of the sun and found that it was

twenty-five degrees and thirty minutes of height in the border on the back. Then I turned my astrolabe around, and because it was before midday, I turned my rete and set the degree of the sun, that is, the first degree of Aries, on the right side of my astrolabe upon twenty-five degrees and thirty minutes of height among the *almucantars*. Then I laid my label upon the degree of the sun, and found the point of the label in the border upon the capital letter X. Then I counted all the capital letters from the line of midnight to this letter X and found that it was nine o'clock in the morning. Then I looked down upon the east horizon [on the *horizon obliquus*, not the east line] and found there the twentieth degree of Gemini ascending, which I took for the ascendant. Thus I learned once and for all how to find out the time of day, and also the ascendant.

Then later on that same night I wanted to know the hour of the night, and this is how I did it. Among all the quantity of stars I decided I wanted to take the height of the fair white star that is called Alhabor [Sirius], and I found it situated on the west side of the line of midday [the south line], at twelve degrees of height taken by the ruler on the back. Then I set the center of Alhabor [its pointer on the rete] upon twelve degrees in the *almucantars* on the west side, because it was found on the west side [of the sky]. Then I laid my label upon the degree of the sun, which had descended beneath the west horizon, and counted all the capital letters from the line of midday to the point of my label in the border, and found that it had passed 9 o'clock by the space of ten degrees. Then I looked down upon the east horizon [of the instrument] and found there ten degrees of Scorpio ascending, which I took as my ascendant. Thus I learned once and for all how to find both the hour of the night and the ascendant, as accurately as could be done with so small an instrument.

Nevertheless, I caution you to pay strict attention to this rule, without exception. Do not be so bold as to assume that you have taken an accurate ascendant by your astrolabe, or that you have set a clock accurately, when the celestial body by which you intend to calculate such things lies near the south line. For you may be sure that when the sun is near the meridian line, the degree of the sun runs concentric upon the *almucantars* for such a long time that you will certainly make a mistake about the exact ascendant.[26] The same is true of the center [pointer on the rete] of any star by night. Moreover, I know very well from experience that in our latitude, from eleven o'clock until one o'clock, the taking of an exact ascendant by a portable astrolabe is too difficult to perform (I mean from eleven o'clock before noon until one o'clock following). For a fuller explanation, here is a figure [see Figure 19, next page, with 20 degrees Gemini rising at 9 A.M.].

Figure 19. To Find the Hour of Day or Night.

4. A special explanation of the ascendant.[27]

The ascendant is definitely something to which astrologers pay much attention, in all nativities as well as in questions and the selection of auspicious times. Therefore it seems to me suitable, since I am speaking of the ascendant, to include a special explanation of it.

The ascendant, to describe it most generally, is that degree [of a sign] which is ascending upon the eastern horizon at any stated time. Therefore, if any planet should ascend at the same time in that degree, it has no latitude from the ecliptic line, but is in that degree of the ecliptic which is the degree of its longitude.[28] People say that such a planet is *in horoscopo* [the degree of the ecliptic just rising].

But certainly the house of the ascendant, that is, the first house or the east angle, is something both broader and wider. For whatever celestial body is five degrees above the degree that is ascending, or within that number, that is, near the degree that is ascending, astrologers according to their laws take that planet to be in the ascendant. And whatever planet is within twenty-five degrees under that degree that is ascending, they say that such a planet is like the one that is in the house of the ascendant. But if it passes the bounds of these spaces, above or beneath them, they say that the planet is falling from the ascendant.

The astrologers say, moreover, that the ascendant and also the lord of the ascendant [the planet that "rules" the zodiacal sign now rising, that is, whose domicile is there] may be fortunate or malefic, like this: They call an ascendant fortunate when no wicked planet, like Saturn or Mars or the Tail of the Dragon [the point at which the moon crosses the ecliptic when moving southward], is in the house of the ascendant, and when no wicked planet has any aspect of enmity [bad angle] upon the ascendant. They will cast [see] that they have a fortunate planet in this ascendant, and also in its felicity [when the planet is in a favorable aspect], and then they say that it is good. Furthermore, they say that the malefic aspect of an ascendant is the contrary of these things. The lord of the ascendant, they say, is fortunate when it is in a good place from the ascendant, like in an angle [the first, fourth, seventh, or eleventh house] or in a succident [in a house following the first, fourth, seventh, or eleventh house] where it is in its dignity and comforted with the friendly aspects of planets and well received. And also it is fortunate when it [the planet that is the lord of the sign] may see [be in good aspect with] the ascendant, and it should not be in retrograde [moving west to east], or combust [obscured by the light of the sun and hence diminished in power], or joined with some evil planet in the same sign. And it should not be in its descent or joined with any [other] planet in its descent, or have upon it any malefic aspect, and then they say that it is well.

Nonetheless, these are observations of judicial astrology [concerning the influence of heavenly bodies upon human affairs] and pagan rites, in which my spirit has no faith—or understanding of their "horoscopes." For they say that every sign is divided into three equal parts having ten degrees, and they call each part a *face*. Although a planet might have a latitude [declension] from the ecliptic, yet some people say that so long as the planet rises in the same sign with any degree of the face in which its longitude is reckoned, then the planet is *in horoscopo*, whether it is a nativity or an election [that is being calculated], etc. And for a fuller explanation, here is a figure [see Figure 20, next page with Taurus rising].

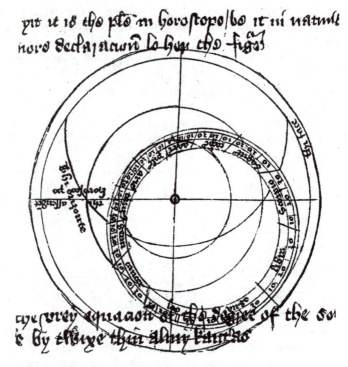

Figure 20. The Ascendant.

[Note that Chaucer does not end Part II with this operation; there are forty
sections in this part, plus a few more less certainly attributed to Chaucer. So
the *Treatise* itself does not end here, only this abbreviated translation does.]

Notes to Translation (Osborn)

1. For a complete discussion of the astrolabe, its parts, and Chaucer's treatise,
    with fine diagrams, the reader is referred to North, *Chaucer's Universe*,
    38–86. I would like to record here my enormous debt to that book and also to
    the work and kindness of Professor Sigmund Eisner.
2. Except for the illustrations of the front and back of the astrolabe that are
    based on drawings in MS Rawlinson, 913, and the "horse" that is copied from
    a drawing in MS Camb. Univ. Library II.3.3 of Masha'allah's treatise (upon
    which Chaucer based much of his), all the diagrams printed here are from MS
    Cambridge Dd.3.53 by way of Gunther.
3. This phrase, occurring in four of the many manuscripts of Chaucer's treatise,
    is a standard rhetorical indicator that the contents of what follows will be
    simple. J. D. North supposes that it was the addition of "an ironical scribe"

(*Astronomy and Cosmology*, 214), but in fact the part of the treatise translated here, at least up to II:4, really is far easier to comprehend than Chaucer's sources are.

4. Chaucer's main source is the twelfth-century Latin translation by John of Seville of an Arabic treatise ascribed to Masha'allah, though the author's actual identity remains unknown. The slim treatise that Pèlerin de Prusse wrote in 1362 in French for the future Charles V was based on the same source (see Laird and Fischer).

5. The height in degrees of the sun at noon, varying from season to season.

6. Although both Oxford scholars created important calendars, Chaucer is known to have been especially familiar with that of Nicholas of Lynn, upon which he based some of the astronomical detail in the *Canterbury Tales* (see Eisner, *Kalendarium*, 29–34, and Osborn, "Chaucer's Dantean Presentation of Time"). *The Kalendarium of John Somer* has recently been edited by Linne R. Mooney for the Chaucer Library.

7. If one points twelve noon on an analogue watch to the south, remembering that the sun is at the southernmost point of its daily arc across the sky at noon, this unfamiliar orientation becomes more comprehensible as one sees that morning lies east and evening west even on a watch. (That is why it is called an "analogue" watch; unlike a digital watch, it still bears some analogical relationship to the apparent daily course of the sun across the sky.)

8. The astronomer whom Chaucer names Alkabucius is Al-Qabisi, a tenth-century Arabic astronomer whose popular treatise on astrology was translated into Latin in the twelfth century. North suggests that Chaucer might have been thinking of using this treatise for his Part V (*Chaucer's Universe*, 192).

9. For an explanation of the factual errors in this statement, not relevant to the astrolabe, see Reidy's note in his edition (*Riverside Chaucer*, 1096).

10. These holy days, dedicated to saints and the Virgin Mary, are no longer celebrated in our culture, and the diagram places them in the wrong months, so this diagram is not reproduced.

11. In the *Squire's Tale*, Chaucer changes the probably wooden horse of his source into a steed of brass in order to give it certain characteristics of an astrolabe. (See Osborn "The Squire's 'Steed of Brass.' ") It is possible that he originally conceived of a story with the same exotic beginning as a tale for his son Lewis.

12. Although, as Reidy points out in his note, the Latin word *aequator* can be translated *weigher*, it seems "strange for Chaucer to explain an English word with a rare Latin word" (*Riverside Chaucer*, 1096). Here Chaucer may be thinking of the first two stanzas of *Paradiso*, XXIX, where for a fleeting moment the zenith holds the sun in Aries and the moon in Libra in balance, in a striking visual image of a scale. In "Chaucer's Dantean Presentation of Time" I argue that Chaucer uses this same image in the *Canterbury Tales* (diagram on 613).

13. A planetary daytime hour is the time from sunrise to sunset divided by twelve, and a planetary nighttime hour is likewise the time from sunset to sunrise divided by twelve, daytime hour and nighttime hour being of equal length only at the equinoxes.

14. This is a detail with which the rooster Chauntecleer of the *Nun's Priest's Tale* was familiar. He crows on the hour with more certainty than a clock, says the narrator, "For whan degrees fiftene weren ascended,/Thanne crew he that it myghte nat been amended" (For when fifteen degrees had ascended,/He crowed so that it could not be improved on (B². 2857–58).

15. Chaucer is referring to the celestial sphere upon which the visible stars appear to be fixed.

16. Later in Part II Chaucer explains these planetary hours. Briefly, each day begins with the planetary hour of the lord of that day; this is the planetary god corresponding to the name of that day, Saturn for Saturday, the Sun for Sunday, and so on. Then each successive hour is ruled by the planetary god who follows in reverse Ptolemaic order: Saturn, Jupiter, Mars, Sun, Venus, Mercury, Moon, repeated endlessly. It so falls out that thus rotating the seven "planets" through the twenty-four hours causes the appropriate god to fall on the first hour of the day named after that god. The idea is that certain planetary gods are friendlier than others, so that one should take their natures into account when beginning an enterprise. Chaucer dramatizes this belief in the pagan world of his *Knight's Tale*.

17. This curious rule is an effect of the fact that celestial longitude in Chaucer's day was based on the oblique ecliptic, rather than on the celestial equator, as it more sensibly is today, but the situation is even more complicated than that suggests. For Chaucer, stellar longitude is not a coordinate of the star itself but "the degree of the ecliptic which comes to the meridian at the same time as the star" (North, *Chaucer's Universe*, 68; see his further explanation and diagram, 68–69).

18. Chaucer does not fulfill this promise.

19. A modern reader may find it easiest to imagine this "line of the ecliptic" as the central line of a one-way highway. The sun sticks to the line down the center of the zodiacal band, whereas the planets can range over the full width of that highway.

20. On the rete of an astrolabe, the zodiac band represents the six degrees of the zodiac on the northern side of the ecliptic line only, since the outer edge of the band represents the ecliptic itself.

21. Chaucer may derive this idea from the *Consolation of Philosophy* by Boethius, a work that he translated and to which he refers or alludes frequently in his poetry. For one example of many humans referred to as beasts, see his short poem "Truth," 1. 18 (*Riverside Chaucer*, 653).

22. The association of the neck with Taurus explains why the rooster Chauntecleer in the *Nun's Priest's Tale*, knowing as much about celestial mechanics as he does (see n. 14 earlier), ought to have been more cautious about stretching his neck out to sing for the fox when he had observed that the sun was in Taurus (B². 3191–97).

23. The diagram called a melothesic man found in many astronomical and medical treatises connects zodiacal figures to different parts of the body (Greek *meloun*: "to probe a wound"). Skeat provides such a diagram, adapted from Trinity College Cambridge Manuscript R.15.18 (lxvii), and North provides a particularly attractive one in *Chaucer's Universe* (200). Such diagrams con-

tinued to be made well into the sixteenth century.

24. This is a reference to the extremely popular treatise *De Sphaera* by Sacrobosco (John of Holywood; see North, *Astronomy and Cosmology*, 234–35).

25. This March 21 alignment offers a quick way of telling at a glance whether an astrolabe was definitely made after 1582. To check this, one merely needs to see whether or not March 12 falls within the first degree of Aries; if March 21 falls on that date instead, the astrolabe is a later instrument. If the first degree of Aries is aligned with March 12, however, this does not necessarily indicate that the instrument was made earlier than 1582, because the new Gregorian calendar was by no means accepted at once by everyone.

26. The merely "sufficient" astrolabe that Chaucer has procured for little Lewis is not finely enough calibrated to take a precise measurement when the sun apparently slows down at midday around its highest point in the sky.

27. The ascendant, the sign that is rising upon the eastern horizon at any specified time, is crucial to astrological prognostication, as Chaucer says in what follows.

28. See n. 17, earlier.

11

The *Ecloga Theoduli*

PATRICK COOK

The *Ecloga Theoduli*, or *Eclogue of Theodulus*, was one of the most widely
known and culturally significant poems in Europe from the eleventh century,
and perhaps earlier, to the Renaissance. Its content, diction, and prosody
indicate that it was written in a milieu that was either Carolingian or post-
Carolingian, but under the continuing influence of the great cultural revival
initiated by Charlemagne, in or around the tenth century.[1] All other details of
its provenance remain unestablished. Over two hundred surviving manuscripts, most of which were bound up with commentaries on the poem or as
part of the collected *Auctores octo* (*Eight Authors*) used as grammar school
texts, attest to its remarkable popularity. Although the *Ecloga* was, like its
companion texts in the school volume, used for Latin language study, it surpasses the others in importance because it was the principal work used to
introduce young readers to the mythological heritage of pagan antiquity and
the major stories of the Old Testament, and because it offered them their first
extended experience of how these two essential traditions might be assimi-
lated. Since "every medieval schoolboy knew by heart" (Raby, 226) Theodulus's eclogue, it is arguably the most important pastoral poem between Vergil
and Mantuan, and its crucial role in forming a European-wide cultural literacy makes it a text whose influence on medieval culture can scarcely be
exaggerated.

Set in a pastoral landscape resembling that of Vergil's famous *Eclogues*,
this 344-line poem follows the classical "amoebaean" form in which singers
compete in a series of alternating songs. It opens with Pseustis (Falsehood,
according to medieval commentators, from the Greek for "liar'), a pagan
Athenian and therefore the representative of classical rationalism, playing his
pipes and herding his goats into the shade for relief from the midsummer sun.
Across the river, Alithia (Truth), a virginal descendant of David, plays her
great ancestor's harp and tends to her sheep (2). When the girl's sweet play-

ing entrances the animals and the stream, Pseustis, stricken with envy, challenges her to a singing contest. Fronesis (Prudence) enters providentially, agrees to serve as judge, and the contest begins. A series of quatrains follows, as Pseustis sings of twenty-nine incidents drawn from classical lore, each of which is answered by Alithia with a quatrain containing a parallel story or description from the Old Testament. Phaedra's rejection by Hippolytus, for example, is answered by Joseph's rejection of Potiphar's wife, and Hercules' labors find their comeuppance in the allegedly heroic deeds of Samson. Although the poem does not show the contempt for the Olympian deities evident in many earlier Christian writers, including several of Theodulus's demonstrable sources, the contest clearly reveals that Christianity and its God are superior to pagan polytheism. The sequence is interrupted at the mention of Dalilah's perfidy, which prompts Pseustis at line 181 to seek heavenly assistance. The alternating stories resume until at line 245 Pseustis, for reasons now less obvious, again waxes desperate and deplores the delay of nightfall. A brief interchange occurs on matters religious and pastoral, after which each party poses a riddle that remains unanswered. At this point Pseustis rather ungraciously concedes defeat. With the arrival of evening, which seems to have been delayed until the maiden's victory, the interchange ends, and Fronesis offers a few parting words. Some manuscripts also attach a brief prayer by Alithia, probably written several centuries after Theodulus, at the end.

The *Ecloga Theoduli* as Children's Literature

The *Ecloga Theoduli* is interesting to consider as children's literature because it displays a pronounced doubleness of appealing simplicity and provoking complexity. On the one hand, it offers many pleasures for the young student in the classroom. As if he is aware of youthful attention spans, Theodulus mitigates the tedium of his long series of exempla by breaking it into three series of declining length: the reader's heroic march through the first thirty-six stories comes to a halt with the comic relief of Pseustis's first outburst; a mere fourteen stories intervene before his next interruption, and only eight before the third series closes. The poem's hexameters are leonine (the line-end rhyming with the word preceding the line's caesura, an effect I did not attempt to capture in the translation), a feature designed to please listening ears, facilitate memorization, and restrict syntactic complexity to a level that is for the most part manageable for intermediate students but still challenging at times.[2] The narrative unrolls gracefully to represent a world of childhood, and one that surprisingly includes girls, unlike the Vergilian countryside. Theodulus emphasizes the youth and youthful emotions of his characters. Vergil's contest-ending imperative of duty to the flock at day's end, for example, is replaced by Alithia's fear of parental punishment if she returns home late, and Pseustis's initial jealousy and eventual befuddlement are decidedly juvenile. Many of the stories told by both contestants focus quite naturally on parent–child relationships. The perennial children's theme of punishment and reward continues within the quatrains, as figures from both sides of the classical/biblical divide incur divine wrath or favor.

The characters pose riddles (317–24), and the text itself possesses riddling aspects that would challenge young minds. The naming of characters is sometimes avoided (as Alithia charmingly declines to name her ancestral harpist, ll. 193–96), and the poet identifies his classical and biblical figures with periphrases of varying degrees of difficulty. Such practices would reward more advanced readers and stimulate younger students to emulation. Theodulus allows his classical/biblical parallels to range from the obvious to the perplexing, providing ample material to develop students' skills at comparison and contrast. Few readers would be puzzled as to why Alithia answers Cecrops's founding of sacrifice with the Cain and Abel story, or Deucalion's flood with Noah's, but what connects the snatching of Ganymede with Noah's faithless raven and faithful dove? Since the Ganymede story traditionally features Jove's eagle or Jove transformed into an eagle as the abducting agent, the two stories seem to use birds as their connecting link. However, since Theodulus does not mention the eagle, we can only conclude that he intended to teach the story through puzzling his young reader, at least momentarily.[3] That the missing element is an animal is also indicative of the author's careful attention to his audience's youthfulness. Animals are, of course, a staple of the Ovidian narratives of metamorphosis on which Theodulus draws copiously, but they feature less prominently in biblical narratives, and the poem's varied menagerie, which includes not only an abundance of birds and the expected pastoral sheep, goats and bulls, but also serpents, wolves, hares, horses, dragons, foxes, lions, an ass, a gadfly, and a cicada, link the poem continually to the medieval child's familiar world of the beast fable.

Classical Heritage and Christian History

On the other hand, some aspects of the poem are quite sophisticated and clearly directed toward a learned audience. Its allusiveness extends from the situational to the verbal and rewards readers intimately familiar with a wide variety of sources, although one cannot always be sure if a borrowing derives simply from convenience or from an intention to create a richer field of meanings intertextually.[4] The latter is most clearly the case with respect to the works of Vergil and Ovid, which are echoed repeatedly. As one example among many on the most detailed verbal level, the assiduous student of Vergil will delight to observe Theodulus's meticulous revision of the story of Salmoneus from *Aeneid* 6.585ff. in lines 237–41. Vergil's

own "fill in the blanks" technique leads one back to his sources to understand how the king imitated Jove's thunder. Vergil includes the detail of
his four horses, but elides the fact that Salmoneus created a thunderous
clamor by riding them across a bridge of brass, using the four-horse chariot ridden "through the middle of the city" to transfer attention from the
literal sound to the metaphorical thunder of the Roman triumph, in which
just such a chariot was ridden to the city center. Theodulus restores the
bridge and retains the idea of centrality by locating Salmoneus's fall "in
the middle" of it. Vergil's ironic use of the Roman triumph participates in
his meditation over the price of empire, but Carolingian poets turn their
eyes to this trapping of empire without irony, and so Theodulus makes his
representative of mad aspiration follow the common Carolingian image of
Fortune's wheel, whereby the proud are humbled at their moment of greatest height. The poem is filled with such meaningful reworking of borrowed texts, which manifest the poet's efforts to create a text that will
continue to create new appeals as its readers enlarge and deepen their
knowledge of classical literature.

Especially impressive in this appeal to an educated, adult audience is
Theodulus's evocation of providential order. Athenian Pseustis attributes
the timely arrival of Alithia to chance or luck (Latin *sors*, 1. 27), but the
poem's unfolding reveals that Prudence is really allied with Providence,
the idea of divine order that Christianity promoted to replace pagan
notions of a random universe. By allowing Pseustis to claim male prerog-
ative by going first, Fronesis allows him to determine the order of the stories. It gradually dawns upon the biblically literate reader that the order
controlling the poem's progress is the chronology of Old Testament history, as stories drawn with increasing randomness from classical mytho-
graphic history find their biblical counterparts, as if by miracle, in stories
that move with steady progress toward the Christian era. Moreover, the
stories are answered first by twelve stories from Genesis, then by twelve
from Old Testament books from Exodus through the prophets, and finally
by twelve more drawn from post-prophetic biblical texts. Thus is the disorder of polytheistic classicism contrasted with the Christian God's providential movement of history toward the establishment of Christianity, until
both a reference to the Incarnation and Alithia's announcement that she
could carry on the story from that point make Pseustis beg Fronesis to stop
Alithia's narration.[5]

Number symbolism, which Fronesis's early reference to the
Pythagorean mystical tetrad (35–36) invites us to expect, reinforces the
impression of providential order and the related message of Christianity's
assimilation of classical culture. As the quatrains progress from the pagan
tetrad toward the divine Tetragrammaton (324), they in all probability deploy
other numbers in meaningful patterns that remain to be uncovered by the dili-

gent researcher, but it must suffice here to consider a few implications of the number twelve. The hours of the day, long an issue in eclogues because the singing must end at nightfall, here become a point of contention, as Alithia's prayer to the sun for more time (36) seems to have been well received. At least Pseustis thinks so, since he interrupts a series that includes the reversal of the sun's course for Hezekiah (228) by lamenting Phoebus's delay. The sun's daily progress is linked to the months of the year when Pseustis twice refers to the zodiac in his complaints: first obliquely, when he refers to a distich of the Roman poet Ennius (288) that named all twelve Olympian gods (Green, 1980, p. 144), and then openly, when he wonders if the Olympians of the zodiac have left their posts (310). Both the daily and annual celestial movements, we are being reminded, and time itself, are ordered and can be manipulated by the Christian God. In addition to contrasting the truth of God to the falsity of the twelve Olympians, twelve also recalls the moment that the three sets of twelve biblical stories point to, when the twelve apostles superseded the twelve tribes of Israel. For an audience steeped in Vergil no less than in the Bible, twelve would also inevitably recall the famous division into twelve books of what was then considered the classical world's greatest literary landmark, the *Aeneid*, which Theodulus's contemporaries believed was written by a proto-Christian.[6] Such linkages through number are common in the most sophisticated literature of the Middle Ages, but it is likely that in Theodulus's hands such a technique was also a resource for developing children's numeracy.

The Carolingian Renaissance

Any such linkage between the Old Testament and Vergilian texts would be embraced by a Carolingian or post-Carolingian poet and audience because both works were essential components of the ideology underlying Charlemagne's renaissance. As conceived by the brilliant Alcuin and a host of talented poets and scholars gathered from throughout Europe to form the "palace academy" around the Holy Roman emperor, the court established at Aix-la-Chapelle in 796 was conceived as the core of a "new Athens," assimilating the classical wisdom of Plato and governed by a Platonic philosopher-king. It was also a "new Rome," ruled by a new Augustus who would administer imperial justice to the Christian nations in the manner defined in a line from *Aeneid* (6.853) that was perhaps Vergil's most famous: to battle down the proud and spare the subjected. Nevertheless, Charles's reign would surpass the previous heights of European culture in wisdom and power because the Christian dispensation had illuminated its souls with superior truth. It would become as well a "new Jerusalem" at the heart of a new "Christian Empire." At the same time that Emperor Charles was likened to Emperor Augustus, he was also considered to be a new David, heading a new dynasty that was the providentially ordained restoration of Old Testament kingship.

Charlemagne's poets eagerly returned to the Roman literary forms that had so effectively shaped and propagated the earlier empire's ideology. The *Aeneid* (despite the irony perceived by many modern readers) was, of course, the great poem of empire, and there were several attempts to write epic poetry in praise of the Christian Empire. But the principal literary effect of identifying Charles with Augustus was the revival of pastoral, which was considered to be the ultimate form of courtly poetry, the form in fact that Vergil had used to win Augustus's patronage. Largely because of Vergil's influential fourth eclogue, pastoral was also associated with the return of the Golden Age through the rule of an enlightened emperor. Charles's imperial coronation at Christmas in 800 initiated a long trend of pastoral poetry celebrating with millennialist fervor the new David's Christian Empire. Some time, perhaps as much as one or even two centuries, after such poets as Alcuin, Angilbert, Theodulf, and Naso created some of the finest Golden Age pastoral poetry ever written, Theodulus continued the tradition. What makes Theodulus's poem especially fascinating, however, is that is continued a literary tradition aimed at very sophisticated readers and, at the same time, functioned as a school text, extending, as it were, the Carolingian renaissance into the minds of children.

We can observe Carolingian vestiges throughout the *Ecloga*. Though by another hand, the quotation of the Vergilian formula for Rome's civilizing mission (350) in the appended prayer reflects the transfer of Roman imperial concepts to the Christian Empire that Charles and his poets achieved. The Orphean power over nature displayed by Alithia's Davidian harp is a staple of Golden Age pastoral, and Pseustis's childish jealousy signifies the limitation of an Athenian who has not added Christian revelation to classical rationalism. When David enters his descendant's narrative, his predecessor Saul is vexed by an evil spirit, reflecting how Charles and his Academy viewed the situation of the Frankish kingdom under the Merovingian kings (Fleckenstein, 45), which they labored to remedy through an integrated program, in Alcuin's words, of "government of the world, protection of the church, and the embellishment of wisdom."[7] A crucial part of the embellishment of wisdom was educational reform. The famous royal mandate "On the Teaching of Letters" reveals the depth of Charles's commitment to the liberal arts, a zeal that resulted in the study and imitation of classical literature to assist in understanding Scripture and in extending the Christian Empire through the conversion of pagans. Theodulus's innovative transformation of the Golden Age eclogue into a school textbook carried on the great Carolingian cultural project. Pseustis's defeat results in the handing over of the classical lute to his Christian vanquisher, which is both an image of the result of this project and an explanation of how it was accomplished.

Notes

1. On the debates over dating and authorship, see Green, *Seven*, 114. The suggestion made early in this century that Theodulus was Gottschalk of Orbais, based principally on the fact that the names Theodulus in Greek and Gottschalk in Germanic mean "slave of God," was effectively refuted by Karl Strecker, who described crucial differences in the two poets' versification. In the later Middle Ages Theodulus was generally believed to be a Christian author of fifth- or sixth-century Athens, and by some to be St. John Chrysostom (Quinn, 384–85). On the general issue of the eclogue's fame and influence, see Hamilton, "Theodulus: A Medieval Textbook," and for specific instances, Steadman. On its relation to classical and medieval traditions, see Hanford, 130–31.

2. As a revision of classical toward nonclassical prosody probably developed during the Carolingian renaissance, leonine hexameter had become a popular technique by the tenth century.

3. Beyond such programmatic difficulties presumably designed to provoke thought, there remain a number of irresolvable conundrums. On the classical side, why is Mulciber assigned Jupiter's role of casting thunderbolts against the Titans (87)? What is one to make of the sharpening of claws replacing the sharpening of teeth (120)? On the latter, Green, *Seven* (129), reviews the possible sources of confusion and in "Genesis" (85) cleverly suggests "gnashing of teeth." On the biblical side, why does Alithia claim that Jezebel blocked Elijah's flight?

4. For extensive lists of possible allusions, though without any attempt to explore the intertextual generation of meaning, see Osternacher, *Funfter* and *Quos auctores*, and Green, "Genesis."

5. The sudden revelation that Fronesis, though earlier referred to as "Mother Fronesis," is apparently Alithia's sister confuses the poem's age dynamics.

6. Alastair Fowler mentions two instances of ancient pastoral play on the number twelve, both of which could have influenced Theodulus in this regard: Vergil's first and ninth eclogues, each with twelve speeches "so that they follow in numerological terms as well as in content the ancient convention whereby pastoral poems ended with nightfall" (136); and Ausonius's two eclogues on the months, one with twelve and one with twenty-four lines. Fowler also believes that twelve's preeminent status as a temporal number led Augustine to divide his commentary on Genesis into twelve books. On the belief in Vergil's Christianity, see Comparetti.

7. This summary description is Alcuin's, in a letter to Charles contained in Duemmler, no. 308, dated 801–4 (my translation). On the educational legacy of the Carolingian Renaissance, see West.

Translation of the *Ecloga Theoduli*

Now hot summer scorched the Ethiopian lands,
While the sun's golden car wheeled its way through Cancer;
The shepherd Pseustis, Athenian born, herded
His goats beneath the pleasant shade of the lime trees.

With his body clad in a dappled panther skin,   5
He puffed on a shepherd's pipe through his two rough
    cheeks,
Sending its resounding voice through a thousand holes.
To a fountain nearby a shepherdess herded
Her sheep. A comely maiden of King David's seed,
Alithia played the king's lute to the swift stream.   10
The current stood still, enraptured by the sweetness,
Hearing the sounding plectrum's dulcet melody,
And even the flock grew weary of the acorn.
Pseustis could not stand it! Aching with jealousy
He blurted out toward the bank on the other shore: 15
"Why, Alithia, do you sing so foolishly
To these mute things? If you delight in vanquishing,
You can compete with me. Win and my pipe is yours;
Lose and I take the lute: we'll play on equal terms."
She replied: "Such words and such prizes don't move me.   20
I come to you now because one thing concerns me:
If you are beaten, you won't admit that I won.
But once a verdict is pronounced it cannot be changed.
Bringing the flock to drink, and to escape the heat,
Here comes my Fronesis! Let her sit in judgment."   25
Pseustis responded: "I see that fate has sent her.
Here you are, Fronesis! The time of day is right
For you to consider our game above your work."
Mother Fronesis replied: "Although both parents   30
Bade me to hasten home once the flock was watered,
And I should find swift punishment if late at all,
With confidence will I bring gladness to these shores.
You start, Pseustis, since you're a boy. She will answer
With pursuing zeal. Let Pythagorean four   35
Order your lines. May Sol, I pray, give us more time.

PSEUSTIS: The first to come was Saturn from the mouth of Crete,
           Meting out the golden age in every land.
           No father had he and none was greater in years;
           The gods' noble race glories in their ancestor.   40
ALITHIA: The first to live in green paradise was a man.
           At his wife's urging he took the serpent's poison,
           Preparing out of these cups of death for us all.
           The offspring still feel what the parents committed.
PSEUSTIS: Such splendors of gold Jupiter could not endure.   45
           He expelled his father cruelly with force of arms.

The face of the world was then shaded with silver,
And now Jove is foremost in the court of the gods.

ALITHIA: Cast from the holy seat, the first-created was
Exiled. Ashes turned nature's glory to ashes.   50
Lest we be spared through the fruit of eternal life,
A flaming sword before the gate forbids approach.

PSEUSTIS: Origins of sacrifice we owe to great Cecrops,
Who first opened the insides of bulls with the sword.
He raised shrines to Jove that posterity honored,
And he founded Athens, naming it for Pallas.

ALITHIA: Cain burned his harvest of crops in the sight of God.
His righteous brother Abel gave a worthy gift,
Freely bearing a lamb (prefiguring Christ's host).
Slain by his brother's sword, after death he still spoke.   60

PSEUSTIS: Arcadian Lycaon provoked divine wrath.
Once when Jupiter entered his house as a guest,
He tested the god's divinity, serving him
Man's flesh and bone; he raged a wild wolf in the fields.

ALITHIA: Enoch, grower of justice in our defiled orb,
Was rapt from the earth out of sight. As God's athlete,
Trusting the second coming of the judge, he will
Proceed with an ally against Leviathan.

PSEUSTIS: Waters rose from the Ocean, submerging all things.
Earth died in the water, and all who lived perished.   70
Deucalion, beyond whom no man can excel,
With wife Pyrrha restored mankind by casting stones.

ALITHIA: When godly revenge burst the founts of the abyss,
God saved Noah and seven others in the ark.
Thenceforth mankind would not suffer such destruction.
To human sight Iris unfolded through the clouds.

PSEUSTIS: On Mount Ida young Ganymede, pursuing hares,
Was snatched up in the air as Jove's armor-bearer.
The assembly of gods granted the abductee
The name of cupbearer, which Hebe had possessed.   80

ALITHIA: The animals all damn the raven's faithlessness,
Noah's messenger who did not wish to be saved.
But the dove brought back in his mouth a bough sprouting
New leaves. Armenia rose above as witness.

PSEUSTIS: Springing forth from mother earth the giants rose up,
Their one wish to overthrow the heaven-dwellers.
Mount was piled on mount, but Mulciber drove the
            whole crew
Into the cave of Vulcan with the thunderbolt.

ALITHIA: On the high citadel of Babylon, Adam's
Descendants built a tower reaching to the sky.   90
It incited God's wrath; their lips were confounded;
And they were dispersed. The town did not lose its name.

PSEUSTIS: For Paeon's slaying, Apollo's verdict was death
For the Cyclopes, who fashioned the bolts of great Jove.
Stripped of his deity by his fellow gods' wrath,
He was sentenced to a term of heart-rending woes.

ALITHIA: Ordered to leave his native land, Abram set out
With Sarah, without hope of receiving an heir.
At last to the couple wearied with age a son
Was born. She gave suck to the child she had carried.   100

PSEUSTIS: On crafted wings Daedulus cut the liquid air.
His son followed, but the fragile wax melted
He dropped into the sea. Under the weight of the flood
He sighed, while his steadfast father reached the cold north.

ALITHIA: The patriarch was unmoved by the sight of his
Son, and would have slain him, but a voice from above
Ordered that he be spared. He seized a ram with horns caught
In the thorn-bush. This child too followed his father.

PSEUSTIS: Stricken with passion for proud Demophon, Phyllis
Mournfully exchanged stiff bark for her human form.   110
Returned, he bedewed the trunk with reverent tears.
As if she felt the kisses, Phyllis sprouted leaves.

ALITHIA: Set to make Sodom ashes, the divine power
Agreed with the patriarch to spare Lot alone.
Segor sheltered him, but his faithless wife was turned
Into a statue of salt. Beasts licked at the rock.

PSEUSTIS: When Citharea battled the Argive forces,
She was gravely wounded at Diomedes' hands.
His companions lamented their mad leader's deed:
Turned into birds, instead of teeth they sharpen claws.   120

ALITHIA: Jacob encountered God and wrestled with him long.
When God could not prevail, he struck his thigh's sinews.
To lament the wound received by their ancestor,
His whole line of children declines to eat that meat.

PSEUSTIS: Charged by his cruel stepmother Hippolytus died,
Ripped by his team startled by a seal from the sea.
Diana's wrath could not bear the slur on his name.
She recalled him, but with the new name Virbius.

ALITHIA: Sold into slavery through his brothers' envy,
Joseph spurned advances from a lustful lady.   130

Bound in fetters, he interpreted the king's dream
And all of Egypt was put under him.

PSEUSTIS: Cadmus first discovered the letters of the Greeks.
Then he sowed the teeth of the seven-fold serpent.
When fortune was poised to destroy him, he did not
Submit, but made himself a dragon by hissing.

ALITHIA: Snatched from the waters, Moses vanquished magicians.
All feared him in the regions watered by the Nile.
He led forth his people, drowned his foes in the flood.
The Red Sea bears witness to Egypt's destruction.   140

PSEUSTIS: Europa's perfect shape fired Jupiter's marrow,
And turned the garment of his godhead to a bull.
The virgin defiled and Agenor eluded,
Jove gave her the name held by one third of the world.

ALITHIA: Fire and gold together formed the famous calf
From Aaron's fingers, while a mad rebellion raged.
When the stock of Levi restrained the wrath of God,
By perpetual law they received the priestly band.

PSEUSTIS: A priest gave luring bribes to Amphiaurus's wife.
Her breast flamed up when the jeweled necklace   150
    glittered.
A channel to deep Acheron soon drew her down.
The bereft son's hand offered her up to darkness.

ALITHIA: The Fates warned poor Korah to obey his better.
The dry earth devoured him and hell took him in.
But God himself buried Moses clandestinely,
Revealing to no man how to find his tomb.

PSEUSTIS: A gadfly drove Io to toss her horns about,
And wrathful Juno assigned Argos to watch her.
She sprouted bristling hair, bellowed instead of speaking,
Until she at last was restored to human form.   160

ALITHIA: Offended Balaam drove his ass on with his spurs.
An angel blocked his way, forcing the beast to halt.
An astonishing business! The animal spoke
To the man accustomed to producing the words!

PSEUSTIS: To afford Jove time in Amphitryon's bedroom,
Gleaming Phoebe doubled the course of gentle night.
His wife Alcmena allowed her son Alcides
To strangle the snakes sent by indignant Juno.

ALITHIA: Once for the chosen people, that a band alive   170
For battle might rescue Gibeon, for valiant
Joshua Phoebus stood unmoving in his stronghold.
Let all learn what rewards there are for holy faith.

PSEUSTIS: The club of Hercules slew the wakeful dragon,
Seized the pomp of Geryon and vanquished Hydra.
Cacus fell to it, as did the warder of hell.
At last Deianeira burned the proud man to death.

ALITHIA: Bedecked in the hide stripped from the lion, Samson
Slew a thousand men, destroyed the fields with foxes,
Uprooted city gates, burst the chains of sinew.
At last with deceit Dalilah cut off his hair. 180

PSEUSTIS: O gods of a thousand names, come defend your bard,
You who inhabit Dis and the starry regions,
Divisions of earth and pools of sounding ocean,
O gods of a thousand names, come defend your bard.

ALITHIA: Equal, unified God, greatness, glory, virtue,
Who was, is, and will be, may you be praised and served,
Of three persons and three names, you are without end,
Without beginning, bid us to vanquish falsehood.

PSEUSTIS: The wild ash-trees strove to follow, shedding their leaves,
Chanting songs of praise through the woods for Orpheus. 190
He moved hell's rulers, and Proserpina ordered
Euridice returned, with one grave condition.

ALITHIA: An evil spirit ceased vexing the king's body;
The boy harpist helped him with music from his strings.
He applied himself to shearing the hides of sheep.
In time his right hand succeeded to the scepter.

PSEUSTIS: Drawing plant extracts, the Cyllenian hero
With his wand called souls back from darkness into light.
So potent was his art that one can surely claim
The breast of step-dame Juno suckled Maia's son. 200

ALITHIA: Mighty Solomon asked for the gift of wisdom.
He was granted it beyond nature or custom.
The gifted man graced the city with a temple.
His treasure used up, love for women threw him down.

PSEUSTIS: When Dodona's oaks stopped dropping acorns freely,
Ceres, mother of plenty, pitied men's hunger.
Triptolemus she sent in a dragon-drawn car,
Who revealed to the world its first hope for harvest.

ALITHIA: Elijah bound up the clouds of the sky with prayers,
So that no showers dropped moisture upon the grass. 210
Brought to his homeland, the prophet drank from the
 brook.
He was sustained by food served him by the raven.

PSEUSTIS: The Gorgon's face has power to change the human form;
Those who looked upon her were hardened into stone.

                Bellerophon killed the monster with Pallas's help.
                He stroked the horse's plumes and launched himself
                    skyward.
ALITHIA: Jezebel hindered Elijah's flight from the land,
                When the fiery car drawn by horses appeared.
                The flaming chariot carried the prophet up.
                For love, his son's prophetic spirit was doubled.   220
PSEUSTIS: Aurora let Tithonus grace her proud chamber.
                Extending his life, she made him a cicada.
                Their son Memnon was buried at Troy, where each year
                He was venerated at feasts by flocks of birds.
ALITHIA: Sick unto death, King Hezekiah turned his face
                To the wall, weeping precious tears. His hours of life
                Were lengthened. He did not doubt the promised reprieve,
                For the sun turned his panting team back in its course.
PSEUSTIS: Let great praise go forth to that man who first set up
                The games held below the peak of mount Olympus.   230
                Hard-fought-for laurel covers the heads of victors;
                Pomp leads them home, while shame follows the defeated.
ALITHIA: The towns of Judah bewailed Josiah's defeat.
                A spring and a tree curse the plains of Megiddo.
                For laws and noble Easter he was mourned by all
                Ages, but especially by Jeremiah.
PSEUSTIS: Salmoneus aped thunder and brandished lightning,
                Running with frightful torch through the fields of Elis.
                Not suffering such a rival, in the middle
                Of a bridge Jove threw him down with a thunderbolt.   240
ALITHIA: Knowing no god but himself, the Assyrian
                King spent seven summers bedewed and wet with rain,
                A man turned into a beast. From him all should learn
                To be content with powers endowed by nature.
PSEUSTIS: Why do the steeds of Phoebus delay? Is our time
                Again enduring the misfortune of Phaeton?
                Why loiter, evening? The sheep have their fill of grass.
                The flock is fed, but Phoebus forgets to advance.
ALITHIA: The light of the sun is servant to human sight,
                Fixed it the role first assigned it when created.   250
                Why call on night? What do you wish? To deceive me?
                Your sighs pour out because your powers desert you.
PSEUSTIS: Fearing violation of his lovely daughter,
                Acrisius long guarded his tower's threshold.
                Adulterous Jove dropped a shower from above,
                Into the virgin's lap; gold corrupted Danae.

ALITHIA: Angry lions did not touch Daniel in the den,
        Whatever hunger they felt, with God guarding him.
        Habakkuk brought a meal to him through the sealed door,
        Transported to the kingdom on a single hair.   260

PSEUSTIS: Burn incense at the hearth, if you would keep your child
        Unharmed; so Latona commanded her children.
        From Trivia's shoulder hang a thousand points and
        Arrows, the punishment of boastful Niobe.

ALITHIA: Neither the weakness of old age, nor their manly
        Strength and virtue, could hold in check the old men's
           flames.
        But even as she saw herself stripped and fated
        To death, Suzanna triumphed over nature's law.

PSEUSTIS: The robust mind of men falls to women's lightness.
        They draw love-potions and defile themselves eating.   270
        What woman can do Tereus's bitter house knows.
        Wicked Medea knows, who killed her own children.

ALITHIA: Stop fouling the air with these aspersions of yours!
        Duke Holofernes learned to respect female strengths,
        Held by mad love for the illustrious widow.
        The Assyrians wept for his trusting a woman.

PSEUSTIS: Scylla burned with love—Minos twisted her insides.
        She stole her old father's purple lock. Condemned by
        Her man, she grew wings. Her father's sharp beak pursues
        Her everywhere. The air resounds through her curved   280
           claws.

ALITHIA: Offended by his wife's pride, the tyrant of Medes
        And Persians was moved by the beauty of Esther.
        Earning her way to Vashti's seat, she deflected
        A blow to her people by the first minister.

PSEUSTIS: The meadows turn green, trees spout leaves, now all things
           laugh.
        Come Helicon Muses! Proteus send your nymphs!
        Come chiefly, if you care for flowering Tempe,
        Olympians embracing in Ennius's verse.

ALITHIA: Fear and carnality are the roots of error.
        If hell has its gods, and heaven its own gods too,   290
        If the earth has some, or a bridge, where does it end?
        Are there as many parts as you think there are gods?

PSEUSTIS: On their own the bulls long to return to their roofs.
        Evening guides sheep to the clover, goats to the elm.
        If you don't go soon, the wolf will ambush your sheep.
        Pass, day, from the sky, since the maiden will not pass.

ALITHIA: If the wolf frightens you, sheep, on your journey back
              To the fold, seek him out, my cares, with upraised horns,
              Whom the holy Paschal Lamb conquered without harm.
              Hold your course, day, lest the maiden lose her triumph.   300

PSEUSTIS: Baneful to the sailor is glimpse of Helen's star,
              As is rust on crops, and serpent's hiss in the field.
              The mole roots up gardens, nettle stings the fingers.
              What god wished that all come into conflict so much?

ALITHIA: Sweet is a wife to a man, rain to the dry meadows,
              Mandrake to the barren, fountain to parched field hands.
              Surpassing all is that after our souls have shed
              Their fleshy garments, the judge's wrath is appeased.

PSEUSTIS: What pleasure has diverted the heavenly gods?
              Has the great crew of the zodiac absconded?   310
              Or do they all snore and drain the Lethean cup?
              Pass day, from the sky, since the maiden will not pass.

ALITHIA: The vault of heaven attends with vigilant gaze.
              He who sustained the earth and produced the abyss
              He knows not sleep, who created all with his word.
              Hold your course, day, lest the maiden lose her triumph.

PSEUSTIS: Tell me: when Proserpina went to her sad seat
              With a rule given her mother for her return,
              Who revealed her faithless tasting? Tell me, and you
              Will be praised as if you knew the secret of Troy.   320

ALITHIA: Sea is below land, land below heaven. Air stays
              Suspended ever in between. Say where the earth
              Overtops the sky's light axis, and I will grant
              That you can speak the divine Tetragrammaton.

PSEUSTIS: You have so overcome me with your arts today,
              I will grieve like Calcas when he lost to Mopsus.
              But I will not lose through a girl's deceit. Respond
              I will a thousand times, unless nightfall stops me.

ALITHIA: Would that Thales were here now, maker of falsehoods.
              Would that I might lean on the four evangelists'   330
              Books of reason, which state that God took human form
              From a virgin, and that task will not weigh me down.

PSEUSTIS: I beg, Fronesis, that you bid your sister hold
              Her peace, for love of Mercury, whose great son you
              Add to the rank of gods, as Capella holds.
              I concede it all and will not deny the fact.

FRONESIS: That which every mortal struggles to attain,
              And which to achieve will ignore mortal danger,
              Unexpectedly has God has brought you on His own:

To urge you to cease, the vanquished bows to his foe.   340
The Thracean bard moved a soul of the dead with
His lute. May my tears move you. Phoebe lifts her horns.
Sol seeks the ocean, submerging in the cold shade.
Give over what remains; despair brings no danger.

[Then Alithia, her foe calm though defeated,
Took up with her plectrum a sacred song to God:
Loving God, triune, almighty, holy, at one,
Who duly rules heaven, lands, sea, and Tartarus,
And who reigns over all things with unique virtue,
Raise all the humble to you, castigate the proud.   350
Forever will last your praise, virtue, peace, glory,
Your eternal kingdom without end forever.]

12

"The Child Slain by Jews" and "The Jewish Boy"[1]

JULIE NELSON COUCH

A child sings a hymn to the Virgin Mary, despite the fact that his throat has been cut, and he has been thrown into the hole of a privy. Another child, a Jewish boy, suffers not the slightest scorch when his father, enraged at the discovery that his son has participated in the Eucharist, throws him into a hot oven. Queen Mary has kept him safe. These two narratives, "The Child Slain by Jews" and "The Jewish Boy," exemplify the boundless power attributed to the Virgin Mary in the Middle Ages. Mary as Redeemer fascinated monk and miller, nun and mother, cleric and bureaucrat. In the Marian miracle tales written, collected, and disseminated for four centuries, Mary often saved an ignorant monk or promiscuous nun, but just as often she rescued secular characters: a mother, a noblewoman, a robber, a merchant, a Jew, a child.

The Vernon manuscript, c. 1390, a Middle English "spiritual encyclopaedia,"[2] supplies an exemplary cross-section of the Virgin's sympathies. In its extant tales, Mary saves the population of a city, a Christian child, a harlot, a Jewish child, a man with an amputated foot, a Christian borrower, a priest who has had sex with a nun, a man with quinsy, and a sexually incontinent monk. The predominant characteristic of Mary's interventions is her deliverance of the least deserving and the most helpless: the criminal and the ignorant, sick people and children. Although to an extent didactic, with occasional reiterations of simple, orthodox theology, the tales are more reassuring than pedagogical. They invite everyone to revere Mary as one would a loving mother, and they hold out the assurance of salvation no matter how insignificant, how little schooled, or how sinful a person may be.[3]

The diversity of Mary's beneficiaries matches the perception of the diverse audience of the miracle tales, one that consisted of both clerics and the unlettered.[4] The elaboration of child characters in the poems edited here suggests the inclusion of child readers in particular. The poems' focus on a child's devotional experience invites the young reader to participate in affective religious practices in his own terms of play and sensuous pleasure. In these poems, the unregulated forms of praise and worship exercised by the child character lead him beyond social and religious boundaries. In transgressing society's limits, the vulnerable child leaves himself open to murder and abuse. These narratives, however, are quick to assure that the firm hand of civil and ecclesiastical authority will defend the devout child. Thus, while child readers are allowed to imagine the ideal of a devotion that transcends fractious society, the poems also insist on the authority of the adult figures who maintain society's divisions.

In a larger medieval literary context, the representation of children in these two poems demonstrates that some medieval authors granted an active subjectivity to their child characters. Rather than mere objects of pathos, these children appear as subjects who manage their own voices and experiences. Even the Virgin Mary does not displace their narrative centrality.

Vernacular Mary

Tales of Mary's miraculous interventions were first composed in Latin and collected into large volumes, called *mariales*.[5] Told and retold in homilies during the weekly masses and the special days devoted to Mary, they soon found their way as narrative poems into Middle English miscellanies.[6] The Vernon manuscript originally contained a collection of forty-one Middle English Marian tales, each accompanied by an illuminated miniature.[7] "The Child Slain by Jews" and "The Jewish Boy" remain as two of the nine surviving tales in this late-fourteenth-century manuscript. In addition to its Marian collection, the Vernon manuscript contains collections of saints' lives and homilies (which include some Marian tales), as well as other religious verses, with many prayers and poems in honor of Mary.[8]

The idea of a child reader complements the hypothesis of a largely female audience for the Vernon manuscript. Its large size and high quality point to a well-endowed religious or educated lay group as commissioner or at least ultimate owner of this book.[9] Derek Pearsall sums up the critical consensus on the Vernon, contending that the manuscript was compiled and written in a religious house as a lay group's comprehensive "book of reading in the Christian faith" (*Studies*, x).[10] Specifically, the emphasis on female characters in the manuscript texts has suggested to critics that the intended audience was a group of devout women, either nuns or laywomen, perhaps associated with a monastery.[11] Both as mothers and as devouts, medieval women were often the prime teachers of children (Herlihy, "Domestic Roles," 121–23). Emphasis on the mother–child bond in these tales makes it plausible to suppose that this book was used by women to teach children. The active presence of children in these narratives highlights their participation in the learning of devotion.

In their earlier Latin forms, miracle tales were often given only in brief synopsis, with little narrative action. The Middle English verse translations add literary characteristics more familiarly associated with metrical romances: fuller characterization, direct dialogue, and enhanced dramatic unity.[12] One late-fourteenth-century analogue of the "The Child Slain by Jews," Chaucer's *Prioress's Tale*, predominates as the most famous of these poems, in part for what critics consider its superior pathetic and realistic portrayal of the little boy, Chaucer's *litel clergeon*.[13]

The two poems edited in this chapter merit the scrutiny of literary criticism because their representations of the child-protagonist are in fact more sympathetic and more detailed than Chaucer's.[14] The prominence of the narrator, Chaucer's Prioress, ultimately eclipses the role and voice of the little schoolboy. Her loud religious knowledge, rich with allusions to saints' lives, scripture, and liturgy, usurps the boy's narrative and highlights his contrasting ignorance. In contrast, the Vernon manuscript's miracle tales dramatize a child's receptiveness and minimize his ignorance.

The Child Slain by Jews

The Vernon analogue of "The Child Slain by Jews" is listed in the manuscript's table of contents as *Hou the Jewes in despit of ure lady threwe a chyld in a gonge*. In this tale, a beggar child sings in the streets to earn food for his family. Angered by the boy's incessant singing of a hymn to the Virgin Mary, a Jew lures him into his house and cuts his throat; miraculously, the boy continues singing. Further enraged, the Jew throws the body into the pit of a privy (*gonge put*). The boy's mother searches frantically for the child and finally approaches the Jew's house because she hears her son's voice issuing from it. The Jew denies any knowledge of her son, so she goes to plead her case before the mayor and his bailiffs. They force entry into the Jew's house and draw up the boy's body. The boy continues his miraculous singing until the bishop extracts a lily from his mouth on which the words of the song (*Alma Redemptoris Mater*) are engraved in gold. The boy sings miraculously once more during his funeral mass. (See Figure 21, next page).

The legend of the "The Child Slain by Jews" arose comparatively later than "The Jewish Boy," first appearing in early-thirteenth-century manuscripts.[15] In his study of the analogues, Brown divides the texts into groups A, B, and C. He identifies the A group as the oldest form of the story; its main features include the prominence of the mother's role, the burial of the boy's body by the murderer, and the resurrection of the boy. Group B represents a continental tradition that features a choirboy singing in church rather than a schoolboy singing in the streets; the priests, rather than the boy's mother, are involved in the discovery of the miracle. Group C, the latest version of the

Figure 21. The child slain by the Jews.

story, adds the detail of the boy's body being thrown into a privy, as well as the funeral scene (Brown, *Study,* 57–62). The tale is apparently related to the expulsion of Jews from England in 1290 (Brown, *Study,* 55–56).[16] Both the Vernon tale and Chaucer's *Prioress's Tale* are included in the latest analogues, Group C, a group even more explicitly linked to England through the chronicled event of the death of Hugh of Lincoln in 1255, for which King Henry III executed nineteen Jews on charges of murder. All but one of these C tales were written in England, yet the one exception, written in Spain, links the tale to the expulsion of English Jews from Lincoln. The change from the miraculous resurrection of the boy in earlier versions to the dead boy's posthumous singing is attributable to Hugh's narrative (Brown, *Study,* 60–62; 86; 94–95).[17]

The Jewish Boy

In contrast to "The Child Slain by Jews," the child does not die in "The Jewish Boy," which is listed in the table of contents as *hou a Jew putte his sone in a brennyngge ouene, for he was communed wit othur cristene on the pask day.* A Jewish father, discovering that his son has taken communion at an

Easter mass, casts him into a hot oven. The Virgin Mary keeps the boy safe, and after a rescue instigated by his mother, he, his mother, and many Jews convert to Christianity. (See Figure 22).

This is one of the oldest and most perennially popular of the Marian tales. Four branches of the tale have been classified, with the oldest, "Lady Dressed in Purple," hailing back to a Greek tale of the sixth century. The latest of the versions, "Jew of Bourges," naturalized the tale in the West and became associated with Easter.[18] Long before versions of the more anti-Semitic "The Child Slain by Jews" appeared, "The Jewish Boy" imagined a scenario wherein Jews were converted to the "truth" through the experience of a child. Though this tale still relies on a Jewish villain (the child's father), the earliest versions of the tale made his villainy less a Jewish act than one arising from the explosive combination of his vocation as a glassblower (with his own furnace) and his moment of unpremeditated wrath.[19] The later versions, including the recension in the Vernon, reflect the progressively deteriorating relationship between European Christians and Jews: In these versions, the father's original vocation drops

Figure 22. The Jewish Boy.

out so that his anger derives from his unconverted Jewishness more than the happenstance of his craft.[20]

The Child in the Miracle Tale

Child characters in medieval texts often appear as marginal characters, outside the proscriptions of a given social or vocational identity.[21] In both "The Child Slain by Jews" and "The Jewish Boy," the child character's receptiveness to devotion follows from his loose attachment to social identity, which allows any child, whether Christian or Jewish, to transgress societal boundaries. Both of these miracle tale children—a beggar and a Jew—are outsiders. The depiction of the singing boy as a beggar is unique to the Vernon; in the other versions, including Chaucer's, he is a schoolboy (Brown, *Study*, 105). As a Jew, the boy in the other tale falls into a group relentlessly persecuted for its "heretical" religion.

Though outsiders in the social hierarchy, both boys possess narrative agency within the poems. Granting the beggar agency in his singing of the song, the Vernon poem esteems him as an artist. In fact, the narrative emphasis quickly shifts from his work as *beggeri* (9) to his work as *craftus* (13). Celebration of the child's sweet voice overshadows the image of the child as a beggar; the unceasing commentary on this wonderful voice serves as a refrain throughout the poem. Moreover, the child's singing is something *he* does, not simply a circumstance that happens to him: *he* sings the hymn everywhere, *he* sings it from house to house, *he* sings it so pleasingly, *he* sings it so eagerly (21, 28, 29, 35, 36). His artistry is something he expresses, and the poem joins him in delighting in its beauty. Praise of the song as *deynteous* (27) highlights its pleasing aesthetic.[22] The poem represents the boy as a conscious artist and locates its devotional and aesthetic center in the child's singing.[23]

The singing child's artistry corresponds to the Jewish boy's ability to apprehend vital religious truths. The outsider status of children, particularly in medieval religious texts, initiates an active responsiveness to what befalls the child or what he discovers on his own initiative, a responsiveness that models the art of learning for a possible child audience and translates learning into a dramatic experience. "The Jewish Boy" stages a child's receptiveness to the effects of an Easter mass, reproducing the visual and liturgical spectacle within the church as a sensual novelty. The reader sees the ritual as if for the first time, through the eyes of a young outsider (52–54). The child is dazzled by the candles, painted altars, and gilded images. The child's mesmerizing experience of mass communicates the poem's overarching desire for a universal Christendom, a potentially utopian vision in which all children could go to mass without fear.

Here a central Christian project, its mission to the unconverted, is centered in the sensitivity of a child.[24]

Uniquely, the Vernon narratives register a longing for an earthly utopia in which a Christian child can sing in a Jewish street, or a Jewish boy can play with Christian children. Other miracle tales in the Vernon manuscript, like the "Harlot's Prayer," mention the idea of a universal Christian community that could include someone as sinful as a prostitute. The hermit includes the harlot in such a vision: "Bothe thou and I and alle othur / ffor eueri cristene is otheres brother" (Horstmann, *Minor Poems,* 146.63–64). Yet in the extant tales of the Vernon manuscript, the utopian ideal is more fully developed in the tales with a child protagonist. As a crossover figure, free from the limitations of social identity, the child exposes and erodes important societal boundaries.

The poem's allusions to Christ are grounded in the boys' crossover roles. The events of "The Child Slain by Jews" and the "The Jewish Boy" take place on Easter Sunday, and in both the relevant allusions are obvious: The Christian boy arises on his bier to sing a requiem mass; the Jewish boy walks out unscathed when the stone of the hot oven is rolled back. The saving of a child reenacts Christ's resurrection.[25] As a Christ-child figure, the boy in "The Child Slain by Jews" is also linked to the idea of Christian experience outside the bounds of clericalism and state authority. The singing child takes the song of a cathedral boys' choir out into the street.[26] He spreads a liturgical hymn to Mary into the city streets and across all walks of life. He sings at the door of a Jew and links hymn singing to the mundane necessity of getting food. Like Jesus not only in death, he imitates Jesus' nomadic, anticlerical life as presented in the Gospels. "The Jewish Boy" presents an idyllic scene of Christian children playing in a field where the little Jewish boy joins them (21–24). The Jewish child plays with them whenever he wants and comes to know all of their games just as if he were one of them, and the Christian children accept his company *With loue* (31–32). Such a harmonious scene assumes a distinct subculture experienced by children, whose playing opposes the surrounding adult culture in which the Jews of the city are confined to one street (15–20).[27]

Yet as in "The Child Slain by Jews," the child—by transgressing a religious boundary—makes visible the cultural fissures that threaten to dissolve this chimera of harmony. The boy's father does not accept his son's assimilation into the exclusively Christian "utopia" and intends to kill his son for his trespass; in turn, the Christian authorities kill the father for his attempt to reassert societal divisions even as their judgment reestablishes those same boundaries. Ultimately, the narrative's longing for harmony and for eroding boundaries is modulated by the anxieties latent in the representation of a vulnerable child, especially when that child stands at the cusp of medieval Christian–Jewish relations. When the free child does cross the boundary— when the Jewish boy attends church and when the Christian child sings in the Jewish section of town—his action provokes chaos and murder, not harmony, and exposes his vulnerability.[28]

To stem the anxiety provoked by the vulnerability of the child, governmental authority intervenes to resolve the violence, apparently confounding the desire for a society without boundaries manifested by the child. Patriarchal order brings resolution by reestablishing the divisions of society: by upholding the dominance of Christianity, and by subordinating the Jew to criminal or convert status in the Christian order.[29] Such a reassertion is anti-Semitic, in that it endorses assimilation or erasure of the Jew. Mary's miracles of saving and protecting the child become reinserted within a containing frame of patriarchy. The illustration accompanying "The Child Slain by Jews" reinforces this frame: Notice how the authority figures enclose the narrative triangle of the Jew, child, and mother, with the mayor and his bailiff on one side and the bishop on the other.[30]

Though the Vernon tales project parental anxieties onto a Jew and defer to secular authority, the enhancement of child subjectivity in these tales correlates with a distinct muting of anti-Semitic passion, refocusing the reader's attention onto the positive, momentarily utopian, affective piety of a child.[31] Despite the reassertion of boundaries brought by legal procedures at the end of each tale, the outsider child has succeeded in bringing diverse segments of society together: In "The Child Slain by Jews" the rich and poor, bishop and beggar, are brought together; in "The Jewish Boy," the Christians and Jews (albeit minus the father) come together, as the boy and his mother and the other Jews who witness the miracle convert to Christianity.

The Child Reader

The muting of anti-Semitism and the concomitant prominence of the child-protagonists' experience acknowledges the presence of an implicit child reader. However, patriarchal order does remain problematic in Marian tales. Often the full salvation of Mary's mercy comes about in miracle narratives without recourse to law and order. Thus, the robber who prays to Mary is saved without enduring any earthly or heavenly punishment; the abbess who has a baby receives no punishment from the bishop when he hears how Mary has already forgiven her and provided for the child. The active presence of civil authority in "The Child Slain by Jews" and "The Jewish Boy" may be directed in part to a child reader. Such an authoritative backdrop presents the societal limits that the child must learn to accept. To this anticipated acceptance the Vernon narratives link a sense of security: In both poems, the mother's pleas to authority are heeded and the child is found and restored. The request for civil aid, the dispassionate trial of the criminal, the traditional funeral procession and mass with all the appropriate accoutrements, the custom of going to church—all these additions in the Vernon tales reassure the child that the adult world around him is just and efficient.

Despite the involvement of legal authority, the child's mother in both poems retains a central role as a bridge or mediator between the utopian experience of the child and the overarching authority of patriarchy. The child's mother parallels Mary as intercessor. Each mother insists that the mayor and his men rescue her child. These tales, framed narratively and visually by the patriarchal order, still celebrate Mary's alternative, feminine practice of boundless mercy to those without social power by valorizing the mother–child bond. In so doing, they provide space for the subjectivity of a child who does not stay put within boundaries and still experiences the salvation of Mary. Ultimately, society's boundaries and exclusions do not affect the experience of the child. Whether alive or dead, the Christian child keeps singing; neither the Jew's actions nor the bishop's authoritative plucking of the lily from his mouth alters his devotional activity. Both inside and outside the oven, the Jewish Boy enjoys the wonder of Mary, no matter what his father does or what authorities do to his father. The result is a poem that teaches children effective practices within (and despite of) a framework of tradition and authority.

Readers as Children

Awareness of the centrality of the child character, with his characteristic vulnerability and receptiveness, refigures the reading of all the Marian tales. Meale has surmised that the attraction of women readers to Marian tales follows from a fascination with the idea of limitless, unpredictable power being held by a female protagonist, especially a mother; the tales display an agency in the maternal role not commonly attributed to it. Mary's "partiality toward her followers overrid[es] notions of justice, as represented by her son."[32] The earthly mother–child bond is strongly developed in the miracle tales, serving as analogues for Mary's bond with her son.[33]

Ultimately, this emphasis on mothering and on the mother–child relationship provides a vital image of Mary's care for all kinds of persons. Under the motherly eye of the Virgin, adults are cast with a childlike vulnerability. In other words, in the Marian tales, all are like children by virtue of their openness to the care of Mary. Such tales recast a religion, often delineated by its stark renditions of sin and punishment, as a perpetual experience of mercy, a perpetual experience of being parented.[34] In the Marian tales, the redeemed adult's vulnerability outweighs the awfulness of his or her sin. That is why alongside a tale about an innocent, curious Jewish boy one can read about a mother conceiving a child by her own son and killing that baby to hide her sin—an episode that should be received as horrific—yet is presented with the same wash of powerful forgiveness that saves the little boy in the oven.

In sum, representations of the child in these tales provide important examples of child subjectivity in medieval literature and good evidence for a child audience. These features in turn provide a valuable point of entry into the fundamental conceptions of the genre as a whole. In the two Vernon texts presented here, a child's experience is central to the didactic and literary movement of the poem. As the Jewish boy imbibes the golden marvels and the Christian boy sings with delight, Christianity is made freshly appealing— as a new, exciting experience of a child—rather than clunking through the poem, heavy with authority. The active, receptive subjectivity of the children in Vernon manuscript tales assumes a child reader, one who is being taught the practices of affective piety, the value of universal Christian harmony, and the sure control of societal authority.

Notes

1. I thank Geoffrey Russom, Maria S. Castellanous, Margaret Kennedy, and Nina Markov for their excellent suggestions and input, and their unfailing encouragement on this essay.

2. Robinson uses this term (borrowed from Gillespie) to describe the amplitude of this manuscript, "both in physical size and the number of its contents, the biggest surviving volume of Middle English writings" (Robinson, 26; Doyle, *Vernon*, 1). Doyle counts 403 items in the manuscript ("Shaping," 2). See Doyle, *Vernon*, 1 for dating of the manuscript (Bodleian Lib, MS Eng. poet. a. 1).

3. See E. Power, *Miracles*, xx–xxv, for her discussion of the wide variety of Mary's beneficiaries. See also B. Ward, Wilson, and Tryon.

4. One thirteenth-century compiler explains that his Marian miracles derive from "diverse times, and in diverse places, upon diverse persons of either sex, of different ages, of different condition and status" (in Wilson, 16). Both William of Malmesbury and Dominic of Evesham, two of the three early English collectors of Marian tales, specify their purpose as the edification of "simple men" (B. Ward, 164).

5. While some Marian tales can be traced back to the early centuries of the Greek and Roman empires (such as "The Jewish Boy"), the practice of collecting them into substantive volumes intended to honor Mary was uniquely a medieval activity. See Whiteford, 10–11. Starting in 1886,

Adolfo Mussafia collated and classified the earliest Marian tales, estab-
lishing the names of three basic groupings of the tales (*Elements*, HM, and
TS), which are still authoritative. R. W. Southern traces the earliest Latin
mariales to three English ecclesiastics—Dominic of Evesham, Anselm the
Younger, and William of Malmesbury—who, within a span of thirty years
in the twelfth century, assembled the three groups of tales that became the
base for all subsequent Marian collections ("English Origins"; 178–204).
Claiming an English origin for these groupings, Southern corrects Mussafia's conclusions about their provenance.

6.   The increase in popularity of these narratives corresponded with the rise in offi-
cial Marian devotion as festivals and the day Saturday were given over to the
Holy Mother. So popular was Mary that a number of miracles originally attributed to other saints or even to pagan legends were ascribed to her. On the history
of the medieval Marian tale, see B. Ward; Southern, "English Origins"; Wilson;
Boyd; and Whiteford. See Meale for a recent concise introduction. For various
manifestations of Marian tales in Middle English manuscripts, see Meale,
115–17, and Whiteford, 18–23. The earliest extant Middle English Marian
tale—*Theophilus*—is found in the *South English Legendary* (a calendrical collection of saints' lives) of Laud Misc. 108, a manuscript dated ca. 1300. The earliest group of Middle English miracle tales is found in Harley 2277 (Boyd, 8;
Tryon, 308–9).

7.   The titles are listed in the manuscript's table of contents, which was probably
added in the early fifteenth century (Doyle, 5–8). Meale corrects the number
listed in the table of contents to forty-one (117).

8.   On the specific contents, see the table on the back flyleaf of Doyle, *Vernon*.
The manuscript contains a version of the *SEL* and the *Northern Homily
Cycle*.

9.   Manuscript leaves measure 21.5 × 15.5 inches and the book weighs almost
49 pounds. Each sheet is a small calf skin with a thick, uniform matte finish.
Doyle surmises that the manuscript likely sat on a lectern desk or table as a
coucher or ledger book (*Vernon*, 1). See Robinson on the extraordinary
expense of the book and on the precise meanings of *coucher* and *ledger* in the
Middle Ages.

10. Both Baugh and Savajaara hold that the manuscript was written in a Cistercian
scriptorium, perhaps in North Worcestershire (Guddat-Figge, 277). Doyle
points out the Cistercian allusions found in the manuscript (*Vernon*, 14).

11. See Doyle, *Vernon*, 14, and Meale, 134–35. Meale cites nun ownership of
vernacular miracle tales (131–33). Doyle does note that other texts in the
manuscript point to a wider lay readership (14).

12. See Tryon, 310, who mentions the increase of "vivid characterization," more
"direct quotation," and better "dramatic unity" in Middle English versions of
the tales. Boyd also notes that the tales conformed to the characteristics of
Middle English narrative poetry when they were transferred into verse (9).
See also Meale, 120.

13. For Chaucer's additions to the tale, see Brown, especially 113–36. Readings of
the *Prioress's Tale* usually adopt Brown's conclusions and assume that

Chaucer's *clergeon* stands out in a genre of "simple moralizing and idealizing functions" (Pearsall, *Canterbury*, xiii–xiv). In the *Riverside* edition of Chaucer's works, Benson echoes the general consensus on Chaucer's realism when he comments that the little boy's interaction with his schoolmate provides an "amusing and convincing vignette of life in fourteenth-century schools" (16).

14. Scholarly focus on Chaucer's analogue has eclipsed the critical reception of other Marian narratives. More recent critics of Middle English miracle tales, including Meale and Whiteford, break this Chaucer-centrism, and both of these critics treat the Middle English miracle tales in a tradition of cultural studies that assesses the meditative and other cultural purposes of medieval religious genres. See, e.g., Woolf.

15. Brown conjectures a date of late twelfth century for the beginning of the legend (55).

16. See the early A group analogues in Brown, 1–20.

17. On Hugh of Lincoln, see Langmuir.

18. See Wilson, 157–59. Thirty-one forms of "The Jewish Boy" have been identified in at least sixty-eight manuscripts by H. Ward and Mussafia. The miracle has been translated into Greek, Latin, French, Spanish, German, Arabic, and Ethiopian. See Tryon, 324–26, and Wolter's collection of "The Jewish Boy" analogues.

19. In both "Lady Dressed in Purple" and the later "Covered with Her Cloak," the father is a glassblower. His calling drops out in all the versions of "Jew of Bourges" (Wilson, 157–59).

20. See Grayzel, 1–23, for a sketch of medieval European Jewish history.

21. Contrast this idea of childhood to the adult identities, for example, in Chaucer's *Canterbury Tales*. As Mann has well illustrated, Chaucer's characters contract their identity from their vocation or profession.

22. *Deynteous* signifies "Delightful, elegant, beautiful" (MED 1.a.), with its alternate meanings shading off into "luxurious, delicious, and epicurean" (MED b. and c.); it is a word that identifies something of artistic, sensual merit, not necessarily of devotional worth. The other references given in the MED under *deinteous* a. include a sword, a tale, a dove, and the sight of a falcon in flight.

23. Contrast this depiction of the child to the absence of agency in Chaucer's little *clergeon*: "Twies a day it [the song] passed thurgh his throte" (*Riverside Chaucer*, B^2.548).

24. See Rex and Grayzel on medieval attitudes toward conversion of Jews to Christianity.

25. Perceiving Christ as a child in this instance was one way devout lay people could grasp the feelings of loss and gain that the crucifixion and resurrection should evoke. See Herlihy, "Domestic Roles," 115. Keeping Christ a child in these tales also maintained Mary at the center of power. In Marian tales, Christ usually remains a baby, ready to do his mother's bidding.

26. See Brown, 132–36, on choir schools in medieval England.

27. The naturalized, idealized scene of children playing together is reinforced by the inclusive listings of all those who go to mass on Easter, a list generously benign in its inclusion of the Jewish boy. The poem includes all social classes, both genders, and all ages in its itemized accounting of the church-going Christians: the more and less, husbands and wives, fathers and children (40–46). This is a fantasy of inclusion; boundaries of age and station are transcended in a universal worship experience. This scene of an all-inclusive Christendom on Easter Sunday displaces onto the Jew the historically documented experience of great prejudice and intolerance erupting against the Jews at Eastertide. In this poem, the Jewish father displays intolerance and murderous, irrational prejudice and the Christians come across as all-inclusive—not only do the Christian children play with the Jewish boy, the Christians pity and aid the distressed Jewish mother on their Easter day. On the perils of Christian holy days for Jews, see Goodich, 7–8.

28. John Boswell has linked the anxiety caused in actual historical experience by the sense of a child being unanchored in identity—a child could so easily descend the social scale if not carefully attended to—to the resolutions found in medieval romance when the true identity of an abandoned child always comes to light at the happy ending (394). In a similar manner, these tales resolve the anxiety caused by the Christian medieval apparition that imagined the Jews as child-killers. Because of accusations of ritual murder against the Jews, the image of a victimized child resided at the center of European Christian intolerance of Jews. Christians justified their accelerated persecution and exclusion of the Jews by demonizing them as child-killers. On the history of medieval Jews, see Grayzel, Hill, and Goodich, *Other.*

29. In "The Child Slain by Jews," the Jew is judged for the murder, and the Bishop presides over the funeral rites of the boy (114, 129–39). In "The Jewish Boy," the mayor holds a trial by jury; the twelve men condemn the Jew to death in the oven (173–80).

30. Interestingly, Mary herself is not depicted in either illustration. The human mother in each case assumes the central, intercessory role, mediating between her child and the civil authorities.

31. By contrast, other analogues ratchet up the anti-Semitism. In the *Prioress's Tale*, for example, all the Jews conspire to kill the child, and the excessive vengeance deployed against them—they are all drawn by wild horses and hanged—falls outside any bounds of justice. In a later fifteenth-century Middle English version of "The Jewish Boy," the father is presented as shrewdly calculating the death of his son, and the Christians kill *all* the Jews. See Tryon, who gives an edition of this version, found in BM Addit. Ms 39996, on 351–52.

32. Meale concludes that the Vernon tales are set within "distinctive forms of female piety" (133–34).

33. In two versions of "The Woman Who Stole Our Lady's Child" (3; Banks, 315–16), Mary recovers lost children—a son who has been imprisoned and a

daughter who was snatched by a wolf—after the mothers take the Christ child from a statue of Mary. Mary becomes the baby-sitter in another tale: The mother has none to entrust her child to when she goes out to the field to take her husband his food. Their house burns down and they find their boy unhurt (Power, *Miracles,* 33–34).

34. In the Middle Ages, Mary aids the sinner who requires a maternal, merciful go-between to approach the stark justice of the Son. Devotees of Mary shifted the elemental mercy of Christ to his mother: Her *female* mercy—powerful, perennially sympathetic, even wily—completed a religious equation in which her infant son must finally concede to his mother's wishes. See Meale, 133–34. In the general imagination, the Trinity was often eclipsed by this more accessible family drama (see Power, *Miracles,* and B. Ward, and Herlihy and Bynum, for further examples of family imagery used in medieval devotional practices).

"The Child Slain by Jews"[1]

Wose loueth wel ur(e) ladi		*Whosoever, Our Lady*
Heo wol quiten his wille wel whi,		*She will requite*
Othur in his lyf or at his ende,		*Either*
The ladi is so freo and hende.		*gracious; courteous*
Hit fel sum tyme in parys,	5	*It befell; Paris*
As witnesseth in holy writ storys,		*city; befell; case*
In the cite bi-fel this cas,		
A pore child was of porchas.		*a poor beggar child*
That with the Beggeri that he con wynne		*what he could gain*
He fond su(m)del what of his kinne,	10	*supported some; kin*
His ffader his moder and eke hi(m)-self.		*also himself*
He begged in cite bi everi half.		*everywhere*
The child non othur craftus couthe		*was craft; competent*
But winne his lyflode with his mouthe.		*livelihood*
The childes vois was swete and cler;	15	
Men lusted his song with riht good cher.		*listened to*
With his song that was ful swete,		
He gat mete from strete to strete.		*food, bread*
Men herked his song ful likyngly;		*listened to*
Hit was an antimne of ure lady.	20	*sacred hymn; over*
He song that antimne eueri wher,		*sang*
I-called *Alma Redemptoris Mater.*		
That is forthrihtly to mene		
Godus moder mylde and clene,		*merciful; pure,*
Heuene gate and sterre of se,	25	*Heaven's gate; sea*
Saue thi peple from synne and we.		*woe*

That song was holden deynteous.   *considered; delightful*
The child song hit from hous to hous;
Ffor he song hit so lykynglye   *pleasingly*
The Jewes hedde alle to hym Envye.   30   *ill-will; hatred*
Til hit fel on Aseters day   *befell; Easter*
The childes wey thorw the Jewerie lay;   *through*
The Jewes hedden that song in hayn,   *hated that song*
Therefore thei schope the child be slayn.   *contrived; proposed*
So lykingly the child song ther   35
So lustily song he neuer er.   *eagerly; before*
On of the Jewes malicious   *One*
Tilled the child in-to his house;   *Lured*
His malice there he gan to kuythe,   *began; exhibit*
He cutte the childes throte alswithe.   40   *swiftly*
The child ne spared nout for that wrong,
But neu(er) the latere song forth his song;   *nevertheless*
Whon he hedde endet he eft bigon.   *again*
His syngyng couthe stoppe no mon.   *could no man stop*
Th(er)of the Jeuh was sore anuyet;   45   *keenly vexed; annoyed*
Leste his malice mihte ben aspyet,   *Less; might be espied*
The Jeuh bi-thouhte him of a gynne.   *scheme*
Into a gonge put fer with-inne   *hole of a privy*
The child a-doun ther-inne he throng;   *threw*
The child song euere the same song.   50
So lustily the child con crie
That song he neuer er so hy*gh*e,
Men mihte him here fer and neer,   *hear; far and near*
The childes vois was so heig*h* and cleer.
The childes moder was wont to a-byde   55   *accustomed to wait*
Euery day til the non-tyde;   *noon*
Then was he wont to bringe heom mete   *habit; them food*
Such as he mihte with his song gete.   *might; get*
Bote that day was the tyme a-past;   *But*
Th(er)fore his moder was sore agast,   60   *afraid, aghast*
With syk and serwe in eueri strete   *sighing; sorrowing*
Heo souhte wher heo mihte with hi(m) mete.   *she; sought; meet*
Bote whon heo com in-to the Jewery,   *when*
Heo herde his vois so cler of cry;
Aftur that vois his modur dreuh,   65   *went, drew*
Wher he was inne therbi heo kneuh.   *she knew*
Then of hire child heo asked a siht;   *her; sight*
The Jew with-nayted him a-non riht,   *denied; right away*

And seide th(er) nas non such child thrinne.		*there in*
The childes moder yit nolde not blinne	70	*would not; cease*
But euer the moder criede in on;		
The Jeuh seide euere ther nas such non.		*never was*
Then seide the wo(m)mon "Thou seist wrong,		*sayest*
He is her-inne I knowe his song."		*herein*
The Jeuh bi-gon to stare and swere	75	*swear*
And seide ther com non such child there.		
But neuer de latere men mihte here		*hear*
The child song eu(er)e so loude and clere,		
And euer the lengor herre and herre		*longer; higher*
Men mihte hi(m) here bothe fer and nerre.	80	*far and near*
The modur coude non othur won		*knew; no other way*
To meir and baylyfs heo is gon;		*mayor; bailiffs*
Heo pleyneth the Jeuh hath don hire wrong		*charges*
To stelen hire sone so for his song.		*steal her son*
Heo preyeth to don hire lawe and riht	85	*to administer justice*
Hire sone don come bi-fore heore siht;		*to cause to appear*
Heo preyeth the meir p(or) charite		*for charity*
Of him to haue freo lyuere.		*deliver*
The(n)ne heo telleth the meir among	90	
Hou heo lyueth bi hire sone song.		*how she knows*
The meir then hath of hire pite		*pity*
And su(m)neth the folk of that cite;		*summons*
He telleth hem of that wo(m)mons sawe		*speech, testimony*
And seith he mot don hire the lawe		*must*
And hoteth hem with hym to wende	95	*commands; go*
To bringe this wo(m)mo(n)s cause to ende.		*conclusion, resolution*
Whon thei cu(m) thider for al heore noyse,		*despite; noise*
Anon thei herde the childes voyse,		
Riht as an angls vois hit were,		*Like; angel's*
Thei herde hi(m) neuer synge so clere.	100	
Ther the meir maketh entre		*forces entry*
And of the child he asketh lyuere.		
The Jeuh may nought the meir refuse		
He of the child hym wel excuse;		*claims innocent*
But nede he moste knouleche his wro(n)g	105	*must acknowledge*
A-teynt bi the childes song.		*convicted*
The meir let serchen hym so longe		
Til he was fou(n)den in the gonge,		*privy*
Fful depe i-drouned in fulye of fen.		*in filthy dung*
The meir het drawe the child vp then	110	*commanded; drawn up*

With ffen and ffulye riht foule bi-whorue(n)   *having become*
And eke the childes throte i-coruen.   *cut*
Anon riht er thei passede forthere,   *left from there*
The Jeuh was jugget for that morthere;   *judged; murder*
And er the peple passede in sonder   115   *before, separate ways*
The bisschop was comen to seo that wo(n)der.
In p(re)se(n)ce of Bisschop and alle i-fere   *all the company*
The child song euere i-liche clere.   *equally*
The Bisschop serchede with his hond,   *reached; hand*
With-inne the childes throte he fond   120   *found*
A lilie flour so briht and cler.   *lily flower*
So feir a lylie nas neuere seyen er   *fair; never seen before*
With guldene lettres eueri-wher   *golden*
Alma Redemptoris Mater.
Anon that lilie out was taken,   125   *Immediately*
The childes song bi-gon to slaken;   *slake*
That swete song was herd no more,
But as a ded cors the child lay thore.   *dead corpse; there*
The Bisschop with gret solempnete   *solemnity, ceremony*
Bad bere the cors thorw al the cite,   130   *ordered; be borne*
And hym-self with p(ro)cessioun
Com with the cors thorw al the toun.
W(i)th prestes and clerkes that couthe(n)
    syngen
And alle the belles he het hem ryngen;
With torches bre(n)nynge and clothus riche 135   *burning*
With worschipe thei ladden that holi liche.   *led; body*
In-to the munstre whon thei kem   *church; came*
Bi-gonne the masse of Requiem
As for the dede men is wont.   *the custom*
But thus sone thei weren i-stunt   140   *astounded*
The cors arros in heore p(re)sens   *arose; their*
Bi-gon then *salue sancta parens.*   *Begun (to sing)*
Men mihte wel wite(n) the sothe ther bi,   *know, learn; truth*
The childe hedde i-seruet vr swete ladi   *served; our*
That worschipede hi(m) so on erthe her   145   *who honored*
And brouhte his soule to blisse al cler.   *bliss, heaven*
Th(er)fore I rede that eueri mon   *advise*
Serue that ladi wel as he con   *serve*
And loue hire in his beste wyse;   *as best he can*
Heo wol wel quite him his seruise.   150   *repay*
Now Marie for thi muchele miht   *with; great power*
Help us to heuene that is so briht.   *bright*

The Jewish Boy

Lord makere of alle thing,		
Almihti God in maieste		*almighty; majesty*
That eu(er) was with-oute biginning		
And art and euermore schal be,		
Grau(n)te vs bothe miht and space	5	
So to serue the to pay		*thee; to satisfaction*
That we mowe thorw thi grace		*may be able to*
Wone with the for euere and ay.		*dwell*
Of the miracles of vre ladi,		*Our Lady*
We ouhten wel to hauen in muynde	10	*mind*
That writen beth in soth stori,		*are; true story*
Hou helplich heo is eu(er)e to mo(n)kynde.		*helpful*
Sumtyme fel in on cite,		*(it) befell; a*
Herkneth wel and ye may here,		*hear*
As Jewes weren i-wont to be	15	*where; accustomed*
Among the cristen and wone i-fere:		*Christians; lived*
The cristene woneden in on halue		*one half*
Of that cite as I the hete,		*tell you*
And alle the Jewes bi hem-selue		*by themselves*
Were stihlet to wone in a strete.	20	*compelled; divine*
The cristene children in a crofte		*small, enclosed field*
I-mad hem hedden a wel feir plas;		*had made themselves*
Ther-inne a Jewes child ful ofte		
With hem to pleyen i-wont he was.		*them; play*
The childes ffader nom non hede,	25	*father; took no heed*
He to his child he sette non eiye.		*eye*
Therfore the child bothe com and eode		*came and went*
As ofte as euere hem luste to pleye;		*it pleased them, wished*
So ofte to pleyen hem fel i-fere		*befell to play together*
The Jewes sone on heore pleyes coude	30	*games; knew (how to do)*
That riht as on of hem he were;		*as (if) one of them*
With loue therfore thei him alouwede.		*love; they allowed him*
At an Aster tyme bi-tidde		*happened at Easter*
Whon cristen made solempnite,		*religious rites*
A menskful munstre was mad amidde	35	*exalted church*
As semed best in that citéé;		
Therto the cristene peple can drawe		*did draw, drew*
To here bothe mateyns and eke masse		*matins; mass*
As falleth bi the cristene lawe		*in keeping with*
Bothe to more and eke to lasse.	40	*(everyone)*
Eueri mon in his array,		*position, proper order*

Bothe housbonde and wyf also,
As falleth wel for aster day,
And al as cristene men schul do;
The children foleweden heore fadre(s) i-fere   *45*   *followed their fathers*
As thei weore euere i-wont to do.   *their habit*
The Jewes child with wel good chere
With hem wel fayn was for to go.   *with them; happy, eager*
With-inne the chirche whon he was riht
Him thouhte he nas neu(er) er so glad   *50*   *he was never before*
As he was of that semeli siht;   *splendid, seemly sight*
Such on bi-fore neuer seye he had,   *(a) one; seen*
Bothe lau(m)pes & tapers bre(n)ni(n)de briht,   *burning bright*
And Auters curiousliche de-peynt,   *altars; skillfully*
                                                                 decorated

Images ful deinteousliche i-diht,   *55*   *beautifully made*
And guld of moni a good corseynt.   *gilt; saint's body, relic*
A comeli qween in o chayer   *chair*
Fful semeli sat al greithed in golde,   *dressed*
A blisful Babe on arm heo beer   *on (her) arm she bears*
Fful kyngly corouned as he scholde.   *60*   *crowned*
Of that ladi the child tok hede   *paid attention*
And of that blisful Babe also,
Hou folk bi-foren heore bedes bede   *offered their prayers*
As cristen men beth wont to do.
The Jewes child eu(er)e tok such yeme   *65*   *heed*
To alle sihtes that he ther seih,   *saw*
Him thhou*h*te hem alle so swete to seme
For joye hi(m) thou*h*te i-rauessched neih.   *Enraptured, transported*
Whon hei*h* masse of that day was do,   *when high mass; done*
The prest bad alle men knelen a-doun,   *70*
With "confiteor"[2] as falleth ther to
He giueth hem absolucioun.   *absolution*
He biddeth hem more and lasse also
To vengen heor sauiour buske(n) he(m) bou(n).   *savior; prepare*
                                                                 themselves

The Jewes child tok tente ther-to   *75*   *paid attention*
Among the cristene he dude hi(m) doun.   *did (knelt)*
Among the pres thauh he were poselet,   *crowd; jostled*
He spared no thing for no drede,   *fear*
Among the cristene til he were hoselet.   *received Communion*
Of such a child me tok non hede.   *80*   *men*
To ende whon alle thing was brouht

And eueri cristene drouh him hom,		*went, drew*
The Jeuh thorw toune his child hath souht		*sought*
And saih wher he from chirche com.		*saw*
He asked his sone wher he hedde ben	85	
Whil he hedde souht hi(m) al that day;		
Al riht as he hedde i-don and seon		*just*
The child him rikenet al the aray.		*told; festivities*
His ffader th(er)fore wox wood wroth		*mad (with) anger*
And seide anon, "Thou getest thi mede!"	90	*said; reward*
And to his houene al hot he goth,		*oven; goes*
That glemede as glowyng as a glede.		*gleamed; live coal*
In-to the houene the child he caste,		
To askes he thoug*h*te the child to brenne;		*ashes; to burn*
And with the mouth ston he steketh hi(m) faste	95	*locked him up securely*
And thouhte th(at) neu(er) couth scholde hi(m) kenne		*kin should find him out*
Th(er)of whon his moder herde		
In a stude ther as heo stood,		*In a stupor*
As ffreyed in ffrenesye heo ferde,		*frightened, frenzy; fared*
Ffor wo heo wente as waxen wood.	100	*woe went crazy*
Euer hotyng out heo tar hire her		*calling; tore her hair*
In eueri stret of that citee,		
Nou in nou out so eueriwher;		
Men wondret on hire and hedde pite.		*wondered; pity*
Bothe meir and Bailifs of the toun,	105	
Whon thei herden of that cri,		
Thei aresten hire bi resoun,		*stopped*
Amaden chalange enchesun whi		*questioned why*
Heo criede so in that cite		*she cried*
And putte the Peple in such affray	110	*consternation*
To serwen in such solempnite		*sorrow; during*
And nomeliche on heore Aster day.		*namely*
As sone as heo mihte sece of wepe,		*could cease weeping*
This was the seyinge of hire sawe:		*speech, story*
"Sires ye han this citéé to kepe	115	
As lordus han to lede the lawe.		*uphold*
Allas! Allas! I am i-schent		*destroyed*
And help of ow me mot bi-houen;		*you; I require*
I prey ow of just juggement,		
Mi cause I schal bi-fore you p(re)uen.	120	*prove*
Mi hosebonde hath my child i-brent,		*burnt*
I-stopped him in a glouwyng houen.		

Goth seoth sires bi on assent   *go see; one assent*
And I schal giue ow gold to glouen."   *a bribe*
Bothe meir and Baylifs with folk i-fere   125
To the Jewes houene ben gon;   *oven*
As sone as thei thider come were,
The meir comau(n)det, "Doth doun the ston!"   *move the stone*
Ther eu(er)i mon wel mihte i-seo
The houene roof that was so rou(n)d,   130
Hou hit was Blasyng al of bleo   *with brightness*
As glouwyng glos from roof to grou(n)t.   *glass*
The child sat th(er)e bothe hol and sound   *whole*
Ne nouht i-harmet hond ny her,   *hand, hair unharmed*
A-midde the gledes of the ground   135
As he seete in cool erber.   *as if; sat; arbor*
The childes moder whon heo that seih
Hire thouhte heo nas neuer er so glad;
Into the houene heo sturte him neih   *jumped to him*
Thus sone with hire him out heo had.   140   *soon*
And al the peple there present
Wondred on that selly siht   *surprising, marvelous*
And heried god with good entent   *praised God*
Ffor miracle is more then monnes miht.   *beyond man's power*
Hou he hath non harmes hent   145   *received no harm*
Among the brondes that bre(n)neth so briht,   *flames*
Thei asken of him bi on assent;   *ask him together*
The child onswered a non riht.
"Of alle the murthes that I haue had mirths,   *pleasures*
In al my lyf yit hider-to,   150
Ne was I neuere of gleo so glad   *merriment*
As aftur I was in the houene i-do.   *put*
Bothe Brondes and Gledes   *brands and embers*
That weren bi-nethen vnder my fote
As feire floures feithfully   155   *fair, beautiful; flowers*
As special spices me thhou*gh*te he(m) swote.
The blisful Qwen that maiden milde,
That sitteth in chirche in hih chayer,
With that comely kyng hire childe,
That Blisful Babe on Barm heo ber,   160   *bosom*
Ffrom alle the schydes thei cu(n)ne me schilde,   *firewood, shield*
Ffrom gledes and brondes th(at) bre(n)de
    so cler,
Ffrom alle the flaumes that flowe(n) so wilde,

That neuer non mihte neihhe me ner."   *draw too close to me*
Bothe men and wy(m)me(n) al that ther were   165
Thei herieden God hertily,
Bothe luytel and muche lasse and more,
Of this miracle witerly.   *certainly, indeed*
The Jewesse thorw hire sones sawe   *through, testimony*
Was conuertet to crist a-non;   170   *converted; Christ*
The child tok hym to cristes lawe   *betook himself*
And alle the Jewes euerichon.
The meir sat on the Jeuh him-selue   *sat in judgment*
Fforte beo juge of his trespas,   *judge*
To siggen the sothe i-sworen were twelue   175   *to tell the truth; sworn*
To giuen heore verdyt in that caas.   *verdict; case*
Thei counseiled i-vere vppon that caas   *together*
And comen ageyn bi on assent;
The wordes of that verdyt was   *verdict*
In that same houene he schulde be brent.   180
Thus is endet this stori
Of the miracle
I-writen a-boue.
God graunt us joy
In heuene an hih,   185   *on high*
Jh(es)u for thi moder loue. A M E N

Notes

1. The two poems were edited from *The Vernon Manuscript: A Facsimile of Bodleian Library, Oxford, MS. Eng. Poet. a. I*, Introd. I. A. Doyle (Cambridge: D. S. Brewer, 1987). I am grateful to the publisher, Boydell & Brewer, for permission to transcribe the poems from this facsimile. I also thank the staff of the Rockefeller and John Hay Libraries of Brown University for their assistance in acquiring this facsimile for our library and in facilitating my use of it. I especially thank Elizabeth Bryan for generously sharing her paleographical expertise as she helped me decipher the anglicana script. I collated my reading with the two earlier editions by Horstmann and Boyd.

    I adhere to the original spelling of the manuscript text with the following exceptions: (1) I differentiate between the various uses of the capital letter *I*: when it is used for the first person pronoun (*I*), when it is used for the verbal prefix (*i-*), and when it is used for a capital or lower case *J* (*J, j*). In the manuscript, a capital *I* is used in most of these instances, and it is followed by a *punctus* when it is being used as the pronoun or prefix. (2) I substitute *th* for the Middle English letter thorn. (3) I substitute an italicized *y, h,* or *gh,* as appropriate, for the Middle English letter yogh. (4) I have expanded abbreviations, putting the additions in parentheses, and I have added hyphens to attach prefixes to their words. (5) I have added modern punctuation marks. (6) I have added italics to indicate the names of the songs sung by "The Child Slain by Jews."

2. A prayer beginning, "I confess to Almighty God. . . . "

13

Ypotis: A Middle English Dialogue

JUDITH DEITCH

It is a truism of scholarship that the context in which a work of literature is studied affects its interpretation. Thus, it is salutary to consider the Middle English *Ypotis* as a work of medieval children's literature. In this simple poetic dialogue, the child Ypotis answers questions put to him by the emperor Adrian (Hadrian) on topics ranging from how many heavens there are to why people fast on Friday.[1] Hitherto, *Ypotis* has been situated in two main traditions of question-and-answer dialogue, both widely reproduced in the Middle Ages: the medieval Latin *Altercatio Hadriani et Epicteti Philosophi (AHE),* surviving in over one hundred manuscripts (Daly and Suchier), along with the related texts of the *Joca monachorum tradition* (Suchier, *Mittlellateinische*); and the texts of *L'enfant sage* ("wise child") tradition, considered derivative of *AHE* and found in many vernaculars across Europe (Suchier, *L'Enfant*; Utley). The popular Middle English *Ypotis* is extant in fifteen manuscripts dating from the first half of the fourteenth century through the fifteenth century (Utley, 740; Sutton, 115) and is found in a variety of manuscript contexts, from the poetry of the august Vernon manuscript, to the personal accounts of the Brome commonplace book.[2]

Despite contemporary popularity, the poetic dialogue is best known today from Chaucer's reference to it in the third, aborted fit of *Sir Thopas.* Here *Ypotis* stands out as the seeming anomaly in a catalogue of English romance heroes:

> Men speken of romances of prys,
> Of Horn child and of Ypotys,
> Of Beves and sir Gy,
> Of sir Lybeux and Pleyndamour—
> But sir Thopas, he bereth the flour
> Of roial chivalry! (B[2].897–902)

Significantly, *Ypotis* is found among these same romances in several manuscripts, including Cotton Caligula A.ii, the version edited here. However, since *Ypotis* contains nothing "[o]f bataille and of chivalry, / And of ladyes love-drury" (894–95), scholars have posited various hypotheses for its inclusion in *Sir Thopas*: from the redefinition of the term *romance* to mean any kind of tale (Everett, 446), to the use of the more inclusive category of a religious legend; from an intentional mistake—a Chaucerian burlesque (Everett, citing Manly, 446)—to an unintentional mistake, a confusion of the name Ypotis with Ypomedon, a bona fide romance hero (Gruber, citing Schröder, 72). As Everett says, "It seems probable, therefore, that Chaucer may have read *Libeaus Desconus* in a book which also contained *Ypotis*"; thus when "needing a rhyme to 'prys,' he wrote 'Ypotis' " (448). Thematically, it has also been noted that the one thing all the previously mentioned characters have in common is their youth (Burrow, Explanatory Notes, 922).

Despite these intersections with Chaucer's *Sir Thopas*, scholarship on *Ypotis* has focused primarily upon philological study. Between 1881 and 1991, all the extant manuscripts received a modern edition, and while the content is frequently considered too uninteresting for examination, such editing has occasionally led to comment beyond the taxonomy of families of manuscripts—most recently, the interesting suggestion that *Ypotis* was, in one case at least, potential sermon literature (Gardiner-Scott, 237–38). Now that a stemma of manuscripts has been established (Sutton, 154; Gardiner-Scott, 240), a turn to codicological research—studying the different manuscript contexts for *Ypotis*—can shed light on medieval concepts of genre and audience, literacy and reading, as well as book production. *Ypotis* epitomizes the medieval text through its multiplicity of generic markings: both internally, in the network of traditions it taps into, and externally, in its multiplicity of manuscript contexts. Some of that generic encoding is directly related to the question of how *Ypotis*, as a formal dialogue, functions as children's literature.

The Depiction of Childhood in Ypotis

The Ypotis of the poem is, without a doubt, a child in the sense of being young and small. In the opening, Ypotis sits upon the emperor's knee ("On hys kne he hym sette," l. 15). The word *chyld* is used regularly throughout *Ypotis*, both in the direct address of the Emperor Adrian (e.g., "Chylde, tell me thy ryght name," l. 30), as well as in the indirect address attributed to Ypotis (e.g., "The chylde answered wyth mylde spech," l. 26). Thus, repetition of the word *chylde* forms a kind of discursive heading to each section, calling attention to the introduction of a new question, and separating each question-and-answer set from the previous one.

The youth of the speaker is necessary for thematic reasons and for the communication of religious doctrine, and is not merely "filler" (*pace* Gardiner-Scott, 238). Much of the text's appeal is in the interlocutors' inversion of the natural order of authority and subordination, wisdom and ignorance, age and youth: We can imagine the delight of the medieval audience as the child instructs the adult, the innocent instructs the emperor. The "surprise" of the ending also depends upon this interlocutor being a child, small and young, but wise beyond his years, rather than immature. Like the *Pearl*-child, the precocious debater of another Middle English dialogic poem, Ypotis draws attention to Jesus' association with children and his privileging of children as a social class, thus inverting the natural order. However, it is revealed at the end of the dialogue that Ypotis is an incarnation of Christ, a member of the Trinity in the body of a child. Or rather, Ypotis is a child who unites two persons of the Trinity, God the father and God the son: "I am he that the[e] wroghth / And on the Rode the[e] dere bowghth" (597–98). The revelation is a correlate to the incredulity of the emperor at the beginning of the poem ("Then art thou wyse wysdome to teche?" l. 24–25). This familiar inversion of youth and age, child and adult, is immediately available through commonplaces about the wisdom of the young Christ.

This suggests that the emphasis on *chylde* throughout *Ypotis*, while concealing his identity and emphasizing the surprise revelation, also anticipates the final revelation of identity for those who pick up the clues. The inverted nature of the interlocution throughout, with youth instructing age, is directly assignable to the childhood of Jesus, based on the New Testament scene of teaching in the temple. *The disputisoun bitwene the child jesu and maistres of the lawe of jewes* is another Middle English dialogue that presents Jesus as "twelf yer age" (10). Like the mystery plays of Jesus and the Doctors, *The disputisoun* also refers to the divine interlocutor as "child," for example, when the masters ask, "Child, what destou [th]ere? / [Th]ou sittest stalled in vre [our] stage" (15–16). By noting this displacement from their rightful position, the masters call attention to the inversion of proper roles. The youthful Jesus enters the temple expressly to teach ("to lere," l. 11]); and the masters remark, "[Th]ou scholdest lerne and nou[gh]t teche, / [Th]ou spillest speche—what seystou" (18–19). While the Pharisees' incredulity in *The disputisoun* has a different polemical force from the Emperor Adrian's surprise in *Ypotis*, it is based on the same motif of the precocity of this particular child.

In addition, the name "Ypotis" itself reinforces the child's divine identity. This unusual name is usually described as a corruption of "Epictetus" from the Latin tradition of the *AHE*. Alternatively, it is read as a corruption of the Greek "Hypostasis" or perhaps "Hypostatis," for "The former was a common word with the Greek ecclesiastical writers for a person of the Trinity; the latter is used by them for a creator" (Gruber, citing Hales, 71), and the term *hypostatic union* was used to describe the uniting of divine and human natures in Christ. Such a fluid divine identity perfectly suits the wise child of this dialogue.

Thus Ypotis, as an incarnation of Christ, as well as a figure for the child Jesus, is not only precocious, but also singular, and does not seem to yield direct access to a definition of medieval childhood. For, like the virginity and womanly ideal of Christ's mother ("alone of all her sex"), the child Jesus ("alone of all his age") is less a model for imitation than a sign of divine potency. As an (unattainable?) ideal he may allow a possible construction of medieval childhood through contradiction; for example, his extraordinary state of wisdom implies the ordinary state of ignorance. The figure of the wise child can be read as a model to imitate, insofar as proper application to one's studies; an argument *a minore ad majore*—that even a child can learn this—provides a stimulus to learning for a reader of any age. Moreover, the motif of the "wise child" can also be seen to have a leveling effect with regard to age, for it shows that a child could just as easily be a vehicle for divine knowledge as an adult. The whole tradition of the "wise child," therefore, seems to caution against using it in any direct way to uncover a subjectivity of medieval childhood.

Ypotis as Children's Literature

Ypotis, then, can be seen as children's literature because of the appearance of the eponymous, atypical child speaker and didactic aim of the poem, and like other question-and-answer dialogues, it has been called "childish." While modern readers disparage the unsophisticated "jog-trot" metre—something that links it to the Middle English romances parodied by Chaucer (Everett, 447)—perceived lack of sophistication cannot be used as an indication of juvenile literature, while simplicity of subject matter and expression can. This judgement of the meter, moreover, ignores the fact that many of the other romances and serious religious poems collected in the same manuscripts as *Ypotis* are composed in the same meter.

The dialogue form itself directs attention to the educational aim of the poem. Dialogue was used for both oral method and written texts of instruction from antiquity through the Renaissance. Likewise, it was important from the very first, formative stages of literacy, from the Latin grammar "donet" (the *Ars Minor* of Aelius Donatus), through the advanced level of study in philosophical, theological, and encyclopedic texts, and in the oral form of university disputation. In his study of the *AHE*, Daly cites patristic question-and-answer dialogues concerning biblical interpretation, which are descended from hermeneutical texts on Homer. These compendia answered the want "for a condensation of learning" (Daly, 19) and were composed by such authors as Athanasius, Augustine, and Isidore (Daly, 28–31). The latter's *De Veteri et Novo Testamento Quaestiones* Daly calls a collection for students of an "extremely elementary, not to say childish character" (31). Nonetheless, while didactic, these texts were probably not written exclusively for children. Daly also cautions against viewing the texts of the *AHE* tradition "as unsuccessful attempts at imitation of the classical dialogues" (18); rather, they were "essentially for popular consumption" by the literate but unlearned (16). I would posit these dialogues achieve the same purpose as that ascribed to other medieval encyclopaedias, that of *specula* through the ordering of knowledge itself. Brian Stock asserts that encyclopedic catalogues, listing all things in the world proceeding from matter and form to the immense diversity of the universe, imitate the rational design of the universe through the ordering of facts; and through the catalogues the logical and harmonious pattern of the world can be apprehended (20–21). Not only linked to educational procedure from antiquity through the Renaissance, question-and-answer dialogues like *Ypotis* and those of the *AHE* must also be seen as repositories of knowledge and the structures of knowledge for the unlearned, and therefore a replication of the divine order of the universe.[3]

Ypotis is meant for instruction, but it is doubtful that the modern notion of educational literature geared to a certain age applied in the Middle Ages. What strikes modern readers as "childish" might better be called appealing to an elementary level of literacy. Discussion of the catechism, another elementary form of dialogue, may help clarify this distinction. *Ypotis* has been classified as a catechism (Utley) because the modern mind identifies rote (doctrinal) knowledge packaged in questions and answers with this form. However, it is only a partially successful category. First, as Daly notes, the *catechismus* was not established as a form for children until the sixteenth century (13–14). *Catechesis* had always been a form of instruction for adults to be received in the Christian faith. In the Middle Ages, when large numbers of uneducated pagans were converted, some elementary form of instruction became necessary (Daly, *Contributions,* 37). It was not until the Reformation that the questions were standardized and prescribed for every schoolboy. Daly does note at least one exception, however, in Alcuin's *Disputatio Puerorum per Interrogationes et Responsiones*, which includes questions on the *credo* and *pater noster*, the essentials of the catechism (38). These rudiments of the faith were often the basis of medieval schooling.

While "catechism" underlines the intrinsic educational procedure of the dialogue, Ypotis, like the child Jesus, has come to teach, not to repeat the master's lesson; thus, formally, we do not have a catechism at all. Because of the status of the interlocutors, the dialogues of the *AHE* are not, logically speaking, catechisms either. For in the *AHE*, the philosopher Epictetus cannot in any way be considered to be repeating instruction to a more learned superior. On the contrary, as the answerer in dialogue he is the *magister*, providing the emperor Hadrian as *discipulus* with access to arcane wisdom. Unlike *Ypotis* and the child Jesus, however, we do have a proper arrangement of the power/knowledge dynamic: the emperor/disciple deferring to the philosopher/teacher.

Besides the inverted configuration of interlocutors and the figure of the child, *Ypotis* differs in another important way from *AHE* and from the English texts properly derived from it—the Old English *Solomon and Saturn* and *Adrian and Ritheus*, and the Middle English *Questiones by-twene the maister of Oxenford and his clerke* (Utley, 740; see Wülcker). These texts make absolutely no effort to frame the catalogue of information other than schematically assigning initials or names to the interlocutors (e.g., "H" and "E" or "Clerk" and "Maister"). In *AHE* the question is frequently introduced with a mechanically repeated *"quid est"* ("what is?") or *"dic mihi"* ("tell me"), and the answers are frequently one word or lists of words. Thus there is much more emphasis on these texts as repositories of knowledge; their authors have not taken the same care to engage the reader's imagination by characterizing the interlocutors or dramatizing the situation as in the "wise child" tradition. Nor do they provide meter and rhyme for the reader's delectation.

Therefore, *Ypotis* offers a different experience of reading (aloud or silently) from the "bare bones" question-and-answer dialogues of the *AHE*; it offers instruction in basic doctrine in a form that is appealing to an unlearned audience, including youth. I would say that *Ypotis* is medieval literature for children, but not *only* for children. The category should not be seen as restrictive or exclusive of other age groups; the audiences for a single text in the Middle Ages were often multiple, as can be demonstrated from a brief examination of *Ypotis*'s manuscript contexts.

Two Manuscript Contexts for *Ypotis*

Codicology provides another way of answering the question "What readership or audience was envisioned for this poem?" First, in studying *Ypotis* in the context of the York Minster MS, which contains *The Lay Folks' Catechism* with a Lollard emphasis, a treatise on Holy Scripture, a reading for the Eve of Easter, and an explication of the Sacrament of Holy Baptism (235–36), Gardiner-Scott suggests this aggregation of texts "implies potential sermon use, consistent with the clerical provenance of the Holy Saturday liturgy and sermon in the preceding folios" (238). The manuscript context of the York Minster MS thus weighs against viewing *Ypotis* as a text intended only for children.

Second, MS Cotton Caligula A.ii is one of the most complete versions of the text and may belong to the oldest strata of surviving witnesses (Sutton, 160). Although post-dating Chaucer, it exists in the kind of medieval book combining romances and religious material in which Chaucer could have read it and therefore drawn upon it for his reference in *Sir Thopas*. Moreover,

Cotton Caligula A.ii contains four medical recipes, a short chronicle, a poem by Lydgate, and—most interesting for present purposes—Lydgate's transla-tion of "Stans puer ad mensam," an advice poem for medieval youth.[4] Apart from the seven romances, the "religious matter" that makes up the rest of the book is quite diverse, ranging from the story of Susannah, to saints' lives, prayers, and visions.[5] While Cotton Caligula A.ii cannot as a whole be regarded as a children's book, if read with "Stans puer ad mensam," *Ypotis* can be seen as a work for children; studied with the poem on the Ten Com-mandments as biblical lore; interpreted with the confession of sins as instruc-tion in religious practice; glossed with the stations of Rome as a literary pilgrimage; examined with *The Siege of Jerusalem* as a romance of conquest; looked at with the five wounds as a poem on the second person of the Trinity; and so on.

In other words, one's reading experience of *Ypotis*—as well as the inter-pretation of the text and assessment of its generic attributes—could vary con-siderably, depending upon the textual associations of its manuscript context. These remarks merely suggest areas for further investigation. Such study is salutary, since it cautions against imposing modern frames of reference upon past texts, while considering *Ypotis* as children's literature sharpens issues of audience, genre, and manuscript context. All three areas reinforce the uses of the medieval text as multivalent, adaptable to widely differing purposes and readers. Such study also underlines the generic fluidity of the medieval text, or rather, the multiple networks of generic links that exceed our notions of classification. Like the precocious, energetic child of the text, *Ypotis* is a text that just will not stay put.

Notes

1. Gardiner-Scott provides a detailed synopsis of the carefully planned move-ment of the dialogue:

   > It begins . . . with sections on God, the heavens and the angelic orders, and then moves into God's intervention in historical time in the Creation of the world and man. It then recounts the timing and nature of Original Sin, and the resultant plan of salvation in Christ, showing how Christ saved Adam. Then comes an exploration of the Devil's counterattack in the form of temptation to the seven deadly sins, and the temporal and eternal results of succumbing to that tempting. The bond with God can further be broken once a man has severed it by sinning—either because man will not repent, or because God will not forgive (the latter only in certain circumstances)—and thus the importance of the sacrament of penance is stressed. Sin results in death, and another section deals with the different types of death awaiting man.
   >
   > However, an alternative of will is presented, in that it is possible for

man to meditate on the plan of salvation as revealed in Christ and his Passion, and to try actively to please God by his way of life. One practical method of showing devotion is the Friday fast, and the child gives thirteen reasons for observing the fasts that range from Creation to Judgment Day, with a special section on selected saints and an eulogy of the Virgin. The practical method of showing devotion is accessible to all Christians, whatever their estate. (237–38)

2. I omit here the early print edition because it is not the same text as *Ypotis*, although it is in the "wise child" tradition, perhaps a translation from another language. See Utley.
3. Other encyclopaedic dialogues include *Sidrak and Bokkus*, recently edited by EETS, and the *Elucidarium*. See Utley.
4. Other works that occur in both manuscripts include a medieval recipe, a Trental, poems by Lydgate, prayers, and some rules for conduct. This all requires further examination. In terms of texts depicting children, Brome also contains a play of Abraham and Isaac; in terms of texts for children, it contains a number of puzzles. For a discussion of the contents, see L. Smith.
5. Mearns has suggested that one section of the MS (ff. 89–108) might be separated as the "Eschatological booklet" (45).

Ypotis: A Middle English Dialogue[1]

He th*at* wyll of wysdome lere		*learn*
Herkeneth now & ye may here		*Hearken, listen*
Of a tale of holy wryte—		*holy writ*
Seynt Jon the euangelist wytnesseth hyt—		*it*
How h*yt* befell yn grete Rome,	5	
The chefe cyte of crystendome:		*chief city*
A chyld was sent of myghtes most		
Thorow vertu of the holy gost		
Vnto the empe*rour* of Rome,		
A nobull man & wyse of dome—	10	*judgment*
The emperour of Rome than		
Men called hym syr Adryan—		*Hadrian*
When th*at* chyld of gret honour		
Was comen before the emperour		
On hys kne he hym sette,	15	
Well fayre the empe*rour* th*er* he grette.		*greeted*
The e*mperour* wyth mylde chere		*pleasant disposition*
Askede the chylde of whens he were.		*where he came from*
The chyld answered hym aplyght,		*truly*
"Fro my fadur y come now ryght,	20	
And that ys fro the hygh justyse,		*high justice*

To teche them th*at* ben vnwyse
Ne nowght fulfylled of the lawes."
    Then sayde the emp*er*our yn hys sawes,   *wisdom*
"Then art th*ou* wyse wysdome to teche?"   25
The chylde answered w*yth* mylde spech,
"He ys wyse th*at* heuen may wy*n*ne   *gain*
And kepe hy*m* out of deedly sy*n*ne."
The e*m*perou*r* sayde w*yth*out blame,
"Chylde, tell me thy ryght name.   30   *true name*
My name, he sayde, ys ypotyse   *Ypotis*
Th*at* mych kon telle of heuen blysse."
    The e*m*perour sayde, what may heuen be?
"Syr, sayde the chyld, goddys pryuyte."   *sacred mystery*
      "What," he sayde, "ys god allmyght?"   35
The chylde answered anon ryght,
"He ys w*yth*oute begynnynge
And shall be w*yth*oute endynge."
    The emperour sayde, "Y haue g*r*et selkowth   *wonder*
What come fyrst of godd*us* mowth?"   40
The chyld answered & sayd anon*e*,
"Therof speketh the apostell John*e*
In h*ys* gospell all & su*m*me,
In principio erat verbu*m*.   *beginning was the word*
Thys was the fyrst bygy*n*ny[n]ge   45
That eu*er* spake our heuen kyng,
W*yth* th*at* word was the fad*ur* & the sone
And the holy gost togedur kome,   *together come*
Thre persones in trinite,
Ther may none fro oth*ur* be."   50
    The e*m*perour sayde full eue*n*ne,
"Chyld, th*ou* hast be yn heue*n*ne,
How fele heuens hath god almyght?"   *many*
"Seuen," sayde the chylde aplyght.
"The *hy*este heuen th*at* may be   55
That ys of the holy trinite,
Ther ys the fadur w*yth* the sone,
The holy gost to ged*ur* they wone   *live*
As these clerkes both syng & rede,   *priests*
Thre p*er*sones in on godhede—   60
That joye may no man dyscryue   *describe*
Lered ne lewed th*at* ys on lyue   *learned; unlearned*
That oth*ur* heuen ys gostly wrowght   *spiritually fashioned*
Of lower degre b*v*t hygher nowght,

That joye may no man telle   65
Thyll dommus day, thowgh he wold spelle.   *Judgment Day; tell*
The thrydde heuen shyneth as cristall,   *shines like crystal*
Full of joye & swete smelle,
For confessores that place ys dyght   *confessors; built*
Ther euur ys day & neuur nyght.   70
The fowrthe heuen ys gold lych   *like gold*
Full of precyows stones rych,
For innocentes that place is sette
And euur yn joye wythowten lette.   *cessation*
The fyfthe heuen ys long & brode,   75
All fulfylled wyth goddus manhode;   *humanity*
And ner goddus manhode were
All thys worlde were forlore,
For thorow hys passyon & hys manhede
Heuen blysse shall be her mede.   80   *reward*
The sixte heuen holy chyrche ys,
Full of holy angeles, ywys,   *indeed*
That syngyn both day & nyght
Of hys strengthe & off hys myght.
The seuenth heuen, as sayth the story,   85
Is paradys aftur purgatorie,
When sowles haue done here penance   *their*
They come thydur wythoute dystance.   *thither*
Thes ar the heuens, syr emperour,
That Jhesus hath, our sauyour."   90
        The emperour sayde anon ryght,
"How mony orderus ar ther of angelus bryght?"
The chylde answered anon tho,
"Tenne orderes syr & no mo.
The fyrste ordur ys cherubyn,   95   *Cherubim*
And that othur ys seraphynne,   *Seraphim*
The thrydde ys tronus,   *Thrones*
The fowrthe ys dominaciones,   *Dominions*
The fyfte orthur ys principatus,   *Principalities*
The sixte potestates, ywys,   100   *Powers*
The seuenthe orthur virtutes ys,   *Virtues*
The eythe angelica called ys thus,   *Angels*
The nyneneth ordur archa[n]gely;   *Archangels*
And euery pryns hath hys party,   *prince*
Mony a thowsand to hys banere   105
That seruene god both fer & nere.
The tenth ordur shall ma[n]kynde be

And fulfylle the place on hyghe
Heuen by th*at* oth*ur* syde
That Lucyfer lost for h*ys* pryde;   110
Ther shall the manhede of god almyght
Be our p*r*inse & that ys ryght."
    The *emper*our sayde, "Chyld, y the p*r*ay,   *thee*
What made god the fyrst day?"
The chyld answered hy*m* full euen,   115
"Angelles, archangelles & heuen,
That same werke of g*r*et nobylye   *nobility*
God made hy*t* on the sondaye.
The monday aft*ur*, verament,   *truly*
God made the fyrmament,   120
Mone & so*n*ne to shyne bryght,
And the sterres th*er*on he dyght.
The tewesday, y vnd*ur*stonde,
He made both see & londe,
Welles fayr w*yth* wateres fresh   125
To temper the erthe harde & nesh,   *soft*
Erbes, trees and also gras,
And oth*ur* thyngus as hys wyll was.
The wednesday made god a[l]myght
Fysh yn wat*ur* & fowle of flyght   130
And bad hem abowte wende   *to go about*
For to helpe all mankynde.
The thursday god made g*r*et & small
Bestes bothe by downe & dale,   *hill and dale*
And yaf hem erthe to her fode,   135   *gave*
And badde hem turne man to gode.
On a fryday god made Adam
Aft*ur* hys shappe & yaf hym name.   *gave*
Sythen hy*s* on rybbe gan he take   *one*
And made Eue vnto h*ys* make.   140   *mate*
And made hy*m* man of myghtest most,
And yaf hy*m* lyf of the holy gost;
A g*r*et lord he gan hym make,
All p*a*radys he ded hym take.
The saterday god forgate noght   145
The workes th*at* he hadde wroght,
He blessed hem w*yth* gode wyll
Bothe lowde & eke styll,
And badde he*m* wex & multyplye,
Euery thyng yn h*ys* partye.   150   *after his kind*

That oth*ur* sonday god reste toke,		
As we fynde yn holy boke.		
That day shuld no mon werke,		
But serue god & holy kerke,		*holy church*
And kepe hym fro deedly sy*n*ne,	155	
That he fall not ther*e*inne."		
The *e*mp*er*our sayde, "Th*ys* may well be,		
But oo thyng, chylde, tell th*ou* me,		*one*
What mon dyed & was not born?"		
The chylde answered hym byforn,	160	
"Adam, our*e* forme fadyr, ywys,		*first, truly*
That god yaf lyue yn p*a*radys,		*gave paradise to live in*
He was not borne, y vnd*ur*stonde,		
For god made hym w*yth* h*ys* honde."		
The *e*mp*er*our hereof was gladde,	165	
Chylde ypotys full sone he badde,		
Yyf he kowthe telle hym owght		*know*
Of how many thy*n*g*us* mon was wrowght.		
The chylde sayde, "Syr of seue*n*ne,		
Whych they be y shall the neuen:	170	*name*
Eerthe slyme forsothe ys on of tho,		
Water of the see god toke th*er*to,		
And of the so*n*ne & of the wynde,		
And of the clowth*us*, wrytyn I fynde,		*clouds*
And of the stones by the see coste,	175	
And also of the holy goste.		
Of the erthe slyme ys mo*nn*us flesh,		*man's*
Of the watyr h*ys* blood nesh,		*fluid*
Of the so*n*ne h*ys* herte & h*ys* bowelys,		*internal organs*
Hys mekenes & h*ys* gode dewes,	180	*just acts*
Of the clowdus h*ys* wytt*us* beth,		
And of the wynde ys made h*ys* breth,		
And of the stone ys made h*ys* bone,		
Of the holy gost h*ys* sowle alone;		
Of these seuen thyng*us* ys made ma*n*ne.	185	
Beholde syr emp*er*our Adryan		
Therfor*e* eu*ery* man here		
Ys of dyuers manere:		*different types*
The mon th*at* hath of the erth most		
He shall be heuy, well th*ou* wost,	190	*heavy*
Both yn worde & eke yn dede		
And yn oth*ur* thyng*us*, as we rede.		*things*
The man th*at* hath most of the see		

Eu*ur* yn trauell shall be he		*travail*
And coueyte both londe & lede,	195	*covet, riches*
That shall hym fayle at h*ys* nede.		
Who of the wynde hath most mygth		
Be ryght reson he shall be lyghth,		*light*
Wylde yn worde & eke yn thowghth,		*thought*
And speke moche & waylys nowghth.	200	*lament*
Who of the clowth*us* hath moste foyson,		*abundance*
He shall be wyse be ryghth reson		
And be ware yn worde & dede		*cautious*
And yn oth*ur* thyng*us*, as we rede.		
Who of the so*n*ne hath most plente	205	
Hote & haste he shall be,		*temperamental; hasty*
Also stalleworth mon & mykyll of mygth,		
And be ryghth reson a p*ar*ty lyghth.		*somewhat*
Who so of the stone ys most wroghth,		
He shall be steddefast yn h*ys* thowghth	210	
And yn t*ra*uayle trusty & trewe,		
And be ryghth reson pale of hewe.		*pale complected*
Who th*at* hath most of the holy gost,		
He shall haue *y*n herte most		
Good worde, good thowght & good dede,	215	
The pore & naked to clothe & fede,		
And loue well god & holy chyrche,		
And oth*ur* penaunce for to wyrche."		
The emp*erour* sayde w*yth* word*us* mylde		
Anon*e* ryght to the chylde,	220	
"Thow speke fyrst of the see,		
I wolde wyte what h*yt* myght be."		*would know; it*
The chylde sayde w*yth*out lesyng,		*falsehood*
"A wylde way of wendynge—		*going*
For such way th*ou* myghth take th*er*inne,	225	
That th*ou* shalt neu*ur* to londe wynne."		
The emp*erour* sayde w*yth*out delay,		
"Tell me, chylde, y the pray,		
What tyme dyde Adam amys		*time did; sin*
That he loste paradys?"	230	
The chylde sayde, "At mydde morrow t[yde],		*morning hour*
And or mydday he loste h*ys* pryde—		
An angell drofe hy*m* yn to desert		*drove*
W*yth* a bryghth bre*n*ny*n*g swerde,		
Ther to be yn care & wo,	235	
He & h*ys* ofsprynge for eu*er* mo."		*offspring*

"Alas," sayde the emp*er*o*ur*, "for dole — *sorrow*
That Adam was so mykyll a fole. — *great a fool*
How mony sy*nn*u*s* dyde Adam, — *many sins*
Byfore th*at* god bekam ma*nn*e?" 240
"Seuene," sayde the chyld, "w*yth*out mo,
And sacrylege was on of tho,
Lecherye was on of these,
Auaryce and couetyse, — *avarice, covetous*
In glotenye & yn g*re*t pryde— 245
These seuene sy*nn*u*s* all Adam dyde. — *Seven Deadly Sins*
In pryde he sy*n*ned vyle — *vilely*
When he wroghth h*y*s owene wylle, — *worked his own will*
And nowght aft*ur* the heste of god, — *after the will, behest*
He ny helde nowght godd*us* forbodde. 250 — *withhold, forbidden*
In sac*r*ilege he sy*n*nede sore
When he wroghth the fendes lore — *fiend's bidding*
And fulfylled h*y*s owene talent
And dyde the fend*us* co*m*maundement. — *fiend's*
Man slawghtur he dyde ynowghth 255 — *enough*
When he h*y*s owene sowle slowghth— — *sloth*
And all th*at* of hym come—
The fende to helle to hym nome. — *took*
A thefe he was ayeyns god — *thief; against*
When he stale th*at* he hym forbode— 260 — *stole*
Certaynlyche, as y the saye, — *Certainly*
He was worthy for to dye.
Fornycacyon he hadde yn mynde,
When he wroghth aft*ur* the fende
And helde th*at* godd*us* lore was false. 265 — *God's law, word*
And yn Auaryce he sy*n*ned alse
When he coueyted to haue more
Then he hadde nede fore,
When*e* all p*a*radys was at hys wyll—
No wo*nth*u*r* thowgh god lykede yll.
In glotenye he sy*n*ned full yll 270
When he putte hym yn th*at* peryll
For the appull th*at* he gan take, — *apple*
That god forbadde hy*m* & h*y*s make. — *mate*
In slowthe he dyde worste of all 275
When hem th*at* synne was byfall,
He ne hadde no g*r*ace to ryse
When god come to hy*m* yn thys wyse — *in this manner*
And sayde, 'Adam, what thost th*ou* now?'

Adam answered ayaeyn & se how: 280
'Lord, y here the speke aplyght,
But of the haue y no syght.'
Owre lord than to Adam sayde,
'Man, why dedest th*ou* th*at* y the forbayde?'
Adam answerd ayeyn wyth wyll, 285 *again*
'Thys wo*m*man tysed me th*er* tyll *tempted*
And made me to do th*at* dede.'
Our lorde then to Eue sayde,
'Who*m*mon, why wroghtest th*ou* thy wyll?'
'The edder, lord, tysed me ther tyll.' 290 *adder*
Our lorde sayd to the edder tho,
'Worme, why wroghtest th*ou* he*m* thy*s* wo?'
The fend answered, by maystry, *to get dominance*
'For th*at* y hadde to hem enuye *envy*
That they shulde haue th*at* g*r*ete blysse 295
That y for p*r*ide gan to mysse.'
Our lorde sayde to Adam than,
'For thy gylte,' he sayde, 'man,
Thow shalt gete thy mete w*yth* swete *food, sweat*
And suffre both colde & hete.' 300
To Eue sayde our heuen kyng,
'Wo*m*man, for thy wykkyd tysyng
Thow shalt euu*r* be ma*nn*us thrall, *servant*
And haue moch wo & t*r*auell w*yth*all, *woe and travail*
And bere thy fruyt w*yth* grony*n*g & care 305 *children*
Th*ou* & thyn ofspryng for euu*r* mare.'
Our lorde then sayde to Satan,
'In forme of a worme th*ou* temptest man*e*,
Th*er*for on thy wo*m*be th*ou* shallt glyde *belly*
And all th*at* the sene on eche a syde 310 *everyone who sees you*
Of the shall be sore aferd
When they come yn to myddul erthe; *middle earth*
A virgyn shall be borne blyue
That all thy powste shall to dryue.' *dominion*
Thus Adam lyued here 315
Nyne hondrede & ii & thrydty yere,
Whe*n* he was deed to helle he nam, *was taken*
And all tho th*at* of hym cam. *them*
Hys sowle was yn helle there
Fowr*e* thowsand & fyfe hondred yer*e* 320
And fowr*e* & tydes seuene,
Tyll the myghtyfull kyng of heuene

Kydde th*at* he was of myghtys moste,   *knew*
And sende down the holy goste
And lyghte yn the mayde marye   325   *descended*; *Maid Mary*
Wythoute we*m*me of her*e* bodye.   *blemish*
Fowrty dayes for vs he faste,
The jewes toke hym at the laste
And dede hym vpon the rode   *cross*
And so he bowghte vs w*yth* hys blode.   330   *bought*
And sythen he lyghth yn to helle   *descended*
The fendes powste for to felle,   *fiend's power*
Ther he vnbonde Adam & Eue   *unbound, freed*
And oth*ur* mo th*at* hym wer leue   *beloved*
And ledde hem yn to *p*aradys,   335
Ther eu*ur*more ys joye & blys.
Sythen aft*ur* hy*s* vp rysynge   *Soon*; *resurrection*
He styed to heuen ther he ys ky*n*g,   *ascended*
On h*y*s fad*ur* ryghth hond sytte he than,
There he ys sothfast godde & man.   340   *truly*
That sone, god omnipotent,
Shall come ayeyn yn jugeme[n]t
And deme all men aft*ur* her dedes—   *judge*
He ys vnwyse h*yt* not dredes—
The gode to Joye, the wykked to pyne;   345
That joye may no man dyuyne,   *divine, know*
He shall haue th*at* for h*y*s seruyse   *service*
That seruyth god yn all wyse."

The emp*erour* seyde, "Be heuen kyng,
Chylde, th*y*s ys fayr sayynge.   350
But telle me, chyld, yyf th*ou* can
Wher w*yth* the fende begyled man?   *fiend beguile man?*
And y the p*r*ay th*at* thou me telle
What draweth ma*nnus* sowle to helle?"
The chylde sayde, "Sy*nn*us fyfe,   355   *five sins*
That among manky*n*de ys ryfe:
Wykked thowght yn ma*nnus* herte
Whyll th*at* he ys hole & qwarte.
Man slawght*ur* ys anoth*ur* of tham
That bryngeth a man to wykke fam;   360
But shryfte make hy*m* therof clere,   *Unless confession*
Forsoth he goth to helle fere.
Pryde, y wote, ys anothur,   *I know*
Glotenye ys the thrydde broth*ur*,

Lecherye than ys the ferthe,	365
On the worste abouen erthe.	
The fyfte ys couetyse, y the tell,	
That draweth ma*nn*us sowle to helle.	
Seynt poule wytnesseth yn h*ys* story	*Saint Paul*
Of the paynes of purgatory,	370
That couetyse by hy*m* self ys dyghth	
As a welle of bras bren*ny*ng bryghth,	*brass burning brightly*
Full of sowles hy*t* ys hongynge	
As ych by oth*ur* may thrynge,	*push*
A wylde fyr among he*m* thoth re*nn*e	375 *doth*
All that hy*t* towchyt hy*t* doth brenne;	*touches*
And why coueytyse ys lykned to a whyle	*a well*
I wyll yo*u* telle fayr & wele:	
In h*ys* yowthe he wy*nn*eth the price	
And yeueth hym all to couetyce,	380 *gives*
And in no tyme wyll bly*nn*e	*cease*
But endeth all hys lyf therinne;	
Certeynly, as y the telle,	
Yyf he dye so, he goth to helle.	
Theref*or* hy*t* ys lykned to a whele	385 *wheel*
For coueytyse hath ende no dele."	
The e*m*perour sayde, "Thys ys hard chanse—	
What letteth a man to do penance	
To sawghte vs wy*th* our sauyour?"	*reconcile*
The chylde sayde, "sy*nn*us fowr:	390
Slowthe ys on, shame ys th*at* oth*ur*,	
Wanhope the thrydde brodur,	*despair*
The fowrthe ys wy*th*out fabull	
That god ys so mercy[a]bull	*merciful*
He wyll of hym take no wreche	395
Yyf shryft of mowthe may be h*ys* leche."	*confession; physician*
The empero*ur* sayde, "Soth hy*t* ys.	*it is true*
What bry*n*geth a ma*nn*us sowle to blys?"	
The chylde answerd hy*m* & sayde,	
"Good word, good thowght & good dede.	400
Ther was neu*ur* so euell thyng wroghth	
But the begy*nn*yng was euell thowghth,	
Ne neu*ur* non good doyng	
But good thowghth was the begy*nn*yng.	
Who so hath wy*th* hym good speche	405
And h*ys* foo of hym wolde take wreche,	
Wy*th* good speche he may, er he wende,	*before he goes*

Of hy*s* foo make hys frende.

A good dede ys moche of myghth

Ayeyn god yn heuen bryghth,   410   *bright*

For a man may w*yth* on good dede

Wy*n*ne heuen to hy*s* mede."

    The e*m*pero*u*r sayde, "Th*ys* wele y beleue.

But, chylde, take hy*t* not a-greue,   *grief*

Tell me, y the pray, yyf th*ou* kan,   415

On how mony dethes may dye aman?"

The chylde sayde, "Dethes thre,

And I woll the telle whych they be.

That on deth ys bodyly here,

That ys streyte & of grette fere,   420   *strict*

That ys a sy*n*full man*n*e wyth inne

Or body & sowle may p*a*rte atwy*n*ne;   *before*

That oth*er* deth ys deth of shame,

Yyf a man dye yn wykked fame;

The thrydde deth ys, as seyth these clerkes,   425

Yyf he haue no part of goddes werkes."

    The e*m*pero*u*r sayde, "I beseche the,

On thyng, chylde, telle th*ou* me,

How many sy*nn*u*s* th*at* ben*e* vnshryuen*e*   *unconfessed*

Agayn god shall not be foryeuen?"   430

The chylde sayde, "Sy*nn*u*s* two,

Mysbyleue ys one of tho.   *unbelief*

Mony a man wyll for no Reson

Byleue yn C*ri*stys yncarnacyon*e*,   *incarnation*

That he lyghth ynto the mayde Marye   435

W*yth*owte wem of her body,

And th*at* he styed th*er* as he ys kynge.

But he hy*t* leue yn all thynge,   *unless/believe*

Certeynly, as y the telle,

W*yth*owte ende he goth to helle.   440

Wanhope ys th*at* oth*ur* synne   *Despair*

That mony a man ys bou*n*den inne—

And [he] hath ayeyn god so mykyll gylt,   *much guilt*

The fende to wanhope he hym pylte,   *drives*

And than he wyll no mercy craue   445

For he weneth non to haue;   *supposes*

For th*at* wanhope wrytene y fynde

He goth to helle w*yth*outen ende."

    The e*m*pero*u*r sayde, "Syn hyt ys so

Sy*n*ne thoth mony a man myche wo,   450

Chylde, where w*yth* may a man hy*m* were   *defend*
That the fynde ne shall hy*m* dere?"
The chylde sayde, "W*yth* good deuocione.   *devotion*
Thenk wele on C*ri*s*t*us passyone,
How he kneled on the hyll of Olyuete   455   *Mount of Olives*
And for drede of deth blood gan swete;
Stode bou*n*den to a pyler longe,   *pillar*
Beten he was w*yth* skou*r*ges stronge   *beaten; stiff whips*
That h*ys* body th*er* hy*t* stode
Was dypped yn h*ys* swete blode;   460
Also crowned w*yth* thornes kene   *sharp*
That the wond*us* yn h*ys* hedde wer*e* sene,   *wounds*
And bare the crosse to Caluarye
On the whyche hy*m*self moste dye.
Thenk vpon h*ys* wondes smerte,   465
Haue h*ys* passyon yn thyn herte,
Therwyth may a man hym were,
That no fynde shall hym dere."
      The e*m*perour sayde, "I leue the well   *believe*
That th*ys* ys soth euery dele.   470
But tell me, chyld, yyf th*ou* kan,
What pleseth best god & man?"
The chylde sayde, "Penau*n*ces thre—
I wyll you telle whych they be.
Yyf a man be yn trewe chaunse   475
And lede h*ys* lyf yn ryghth penance,
And weres hy*m* ayeyn the fendes fondy*ng*,   *temptation*
And kepeth hy*m* fro fowle lykynge,   *desires*
God ys payd w*yth* th*at* empryse   *enterprise*
And yeueth hy*m* heuen for h*ys* seruyse.   480   *give; service*
Anoth*ur* thy*ng* payeth god yn herte:
He th*at* ys large yn h*ys* pouerte,
And taketh h*ys* pouerte stylle,
And thanketh god w*yth* good wylle,
And wolde gladly helpe & restore   485
Hys euen crysten th*at* are pore.   *fellow*
Yyf he ne may do no more
But here pouerte rewe sore,
He shall haue for hys good wyll
Heuen at h*ys* endy*ng*, as ys skyll.   490   *fitting*
The thrydde payth god so myche: *allows*
A man th*at* ys yn erthe ryche
And ys come of hygh kynne,   *high-born family*

And forsaketh all thy*s* world*us* wy*n*ne
And yeueth hym to pouerte—   495
Therfor yn heuen shall he be."
    The e*m*pe*ro*ur sayde yet to the chylde,
"Tell me fayre w*yth* wordes mylde,
Why fasteth men the fryday so moche
For by any oth*ur* day yn the woke?"   500
The chylde a*n*swered & seyde ayeyn,
"For thryttene resones tell I kan.   *thirteen*
The fyrste reson ys ha*m*me,   *suitable*
For on the fryday god made Adam
In the vale of Ebron thorow h*ys* gr*a*ce   505   *Hebron valley*
And formed hym aft*ur* h*ys* face.
The secou*n*de reson, th*ou* may me leue,
Vpon a fryday Adam & Eue
Losten p*ar*adys, the sothe to telle,
And both wer dampned to helle.   510   *damned*
The thrydde reson, y the telle,
Vpon a fryday Caym slowgh Abelle,
The fyrste martyr for sothe aplyght
That was martered for god almyght;
And Cayme for th*at* same thyng   515
Hadde the curse of our heuen*e* kyng.
The fowrthe reson ys full swete,
How Gabryell our lady dede grete,
Vpon a fryday w*yth* mylde mode
Goddes sone toke flesh & blode   520
Of th*at* swete mayde Marie
W*yth*owten we*m*me of her body.   *blemish*
The fyfte reson I telle beforn,
Vpon a fryday Jh*esus* was born
Of that swete holy vyrgyne   525
To borow our sowles out of pyne.
The syxte reson ys of hygh e*m*pryse:
When Jh*esus* toke h*ys* cyrcumcise
Vpon a fryday blode gan he blede
For the gylt of our mysdede,   530
And for the sy*n*ne of Adam & Eue,
That blode he bledde for o*ur* beleue.
The seuenth reson, tell y kan,
How seynt Steuen, goddes man,   St. Stephen
Vpon a fryday was stoned to dede   535
Thorow Herode & h*ys* fals rede.   *decree*

The VIII reson y kan telle
Yef ye wyll a stounde dwelle,   *moment*
Vpon a fryday saynt Jon the baptyst
Was martered for the loue of Cryst   540
Yn harueste aftur the Assumpcyon—   *feast*
Hys day ys called decollacyoune.
The IX reson ys full gode,
That goddes sone dyed on the Rode
Vpon a fryday, as y you telle,   545
To bye our sowles out of helle.
Thys ys the tenthe reson:
Of our ladyes assumpcioune:
On a frydaye she yolde the gost   550
To her sone that she loued most,
Ther he ys kyng, she ys qwene—
Iblessed mot that tyme bene.
The XI reson ys full trewe,
That the Apostell saynt Andrewe
Vpon a fryday was don on crosse,   555
To god he called wyth meke voys   *quiet voice*
And sayde, fadur yn trynyte,
Thys suffre y for the loue of the.
The XII reson, wyth mylde mode
Seynt Elene fonde the holy Rode   560   St. *Helen*; *Holy Cross*
Vpon the mounte of Caluarye—
On that Rode Jhesus gan dye,
And was born to that cyte
Wyth Joye & grete solempnite.
The XIII reson ys verament,   565   *truly*
That god shall sytte yn Jugement
Vpon a fryday wyth mylde mode,
Wyth feet & hondes & sydes all blode.
Man, haue thou fryday yn mynde
For these resones that y fynde.   570
For the fryday ys a day of chaunce
Best to faste & to do penaunce.
The satyrday aftur sykurly,   *truly*
Is beste for to faste for our lady,
Thorow her we bene of bale vnbonde   575
And browght out of helle grounde.
She ys called welle of mercy
To alle that wyll to her cry,
To wash & to make clene

All tho th*at* yn sy*n*ne bene;   580
The see sterre called she ys   *sea star*
The ryghth way vs to wys;   *guide*
Of her sprong th*at* swete flo*ur*,
Jh*esus* cryste, our sauyour—
Iblessed mote they all be   585
That seruen Marye mayden fre."   *generous*
　　　　The *emperour* w*yth* wordes sterne
To th*at* chylde he sayde yerne,
"Chylde," he sayde, "I co*n*iure the
In the name of the trynyte   590
And of the passyon of Jh*esus* Cryst—
And of h*ys* deth & h*ys* vpryst,
That th*ou* me the sothe say
Ere th*ou* fro me wende away: *Before you go away*
Wheth*ur* th*ou* be wykked angell or good?"   595
The chylde answered w*yth* mylde mood,
"I am he th*at* the wroghth   *that made thee*
And on the Rode the dere bowghth."
The chylde styed yn to heuen tho,
In to the place th*at* he come fro.   600
The emp*er*o*ur* kneled down to the g*r*ounde
And thanked god th*at* same stounde,
And by cam a good man, as we rede,
In bedes byddyng & almesse dede,   *saying prayers*
And serued god yn all wyse,   605   *every way*
And kam to heuene for h*ys* seruyse.
God yeue g*r*ace yt so mote be,
Sayth all amen for charyte.
Explicit.

Note

1. Textual note: Thorn has been replaced by th, yogh with y at beginning of a
    word and gh in middle or end; all punctuation and paragraph separation added.

14

Occupation and Idleness

BRIAN S. LEE

The play is edited from MS Winchester College 33A, ff. 65r–73v. There is a transcript (with facsimile) in Davis, *Non-Cycle Plays*. The manuscript seems to date from shortly after the middle of the fifteenth century and is written in an East Midland dialect (see Davis, "Two Unprinted Dialogues," and Utley, *Manual*).

The manuscript remains in the library of the school for which perhaps the play was written, and where, one presumes, it was performed. The dialect, however, suggests that the author was not a local man, and the play may, of course, have been imported from farther Northeast because of its suitability as a vernacular school text. Winchester College was founded about 1373 by William of Wykeham, together with New College at Oxford, for "the cure of the common disease of the clerical army, which we have seen grievously wounded by lack of clerks, due to plagues, wars, and other miseries" (Leach, 203). The foundation charter, sealed in 1382, also makes provision for "seventy poor and needy scholars, clerks, living college-wise therein and studying and becoming proficient in grammaticals or the art, faculty or science of grammar" (Leach, 204). The present buildings were not entered until 1394.

Grammar, of course, meant Latin grammar. Some idea of the mid-fifteenth-century curriculum may be gleaned from the play, which is concerned with how to get a living, whether through labor, trade, or in a clerical career; in all cases, the fundamentals of the Christian religion are seen to be prerequisite (cf. ll. 361–66). Doctrine's instruction is liberally sprinkled with Latin quotations from the Vulgate Bible, but he does not trouble his pupils with Greek. Greek was on the curriculum in the later fifteenth century, taught by William Horman, scholar of Winchester in 1468, who was headmaster of Eton from 1485 to 1494 and of Winchester from 1494 to 1502. His *Vulgaria* reproduces exercises he gave and not only is full of Greek phrases, but even refers to the performance of a Greek play. One likes to think that when he was a scholar at Winchester, he may have seen *Occupation and Idleness* performed.[1]

The Morality Play

The vernacular religious drama of the later Middle Ages consisted mainly of biblical craft-cycle plays known as "mysteries" and of homiletic allegories called "moralities." These latter generally showed the life in sin and subsequent conversion and redemption of a representative figure like Everyman, Mankind, or Youth. The other characters were usually personified vices and virtues; but later on, one Vice (e.g., Folly, Hypocrisy, or Iniquity), as the most dramatically interesting character, came to dominate the performances:"proclaiming the superiority of virtue, [the moralities] uniformly demonstrated the dramatic superiority of vice" (Spivack, 123). Entertaining though they were, and enlivened by comedy and contemporary allusion, medieval morality plays were primarily didactic; as such, they were meant to relate directly to the lives of those watching the performance. Mimetic drama, such as Shakespeare's, in contrast, concerns the lives of other people. One may learn from Viola or Othello, for example, but their lives are not, like Everyman's, representative of the audience's and insistently admonitory. Mimetic drama invites critical reflection, whereas didactic drama enjoins decisions and demands assent much like the medieval sermon. The Fourth Lateran Council of 1215 directed parish priests to instruct their parishioners in the fundamentals of the Christian faith; according to *John Gaytryge's Sermon* (1357),[2] Sunday preaching was principally to consist in

> theis sexe thynges: in the fourtene poyntes that falles to the trowthe; in the ten commandementes that God hase gyfen us; in the seven sacramentes that er in Haly Kyrke [Holy Church]; in the seven werkes of mercy untill oure even-crystyn; in the seven vertus that ilke man sall use [each man shall practice]; and in the seven dedly synnes that ilke man sall refuse. (Blake, *Lay Folks,* 75)

Moreover, parishioners were expected to "here and lere thise ilke sex thynges and oftesythes reherse tham till that thay cun [know] tham, and sythen teche tham thair childir, if thay any have, whate tym so thay are of elde to lere tham" (Blake, *Lay Folks,* 75). As a later distich that a child could easily commit to memory more briefly advises,

> Kepe well x & flee from sevyn,
> Spende well v, & cum to hevyn. (Dyboski, 140)

The allusion, of course, is to the Commandments, the Deadly Sins, and the Senses (cf. ll. 378–89 and 801–2); the "five wits" or senses were regarded less as gateways to knowledge than as loopholes for temptation. Morality plays generally assist the work of preachers by introducing some or other of "thise ilke sex thynges."

However, moralities are not homilies, but dramatic allegories.[3] Virtues and Vices contend for the soul of Man, whose life in sin is generally fun and whose conversion is sudden and inevitable. Thus *The Castle of Perseverance* (in, e.g., Eccles), a long and elaborate morality play from the early fifteenth century, follows the career of the protagonist Mankind from infancy to death and indeed into Heaven; the Three Enemies of Man—the World, the Flesh, and the Devil— assail him with their henchmen, and the Castle where he takes refuge is attacked by all Seven Deadly Sins and protected by the corresponding Seven Virtues.

The play that follows has no title in the manuscript: it is called *Occupation and Idleness* for convenience. There is no indication of authorship. However different it may seem from a full-scale morality like *The Castle of Perseverance*, which has numerous allegorical personifications and contending groups of Virtues and Vices, *Occupation and Idleness* is a typical morality play, in that it concerns the punishment and conversion of a representative, willful figure with whom the audience is closely involved: He is clearly one of them. It is an early example of the educative morality, a morality play that is concerned particularly with the moral (and, in this case, religious) education of a youthful person. Elsewhere in the moralities, Virtues and Vices are usually distinguished from the protagonist, who is morally neutral until he chooses to incline first one way and then the other; here roles are combined, and the Youth figure starts out as a Vice, Idleness, and is eventually converted into a Virtue, Cleanness.

The play should be especially diverting for an audience of schoolboys who wait in presumably gleeful anticipation for their unruly fellow pupil to receive the inevitable beating from the master whose tuition he does all he can to avoid. The play is at the same time instructive, in that the audience, of course, hears Doctrine's religious teaching and witnesses the change of heart of the lively pupil Idleness, with whom it has been so easy for the schoolboys to identify. Idleness would probably be played by a precocious pupil, Doctrine probably by a master, Occupation either by a less senior master or an older pupil. Although the play has only three acting parts, and a naughty child for protagonist, it is both theatrically and didactically rewarding, featuring lively dialogue, frequent action or stage business, and subject matter that ranges from Occupation's distress at the hardship of peasant labor to Doctrine's latinate discourse on the mysteries of salvation and the praise due to the Virgin Mary.

The Dramatic Structure of *Occupation and Idleness*

The play is constructed in three movements, as it were, each dominated by a different prop or symbol: namely, the purse (l. 152) that Idleness misappropriates, the book (468) he refuses to study and eventually spoils ("shent," 731), and the birch (implied at 756) with which he is beaten before his conversion.

The first movement, in which bibulous Idleness embezzles his master's money instead of investing it in a lucrative rustic business, may not seem to modern readers to have much to do with the normal concerns of schoolchildren. However, in a rural economy, the more quickly a child could be put to work in the fields, the better for the family. Peasants had to "laboure for [their] mete [food]" (19) in all weathers (32–33) and "with grete greualise [hardship]" (34). Vivid confirmation of the hardships Occupation complains about may be found in *The Second Shepherds' Play*, by the so-called Wakefield Master, and in Langland's *Piers Plowman*, B text, Passus 6.[4] According to Doctrine (ll. 427–29), their lives should consist of work, prayer, and not much play!

In his assumed character as Busy-ness, Idleness claims to be used to all the hard labor farming involves: He says he is willing to thresh, plough, reap, mow, and sow (132–35). He is lying, of course, but Occupation offers him a managerial position as steward or bailiff. In fact, however, Idleness is the college dropout, and to the delight of the schoolboy audience that would scarcely dare to adventure so far, he wastes the money entrusted to him at a cook-shop or inn and swaggers home thoroughly drunk ("verry kuppe shote," 237). His antics are amusing, but alarmingly like those of the wastrels in *Piers Plowman*, B 6, who provoke famine by their unwillingness to work.

The second movement of the play brings the audience closer to the realities of school life. The book that Idleness is unwilling to study is a theatrical prop that focuses attention on the lengths he is prepared to go to escape the main purpose for which he is at the college at all. Here it is less easy to sympathize with him, for the authoritative figure of Doctrine, however alarming to idlers, is obviously right in his teaching and cannot be lightly dismissed. Idleness's efforts to discredit him are too feeble to convince anyone in the audience that he should be regarded as a figure of fun. Few schoolboys would dare to disrupt his classroom.

Idleness is expected to learn the precepts in his book by heart (l. 471). He has evidently been given a primer or ABC, which would have begun with a representation of the Cross (490) and would have contained some elementary prayers and outlines of Christian doctrine (501–2). At his age, Idleness should not be unfamiliar with such beginners' work: His guardians, as well as he, are to blame that he has learned so little (507–8). Perhaps at this point the boys in the audience, already studying their *Donat*, "Cato,"[5] or even Ovid and Virgil, would begin to realize, in their contempt for his ignorance, that their enjoyment of his lifestyle was misplaced. They might even share the master's annoyance at Idleness's stupid reluctance to study his book. Idleness expresses more interest in passing birds and butterflies, and foolishly, or perversely, attempts to destroy his book by washing out the ink written on the pages under pretense of cleaning them. The schoolboys would surely gasp at this wickedness, however often they themselves might have wished a tedious task could be so summarily dealt with.[6]

In the final movement of the play, Idleness receives a good hiding and is immediately repentant. The theatrical effectiveness of this denouement cannot be denied, for conflict, and action that leads to a planned or expected conclusion, is the stuff of drama. However, since we no longer consider beating to be the most effective way of encouraging education, we probably doubt the sincerity of a conversion brought about by force and intimidation. We should be careful, however, not to allow such a view to obscure the message of the play. First, physical correction is endorsed in the Bible (Proverbs 13:24 and 23:13–14), and so parents who failed to chastise their children, like the mother in *Nice Wanton* who allows her spoiled darlings to run wild until they come to ruin,[7] were regarded as foolishly overindulgent. Second, conversions in the morality plays are not as sudden as they may seem, for in fact the thoughtless protagonists are only brought to admit what they and the audience have known from the beginning: that obedience to legitimate authority is necessary if they are to fulfill their moral and intellectual potential. Feckless misbehavior may seem like fun at first, but would be disastrous if the advocates of Christian teaching did not triumph in the end.

Idleness is an attractive character because of his infectious love of fun. But he is also willfully disobedient to authority. Willfulness was thought to be characteristic of children and contrary to reason. Society requires order and reason demands discipline, so willful children had to be punished until they learned to discipline themselves. What nowadays is called social responsibility, the Middle Ages called virtue: the moral consequence of the highest human faculty, reason. In lines 534–35 virtue is linked with reason, reminding us that in medieval times reason was a spiritual and not merely an intellectual faculty, as it usually is today. In other words, Idleness is a naughty boy who shows a promising independence of spirit. All he needs is guidance and correction; without them, he would be a social outcast instead of the "good man" he is destined to become (793–96).

Doctrine's teaching is an essential part of the play that modern readers should not be tempted to gloss over. His first concern is to warn Idleness of the dangers of the Seven Deadly Sins, of which he says sloth, or idleness (the besetting sin of schoolboys!) is the worst (396), and sets him to reading his book. When Occupation asks for the kind of teaching preachers usually gave "the comoun people" (550), Doctrine passes briefly over the Trinity and the nine orders of angels; being more interested in practical Christianity, he elaborates with poetic fervor on the examples of the various orders of saints (566–625), on the divine work of mercy accomplished by Christ on the cross (640–65), and on the Last Judgment (682–710). Uninterested in all this, the feckless Idleness threatens to wash out the instruction written in his book and has to be brought to heel by physical coercion. Converted, he becomes eager

for improvement, and Doctrine obliges him with a description of the Virgin
Mary conventionally derived from the Song of Solomon (822–62).

Notes

1. On medieval schools, see Leach and Orme, *English Schools*.
2. Also known as *The Lay Folks' Catechism*, translated from the Latin by Archbishop Thoresby of York; see Blake, 73–87.
3. On morality plays generally, see Southern, Potter, and Davenport; collections
   of plays are in Eccles and Happé.
4. For conditions that peasant children were subject to when growing up in a
   medieval village, see Hanawalt, *Ties That Bound*.
5. *Donat*: The *Ars Minor* of Aelius Donatus (fourth century A.D.), intended for
   beginners, deals, in the form of question and answer, with the eight parts of
   speech; the more advanced *Ars Major* or *secunda* includes *vitia et virtutes ora-
   tionis* (faults and felicities of public speaking). These were favorite schoolbooks in the Middle Ages. The *Distichs*, supposedly written by Dionysius
   Cato, were a collection of two-line moral maxims used in medieval schools to
   teach both Latin and wise principles. "Cato" is best remembered today as the
   subject of a joke in Chaucer's *Nun's Priest's Tale*.
6. On *Occupation and Idleness* as children's literature, see Lee, especially pp.
   43–45.
7. *Nice Wanton* [Silly Scapegrace] is an early Tudor Morality play about two
   undisciplined children, Delilah and Ismael, and their exemplary brother Barnabas. When a good neighbor advises their mother to beat them, she replies that
   they get enough of that from their schoolmaster, and why should she make
   them lame? Beating need not mean laming, the neighbor retorts. In the end
   Delilah becomes a prostitute and dies of pox, and Ismael a thief and is hanged.
   Barnabas then rescues their mother from suicidal despair.

Occupation and Idleness

*[Occupation, a hard-working farmer, enters the acting area, probably the
school hall (see l. 272) crowded with pupils and their masters and parents]*

OCCUPACION:	The myghty Maker that made al thynge	
	He medle his mercy euer in oure mende,	*instill; mind*
	Oure balis he abate and to blys vs brynge,	*troubles*
	As he was oure founder and we come of	*Creator*
	his kende,	*nature*
	For al the welthe of the world is turned to	
	wranglynge	
	And frendship is ful faynte now for to fynde,	
	Ayen equyte and right the peple be ianglynge,	*squabbling*

And ful fewe ther be that here of haue mynde.	*consideration*
The cause is this,	
For now regneth tresoun 10	
There that shold be resoun,	
But ye be ware in sesoun	*unless; in time*
Ye laboure al amys.	*wrong*
For we may se a grete example euery day	
Of hunger & deth before oure ye,	*eye*
Fro the prikkyng of pestelence ascape we	*attack*
ne may,	
Fro wyndis and wederis that comyth fro	*storms*
the sky,	
Therefor lete right regne and forsake symony	*reign; graft*
Rewle you be resoun and laboure for	
youre mete,	*food*
In trewe occupacioun selle thou and by, 20	
Deseyue no man with sotelte in colde ne	*craftiness*
in hete	
But sewe resoun and trewthe,	*follow*
Lete ese and fauour fro the fle	
And take counseyle and equyte,	
Ellis lese ye heuen so fre	*lose*
And me semyth that were rewthe	*a pity*
And eke grete shame.	*also*
Now if ther be eny here	
That my name wolde aspere,	*ask*
Y telle you, sovereynes al in fere, 30	*together*
Occupacioun, that is my name.	
Y besy ful besely in colde and in hete,	
Wyndis ne wederis we may nat spare.	*avoid*
With grete greualise y go my leuynge	*hardship*
to gete,	
Ofte wery and wetshode y suffre mochel care.[1]	*weary; much*
To sessioun or syses if that y fare,	*lawcourts; go*
Because y haue a litel gadered to hepe,	
In suche ple no skyle y kan, thus am y in care,	
There y stonde and studye as mad as eny shepe	
ffor woo.[2] 40	
ffor y had lever ben at plough,	*rather*
To God y make a vow,	

Thresshe in a berne, ripe & mow,   *reap*
& therefore y hote Occupacion where so   *am called*
   euer y go
On grounde.
Here y thynke to abyde,
To reste me a litel tyde   *while*
In pees bothe saf and sounde.

[*Occupation stands aside, and Idleness bursts in and appeals to the audience*]

IDELNES: A, reste you mery, y make a vow,
Whi sey ye nat welcome now?[3]   50
Be God, ther ben many of yow
That y knowe wel & fyne.
This worthy man, though y it say,
He hath know me many a day,[4]
For he and y spente, in fay,
Oure bothis thryft[5] at wyne.   *both; money*

A, syr, God yeue you good morowe.   *give you*
Lo, siris, this good man wyl be my borowe   *guarantor*
& y had nede.   *if*
Nay, good sir, laugh me nat to scorne,   60
Ytrowe ye haue youre knowlych for lorne   *believe; lost*
For my symple wede.[6]   *clothing*

Ye, this wede wil serue me wel and fyne.
Ofte thou hast be wette sith thou were   *since*
   myne,
Bothe at the ale and atte the wyne
In the hye strete.
While y haue aught y wyl spende,
Whan y haue non God wyl sende.
Thus euery company y wyl amende   *improve*
& gadere felawship to hepe.   70   *friends*

For y haue good mete & drynke,
Whan y am ful y wyl swynke.   *labor*
Now, be my trouthe, as y thynke,   *indeed*
Y am a sly clerke.   *student*
Therfor y tel you expresse,   *particularly*
My name is called Ydelnesse.

Y kepe nat to arise to matynes ne messe   *matins nor mass*
Ne to non other werke.

For to no laboure y kaste me,   *address*
But euer to slowthe y fast me,   80   *sloth; engage*
And if ye wyl ataste me   *examine*
Ye shul fynde me queynte.   *attractive*
Queyntly go y, lo,
As prety as a py, lo.   *magpie*
What sey ye therto,
Who koude make me ateynte?   *find fault with*

Beholde now this gracious face,
Hou galantly y take my trace.   *way*
There is now non such in this place.
Sholde y nat do thus?   90
Lo, how ioly gette y,   *gaily; strut*
& non felaship let y,   *fellowship*
& but fewe mette y
But they wyth me trusse   *pack up*
And gone.   *go*
Ey, what is that yonder gadelynge   *coarse fellow*
That stondith yondere al stradelynge?   *straddling*
Y wyl wite for al his babelynge   *know; chatter*
What he is anone.   *at once*

Al haile, good man, & wel yfounde.   100   *met*
OCCUPACIOUN: A, welcome, yonge man, on this
                  grounde.
YDELNESSE: Whi, sire, tel me this stounde   *time*
              Know ye nat me?
OCCUPACIOUN: Of the, sonne, what is thy name?[7]
YDELNES: Lo, now ariseth game.
              Y am like to take blame
              But y the better ware be.   *unless*

Y must change my name, y wis,   *indeed*
& telle hym Besynesse my name is,[8]   *Industry*
Ye, for God, thus it is,   110   *yea, before*
This is a prety while.   *trick*
& whan y am with hym at fese   *at odds*
Y wyl take myn owen ese.
To slepe ynough he shal nat chese,   *choose*

| | Y thynke hym to begile. | *trick* |

Syr, y wonder ye haue foryete me, ywys,   *forgotten; truly*
And y haue serued you er this,
For Besynes my name is.
Sir, know ye that name?

OCCUPACIOUN: Besynesse, ye, in good fay,   120   *yes; faith*
He hath serued me many a day.

YDELNES: Now, in good fay, leve me ye may,   *believe*
Y am the same.

OCCUPACIOUN: Art thou Besynesse? y trow nay,   *believe*
Me semyth be thi symple aray.   *attire*

YDELNES: Syr, sholde y were my best euery day?   *wear*
Y haue x or twelf
Of good gownes in my presse   *clothes press*
& furres of grete richesse,
Of this man y take wytnesse,   130
Ye may aske hym yourself.⁹

OCCUPACIOUN: Than what labour kan ye best now?   *most skilled in*
YDELNES: Thresshe in your berne or go to plow,
Ripe, mowe and eke sowe,
& other husbondrye,   *farming*
Go to market, bey and selle,
And kepe an household y kan welle,
With shepe and swyne y kan melle.   *concern myself*
Wherto sholde y lye?

OCCUPACIOUN: Wilt thou be with me al this yere   140
& thou shalt be my partenere?
YDELNES: Ye, be my trowthe, with good chere,   *yea*
But y haue no money in store.
OCCUPACIOUN: Yeue me thi trowthe in this stounde,   *give; occasion*
And haue here x pounde.
& thou gouerne it wel on this grounde,   *if*
& thou haue nede, com fech more.

YDELNES: Yis hardely, syr, haue ye no dowte.

[He moves away from Occupation]

Now haue y nede to loke abowte
Bothe within & withowte,   150
That no thynge be a mys.
Y haue here in this purse
X li¹⁰ of golde, it is no worse.   *£10*
To the kokis wil y me trusse   *cooks; pack*
Anon, so haue y blys.   *at once*

Yit, good syr, tel me in same,   *in a word*
What shal y clepe youre name?   *call*

OCCUPACIOUN: Sir, y sey be seynt Jame,   *St. James*
My name is occupacioun.

YDELNES: Occupacioun, be my fay,   160
Is a good name & a worthy
To be commendid honestly
In felde & eke in toun.   *field; also*

But, syr, go ye home or ouere the se,
Your household and your meyne,   *servants*
& than in haste come hider & se.
Tary nat to longe.

OCCUPACIOUN: Fare wel than, in Goddis name.

[*Occupation goes out*]

YDELNES: Now in feithe, he were to blame
That wold do the eny wronge.   170

Walke on, God lete the neuere the,   *prosper*
Thou art ful madde to truste me,
For this gold shalt thou neuer se,
So God me amende,
ffor in Bredestrete, samfayle,   *without fail*
It shall be spent in good vytayle.   *food*
Of wyne & ale y wyl nat fayle.
Thider now am y bent.   *to there*

For and y wolde beset this gold here   *if; lay out*
On sheepe or lambe, thei be dere,   180
And also a badde yeere
Sone wolde hem stroye.   *them; destroy*

If y besette it in kow or veel,
Parauenture some theef myght hem steel.   *perhaps*
Nay, nay, therewith wyl y nat deel,
Such marchauntise y defye.   *merchandise*

Yf y wolde belde eny hous, then   *build*
Myght come some fire & it bren,   *burn*
That makith many awey to ren   *run*
& take the tounnes ende.[11]   190 *town's*
Nay, nay, y wyl nat so, in fay,
But to the tauerne wyl y go my way,
And to the cokes, parmafay,   *by my faith*
Thider wyl y wende.   *go*

But & Occupacioun come by the way?   *what if*
Aske me, syr, y the pray,   *thee*
For we two haue loued many a day,
Thes yeeris foure or fyve!
Tyl this be spente euerydel,   *entirely*
ffal happe falle hel,   200 *(mis)fortune*
Y wyl no lenger with hym mel.   *deal with him*
Y go hennys wel blyve.[12]   *swiftly*

[Idleness goes out, and Occupation reenters]

OCCUPACIOUN: The roy reuerent that on the rode   *revered king;*
                  was rente   *cross*
               He saue you, my souereynes semly in se,   *gracious; seat*
               That was blyndfelled & bofettid & his   *blindfolded;*
                  blood spente   *spilled*
               Fro the thretnynge of thraldom to
                  Make us all fre.
               And the brennynge blossom that bright   *burning flower*
                  is of ble,   *(Mary)*
               With hire feturis so fortunate, voyde   *expression;*
                  vs of oure foon,   *free; foes*

               Excellent emperyse of high dygnete,   *empress*
               Conclude here conclusiones as ye   210 *end their plans*
                  wel kan,
               Thurgh youre Sonnes myght,
               For treuly y wyl euery day,
               Whither so euer y take my way,

In holy chirche, if that y may,
Of thi Sonne haue a sight.[13]

Than to my labour wyl y go,
Tylle & trauayle in moche wo   *work; anguish*
My lyflode to gete.   *livelihood*
We may nat spare, wynde ne rayne,   *refrain*
But go to plow in crofte & playne,   220   *farm*
& ofte we laboure ayen mayne   *beyond our*
In dry & in wete.   *strength*

& y pray you telle me, & ye kan,   *if*
Sey eny you Besynes my man   *see*
Syn y was laste here?   *Since*
For he is so longe oute
With my golde walked aboute,
Be my trouthe y am in doute   *fear*
He is in some daungere.
Y note what is best.   230   *do not know*
Tyl y some tydyngis of hym
              here,   *hear*
Here y thynke to rest.

[Occupation stands aside, and Idleness staggers drunkenly in]

YDELNES: A ha, God spede, y am come.
                         Y haue riȝt wel wette my throte.
                         A ware, a litel stonde a rome,   *stand back*
                         For y am verry kuppe shote.   *drunk*
                         A, my brayne gynneth to rowte   *spin*
                         & turneth as rounde as eny balle.
                         Be my trouthe y am in grete doute,   *fear*
                         Me semyth the sky wyl on me falle.   240
                         Y am ille agast.   *frightened*
                         Y come fro the cokis now,   *cook's*
                         & to God y make a vow
                         Ther haue y wel broke my fast.

                         Y haue ete & drunke of the best
                         Til me thought the dry wey slither,   *slippery*
                         & my maistris golde, so haue y rest,   *master's money*
                         It is spente all to gyder   *altogether*
                         On good mete & drynke.

For be God and oure Lady bothe,   250
Y boght therwith neyther clowte ne   *cloth nor*
   clothe,   *clothes*
For be my partenere neuer so wrothe,
A while wyl y go wynke.   *sleep*

OCUPACIOUN: Abyde, a worde with you.
YDELNES: A, welcome, y make a vow
   Y haue sought you wyde ynow   *enough*
   Thes two dayes or thre.
OCUPACIOUN: Soughtist thou me? y pray the, where?
YDELNES: Be God, no foot there ye were.
OCUPACIOUN: Such a messanger euel he fare   260
   So to seek me.

   Me semyth thou comyst late fro the nale.   *alehouse*
YDELNES: Be God, that is a trewe tale.
   Ther haue y wel fare.
OCUPACIOUN: Now, be God, y stonde in doute
   That thou hast spendid my money
      oute,
   Than am y in grete care.
YDELNES: Sir, that money is a go,
   They there had be such two.   *though*
   Therfore myn herte is sore.   270

OCUPACIOUN: A, sire, foule mote the befalle   *may*
   That euer y mette the in this halle.
   My golde thou hast lore.   *lost*

   What, thou seidest Besynes thi name
      hight?   *is called*
YDELNES: So y dede, be this lyght,
   & yit y dede lye.
   But now y telle the in game   *sport*
   Ydelnes is my name.[14]
OCCUPACIOUN: Y swere be seynt Jame,
   Thou art a wyli pye.   280   *cunning thief*

   Sonne, & thou wylt to me herke   *if; listen*
   Y wyl teche the some other werke.
YDELNES: What, woldist thou make me a clerke?   *student*

	That wyl y nat begynne,	
	For y wyl go pley me	
	And rialy aray me.	*regally*
OCCUPACIOUN:	Herk, sonne, thou say me,	
	Wylt thou worship wynne?	*honor*

YDELNES:	Worship? hou sholde y come	
	therto?	
OCCUPACIOUN:	With manere & manhod, sonne, lo,	290
	& be neuer thyn owen fo.	
	To my wordis thou herk.	
YDELNES:	Who techith that manere, y pray the?	
OCCUPACION:	Treuly, sonne, as y say the,	
	Doctrine, that worthi clerk.	

YDELNES:	Doctryne? what man is he?	
OCUPACION:	A maister of dyuynete	
	Of the vnyuersyte,	*university*
	To teche the to wex wyse.	*become*
YDELNES:	A, a, wylt thou so?	300
	Nay, y wyl nat with the go,	
	Y haue aspied the to wyse.	*for certain*

OCUPACION:	Sonne, leue thi fantasy	*folly*
	& turne to grace, y say the.	
YDELNES:	Y nel, y make to God a vow,	*do not want to*
	Y wyl ete as good as thow.	
	Go sette to gras thi hors or thi kow,	
	Or ellis, syr, go play the.	

OCCUPACION:	Who[15] shal fynde the mete & drynke	*provide*
	al day?	
YDELNES:	Be my fay, Ionet and Gyll.	310 · *by; faith*
OCCUPACION:	What wilt thou do, kan thou me say,	
	Whan Ionet and Gill ys away?	
YDELNES:	Than be it as be may,	
	Therefore care y nell.	*do not want to*

	Y shrew hym that therefore cares.[16]	*curse*
	Some for labour wexith wode,	*go mad*
	And they haue nat an hole hode.	*hood*
	Y know non that better fares.	

	Tunc venit Doctrina.		*Then comes* *Doctrine*

DOCTRINA:	What, siris, what pley is this		
	That ye make in this place?	320	
	Y am come to mende al mys		
	Bi the helpe of Goddis grace.		

YDELNES:	A, that man hath an angry face.[17]		
OCCUPACION:	Pees than, fool, and stonde a syde.		
YDELNES:	Y pray God yeue the euel grace,		*give thee*
	Begynnyst thou now for to chyde?		*find fault*

OCUPACION:	Sir, welcome mote ye be,		
	And of youre name y you prayn.		
DOCTRINE:	Doctryne men clepen me,		*call*
	To teche kunnynge y am fayn.	330	*knowledge*

OCUPACION:	Doctrine, syr, ye be welcome.		
	Y haue besied me ful sadde		*consistently*
	For to study & stire wysdom,		*try to get*
	Now of youre company y am ful		
	gladde.		

DOCTRINE:	What is youre name, gentil brother?		
OCCUPACION:	Treuly, my name is Occupacion.		
DOCTRINE:	Welcome be ye aboue all other		
	With you to haue communycacyoun,		

	For al that to good occupacion long		*belong*
	God is plesed and so am y,	340	
	But occupacion that tuchith to wronge		*tends toward*
	Doth men no good, but vylany.[18]		

	For & thou wilt the occupy		*if*
	In bodely workis or almasdede,		*work; charity*
	In penaunce or prayeris wilfully,[19]		*voluntarily*
	Y, Doctrine, to the wyll take hede,		

	For Doctrine techith openly and clere		
	Vertuous lyf amonge vs to sette.		
YDELNES:	Herke, siris, ye shull here,		
	For now two shrewis ben mette.	350	*bullies*

	Be my trouthe[20] y wil me hide	
	Like a mows in yonder yerde,	
	For of hym that gapith wide	
	Yn feithe y am euel aferde.	*afraid*
	Y wyl be go.	
DOCTRINE:	Be my feith thou shalt abide,	
	& ere thou passe fro me this tyde	*before; time*
	Y wil the teche a worde or two.	

YDELNES:	Whom, me, syr? y know the nat,		
	Ne neuer y kepe, be heuen kynge.	360	*wish to*
DOCTRINE:	Sonne, y wyl teche the som what		
	For to get thy leuynge.		*living*

OCCUPACION:	Sir, in the name of heuen kyng,	
	Yeue hym som informacion	
	Hou he may gete his leuyng	
	In the wey[21] of his saluacion,	
	That is al my desire.	
DOCTRINE:	Treuly, brother Occupacion,	
	That wil y do without eny hire,	

For euery good man is bounde	370	
To occupie hym in clennes,		*virtue (purity)*
For & he in good occupacion be founde		
The feend temptith hym moche the les.[22]		*much less*

Euery man hath enmyes thre,	*three enemies*
The deuel, the world, & his owen flessh.	
Which thei ben y wyl telle the,	
& hou thon they enbateyl hem fressh.	*then; renew*

In pride & wreth the feend temptith man,	
And in envye that is so badde.	
Thes thre synnes in heuen began	380
Sone after Lucifer was made.	

The world temptith man to slouthe[23]	*sloth; avarice*
& couetyse,	
That Adam & Eve first vp broght	
Whan thei wolde be as wyse	
As was oure Lorde that hem wroght.	*made them*

The flessh of glotonye fayled noght,
Lechery was in Sodom & Gomor²⁴
   & other mo,
For these, wyte wel in oure thoght,   *know well*
Ful moche harme there hath be do.   *been done*

For & thou the in temptacion fele,   390   *feel tempted*
Occupie the in clennes,
For the feend on no man may stele   *surprise*
Saue in tho that he fynte in ydelnes,   *except; finds*
In hem wil he hide.
For al the vices that ther be
Ydelnes is the worste, y telle the.

YDELNES: Out, whider may y fle?
This angry man wyl bete me
& y lenger abyde.   *if I stay longer*

DOCTRINE: Of ydelnes comyth this,   400
Thefis & strumpettis, so haue y rest.   *thieves; harlots*
Ayen this defaute, ywys,   *against; indeed*
Occupacion y holde the best.

But the moste defaute nowadayes
On the peple that y fynde,
Men techen hire children wanton playes   *conduct*
& nat as they sholde in kynde.   *by nature*

Some shal beshrewe fader & moder   *abuse*
& be ful wantoun, as ye may se.
Such poyntis and many other   410   *habits*
Makith many children neuer to the.   *prosper*

Sette youre children vnto scole,²⁵
Ye that ben good men of fame,
Mayntene hem nat to pley the fole,   *support*
But lete hem lerne some good, for
    shame.

For he that hath neither londe ne rente,   *income*
Koyne ne catel hym to fynde,   *coin; goods*
Of large spense but he repente   *expense; unless*
Sone shal he begge be kynde.   *as is natural*
That were reprefe,   420   *blameworthy*
For whi and²⁶ thi good be lore   *because if; lost*

& wylt nat laboure for no more,
But in ydelnes sett hym sore,
Than must he wexe a thefe.   *become*
Y lye nat, expresse.   *indeed*
Beware, draw you to good,
& laboure for youre lyfis food,
& pray to hym that deyde on rood,   *cross*
& beware of ydelnesse.

OCCUPACION: Ydelnes is nat ferre, as thynkith me,   430   *far off*
               & so y tolde one ryght now.
DOCTRINE: Ydelnes, where is he?
OCCUPACIOUN: Yonder, syr, as ye may se,
               & scorneth both me & yow.

DOCTRINE: Ydelnes, come nere
               And lerne of me som curtesie.   *courtesy*
YDELNES: Y shrew me & y come ther   *I won't go*
               While thou art so angry.

DOCTRINE: Thu shalt come hider mawgry thyn hed   *willy-nilly*
               & lerne some good in thi youthe.   440
               Thou wylt be like to begge thi brede
               But thou drawe the fro slouthe.   *unless*
               Y sey, boy, aryse.

YDELNES: Y pray the syr, go thi way,
               Me lyst nat with the to play.   *I don't wish*
DOCTRINE: Y wyl the teche, in good fay,
               Now for to wexe wyse.   *grow wise*

               Therfor, boy, y sey stonde stille
               & some vertu that thou lere.   *learn*
YDELNES: Go forthe & do me non ylle.   450
               Y wolde ye were in the diche both   *ditch*
                  in fere.   *together*

DOCTRINE: Y sey, boy, scorne thou me now?
OCCUPACION: He dothe as euel as he kan.
YDELNES: He lieth, y make God a vow
               In recorde of this worthy man.   *as this fellow*
                                                                   will attest

               Syr, saw ye me mokke hym to scorne?
               Nay, he lieth in his face.[27]

| DOCTRINE: | Y trow, boy, thi thryft be lorne. | | *believe; thrift* |
| | To goodnes thou hast no grace. | | |

OCCUPACION:	Syr, euer to sleuthe & ydelnes	460	*sloth*
	He drawith hym morow & eve,		
	& y bidde hym ofte,[28] expres,		*tell; often*
	Al that foly for to leve.		

DOCTRINE:	Sonne, to what levynge were thou borne?		
YDELNES:	With mylke and floure y began, y wene.		*suppose*
DOCTRINE:	What, this boy dryveth me to scorne.		
YDELNES:	Nay, God forbede, lete that bene.		*overlook that*

DOCTRINE:	Haue, sette honde on this book,		*take*
	& to thi lore that thou lowte.		*attend*
YDELNES:	A, se, syr, how y look.	470	
	Nere hande y kan it thurghowte.		*nearly know*
	A, se, here sitt a pye.		*magpie*
DOCTRINE:	But thou the better to thi book lowte,		*unless; attend*
	Be my fay thou shalt abye.		*suffer for it*

OCCUPACION:	In good fey, ye sey wel		
	Euery man to labour in his kunnynge.		
	This matere y trow wel y fele,		
	Ellis can we haue but hard levynge.		

	And ydelnes in household wende		*if; comes*
	Me semyth it moche the worse.	480	
YDELNES:	Ye be euer my bak frende,		*false friend*
	Therfor haue ye Goddis kurse.		

DOCTRINE:	Sonne, haue this book in thi hande		*take*
	& lerne in the name of God,		
	Ellys y do the to vnderstonde		
	Thou shalt be chastised with a rod		
	Bothe even & morowe.		
YDELNES:	A, syr, he that the hider broght		
	Y pray God yeue hym sorowe.		

DOCTRINE:	Sey on,[29] crosse Crist me spede,	490	*repeat; prosper*
	& in thi mynde that it kepe.		
YDELNES:	Be my trouthe,[30] y stonde in drede		*indeed*
	Hou y shal brynge it to hepe.		*accomplish it*

	First lete me reste a litel while,		
	Myn eyen be hevy as eny lede.		
OCCUPACION:	Sir, this boy wyl you begyle.		
	In the name of God take hede		
	And lerne hym som lore.		*teach; learning*
YDELNES:	A, sir, the deuel be thi spede,		
	Thou art ayen me euer more.	500	*against*

DOCTRINE:	Sonne, lerned thou neuer thi beleve,		*doctrine*
	Thi Pater noster, Aue and crede?		
YDELNES:	Nay syr, so mote y cheve,		*may; achieve*
	Therto toke y neuer hede,		
	Y not what it is.		*do not know*
DOCTRINE:	Now be swete seynt Jame		*St. James*
	Thi fader is the more to blame		
	& thi frendis al in same		*likewise*
	That shold haue taught the er this.		*before*

OCCUPACION:	Me semyth it were an almasdede	510	*a kindness*
	To make hym leve this lewde rote.		*rough crowd*
YDELNES:	Y wyl nat do be thi rede.		*advice*
	Olde fole, thou begynnest to dote,		*fool*
	Thi berd begynnyth to hore.		*grow gray*
	Som forwery fallith doun,		*worn out*
	Bothe in cyte, burgh and toun,		
	& rise parauenture no more.[31]		*perhaps*

DOCTRINE:	Treuly ther leuyth no man in ground,		*lives*
	Be he neuer so hye of state,		
	But he be strongly bound	520	
	To occupye erly or late,		*keep busy*

	Prestis to pray & preche also		*priests*
	In penaunse & masse to shewe,		
	Dukis, erlis, baronnes & knyghtis therto		*also*
	To mayntene the land in vertu,		*keep*

	& to fight therfore if nede be		
	& stonde be euery trew cause, ywis,		*uphold; indeed*
	& take no mede of me ne the,		*bribe*
	But to maynten hem there right is.		*where; justice*

| | But now trewthe is dryve abakke | 530 | |

& symony is set vp as a sire.   *symony*
Ther mede is maister ther is no lakke   *bribery*
Of frendship nother in session ne shire.   *assize court*

But wolde God resoun regned aye,   *always*
Than wolde ye gadre al vertues to hepe.   *virtues; together*
To the wordis that ye shew me
Euery man is bounde to take kepe.
Lo, sonne, thou mayst se
To Occupacion thou art bounde.[32]

YDELNES: A, sir, God lete the neuer the,   540   *prosper*
Thou woldist make me weré   *weary*
As is eny hounde,
And that y hate.
For aught that thou kan telle me   *anything*
Shal noon of yow felle me,   *overcome*
Nother be strengthe compel me,
Erly ne late.

OCCUPACION: Doctrine, syr, y pray you,
Tel vs some of Goddis werkis
That the comoun people may knowe   550
As don thes worthi clerkis.   *do; scholars*

DOCTRINE: *Summe Trinitati*[33] y wyl begynne,
That with his myght wroght al   *created*
   thyng,
Nouem ordines without synne   *nine orders*
Angelorum to hym obeyng,[34]   *of angels*

Ad Dei iudicia for to abide,
Misteria complenda, ful of lyght.
Yit fille many one that tide,   *fell; time*
Fro the place that mankende shal   *regain; justly*
   restore ful ryght.

OCCUPACION: What maner men, y wolde wyte,   560   *I'd like to know*
Shal restore that place ayen?
DOCTRINE: Hire names ben in legende wryte,   *written*
& are cleped al halowen, certeyn.   *called; all*
                                                        saints

OCCUPACION: Alle halowes, what be they?
Y pray you, declare hem openly.

DOCTRINE:	Angelis, patriarkis & prophetis to sey, Martiris & confessoris trewly,	*say*

	Virgines & other of clene lyf	*pure*
	That deide in pure chastité,	
	That leved here without stryf	570 *lived*
	In clennes and humylité.	*purity*

	Viri religiosi[35] the patriarkis called	*holy men*
	Atque gloriosi in hire levynge,	*and famous*
	Thei tolde what wolde befalle	
	Of dyuerse prophetis, & Cristis comynge.	

	John the Baptist seide in his steuen	*preaching*
	To al that *veram penitenciam*[36] wold chesen,	*contrition*
	Penitenciam agite that ye nat lesen,	*penance*
	Quia appropinquabit the kyngdom[37] of heaven	*approach*
	The postelis were in erthe goynge	580 *apostles*
	& Iesu Cristis lawes redde,	
	Estote fortes, seide Iesu oure kyng,	*be brave*
	Loke no tribulacion make yu ferde.[38]	*afraid*

OCCUPACION:	Y pray you, telle me in this place Hou apostlis suffred tribulacion.	
DOCTRINE:	Some *ferro perempti*[39] heded was,	*beheaded*
	Some *flammis exusti* brent in toun,	*burned*
	Flagellis verberati, some forbeten,[40]	
	Hij sunt triumphatores, Goddis frendis on[41] heth,	*they are*
	Here good dedis shal neuer be foryeten,	590 *their* *forgotten*
	For hir blissed name *in eternum manet*.	*remains*
YDELNES:	Heere ye, siris, al this breth?	*hear*
	A draght of ale y had leuer.[42]	*draught; rather*

OCCUPACION:	This were a worthy company That the apostel loued day & nyght.	
DOCTRINE:	*Vos estis lux mundi*,[43]	*light*
	To al the world thei shal yeue lyght.	*give*

OCCUPACION: The martiris had a glorious lyf   *martyrs*
That for Goddis loue wold dey so.
DOCTRINE: A, sir, *hij sunt sancti*[44] that neuer   600   *they are holy*
dred knyf,
But *pro Dei amore* thei suffred wo.   *love of God*

O *quam gloriosa* hire deth is,   *how glorious*
& hire blod shedynge ded vs moche
good.
The blood shedyng wolde brynge
vs to blys
If that we ben mylde of mood.   *meek*

Thes blissed confessouris leued clenly
& taught aboute the worde of Crist,
Therfore thei sitte in the grete glory
Where that al ioy & myrthe is most.   *rejoicing*

Virgines in hire clennes   610
Mekely in erthe here leued.   *lived*
Thes be kleped al halowes, ywys,   *called; saints*
That we befor meved.   *referred to*
& al holi chirchis pardoun
Relevith men out of synne,
Of thes seyntis that is come
That is tresore the holy chirche withynne.[45]

At Cristis owen blode y wyl begynne.
His postelis, his marteris, & afterwarde
His officeris that ben out of synne.   620
Ledde hire lyf here ful harde,

& the clennes of the maydenes alle
Make vs good weies into heuen.   *ways*
Al Halowen Day hire day men calle,   *All Saints' Day*
& worship hem with myld steuen.   *voice*

OCCUPACION: A, syr, of men that leuyth a day, now,
Shul they in that number be?
DOCTRINE: Ye, syr, and wyl ye se how?
Fulgebunt iusti[46] & thus sey we.

Rightwys men may nat fayle, ywis,   630   *righteous*
To han heuen for hire trauayl,   *have; suffering*

Rightfulnes so hie a vertu is   *exalted*
That *iusticia manet* may nat fayl.   *justice awaits*

OCCUPACION: & how do they that haue do synne
     & amende hem here ere they dey?   *reform*
DOCTRINE: Fro heuen blis thei may nat wynne,   *cannot decline*
     To aske mercy thei were redy.

OCCUPACION: What is mercy? That wolde y know,
     Y pray you, do me to vnderstonde.
DOCTRINE: Mercy is the best seed sow,   640   *sown*
     Fore aboue al workis he shal stonde.[47]

Fore as *per lignum moriebatur mors*[48]   *by a tree death*
  certayn,   *introduced*
Thurgh a tree oure deth first aroos,
And *per lignum quoque* there agayn   *also by a tree*
By a tree oure lyf was chose,   *restored*

& broght oure blys fro deth and stryf,   *was brought*
For even as Adam by a tre dede falle,
To turne oure deth to euerlastyng lyf
On a tre God deyde for vs alle.[49]

Ther was *oleum promissionis*[50] shewde   650   *oil of promise*
That fro Cristis body ran.
Take hede, thou man, & be nat lewde,   *foolish*
For al our grace ther first began

Goddis body therto was al torente,   *torn*
& made ful of holis that euer shal renne   *run*
To the blode of mercy that neuer shal
  stente   *be staunched*
In the saluacion of synful men.

For his passion, til domys day   *Judgment Day*
His body shal neuer leue rennyng,
& of his blode of mercy euery man   660
  gete may
If thei repente hire euel leuyng.

Ther shal noon be warned that blode   *denied*
  of blys,
Euery man ther of may gete.

This is the licoure of mercy that euery   *[holy] water*
   day, ywys,
In holy chirche thou may it fette.   *fetch*

OCCUPACION: Y thanke Jesu my sauyoure
With al my herte & my speche,
So fre of that worthy lycoure   *liberal*
As wel to pore as to ryche.

DOCTRINE: Nay, sir, ye fayle ther,   670
Ther is no disseuerance, but brother   *distinction*
   & brother.
God boght alle like dere,   *alike; dearly*
& payde as moche for one as for other.

Ther is no pore, God seith before,   *poor*
But tho that be in sinne & out of vertu.   *those who*
Thei thou haue markis in store   *though; riches*
Ther he shal be as ryche as thou.

The riches of heuen is non in gold,
It is in vertu & clene lyf,
As to the before is tolde   680
That shold be vsed in man and wyf.

At domys day God wote   *knows*
Who shal be riche, who shal be pore,[51]
For that day wyl be so hote
That be gold men wyl sette no store.

OCCUPACION: Sir, that is come to my mende,   *mind*
Whi clepe ye that the grete day?   *do you call*
DOCTRINE: For many skile that y fynde,   *reasons*
Y wil declare hem if y may

Than shal sitte the grettest iustise opon   690   *judge*
That euer sate in eny place,
Al other iustisis before hym[52] shal
   stonde,
& al the lordis that euer was.

So many at ones as we ther shal se   *once*
Neuer at ones in oo place come,   *one*

For all that were & euer shal be
In heuen, erthe & helle comyth to dome.   *judgment*

That day wyl be the grettest wepynge
That euer was sey in eny place before,   *seen*
Many thousandis hire hondis shal wrynge   700   *their*
& curse the tyme that thei were bore.

Therfore the grete day clepe y,
For tho that shal be dampned in that rowte   *crowd*
Shul wepe more water with here ye   *their eye*
Than is in alle the world rounde aboute.

Thei shal neuer after sese wepyng,   *cease*
The water fro hire ey shal renne,
Therfor thynke on this day of rekenyng,
& euer after hate thou synne
And in haste thi lyf amende.   710

OCCUPACION: Wyl y neuer worke begynne
              But y thynke on the ende.   *Unless I*

YDELNES: Be my trouthe, no more wil y,
              For y haue no wil to be a clerke.
              Of my book y am wery,
              Y was not wonte to no suche werke.   *accustomed*

              This book is nat worth a resshe,   *rush*
              X suche are nat worthe a beene.   *ten; bean*
              Be my fay, y wyl hym wesshe   *wash*
              & make him feyre & clene.   720

              Good,⁵³ yeue me a litel water   *Good sir*
              That y may wesshe my book,
              For they my maister chide & chater   *although*
              & theigh Ocupacion hereof smatere,   *babble*
              Y wyl no more hereon look.

OCCUPACION: What, sonne, what pley is this?
YDELNES: Be God, it is neuer the worse.
OCCUPACION: Y wyl telle thi maister, ywis.
YDELNES: Therfore haue thou Goddis curse.

OCUPACION: Doctrine, sir, take hede   730

	Hou your clerk shent[54] his book.	*spoils*
YDELNES:	A, syr, the deuel be thi spede,	
	Who badde the hider look?	
DOCTRINE:	A, lewde losell, what iapes ben thes?	*rascal*; *pranks*
	Thou takest the to fantasies.	*follies*
	Fast sit doun, thou shalt nat chese.	*choose*

YDELNES:	A, sire, here be many botter flyes	
	Bothe white & broun,	
	For cokkis blood, take me thyn hode	*God's*; *hat*
	& y wyl smyte hem doun. 740	

DOCTRINE:	A, a, thou dost wel & fyne.	
	Y wil[55] the tame, be seynt Austyne,	*Augustine*
	Be thou neuer so wylde.	
	Ocupacion, ley hond on hym, haue do,	*done*
	And myself wyl helpe therto.	
	Come forth, my feire childe.	

YDELNES:	Come no nere, y charge the now,	*nearer*
	For & thou do, y make a vow,	
	Y wyl stryke the to the hert.	
	Wolde God my dagger were grounde. 750	
DOCTRINE:	Sette honde on hym anon this stounde,	*now*
	Lete him nat sterte.	*escape*

OCUPACION:	Come forthe thou shalt, magre thy teeth.	*despite yourself*
YDELNES:	Out vpon the, stronge theef,	
	Wylt thou me spille?	*kill*
DOCTRINE:	Haue here one, two & thre.	*[beating him]*
	Ydelnes, now thynke on me	
	& holde thi tunge stille.	

YDELNES:	& y lyue y wil be awreke,	*if*; *avenged*
	Some of your hedis wyl y breke, 760	
	For ye haue made me wrothe.	
DOCTRINE:	How seist thou? that lete me se.	
YDELNES:	Nay, for God, it is he,[56]	
	In recorde of al this compané	*witness*
	He dede beshrewe you bothe.	*abuse*

DOCTRINE:	ffy on the, harlot, with thi glosynge,	*rogue*; *lying*
	Thou shalt haue more, be heuen kynge,	

	To teche the wexe trewe.		*honest*
YDELNES:	A, mercy maister, y cry mercy,		
	Foryeue me this & redely	770	
	Your lore wyl y shewe.[57]		

DOCTRINE:	In good feith, thou shalt haue mo		*more*
	But thou leue thi ydelnes.		*unless*
	& but thou study & labour also		
	In al the workis of clennes,		*virtue*

	For God taught his disciplis all,		
	To the & to other teche wyl y,		
	Vigilate ergo, grete & small,		*watch therefore*
	Nescitis qua hora that ye shul dey,[58]		*you do not know at what hour*

	We know non houre of oure deyinge,	780	
	Therefore in prayeris euer shul we be,		
	For with oure Pater noster we shold		*Our Father*
	worship heuen kynge		
	And his blissed moder with an Aue.		*Hail Mary*

YDELNES:	Y sey now mercy, with herte and speche,		
	For euer to you wyl y obedient be,		
	And y wyl do as ye me teche		
	In al the workis of honesté.		
	Pater noster y wil[59] begynne.		

OCUPACION:	Lo, how litel maistry it is		*force*
	To brynge in a childe in yowthe.	790	
	Frendis, take hede to this		
	& euer draw you fro slowthe.		

	& thus had he had no techynge		
	He wold haue cursed his frendis all,		
	& now he may in tyme comynge		
	Be a good man, & so he shall.		

DOCTRYNE:	Art thou sory for thi mys		*sin*
	The which to the y wyl reherce?		
YDELNES:	Ye, syr, that y am, ywys,		
	Therof y cry God & you mercé.	800	*mercy*

DOCTRINE: The x comaundementis thou brake
         euermore,
        Thi v wyttis thou kepte hem ille.   *five senses*

YDELNES: Treuly that y repente sore,
        Y wil amende with al my wylle.

DOCTRINE: The dedis of mercy[60] dost thou
         nat fulfylle
        To poor, seek, presoners also.   *the sick*

YDELNES: Y wyl amende it with good wylle   *make amends*
        And y may haue lyf therto.   *if*

DOCTRINE: Now thou forsakest thyn ydelnes
        & hereafter wilt dred shame,   810
        Here y caste on the a clothe of clennes   *purity*
        & Clennes shal be thi name.[61]

YDELNES: Worthi mayster, y thanke the,
        And yu, Ocupacion, also,
        Of this man that is so fre,   *noble*
        & to you wil y euer drawe to.

OCUPACION: Now am y glad with al my hert
        That euer y mette with the in thys place,
        So feire thou art now conuert
        Fro foly & fantasy turned to grace   820

        With so mylde steuen.   *obedient voice*
YDELNES: Mayster, y pray you for charite
        That ye wolde telle me
        What powere hath oure Lady in heuen.

DOCTRINE: Aboue al the wommen that euer were
        God chese Mary vnto this,
        In hire body hym to bere,
        Et perelegit eam Deus[62]   *God chose her*

        Sicut lilium amonge thornes growyng   *as the lily*
        Sic amica mea inter filias   830
        So is his moder most shynynge,
        Passinge al the wommen that euer was.

        Witnes at hire assumpcion[63]

Whan the angel seide, *que est ista*[64]   *who is this*
Que descendit fro deserte adoun   *who cometh*
Tamquam fumi virgula   *like a branch*
                                                  of incense

& *sicut aurora consurgens*,   *dawn rising*
Neuer sunne shynynge so bryght
With all delites of swetnes
Ther they saw that glorious syght,   840   *where*

But at the ascension of Crist aloon.   *but only at*
Whan she to heuen was come
God seide to his angel anoon,
"*Hec est regina virginum*[65]   *Queen of virgins*

Que genuit regem in hire body so clene   *bore the King*
Cui famulantur angely euery day.   *angels serve*
This same body that ye here sene
Within the blissed sides y lay."

God seide to hire, "*amica veni*,[66]   *beloved, come*
Veni de Libano in flessh & fell,   850
Veni coronaberis[67] in heuen most hy
As quene of heuen & emperes of hell."

& Lady of al the world she is,
Hire power is of grete astate.   *estate*
Whoso honoure hire with Aues   *prayers*
Al his desese she wyl abate,   *distress*

So he be clene & out of synne   *pure*
Or in wille for to amende,
In euery worke that he wyl begynne
Oure dere Lady wyl be his frende,   860

& but he stonde in that degre   *condition*
Y wolde nat yeue for his prayeris a pere.   *give; pear*
CLENNES: Y thanke my Lorde in Tryneté
That euer y mette with you here.

OCUPACION: Thanke we hym of myghtis moste,
Fader and Sonne in Tryneté,
Abatere of the feendis boste,   *boast*

Holy my hert y yelde to the.   *yield*

CLENNES: He vs brynge to good ende
                That deyde for vs on good fryday,   870
                & Mary his moder be oure frende
                Vnto thi sone as ye best may.

DOCTRINE: He that is registred for the ryght eyre,   *lawcourt*
                That doutful domys man that sittith in trone   *terrifying; judge*
                Kepe you euer oute of all dispeyre
                And graunte you his blissynge euerychone.   *every one*
                Amen.

Notes

1. [wetshode] With shoes full of water from tramping in the mire. Lines 32–35 describe typical hardships endured by the medieval peasant laborer. Cf. "Wowerie and wetschod": *Piers Plowman*. C xxi, 1. Only its opposite, dryshod, is current now, indicating perhaps how living conditions have improved since medieval times.
2. Lacking a legal education, Occupation is easily conned. Soon he will unwisely entrust money to Idleness.
3. It is customary for Vices to burst boisterously in and demand the audience's attention. Idleness comes just in time to prevent the schoolboy spectators growing bored with Occupation's long complaint.
4. Singling out and embarrassing a member of the audience was a typical theatrical joke in the role of the Vice. Idleness has already accused the accosted boy's fellows ("many of yow," 51) of the vice (sloth) that he represents.
5. [thryft] Davis reads "thryst" (thirst).
6. Clothing in the Moralities is often indicative of the allegorical status of the wearer. If Idleness were less idle, he would be able to afford to be better attired.
7. 103–4: Idleness addresses Occupation with the respectful plural pronoun *ye*; Occupation replies to the youngster with the familiar singular forms *the* and *thy*. He uses the subject form *thou* at 124; Idleness, consistently respectful, uses the plural object form *you* at 117, and *youre* at 157, but scornfully starts using singular second-person pronouns as soon as Occupation goes out at 168.
8. The Vices typically assume names of opposite Virtues in order to deceive.
9. Here perhaps the actor singles out his bedfellow, who would know how much he is exaggerating the quality of the garments he keeps in the chest or cupboard in their dormitory.
10. [X li] Davis expands to "ten pounde."
11. A reminder that fires in closely built medieval wood and thatch villages or towns could be devastatingly destructive. If once a fire caught hold, the only safe course might well be to get right out of town.
12. 195–202: This stanza is punctuated on the assumption that Idleness, singling out a fellow idler in the audience, asserts: If you're wondering what'll happen

when Occupation comes back, I'll tell you: I'm off to spend his money, and I shan't be here! But he may mean to say: If he asks for me, don't tell him where I've gone (since that is what happens at 223–32); but if so, grammatically he does not succeed in saying it.

13. 203–15: Occupation again uses an ornate thirteen-line stanza, with its intricate rhymes and elaborate alliteration, as he did at the beginning of the play. A Virtue's impressive style on first entering distinguishes him from the more colloquial Vices and signals that he deserves the audience's respect.

14. Now that he has admitted his character to be that of a Vice, Idleness drops his pretense of respect and addresses Occupation with singular pronouns.

15. [who] MS. "whi."

16. The third person singular in *-s* of the rhyme words *cares* and *fares* is a Northeast Midland dialectal form rare in the South at this date, where the usual form ends in *-th*.

17. The first sign in the play that discipline in medieval schools was strict! Cf. 398.

18. Hard work by itself is not enough: Doctrine is careful to distinguish between good and evil occupation.

19. 344–45: The seven works of mercy (see line 805) and deeds of charity (almsgiving) are the outer signs of inward contrition, represented by penance and prayer. These activities make up "vertuous lyf" (348).

20. 351: Ironic: Idleness has little integrity (truth) to swear by, but the phrase is a cliché, meaning little more than "indeed": cf. 73, 492, 713. The synonym *fay* is used at 160, 310, and 719.

21. [wey] Davis reads "way."

22. Cf. 392–94. The Devil proverbially takes advantage of idleness: see, e.g., the Prologue to Chaucer's *Second Nun's Tale*.

23. [slouthe] Sloth is more usually regarded as one of the sins of the Flesh, as in *The Castle of Perseverance*, 2235–38. The three Enemies of Man and the Seven Sins, brought on the stage as personified allegories there, are described, but not personified, here (374–87). They are frequently alluded to in didactic literature.

24. For the sin and destruction of the cities of Sodom and Gomorrah, see Genesis 18 and 19.

25. Advice in the play is directed not only at schoolchildren, but also at their parents. Evidently, the playwright assumed parents might be in the audience.

26. [for whi and] Perhaps "For whi? and."

27. The actor must play the line according to circumstances: If the boy addressed as a "worthy man" in 455 gleefully tells Doctrine he did see Idleness mock him, then the boy is lying; if he takes Idleness's part, then it is Occupation who is lying.

28. [ofte] Davis reads "efte" ("again").

29. [on] "god" canceled in MS after "on."

30. [trouthe] Davis reads "treuthe."

31. 512–17: This insulting speech is doubtless an aside, as Doctrine and Occupation do not seem to react to it.

32. 518–39: This speech, referring to the duties of the various social classes or "estates," to the dangers of meed and to the desirability of the rule of reason,

echoes the themes of the early parts or passus of Langland's popular allegorical poem *Piers Plowman*.

33. 552: *Summe Trinitati* ("At the Supreme Trinity"); 554-55: *Nouem or-dines . . . / Angelorum* ("Nine orders . . . / Of angels").

34. In the *Celestial Hierarchies* (*c.* 500), falsely attributed to Dionysius the Are-opagite, the nine orders, are Seraphim, Cherubim and Thrones, Dominations, Virtues and Powers, Principalities, Archangels and Angels. Only the last two are actively involved with humanity. For the Latin in the following stanza: 1. 556, *Ad De iudicia* ("To God's judgments) and 1. 557: *Misteria complenda* ("fulfilling the mysteries"); (or perhaps the author intended, *Mi[ni]steria complenda* ("Fulfilling their duties").

35. For the Latin in the following stanza: 1. 572, *Viri religiosi* ("Holy men"); 1. 573, *Atque gloriosi* ("And famous").

36. 576: *veram pentenciam* ("sincere contrition"); 577: *Penitenciam agite* ("Do penance"); 577: *Qua appropinquabit* ("Will approach").

37. [kyngdom] MS reads "kyngdon." Cf. Luke 10.11, "Quia appropinquavit reg-num Dei."

38. For Christ's commission to the apostles, see Matthew 10.

39. 586: *ferro perempti* ("slain by the sword"); 587: *flammis exusti* ("consumed by flames"); 588: *Flagellis verberati* ("Beaten with scourges"); 1. 589, *Hij sunt triumphatores* ("They are victorious").

40. 586–88: cf. Hebrews 11: 36–37.

41. [on] Davis reads "an."

42. After Doctrine's impressive biblical citations, the audience is brought to earth with a bump, if only for a moment, by Idleness's feckless mockery; the boys are much less certain now whether they should continue to side with him.

43. 596: *Vos estis lux mundi* ("You are the light of the world," see Matthew 5:14).

44. 600: *hij sunt sancti* ("They are holy); 601: *pro Dei amore* ("For the love of God").

45. 616–17: Saints accumulated a treasury of merit, which was made available to penitents.

46. 629: *Fulgebunt iusti* ("The righteous shall shine," see Matthew 13:43).

47. 640–1: Psalms 144 (145):9. This verse, interpreted as indicating that God's mercy is greater than his justice, is one of the most frequently quoted in medieval texts. After the Reformation, it became less well known as a talis-man; had he been able to make use of it, Marlowe's Dr. Faustus might have escaped damnation. The avaricious protagonist of *The Castle of Perseverance* is saved from the Wicked Angel because he called on God's mercy with his dying breath. Cf. 634–37.

48. 642: *per lignum moriebatur* ("by a tree death was introduced"); 1. 644: *per lignum quoque* ("also by a tree"). The comparison is between the tree in the Gar-den of Eden, by which humanity fell from grace and into death, and the cross of Christ, by which humanity was redeemed.

49. 642–49: The allusion is to line 6 of the hymn "Pange, lingua" (sung at Easter in veneration of the Cross) by Venantius Fortunatus (sixth century).

50. The oil of mercy promised to Adam and provided by Christ is an idea derived from the apocryphal *Gospel of Nicodemus* (James, 117–46).

51. 669–83: The democratic-sounding notion that it is virtue and not rank that counts in Heaven was a religious commonplace: cf. *Piers Plowman*, B 6, 38–49, where Piers warns knights not to oppress the poor, for after death there will be nothing to distinguish poor from rich.

52. [hym] "wyf" or "wys" canceled in MS after "hym."

53. He probably asks one of the college servants to fetch a jug of water so that he may wash out the instruction written on his book.

54. This is the syncopated form of *shendeth*, "destroys" (third pers. sing., present tense).

55. [wil] Davis reads "wyl" in error.

56. Again Idleness points out someone in the audience ("this compané").

57. The conversion seems sudden, as it often does in early morality plays, but it has never really been in doubt. It follows closely on the dramatic climax of the play, the beating of Idleness.

58. 778: *Vigilate ergo* ("Watch therefore") and 1. 779: *Nescitis qua hora* ("You do not know at what hour"). For both phrases, see Matthew 24.42.

59. [wil] Davis reads "wyl" in error.

60. The deeds of mercy are those advocated in the Beatitudes (Matthew 5).

61. As usual in the morality plays, the conversion is dramatically signified by a change both of clothing and of name.

62. 828: *Et perelegit eam Deus* ("And God chose her"); 829: *Sicut lilium* ("As the lily"); 830: *Sic amica mea inter filias* ("So is my beloved among the daughters," see Song of Solomon 2:2).

63. The doctrine of the Assumption of the Virgin was current in the West from the eighth century on. An account of how angels took her immaculate soul up to Heaven at the Apostles' request is attributed to Melito, bishop of Sardis (James, 209–16). The audience would probably recognize some of these passages from church liturgy, contained in the Breviary. They may also have seen mystery plays of the Assumption, which were based on the retelling in the *Golden Legend*, a popular collection of saints' lives.

64. 834: *que est ista* ("Who is this . . ."); 1. 835, *Que descendit* ("who cometh down . . ."); 836: *Tamquam fumi virgula* ("like a branch of incense," Song of Solomon 3:6); 837: & *sicut aurora consurgens* ("and like dawn rising,"? Song of Solomon 6:10).

65. 844: *Hec est regina virginum* ("This is the Queen of Virgins"); 845: *Que genuit regem* ("who bore the king"); 847: *Cui famulantur angely* ("whom angels serve").

66. 849: *amica veni* ("beloved, come," see Song of Solomon 2:10; 850: *Veni de Libano* ("Come from Lebanon"); 851: *Veni coronaberis* ("Come, you shall be crowned," see Song of Solomon 4:8).

67. 852–53: This threefold dominion indicates the Virgin Mary's universal Queenship; similar formulations occur in the N-Town mystery play of the "Salutation and Conception"; in *Pearl* (fourteenth century), ll. 441–42; and in the fifteenth-century lyric *Salve Regina*.

15
Selection from *Math Son* *of Mathonwy,* from the *Mabinogi*

STEPHEN YANDELL

Editors rarely anthologize the tale of *Math Son of Mathonwy*. It falls into too many of the categories that alienate modern audiences—not simply non-English, but Celtic; not merely medieval, but Welsh. Admittedly, many undergraduate readers are already familiar with medieval texts, but few have tackled themes and genres that are distinctly Celtic. An English translation provides a useful start, of course, but still leaves the best-intentioned reader to brave a sea of seemingly unpronounceable names. Yet this particular Welsh text is triply cursed in its marginalization. *Math* is children's literature. It is a tale *about* children; it is believed to have been originally composed *for* children; and, since its rediscovery in the eighteenth century, it has generally been treated as a childish *effort*—the work of an unsophisticated Welsh bard. The image of a child has long been equated with Wales and Welsh texts, and for an English-speaking, post-fifteenth-century, adult audience, the elements of Wales, text, and child have become increasingly interchangeable: objects that are unlearned (needing instruction) and possibly dangerous (needing control). In addressing *Math*'s range of claims to the amorphous category of children's literature, this introduction hopes to provide a brief historical background and to challenge both the myth of *Math*'s inaccessibility and the misperception of its author's naiveté.

Summary and the Theme of Transformation

Math's supernatural setting and its theme of loyalty and betrayal are traditional, but its plot is essentially unique (G. E. Jones, 193). Math is king of Gwynedd (North Wales) and resides at his stronghold of Caer Dathl. Because the king has a condition that requires his feet to rest in the lap of a virgin except during times of war, Math remains at home and relies on the help of his two nephews, the brothers Gwydion and Gilfaethwy, for making regular circuits of the land. One day Gwydion notices how pale Gilfaethwy has become, and after Gilfaethwy admits to having fallen in love with Goewin, the king's virginal footholder, Gwydion vows to give his brother the chance to spend time alone with her. This means starting a war.

Gwydion and Gilfaethwy lead a group of men to South Wales, where they receive a warm welcome from King Pryderi. After reciting tales at the court, Gwydion is offered his choice of gifts, and although King Pryderi initially refuses to part with his herd of swine, he eventually agrees to give them up in exchange for a collection of horses, hounds, and shields. These new objects have been magically created by Gwydion, however, and vanish as soon as the brothers depart. As expected, Pryderi leads an army to Gwynedd, and once Math has left his stronghold, Gilfaethwy enters and rapes Goewin.

News of the violation quickly reaches Math, and he calls Gwydion and Gilfaethwy in front of him. As punishment, Math transforms the boys into a stag and a hind and sends them out to live as animals. Returning a year later below the king's chamber, the brothers bring with them a small fawn produced by their copulation, which Math transforms into a baby boy. For two more years the brothers go out as a new pair of animals, each time leaving with a new gender and returning with a new offspring. Math transforms each new creature into a human boy and at the end of the third year restores the brothers to their original forms, declaring them fit to return to court. The second half of the tale, although not included here, then recounts the evils of Math's niece, Aranrhod.

Math and the *Mabinogi:* History and Composition

Math is the last of four tales known collectively as the *Mabinogi*. Despite their survival in only two manuscripts, the White Book of Rhydderech (c. 1350) and the Red Book of Hergest (c. 1400), the tales are now recognized by scholars as the finest example of Middle Welsh prose and arguably Wales's greatest contribution to medieval European literature. The language of the tales is Middle Welsh, used between the twelfth and fifteenth centuries, and although the physical manuscripts date from the fourteenth century, scholars believe their original composition must have taken place many centuries earlier, roughly between 1050 and 1100 (Charles-Edwards, 53). Who composed the tales is unknown, but stylistic similarities between the four suggest the existence of a single author, a redactor whose skill lay in bringing together, perhaps for the first time, a conglomeration of traditional, related, mythic material (Mac Cana, 32).

Scholarly interest in origins has fueled much speculation about the author of *Math*. Linguistic and textual evidence point to a writer in South Wales (G. E. Jones, 193), and because only a small number of individuals would have been literate in medieval Wales, some assume the redactor must have been a member of the court priests or judges. Both of these groups would have been familiar with the legal terminology and terse prose style typical to the court, and which shows up frequently in the *Mabinogi* (Davies, *Four Branches*, 16).

As with most medieval works, however, the *Mabinogi* comes to us through a manuscript tradition that quickly complicates any easy notion of a single-authored text. Its subject matter, for example, would have been known to all of the professional storytellers in medieval Wales, a group known as the *cyfarwyddiaid*. This prominent class of entertainers was responsible for passing along Welsh culture (G. E. Jones, 189), and once a tale had become part of their repertoire, it could be subjected to any number of revisions and retellings. We cannot know whether the composer had anything to do with the tales' being written down originally (Davies, *Four Branches*, 13), nor can we possibly recreate the centuries of scribal copying and editing they underwent. Scholars are confident, however, that oral versions of the *Mabinogi* must have circulated for centuries before ever taking a written form in the eleventh century.

Our current text, not surprisingly, now displays a combination of literary and oral features. Scholars claim a reliance on writing for the author, for example, by pointing to the tales' great length, their complex narrative patterns, and a general "literariness" (Roberts, 98). The *Mabinogi* need not have been written down to display these features, however, and other critical schools have been equally concerned with identifying a residual orality within the tales. In making a claim for the *Mabinogi*'s oral composition, they point to its loosely attached narrative episodes, the frequent narrative asides, and a duplication of characters and plot elements (R. M. Jones, 225–42).

R. M. Jones has also identified "decentralized continuity" as a characteristic that reveals the *Mabinogi*'s oral nature. According to this feature, narrative units are strung together almost wholly on the basis of chronology, but "not by coherently motivated causality" (243). Medieval audiences, Jones argues, would also have been far more accepting of the kind of narrative heterogeneity we find in *Math* (242), where one event does not necessarily lead logically into the next, and where one finds inconsistencies, unexplained character motivations, and references to background material now unrecoverable. Many of these textual fissures have been explained as an inevitable result of someone trying to synthesize multiple mythic traditions or using forms that make memorization easier for repeat performances.

Math's "Childishness"

Although scholars highlight places where the *Mabinogi* text does *not* fit together smoothly, many are equally interested in identifying connections that unite the tales. Perhaps the most significant of these lies in the short phrase that closes each tale, and from which the collection gets its name: *Ac y uelly y teruyna y geing honn o'r Mabinogi* ("And thus ends this branch of the Mabinogi"). The term *mabinogi* exists nowhere else in Welsh literature, but is believed to have at its root the word *mab*, meaning "child, boy, or son." Some scholars assume the word originally meant "tales describing the life of a boy hero," and that, over time, the term came to indicate simply "a hero's tale." W. J. Gruffydd (*Folklore, Math*) is perhaps the most outspoken proponent of this theory and points as support to a precedent set in Irish tales where a hero's life follows four key periods: birth, youthful exploits, marriage, and death. Several factors argue against any easy claim to unity, however. Although four branches now remain in our extant manuscripts, we do not know whether there were originally more; nor can we identify a specific character who plays a satisfactorily substantial role as "boy hero" in each of the tales.

The term *mabinogi* has also suggested the meaning "a collection of tales *for* boys." The tales might originally have been told for children or explicitly for the edification and entertainment of young noble Welshmen (Davies, *Four Branches*, 18). One can imagine a group of children (possibly girls and boys) gathered around an open fire and listening to the stories, but this claim, however accurate, risks reproducing a long-standing tradition of branding all fantastic literature as juvenile. Far more convincing as an argument for children as an intended original audience is the *Mabinogi*'s subject matter. *Math*, for example, is a story about boys; they not only comprise the central characters, they bring together all of the tale's anxieties about control.

In claiming that the tales served as models for the apprenticeship of young *cyfarwyddiaid*, scholars also point to the technical precision with which the narratives move forward and to the amount of detail given to the actual craft of the bards. The tales not only served as ideal narrative models, they also contained detailed knowledge each bard would have been expected to know. In *Math*, for example, Gwydion's visit to Pryderi lingers over the expectations of an oral performance, details the ritual, and praises the work of the storyteller. *Math*'s narrator also makes frequent asides to provide his audience with a range of useful information: geographical facts, the names of significant Welsh figures, and the origins of archaic words (such as *hobeu*) and place names (such as *Mochdref* and *Creuwryon*).

Whether or not the initial audience was composed mainly of children or adults, for centuries the tales remained unknown outside of Wales. Until the Romantic Revival of the late eighteenth century, Celtic texts were considered valuable only to the degree to which they could provide historical knowledge. Welsh lexicographer William Owen Pughe is credited with turning local attention back toward the tales, and he reinforced the idea that the tales were meant for children by labeling them "Juvenile Romances" in his *Dictionary* (1773–1803). Although Pughe died before having it published, his translation of "The Mabinogion" placed the four *Mabinogi* tales alongside seven other Middle Welsh narratives from the same manuscripts.[1] Pughe chose the title "Mabinogion" because of its single appearance in one of the tales, and it is by this title that many still refer to texts from the White Book and Red Book. However, scholars now use the term less frequently, pointing both to its technical inaccuracy (as a reference to the non-*Mabinogi* tales) and to its now-understood origin as a scribal error (Bromwich, 6–7).

Perhaps not surprisingly, only at the hand of an English writer did the *Mabinogi* tales gain the attention of readers outside Wales. Charlotte Guest, the daughter of an English earl, taught herself Welsh and published a seven-part translation of Pughe's same eleven tales between the years 1838 and 1849. Her enthusiasm for the Arthurian romances drove the project, and yet its success as a whole thrust the *Mabinogi* into public attention. In her dedication of the work to her two oldest sons, she announces her desire for the texts to serve for them as entertainment and moral guidance:

> My dear Children, Infants as you are, I feel that I cannot dedicate more fitly than to you these venerable relics of ancient lore. . . . May you become early imbued with the chivalric and exalted sense of honour and the fervent patriotism for which its sons have ever been celebrated. (Bromwich, 11)

This explicitly maternal agenda made her success as a female scholar more publicly acceptable and also fixed the link between the texts and a children's audience. Guest reveals her genuine fondness for Wales through the dedication, yet this brand of Welsh nationalism could safely grow in England only after several centuries had passed since the last real threat of a Welsh uprising, and after the Celtic borderlands had been thoroughly romanticized.

Victorian modesty, combined with an imagined children's audience, meant that a tale like *Math* had to undergo substantial revisions at Guest's hand. The Arthurian material suited her pedagogical interests relatively effortlessly, but Gilfaethwy's rape of Goewin and the forced copulation between brothers needed to be covered over as discreetly as possible. When Goewin confronts Math about the rape in the Welsh, for example, she says, "They raped me and did shame to you by sleeping with me in your chamber and in your bed." Guest's translation removes any reference to sexual activity—or even a bed: "Unto me they did wrong, and unto thee dishonor" (41). Similarly, Math's punishment of his nephews is necessarily graphic in the original: "Since you are allied together, I will make you go forth together and mate together in the same manner as the wild animals whose form you have taken. And at that time when they have offspring, you also will." Guest's translation anticipates a sensitive audience: "Since now ye are in bonds, I will that ye go forth together and be companions, and possess the nature of the animals whose form ye bear" (42). Nevertheless, Guest's was the only translation available for many years, and with a children's precedent set, a majority of readers since Guest's time have come to know the *Mabinogi* only through collections marketed explicitly for children. Even within collections that "adapt" tales for children, a tale like *Math* frequently finds itself virtually ignored.[2]

In many ways, Charlotte Guest's (and her readers') treatment of the *Mabinogi* mimics the text's own treatment of children (those inside the narrative, as well as those comprising its intended audience). Both are cast as somewhat naïve, unsophisticated, wild, and possibly dangerous. The pre-adult characters in this tale are ruled by selfish passions that cause them to place personal desire above their loyalties to the king and fellow countrymen, and for this reason Math is eager to whisk away the nephews' three infant boys to raise them properly. The tale of *Math* becomes a forum for revealing the ways in which juvenile behavior threatens the lives of everyone in the kingdom, and this risk of social anarchy would have made families eager for children to be exposed to such ideology. Guest's vigilant control of the *text* thus reproduces the perceived need by adult society to control *children*—individuals who would otherwise introduce chaos and disrupt social norms.

Unfortunately, this pattern is not at all unfamiliar to Wales. The English treatment of the *Mabinogi* comes in the wake of many centuries of systematic oppression of Wales by England. Since the Celtic people of Britain first found themselves relocating westward and northward during the Roman invasions of the first century, England's ruling inhabitants (despite their changing identity with each subsequent invasion) prioritized the need for constant vigilance. Keeping alive these suspicions involved creating earthenworks between the countries in the late eighth century (Carr, 28), constructing castles around its borders by Edward I in the thirteenth century (Carr, 79), and drafting fifteenth-century legislation that prevented Welshmen from purchasing land in England, marrying English women, or speaking Welsh freely (J. G. Jones, 57–60).

For centuries, England continued to cast Wales (as well as the texts it produced) in the same role that the *Mabinogi*'s author had cast children—as wild pre-adults in need of training and surveillance. The same agenda of keeping society stable that initiated the tales within Wales was appropriated by an English audience as a way of reinforcing an ideology that controls Wales from the outside. Even today, a great deal remains at stake for the Welsh people in defining themselves on their own terms, instead of being positioned as children beneath a parental England. A text like *Math* thus figures centrally in this ongoing political struggle. Wales wants its people to be taken seriously for the same reasons it wants a text like the *Mabinogi* and the Welsh language to be recognized. Centuries of English control of the text (translating the *Mabinogi* into a more acceptable language and editing it for less offensive content, for example) have literalized English control of Wales.

Modern scholarship continues to subvert the "England-as-parent" model, yet in most studies, the tale of *Math* remains overlooked.[3]

The child's desire for control, similar to that of Wales and the text, is central to *Math*. Gwydion and Gilfaethwy do not defend women, provide for the kingdom, or show devotion to their king and family; and in failing to reflect proper masculine behaviors, these two young brothers are chiefly responsible for the chaos threatening the kingdom. The roles of masculinity that *Math* actively constructs for its audience work to constrain the behavior of men and women alike (Bullough, 33). In his study "On Being a Male in the Middle Ages," Vern Bullough defends the primacy of male relationships in medieval narratives. Manhood is constituted, he argues, by one's performance of "impregnating women, protecting dependents, and serving as provider to one's family." Failure in continually maintaining any of these areas represents a threat to one's masculinity, as well as the introduction of feminizing weakness (34). Perhaps more than any of the other *Mabinogi* tales, *Math* contributes to this masculine emphasis. Once Math has been deceived, chaos touches every part of the kingdom; Goewin cannot be protected, for example, and Math's ability to defend his kingdom is undermined.

Underlying all levels of the brothers' betrayal is transformation. Most immediately, we see that the brothers are a threat because they are engaged in a pubescent transformation from boys to men, a liminal state in which they now hold the power to challenge their uncle but not the maturity to control their passions. They are no longer boys but not yet men, and in this period of heightened desire, self is placed before others. Each fault highlighted by the tale displays a stereotypical feminizing weakness in the brothers. For example, Gilfaethwy's passion saps his strength, and Gwydion's magical creation of gifts casts him in a maternal role.

Math also manipulates appearances to restore the order shattered by Gwydion's magic, though only he is able to employ a phallic wand that represents his proper masculinity. Because both brothers have displayed femininity in their characters, both adopt the feminine role in giving birth during their period of punishment; Gilfaethwy also becomes a female twice in the process, perhaps because his act of rape has threatened order to the greatest degree. The tale is purposely balanced to accommodate the boys' punishment: Having stolen pigs from Pryderi, for example, the brothers must now become pigs themselves; after defiling the king's chamber, they must appear below it. Physical changes become a way of making the brothers' inner sins visible, creating a forced penance through ostracism, and then enacting inner change.

Finally, manipulating the brothers' appearance also literalizes the possible threat to society; the feminizing that has taken place in the brothers' characters is made explicit in their bodies. When the two young men ignore proper masculine roles, all bonds prove to be at risk of breaking down, open-ing the possibility for chaos throughout society. In a single taboo-laden pun-ishment, the threat of social disorder is conflated along multiple lines of shame: not only as mere ostracism for the brothers, but as homosexual desire, incestuous lust, bestial coupling, humiliation in bearing children, and her-maphroditic exchange.[4] For Gilfaethwy and Gwydion, the unnatural is mani-fested sexually, and ultimately the lines between human and animal, boy and man, are revealed as shifting.

Notes

1. *The Mabinogion* includes the four branches of the *Mabinogi* (*Pwyll Prince of Dyfed, Branwen Daughter of Llyr, Manawydan Son of Llyr,* and *Math Son of Mathonwy*), four traditional Welsh tales (*The Dream of Macsen Wledig, Lludd and Llefelys, Culhwch and Olwen,* and *The Dream of Rhonabwy*), and three Welsh prose versions of Arthurian romances (*Owein, Peredur Son of Efrawg,* and *Gereint Son of Erbin*).
2. Gwyn Jones's classic collection of *Welsh Legends and Folk Tales* chooses not to attempt any delicate treading over material as controversial as that found in the first half of *Math*. Instead, it censors the rape and fraternal copulation alto-gether, deleting the first half of *Math* and picking up where the narrative turns to Math's niece, Aranrhod.
3. Roberta Valente's "Gwydion and Aranrhod: Crossing the Borders of Gender in *Math*" concentrates only on the second half of the tale, for example. Andrew Welsh's study "Doubling and Incest in the *Mabinogi*" touches only briefly on the brothers.
4. The idea of gender switching would probably have appeared less threatening to a medieval audience, who believed women to be merely men with internal-ized sexual organs (Ford, *Math uab Mathonwy*, 27).

Math Son of Mathonwy[1]

Stephen Yandell,[2] translator

Math son of Mathonwy was lord over Gwynedd,[3] and Pryderi son of Pwyll was lord over twenty-one cantrefs[4] in the south. Those cantrefs were the seven of Dyfed, and the seven of Morgannwg, and the four of Ceredigion, and the three of Ystrad Tywi. And at that time, Math son of Mathonwy could live only while his two feet remained in the folds of a lap of a virgin, unless the tumult of war prevented it.[5] This virgin who was with him was Goewin daughter of Pebin from Dol Bebin in Arfon. And she was the most beautiful maiden known at that time. And [Math] used to rest at Caer Dathl[6] in Arfon. He was not able to make a circuit of the land, so his nephews Gilfaethwy son of Dôn[7] and Gwydion son of Dôn (his nephews, the sons of his sister) would go with his attendants and make a circuit of the land for him.[8]

And the maiden was continually with Math. And Gilfaethwy son of Dôn set his heart on the maiden, and loved her so much that he did not know what to do about it. And lo, his color and appearance and shape were declining because of his love so that it was not easy to recognize him. What his brother Gwydion did was gaze hard at him.

"Lad," he said, "what happened to you?" "Why?" [Gilfaethwy] answered. "What do you see?" "I can see," he answered, "that you are losing your appearance and your color. What has happened to you?" "Lord, brother," he said, "it is useless for me to confide with anybody about what has happened to me." "What is it, friend?" [Gwydion] asked. "You know," he replied, "about the gift of Math son of Mathonwy: Whatever whispering there is between men, however low, if it meets the wind, he will know of it." "Yes," answered Gwydion, "Be silent now. I know your mind—You love Goewin." What [Gilfaethwy] did then, when he realized that his brother had read his mind, was give the heaviest sigh in the world. "Stop your sighing, friend," [Gwydion] said. "You will not win her over with that. I will arrange," he said, "for Gwynedd and Powys and Deheubarth to be mustered [in war], since without that the maiden cannot be taken. Be happy; I will arrange it for you."

And then they went to see Math son of Mathonwy. "Lord," Gwydion said, "I hear that some sort of creatures have arrived in the south that have never before come to this island." "What is their name?" [Math] asked. "Hogs (*hobeu*), lord." "What kind of animals are they?" "Small animals whose meat is better than the meat of oxen. They are small, and they change names; swine (*moch*) is what they are now called." "Who owns them?" [Math asked.] "Pryderi son of Pwyll. They were sent to him from Annwfn[9] by Arawn, king of Annwfn." (And even now is that name kept in the phrases *hanner hob* and *hanner hwch*[10]). "Indeed," [Math] said, "In what way will they be got from him?" "I will go as one of twelve men in the guise of bards, lord, to ask for the swine." "He can certainly deny your request" [Math] answered. "My plan is not bad, lord, nor will I return without the swine."[11] "Gladly," he said, "go forward."

He went with Gilfaethwy, and ten others with them, as far as Ceredigion, to the place that is now called Rhuddlan Teifi where the court of Pryderi was held. And dressed as bards they came inside; they were welcomed joyfully. Gwydion was placed beside Pryderi that night. "Well," Pryderi said, "we will enjoy hearing stories from some of those young noblemen." "It is our custom, Lord," answered Gwydion, "that on the first night we come to a great man, the chief bard recites. I will happily tell a story." Gwydion was the best storyteller in the world, and that night he entertained the court with pleasant conversation and stories until he was loved by everyone in the court, and Pryderi was pleased to be entertained by him.

When it ended [Gwydion] said, "Lord, is it better for anyone to tell you my errand than myself?" "No," replied [Pryderi], "for yours is quite a good tongue." "Here is my mission, Lord: to beseech you for the animals that were sent to you from Annwfn." "Indeed," he said, "that would be the easiest thing in the world were there not an agreement between me and my people about them. This agreement is that they should not go from me until they have bred twice their number in the country." "Lord," [Gwydion] answered, "I can free you from those words. This is how: Do not give me the swine tonight, but do not deny me them either. Tomorrow I will show you an exchange for them."

And that night [Gwydion] and his companions went to their lodging and held council. "Men," he said, "we will not get the swine by asking for them." "Indeed," they said, "by what plan will they be got?" "I will take care of getting them," said Gwydion. And then he began to practice his arts and began to display his magic. He conjured up twelve warhorses, and twelve hunting dogs, all black with white breasts, with twelve collars and twelve leashes on them. Anyone who saw them would think they were gold. And there were twelve saddles on the horses, and in every place where there ought to have been iron there was solid gold. And the bridles were the same way. [Gwydion] came to Pryderi with the horses and the dogs.

"Good day to you, lord." He said. "God be generous to you," [Math] answered, "and welcome." "Lord," said [Gwydion], "behold, here is your freedom from the words you spoke last night about the swine, that you could neither give them nor sell them. You *are* able to exchange them for something better. I will give you these twelve horses as they are now equipped, with their saddles and their bridles, and the twelve hunting dogs with their collars and their leashes, as you see them, and the twelve golden shields that you see over there." (Those he had created from mushrooms.) "Well," he answered, "we will take counsel." What they decided in the counsel was to give the swine to Gwydion and to take the horses and the hunting dogs and the shields from him.

And then [Gwydion and his men] took their leave and began to travel with the swine. "Lads," said he, "we must travel quickly. The magic only lasts from one day to the next." And that night they journeyed as far as the uppermost part of Ceredigion, the place that is still called, because of that, Mochdref.[12] And the next day they continued their journey and came to Elenid. And that night they were between Ceri and Arwystli, in the town that is also called, because of that, Mochdref. And from there they went out, and that night they went as far as a commote[13] in Powys that is also called Mochnant. And that night they stayed there. And from there they journeyed as far as the cantref of Rhos, and that night they stayed there in a town that is still called Mochdref.

"Men," said Gwydion, "we will approach the stronghold of Gwynedd with these animals. [An army] is assembling behind us." They reached the highest town of Arllechwedd, and there made a pen for the swine. And for that reason it was called Creuwryon.[14] And then after making a pen for the swine, they approached Math son of Mathonwy in Caer Dathl. And when they came there, the country was being mustered. "What news is here?" asked Gwydion. "Pryderi," they said, "is mustering twenty-one cantrefs behind you. It is a marvel how slowly you have come." "Where are the animals you went after?" asked Math. "They have made a pen for them in the other cantref below," said Gwydion. Then, lo, they could hear the trumpets and the tumult in the country. Then they dressed and marched until they were in Penardd in Arfon.

And that night Gwydion son of Dôn and Gilfaethwy his brother returned to Caer Dathl. Gilfaethwy was placed in the bed of Math son of Mathonwy with Goewin daughter of Pebin to sleep together, and the handmaidens were roughly forced to leave. And he slept with her against her will that night.

When they saw the dawn the next day, [Gwydion and Gilfaethwy] went to the place where Math son of Mathonwy and his followers were. When they arrived, those men were about to go into counsel about the place where they would wait for Pryderi and the men of the South. And they entered the counsel. What they decided in the counsel was to wait in the fastness of Gwynedd in Arfon. And they waited in the middle of two districts, Maenawr Bennardd and Maenawr Coed Alun.

And Pryderi attacked them there, and that is where the battle was. And great carnage took place on each side, and the men of the South had to retreat. The place they retreated to was the place still called Nant Coll, and they were pursued as far as there. And then there was a slaughter of immeasurable size. And then they withdrew as far as the place called Dol Benmaen. And there they rallied and sought to make peace, and Pryderi gave hostages for the peace. Who he gave as a hostage was Gwrgi Gwastra, part of the twenty-four sons of noblemen he gave.

And after that, they traveled in their truce as far as Traeth Mawr. And as soon as they had come to Melen Ryd, the foot soldiers could not be stopped from shooting at one another, so Pryderi sent messengers to ask that the two hosts be held back, and to ask that it be left between him and Gwydion son of Dôn, since it was he who had caused that trouble. The messenger came to Math son of Mathonwy. "Yes," said Math, "between me and God, if it pleases Gwydion son of Dôn, I will gladly allow it. I will not compel anyone to fight without our doing what we are able." "Certainly," said the messengers, "Pryderi says it is fair that the man who did this wrong to him should place his body against his and let the two armies remain at rest." "By my confession to God," [Gwydion said], "I will not ask the men of Gwynedd to fight for me, and I myself will fight with Pryderi. Gladly will I put my body against his." And that was sent o Pryderi. "Indeed," said Pryderi, "nor will I ask anyone to claim my right except myself."

Those two men were separated, and they began to arm themselves and then fought. And by the strength of courage and force, magic and enchantment, Gwydion triumphed and Pryderi was killed. And in Maen Tyfyawg, above Melen Ryd, he was buried, and there is his grave. The men of the South traveled toward their country with bitter lamentation. And it was no wonder: Their lord had been lost, along with many of their best men, and their horses, and most of their weapons.

The men of Gwynedd gladly turned back home, exultant. "Lord," said Gwydion to Math, "wouldn't it be right to release to the men of the South their nobleman who was given as hostage to us in the truce? We should not imprison him." "Free him," said Math. And that lad and the hostages who were with him were set free back to the men of the South.

Then Math went to Caer Dathl. Gilfaethwy son of Dôn and the followers that had been with him went on a circuit of Gwynedd (as was their custom), without going to the court. Math went to his chamber and had a place prepared for him to recline in, where he could have his feet placed in the lap of a virgin. "Lord," said Goewin, "seek a virgin who can be beneath your feet now. I am a woman." "What does that mean?" "Lord, an attack was made on me, and that openly, and I did not remain silent. There was no one in the court who did not know it. It was your nephews, the sons of your sister, who came, Lord: Gwydion son of Dôn and Gilfaethwy son of Dôn. They raped me and did shame to you by sleeping with me in your chamber and in your bed." "Well," he said, "First, I will do what I can to make this right for you, according to my right. You," he said, "I will take as my wife, and I will give control of my realm into your hand."

And then [Gwydion and Gilfaethwy] did not come to the vicinity of the court, but instead lived around the country until a ban of food and drink for them was created. At first they did not come near [Math]. Then they did come to him. "Lord," they said, "good day to you." "Indeed," he said, "have you come to make things right to me?" "Lord, we are at your will." "Were it my will, I would not have lost the men and weapons that I lost. You cannot pay me back for my shame, nor for the death of Pryderi. And since you came to place yourself under my will, I will begin your punishment." And then he took his magic wand and struck Gilfaethwy so that he became a good-sized hind. And he seized the other quickly. Though he wanted to escape, he could not. [Math] struck him with the same magic wand so that he became a stag.

"Since you are allied together, I will make you go forth together and mate together in the same manner as the wild animals whose form you have taken. And at that time when they have offspring, you also will. A year from today return here to me."

At the end of a year from that same day, lo, [Math] could hear a commotion below the wall of the room, and the court dogs barking at the disturbance. "See," he said, "what is outside?" "Lord," one said, "I have looked. There is a stag and a hind, and a fawn with them." And with that, [Math] rose and went outside. And when he went, what he saw were three animals. The three animals he saw were a stag and a hind and a strong fawn. What he did was raise his magic wand.

The one of you who has been a hind last year should be a wild boar this year. And the one of you who has been a stag last year should be a wild sow this year. And with that, he struck them with the magic wand. "The boy, however, I will take and arrange to be raised and baptized." The name that was given to him was Hyddwn.[15] "Go; one of you will be as a wild boar, and the other as a wild sow. And let the nature of wild pigs also be yours. And a year from today, be here by the wall, together with your off-spring."

At the end of the year, lo, they could hear the barking of dogs beneath the wall of the room, and the court assembling around them. At this, he rose and went outside. And when he came outside, he saw three animals. The types of animals he saw were a wild boar and a wild sow and a hardy young animal with them. And he was strong for his age.

"Well," [Math] said, "this one I will take and arrange to be baptized." And he struck [the young pig] with the magic wand so that it became a rather swarthy, handsome young man. The name that was given to him was Hychdwn.[16]

"And for you: the one of you who has been a wild boar last year should be a she-wolf this year. And the one of you who has been a wild sow last year should be a wolf this year." And with that he struck them with the magic wand, making them wolf and she-wolf. "And let the nature of the animals whose shapes you have taken also be yours. And be here a year from today by this wall."

At the end of a year from that day, lo, he heard a clamor and barking under the wall of the chamber. He rose and went outside, and when he came, lo, he saw a wolf and a she-wolf, and a strong cub with them. "I will take this one," he said, "and arrange for him to be baptized; and his name is ready. This is his name: Bleiddwn.[17] You have three boys, and these are the three:

> *Three sons of wicked Gilfaethwy,*
> *Three champions true,*
> *Bleiddwn, Hyddwn, and Hychdwn Tall."*

And with that, he struck the two of them with the magic wand so they returned to their own form.

"Men," he said, "if you have done wrong to me, you have had enough punishment, and you have had great shame, each one of you bore children by the other. Prepare a bath for the men and wash their heads, and dress them." And that was done.

Notes

1. **The Sounds of Welsh**

    Pronouncing Welsh names can be intimidating for English readers. The Celtic branch of languages uses a vocabulary that looks and sounds very different from those of the Germanic (English, German) and Italic branches (French, Spanish). However, learning to pronounce Welsh words requires one to understand only a few key points:

    a. **Differences in vowels**: Despite appearances to the contrary, Welsh words *do* require vowels, and most of them represent sounds familiar in English.

        *   Three different Welsh letters are used to represent the sounds of *i* (*i, y, u*), as in English "b*i*t" (also b*ee*t in long syllables, and b*u*t in unstressed syllables). Note: *u* is always pronounced like *i* in Welsh.
        *   The letter *w* can also represents a vowel sound in Welsh, as in English b*oo*t (*pwy* - pooee)
        *   The letters *y* and *w* function as vowels in the middle of Welsh words, but as consonants at the beginning of Welsh words.

    b. **Unique Consonants**: Two Welsh sounds are not found in English:

        *   *ch* represents a guttural sound produced at the back of the throat. Making the sound involves pronouncing *k* while maintaining continual air flow. This sound is common in the Celtic languages, as in Scottish lo*ch* (lake). Note, *ch* is never pronounced as in English *ch*urch.
        *   *ll* represents a single sound produced by keeping the tip of the tongue on the roof of the mouth (as with *l*) and blowing forward (as if trying to hiss).

    c. **Unique Spellings**: Some common English sounds are represented in unique ways by Welsh consonants:

        *   *dd* always indicates *th* (voiced), as in English *th*en (never as *th*in or as a *d*)
        *   *ff, ph* always indicates *f*
        *   *f* always indicates *v*
        *   *c* always hard, as in *c*at (never soft, as in voi*c*e)
        *   *g* always hard, as in *g*o (never soft as in rou*g*e, or ju*dg*e)

d.   **Character and Place Names:**

Character Names		Place Names	
Gilfaethwy	gil-*vahth*-wee	Gwynedd	*gwuh*-neth
Gwydion	*gwi*-dee-on	Dyfed	*duh*-ved
Gwrgi Gwastra	*goor*-gee *gwahs*-tra	Ystrad Tywi	*uh*-strad *tuh*-wee
Hyddwn	*huh*-thoon	Rhuddlan Teifi	*hrith*-lan *tay*-vee
Hychdwn	*huch*-doon		
Bleiddwn	*blay*-thoon		
Pryderi	pruh-*dehr*-ee		
Goewin	*goy*-win		

2. The translation is based on Evans, as provided in editions by Williams and Ford.
3. *Gwynedd*, North Wales.
4. *Cantref*, a land division in medieval Wales, originally determined by the inclusion of one hundred dwellings (from *cant*, "hundred").
5. The king's footholder was a position traditionally held by an officer of the court (Ford, *The Mabinogi*, 191). The presence here of a female virginal footholder makes explicit the importance of the king's heir being assured and having indisputable legitimacy. Because his feet remained constantly in her lap (*croth*, "uterus, womb"), the king very literally maintained control over both the virgin's reproduction and her sexuality.
6. *Caer*, "stronghold or fortress."
7. *Dôn*, a Welsh goddess; in Irish, *Danu*.
8. Frequent circuits of this kind were essential in allowing a medieval Welsh king to maintain his authority throughout a widespread kingdom. Along with his retinue, the king would be provided for by the bondmen of the kingdom as he traveled (Carr, 30).
9. *Annwfn*, the Welsh Otherworld; alternately considered a place of youth and fairies, and of darkness and the dead (Gruffydd, "Folklore and Myth," 8).
10. *Hanner*, "half"; *hanner hob*, "half a pig," or a side of cured meat.
11. The granting of a request was considered standard payment for a bard's performance to a king.
12. From *moch*, "swine"; *tref*, "town."
13. *Commote*, a province or region; together, several commotes comprised a cantref.
14. From *creu*, "sty."
15. From *hydd*, "deer."
16. From *hwch*, "pig."
17. From *bleidd*, "wolf."

16
Sir Gowther (Advocates MS. 19.3.1)

MARY E. SHANER

The fifteenth-century Middle English romance *Sir Gowther* is known to exist
in only two manuscripts, Edinburgh Advocates MS. 19.3.1 and British
Library Royal MS. 17.B.XLIII. The texts of the two manuscripts, however,
differ from each other in substantive readings in more than 50 percent of the
lines. In her analysis of the Advocates manuscript, Phillipa Hardman found
that each of the three romances in that manuscript, *Sir Gowther*, *Sir Isum-
bras*, and *Sir Amadace*, has a text significantly different from the other
known manuscripts of each poem. She concluded that these texts had been
edited, probably by the scribe of most of the Advocates manuscript, Heege.

Hardman also identified the Advocates manuscript as a composite manuscript—that is, a manuscript made up of a group of booklets bound together
to make a single manuscript (Hardman, 268–73). A booklet is defined by
P. R. Robinson as "a small but structurally independent production containing a single work or a number of short works"; the content must form "a self-
sufficient unit" (Robinson, 46–47). The booklets containing the romances in
the Advocates manuscript have one companion piece to each romance: an
instructional work for children. If the content of a booklet must form a self-
sufficient unit, it seems clear that the romances must be considered to have
content congruent with the children's manuals. Therefore, I believe that these
three romances have been emended and edited to make them readable for
children. Of course, the medieval conception of what is suitable for children
has little resemblance to modern ideas. For instance, Hardman found that the
revised romances in the Advocates manuscript were more violent and blood-
thirsty than other texts of the same romances. They also employ more direct
speech, place less emphasis on chivalric and courtly values, and emphasize
domestic values such as loyalty, food and lodging, and marital relations
based more upon equality than upon the courtly-chivalric pattern (Hardman,
268–69).

Sir Gowther as Children's Literature

On the other hand, *Sir Gowther* and the other romances in the Advocates manuscript are homiletic romances, defined by Dieter Mehl as those in which

> the plot is completely subordinated to the moral and religious theme, even though this is occasionally lost sight of . . . and all the adventures of the hero or heroine contribute to it, either by illustrating some particular Christian virtue or by commenting on the exemplary pattern of the action. . . . Several of [the homiletic romances] describe the history of men in whose lives God intervenes very directly, usually by a miracle, in order to chastise them and eventually to save them as in *Robert of Sicily*, *Sir Ysumbras*, *Sir Gowther*, and to some extent, *Sir Amadace*. (Mehl, 121)

It may seem strange to classify as children's literature a work that is not only bloody, but has been edited in a way that increases its violence, yet that is surely comprehensible if we think in terms of what the medieval docent might want to teach his pupils. Modern educators hesitate to use fear or distress as teaching tools, but most previous centuries had no such scruples and indeed would not understand our modern squeamishness. To show the ugliness and randomness of Gowther's evil is appropriate. Just as violent as Gowther's fiendish persecution of Christians is his repentance. He runs afoot from Austria to Rome to confess to the Pope, then undertakes the by no means light penance the Pope imposes, and never looks back. If we must have a penitent hero, his is surely the kind of penitence we want to see.

The increase in violent action in the Advocates version of *Sir Gowther* may also be intended to increase the appeal to an audience of youthful readers. We may not like it, but even today the taste of children in television programming runs to action shows, and thanks to modern special effects, one can lop off just as many heads in a computer game as Gowther does on the battlefield against the Sowdan's men. The edited *Sir Gowther* also contains more direct speech and less narrative, creating a faster pace, another quality attractive to young readers. The piety of the narrator's comments and of the characters' behavior is simple and fairly absolute; the romance has none of the moral complexity of *Sir Gawain and the Green Knight*, nor any abstract thought. There is only right or wrong, with no gray areas. Again, this approach is one suited to the entertainment of the young.

The probable intended audience of *Sir Gowther* as children's literature would be young boys, on the evidence of its companion instructional piece, *Urbanitas*. "This treatise on manners may be 'the booke of urbanitie' mentioned in the Household ordinances of Edward IV, in the section pertaining to the duties of Henchmen. (" 'Henxmen,' or henchmen, are defined in the Household ordinances as 'young gentlemen, Henxmen, VI Enfauntes, or

more, as it shall please the Kinge" [Furnivall, *Early English Meals,* ii])
(Shaner, 12). If this portion of the "self-sufficient unit" of the booklet is
aimed at boys, it seems likely that the other component of the booklet, the
romance, is meant for the same audience.

Literary Attributes of *Sir Gowther*

As a literary work, *Sir Gowther* leaves something to be desired. It is written
in tail-rhyme stanzas, twelve lines arranged in groups of three, the three
lines comprising a rhymed couplet and a "tail," a shorter line. The tails in a
given stanza usually rhyme with one another and serve as the cohesive element of the stanza. This stanzaic form can become somewhat monotonous.
The lines each have four stresses, except for the tails, which have three.
Such stanzas are parodied in Chaucer's *Sir Thopas,* which Harry Bailey
believes may well be "rhyme doggerel." The poetry of *Gowther* itself is
scarcely in Chaucer's "aureate" style; the poet uses very few images and
most of those clichés. The diction is generally simple, but because of the
demands of the stanzaic form not direct; the poet often fills in the length of
lines with "empty" words like "that," "there," and "the." On the other hand,
the dialect of the Advocates' *Sir Gowther* has its own charms. When the
dead maiden "raxeld hur and rase" (659), "stretched herself and rose," this
understated presentation of the miracle has both a pleasing simplicity and a
nearly comic naturalness.

The source of *Sir Gowther* is "a European legend based on the secular
and religious exploits of a fictitious Norman Duke known as Robert the
Devil. Originating in thirteenth-century France, the tale of the demonic
knight who undergoes a dramatic conversion and a gruelling penance can
be found in many versions throughout Europe" (Vandelinde, 139). However, *Sir Gowther* is a much-compressed version of *Robert the Devil*; Sir
Gowther is at most 757 lines long, a suitable length for public performance
by a bard. *Robert* exists in versions over five thousand lines long. This
datum points to the oral performance quality of *Gowther,* supported by the
formulaic quality of the language and the directness of the action, and to
the originality of the romance. Although clearly like *Robert the Devil,*
Gowther is its own story, relying far less on the details of *Robert the Devil*
than some critics assume.

The genre of *Gowther* depends rather upon what aspect of the poem we
look at. It is a metrical romance because of its stanzaic form, a penitential
romance because of its plot. It is also a Breton lay because it so identifies
itself, although it is not set in Brittany. It qualifies as an Arthurian romance
because the fiend who fathers Gowther is the same who fathered Merlin.
Finally, contemporary criticism finds it a monster tale of a cynocephalic
giant. As Jeffrey Jerome Cohen says, romance is

a resolutely hybrid genre, and *Sir Gowther* takes this hybridity to an
extreme. Its protagonist never fights the traditional giant, because his
monstrous body already contains that enemy. The trajectory of the narrative postulates an originary gigantism for the masculine corpus, introject-
ing everything that other romances write as exterior to the hero's body,
and then plunges Gowther so deep into monstrousness that he will emerge
purified, sanctified. This odd but wonderful little romance plots through
the wilds of identity a monstrous route to becoming male in the Middle
Ages. (120–21)

Cohen makes rather more of Gowther's size than the romance does; he is an
unusually large child and grows very rapidly. But in his adulthood, no one
calls him a giant. When he first appears at the emperor's castle, and the
emperor asks the steward, "What is that?" about Gowther sitting under the
table, the answer makes no mention of size:

> "My lord," he seyd, "a mon
> And that the feyryst that ever Y sye;
> Cum loke on hym, it is no lye." (336–38)

Gowther's monstrousness is surely less that of size and appearance than that
of the spirit, prior to his conversion. That he has in his penance become as a
dog, however, is undeniable. He is told by the Pope to take no food save what
he can obtain from the mouths of dogs, until God sends him a sign that he is
forgiven.

Other contemporary critics have focused upon other elements in the tale.
Margaret Robson deals with the story of Gowther's mother, seeing her a
woman sexually frustrated and resentful of her husband's treatment. Her
relationship with Gowther is one of rejection; as a baby, he sucks his wet-
nurses to death and bites off his mother's nipple, thus rejecting feminine nurture (141–43). Robson points out that "Gowther's behaviour as infant and
adolescent bears comparison with modern descriptions and examples of
autism, and . . . the story of a 'demon-child' is a useful and interesting way of
exploring this form of psychosis" (147). Vandelinde deals primarily with the
differences between the two manuscript versions of *Sir Gowther* and finds
the Advocates version generally more concerned with secular aspects of the
action and behavior of the characters (139–47). Corinne Saunders takes a
"non-mimetic" approach to *Gowther*, a way of dealing with the marvelous
and supernatural elements of the Breton lay without dismissing them as
escapist elements; in short, she tries to take the fantastic element of the
romances on their own terms. Saunders is perhaps most interested in the
mother's intercourse with the incubus as an instance of rape by deception;
she cites much medieval debate on the subject of incubi and human women
and concludes, contrary to Robson, that, as Aquinas averred, the woman is

innocent in such events, and that Gowther's mother is more victim, however subconsciously, than partner. Gowther's own career as rapist Saunders sees as the manifestation of his devilish heritage: "Here Gowther re-enacts the sins of his father, but on a larger scale: the veil of romance is torn away to reveal rape and death, specifically directed at those dedicated to God in order to destroy their holiness and chastity" (298). But when Gowther is penitent, he fights the Sowdan to save the emperor's daughter from implicit rape. "By saving a Christian woman from the implicit threat of rape, Gowther both proves his honour and receives his token of divine approval" delivered in the speech restored to the mute princess (Saunders, 299).

This survey of critical views of *Sir Gowther* shows that however varied the approach or the conclusion, most critics are satisfied that the conclusion of the romance is a "righteous" ending, earned by Gowther's penance and creating an appropriate and satisfying retort to the horrific events of the first half of the poem. *Sir Gowther* gives us real sin committed with deliberation; then it shows real redress for sin, performed with passion. Perhaps Cohen's phrase "this odd but wonderful little romance" sums it up rather neatly. *Sir Gowther*, for all its oddity that can charm adult sensibilities, must nonetheless arouse doubts concerning its possible reception among the young. The medieval child would have brought to the story a medieval sensibility that was prepared to believe in incubi and their dangers, the devil and his spite against humanity. Such a child would equally come armed with faith in the Church and the efficacy of its teaching, and in God and His power to intervene directly in time and space. Thus the medieval child would probably both understand and accept the underlying premises that a life can be tainted from birth and lived for only destructive purposes, and yet be reversed, cleansed, and made new and fine. The modern youth, too, may find *Sir Gowther* understandable and even relevant to his condition. Many children know what it is to feel they have been "born bad."

SIR GOWTHER (Advocates MS. 19.3.1)[1]

[God, that art of myghtis most,		*powers*
Fader and Sone and Holy Gost,		
That bought man on rode so dere,		*cross*
Shilde us from the fowle fende		*protect; fiend*
That is about mannys sowle to shende	5	*ruin*
All tymes of the yere.		
Sumtyme the fende hadde postee		*power*
For to dele with ladies free		
In liknesse of here fere		*their mate*
So that he bigat Merlyng and mo,	10	*fathered Merlin*
And wrought ladies so mikil wo		*much*

That ferly it is to here.   *terrible*
  A selcowgh thyng that is to here,   *awesome*
A fend to nyegh] a woman nere   *draw near*
[And] makyd hom with chyld;   15   *impregnated*
Tho kynde of men wher thei hit tane,   *nature; took*
For of homselfe had thei neuer nan,   *themselves; none*
Be meydon Mare mylde,
Ther of seyus clerkus, Y wotte how;   *say scholars; know*
That schall not be rehersyd now,   20   *shall; repeated*
As Cryst fro schame me schyld.
Bot Y schall tell yow of a warlocke greytt,
What sorow at his modur hart he seyt
With his warcus wylde   *works*
Ihesu Cryst, that barne blythe,   25   *child; happy*
Gyff hom ioy that loves to lythe   *hear*
Of ferlys that befell;
A law of Breyten long Y soght   *lay; Brittany; sought*
And owt ther of a tale have Y brought
That lufly is to tell.   30   *lovely*
Ther wonde a duke in Estryke,   *dwelled; Austria*
He weddyt a lade non hur lyke   *lady*
For comly vndur kell;   *headdress*
To [the lyly was likened that lady clere.]
Hur rod reyde [as blosmes on brere,]   35   *complexion red*
That ylke dere damsel.   *same*
When he had weddyd that meydyn schene   *beautiful*
And sche duches withowt wene,
A mangere con thei make.   *feast*
Knyghtus of honowr tho furst dey   40
Iustyd gently hom to pley   *jousted*
For that lady sake;   *lady's*
Tho duke hymselfe wan stedys .x.   *steeds ten*
And bare don full doghty men,
And mony a cron con crake.   45   *crown (head); crack*
  When this turment was yses   *tournament; ended*
Tho ryche duke and tho duches
Lad hor lyfe with wyn;   *joy*
X yer and sum dele mare   *a bit more*
He chylde non geyt ne sche non bare,   50
Ther ioy began to tyne.   *decline*
To is lade sone con he seyn,   *began*
"Y tro thu be sum baryn.   *believe, barren*
Hit is gud that we twyn;   *part*

Y do bot wast my tyme on the   55
Eireles mon owre londys bee."   *heirless; lands*
For gretyng he con not blyn.   *weeping; cease*
   Tho lade sykud and made yll chere   *sighed; countenance*
That all feylyd hur whyte lere,   *faded; complexion*
For scho conseyvyd noght,   60
Scho preyd to God and Mare mylde
Schuld gyffe hur grace to have a chyld,
On what maner scho ne roughth.   *cared*
In hur orchard apon a day
Ho meyt a mon, the sothe to say,   65   *she*
That hur of luffe besoghth.
As lyke hur lorde as he myght be,
He leyd hur down vndur a tre,
With hur is wyll he wroghtth;
When he had is wylle all don   70
   A felturd fende he start vp sonn   *hideous*
And stode and hur beheld;
He seyd, "Y have geyton a chylde on the
Thatt in is yothe full wylde schall bee,
And weppons wyghtly weld."   75   *powerfully*
Sche blessyd hur and fro hym ran,
Into hur chambur fast ho wan,
That was so bygly byld,   *strongly built*
Scho seyd to hur lord, that lade myld,
"Tonyght we mon geyt a child   80
That schall owre londys weld.   *our lands rule*
"A nangell com fro hevon bryght
And told me so this same nyght,
Y hope was Godus sond;   *messenger*
Then wyll that stynt all owr stryfe."   85   *stop*
Be tho lappe he laght his wife   *fold of cloth; caught*
And seyd, "Dame, we schall fonde."   *try*
At evon to beyd thei hom ches,   *evening/hurry*
Tho ryche duke and tho duches,
And wold no lengur wonde;   90   *wait*
He pleyd hym with that lade hende
And ei yode scho bownden with tho fende   *And ever she went*
   bound
To God wold losse hur bonde.   *Till; loose, free*
   This chyld within hur was no nodur   *none other*
Bot eyvon Marlyon halfe brodur   95   *Merlin's,*
For won fynd gatte hom bothe;   *one; begot*

Thei servyd neuer of odyr thyng
But for to temp[t]e wemen yong.
To deyle with hom was wothe.   *danger*
Ylke a day scho grette fast   100   *every day*
And was delyuerid at tho last   *delivered*
Of won that coth do skathe;   *could do harm*
Tho duke hym gard to kyrke beyre,   *caused; church; bear*
Crystond hym and cald hym Gwother,
That sythyn wax breme [and brathe].   105   *renowned and fierce*
Tho Duke conford that Duches heynde
And aftur melche wemen he sende   *milk*
Tho best in that cuntre,
That was full gud knyghttys wyffys.
He sowkyd hom so thei lost ther lyvys.   110   *sucked*
Sone had he sleyn three.   *slain*
The Duke gard prycke aftur sex—   *ride; six*
Tho chyld was yong and fast he wex—   *grew*
Hende, herkons yee: *Gentles, listen*
Be twelfe monethys was gon   115
IX norsus had he slon   *Nine nurses; slain*
Of ladys feyr and fre.
    Knyghtus of that cuntre geydyrd hom samun   *gathered; together*
And seyd to tho Duke hit was no gamun   *game*
To lose hor wyffus soo;   120
Thei hadde hym orden for his son   *decree*
He geytys no more is olde won,   *custom*
Norsus now no moo.
His modur fell afowle unhappe   *misfortune*
Upon a day bad hym tho pappe   125   *breast*
He snaffulld to hit soo   *sucked; violently*
He rofe tho hed fro tho brest—   *tore*
Scho fell backeward and cald a prest,
To chambur fled hym froo.
Lechus helud that lade yare,   130   *Physicians healed; quickly*

Wemen durst gyffe hym sovke no mare,   *suck; more*
That yong chyld Gowther,
Bot fed hym vp with rych fode,
And that full mych as hym beho[de],   *much; needed*
Full safly mey Y sweyre.   135
Be that he was xv yere of eld
He made a wepon that he schuld weld,
No nodur mon myghht hit beyr;   *no other*

A fachon bothe of styll and yron,		*sword; steel*
Wytte yow wyll he wex full styron	140	*merciless*
And fell folke con he feyr.		*many; frighten*
In a twelmond more he wex		*twelvemonth (year)*
Then odur chyldur in seyvon or sex.		*seven or six*
Hym semyd full well to ryde;		
He was so wekyd in all kyn wyse	145	*wicked*
Tho Duke hym myght not chastyse,		
But made hym knyght that tyde		
With cold brade bronde.		*broad sword*
Ther was non in that londe		
That dynt of hym durst byde.	150	*blow*
For sorro tho Duke fell don ded;		
His modur was so wo of red		*sad of condition*
Hur care scho myght not hyde.		
Mor sorro for hym sche myght have non,		
But to a castyll of lyme and ston	155	
Frely then scho fled.		
Scho made hit strong and held hur thare.		
Hor men myght tell of sorro and care;		
Evyll thei wer bested.		*beset*
For wher he meyt hom be tho way,	160	
"Evyll heyll!" myght thei say,		*"Bad luck!"*
"That euer modur hom fed!"		
For with his fachon he wold hom slo		
And gurde hor horssus backus in too		*smite; horses' backs.*
All seche parellys thei dred.	165	*such perils*
Now is he duke of greyt renown,		
And men of holy kyrke dynggus down		*strikes*
Wher he myght hom mete.		
Masse ne matens wold he non here		
Nor no prechyng of no frere,	170	*friar*
That dar I heyly hette;		*earnestly promise*
[Erly and] late, lowde and styll,		
He wolde wyrke is fadur wyll		
Wher he stod or sete.		*whether*
Hontyng lufde he aldur best,	175	*loved*
Parke, wodd and wylde forest,		
Bothe be weyus and strete.		
He went to honte apon a day,		
He see a nonry be tho way		
And thedur con he ryde;	180	
Tho pryorys and hur covent		*prioress; community*

With presescion ageyn hym went
Full hastely that tyde;
Thei wer full ferd of his body,   *afraid*
For he and is men bothe leyn hom by—   185
Tho sothe why schuld .Y. hyde—
And sythyn he spard hom in hor kyrke   *shut*
And brend hom up, thus con he werke;   *burned*
Then went his name full wyde.
    All that euer on Cryst con lefe,   190
Yong and old, he con hom greve
In all that he myght doo:
Meydyns maryage wold he spyll,
And take wyffus ageyn hor wyll,
And sley hor husbondus too,   195
And make frerus to leype at kraggus   *friars; crags*
And parsons for to heng on knaggus   *branches*
And odur prestys sloo.   *priests*
To bren armettys was is dyssyre,   *hermits*
A powre wedow to seyt on fyre,   200   *poor*
And werke hom mykyll woo.
    A nolde erle of that cuntre
Vnto tho duke then rydys hee
And seyd, "Syr, why dose thu soo?
We howpe thu come neuer of Cryston stryn,   205   *believe*
Bot art sum fendys son, we weyn,
That werkus hus this woo;
Thu dose neuer gud, bot ey tho ylle.   *always*
We hope thu be full syb tho deyll."   *offspring; devil*
Syr Gowther wex then throo;   210   *enraged*
Hee seyd, "Syr, and thu ly on mee,
Hongud and drawon schall thu bee   *hanged and drawn*
And neuer qwycke heythyn goo."   *alive go hence*
    He gard to putte tho erle in hold   *custody*
And to his modur castyll he wold   215
As fast as he myght ryde.
He seyd, "Dame, tell me in hye,
Who was my fadur, withowt lye,
Or this schall thoro the glyde."
He sette his fachon to hur hart: 220
"Have done, yf thu lufe thi qwart."   *health*
Ho onswarde hym that tyde:
"My lord," scho seyd, "that dyed last."
"Y hope," he seyd, "Thu lyus full fast."

Tho teyrus he lett don glyde. 225   *tears*
  "Son, sython Y schall tho sothe say;
In owre orcharde apon a day
A fende gat the thare,
As lyke my lorde as he myght be
Vndurneyth a cheston tre."   230   *chestnut*
Then weppyd thei bothe full sare.
"Go schryfe the, Modur, and do tho best   *shrive*
For Y wyll to Rome or that Y rest   *before*
To lerne anodur lare."   *teaching*
This thoght come to hym sodenly: 235
"Lorde, mercy!" con he cry
To God that Mare bare.
  To save hym fro is fadur tho fynde,
He preyd to God and Mare hynde,   *pleasant*
That most is of poste,   240
To bryng is sowle to tho blys
That he boght to all his
Apon tho rode tre.   *cross*
Sythyn he went hym hom ageyn
And seyd to tho erle, withowt leyn,   245
"Tho sothe tale tolde thu mee;
Y wyll to Rome to tho apostyll   *the Pope*
That he mey schryfe me and asoyll;
Kepe thu my castyll free."
This old erle laft he theyr   250
For to be is stydfast heyre.
Syr Gwother forthe con glyde;
Toward Rome he radly ranne,   *quickly*
Wold he nowdur hors ne man   *neither*
With hym to ren ne ryde;   255
His favchon con he with hym take,
He laft hit not for weyle ne wrake,   *better or worse*
Hyt hong ei be his syde.
Toward Rome cety con hee seche;
Or he come to tho powpe speche   260
Full long he con abyde.
  As sone has he the pope con see,
He knelys adown apon is kne
And heylst hym full sone;
He preyd hym with mylde devocyon   265
Bothe of schryfte and absolyscion;
He granttyd hym is bone.

"Whethon art thu and of what cuntre?"   *Whence*
"Duke of Estryke, lorde," quod hee,
"Be tru God in trone,   270
Ther was Y geyton with a feynde
And borne of a duches hende;
My fadur has frenchypus f[one]."   *few friendships*
   "Y wyll gladly, be my fey!
Art thu Crystond?" He seyd, "Yey,   275   *christened*
My name it is Gwother."
"Now Y lowve God thu art commun hedur,   *come hither*
For ellus Y most a traveld thedur   *else*
Apon the for to weyre,   *war*
For thu hast holy kyrke destryed."   280
"Nay, holy fadur, be thu noght agrevyd;
Y schall the truly swere
At thi byddyng beyn to be,   *good*
And hald tho penans that thu leys to me,
And neuer Cryston deyre."   285
   "Lye down thi fachon then the fro;
Thu schallt be screvon or Y goo,   *shriven*
And asoyly[d] or Y blyn."   *absolved; cease*
"Nay, holy fadur," seyd Gwother,
"This bous me nedus with mee beyr,   290   *must*
My frendys ar full thyn."
"Wherser thu travellys be northe or soth,   *Wheresoever*
Thu eyt no meyt bot that thu revus of   *steal; hounds'*
   howndus mothe
Cum thy body within;
Ne no worde speke for evyll ne gud   295
Or thu reyde tokyn have fro God
That forgyfyn is thi syn."
   He knelyd down befor tho [apostoyle]
And solemly he con hym asoyle,
Tho sarten sothe to sey.   300
Meyte in Rome gatte he non   *meat*
Bot of a dog mothe a bon,
And wyghttly went is wey.
He went owt of that cete
Into anodur far cuntre,   305
Tho testamentys thus thei sey;
   He seyt hym down vndur a hyll,
A greyhownde broght hym meyt vntyll
Or evon yche a dey.

Thre neghthtys ther he ley. 310 *nights*
Tho grwhownd ylke a dey
A whyte lofe he hym broght;
On tho fort day come hym non. *fourth*
Vp he start and forthe con gon,
And lovyd God in his thought. 315
Besyde ther was a casstell,
Therin an emperowr con dwell,
And thedurwarde he soght; *in that direction*
   He seyt hym down withowt the yate *outside*
And durst not entur in therate, 320
[Th]of he wer well wroght. *though*
   Tho weytus blu apon tho wall, *trumpeters*
Knyghttus geydert into tho hall,
Tho lord buskyd to his saytte; *hurried*
Syr Gwother up and in con gwon, 325
Att tho dor vschear fond he non, *usher*
Ne porter at tho yatte,
Bot gwosse prystely thoro tho pres. *goes quickly; crowd*
Unto tho hye bord he chesse, *went*
Ther vndur he made is seytt. 330
Tho styward come with yarde in honed, *staff*
To geyt hym thethyn fast con he fonde, *thence; attempt*
And throly hym con threyt *angrily*
To beyt hym, bot he wende awey.
"What is that?" tho emperovr con sey. 335
"My lord," he seyd, "a mon,
And that tho feyryst that ever Y sye *fairest*
Cum loke on hym, it is no lye,"
And thedur wyghtly he wan.
Won word of hym he myght not geyt; 340
Thei lette hym sytt and gafe hym meyt.
"Full lytyll gud he cann,
And yett mey happon thoro sum chans
That it wer gyffon hym in penans," *given*
Tho lord thus onsward than 345 *answered*
   When tho emperowr was seyt and servyd
And knyghtus had is breyd karvyd,
He send tho dompmon parte. *dumb man*
He lette hit stond and wold ryght non. *would (eat) none*
Ther come a spanyell with a bon, 350
In his mothe he hit bare.
Syr Gwother hit fro hym droghe *dragged*

And gredely on hit he gnofe,   *gnawed*
He wold nowdur curlu ne tartte.   *quail nor*
Boddely sustynans wold he non   355
Bot what so he fro tho howndus wan,
If it wer gnaffyd or mard.   *chewed or damaged*
  Tho emperowre and tho emperrys
And knyghttys and ladys at tho des   *dais*
Seyt and hym beheld,   360
Thei gaffe tho hondus meyt ynoghe,
Tho dompe duke to hom he droghe,
That was is best beld.   *comfort*
Among tho howndys thus was he fed,
At evon to a lytyll chambur led   365   *evening*
And hyllyd undur teld;   *sheltered; covers*
At none come into tho hall.
"Hob hor fole," thei con hym call,   *fool*
To God he hym con yelde.
  Bot now this ylke emperowre   370
Had a doghtur whyte as flowre,
Was too soo dompe as hee.   *twice as mute*
Scho wold have spokyn and myght noght.
That meydon was worthely wroght,
Both feyr, curteys and free.   375
A messynger come apon a day,
Tyll her fadur con he say,
"My lord wele gretys the.
Tho Sawdyn, that is of mykyll might,   *sultan*
Wyll wer apon the dey and nyghtt   380
And bren thi bowrus free,   *burn*
And sley thi men bot thu hym sende   *unless*
Thi doghttur that is so feyr and heynde
That he mey hur wedde."
Tho Emperowr seyd, "Y have bot won,   385
And that is dompe as any ston,
Feyrur thar non be feyd;
And Y wyll not, be Cryst wonde,   *wounds*
Gyffe hor to no hethon hownde.   *heathen*
Then wer my bale bredde.   *sorrow begotten*
Yet mey God thoro is myght
Ageyn to geyt hur spech right."   *again get her speech*
Tho messynger ageyn hym spedde
  To tho Sadyn and told hym soo;   *sultan*
Then wakynd ey more wo and wo,   395

He toke is oste and come nere.   *host, army*
Tho emperowr, doghtty undur schyld,
With anodur kepped hym in tho fyld,   *met*
Eydur had batell sere.
Syr Gwother went to a chambur smart,   400
And preyd to God in his hart
On rode that boghtt hym dere,
Schuld sende hym armur, schyld and speyr,
And hors to helpe is lord in weyr
That wyll susstand hym thare.   405   *sustained*
He had [non er] is preyr made
Bot hors and armur bothe he hade
Stode at his chambur dor.
His armur, is steid was blacke color;   *his steed*
He leypus on hors, that styth in stowr,   410   *valiant in battle*
That stalworthe was and store.
His scheld apon his schuldur hong,
He toke his speyre was large and long
And spard nodur myre ne more;   *avoided; swamp*
Forthe at tho yatus on hors he went,   415   *gates*
Non hym knew bot that meydyn gent,
And aftur hur fadur he fore.
Tho emperovr had a batell kene,   *army fierce*
Tho Sawden anodur, withowt wene,
Assemuld, as was hor kast;   420   *purpose*
Bot fro Syr Gwother commun were,
Mony a crone con he stere   *crown (head)*
And hew apon full fast;
    He gard stedus for to stakur   *stagger*
And knyghttus hartys for to flakur   425   *falter*
When blod and brenus con brast,   *brains; burst*
And mony a heython hed of smott;   *cut off*
And owt of hor sadyls, wylle Y wott,
Thei tombull at tho last.
He putte tho Sawden to tho flyghth   430
And made tho chasse to it was nyghth,
And sluye tho Sarsyns kene;
Sython rode before tho emperowr,   *Since*
Non hym knew bot that bryghtt in bowr,
Tho dompe meydon schene.   435   *beautiful*
    To chambur he went, dysharnest hym sone.   *undressed*
His hors, is armur awey wer done,
He ne wyst wher hit myght bene.

In hall he fond his lorde at meyt;
He seytt hym down and made is seytt   440
Too small raches between.   *hounds*
Tho meydon toke too gruhowndus fyn
And waschyd hor mowthus cleyn with wyn
And putte a lofe in tho ton;   *in the one*
And in tho todur flesch full gud.   445   *in the other; flesh*
He raft bothe owt with eyggur mode,   *snatched; eager*
That doghthy of body and bon.
He seytt, made hym wyll at es,
Sythyn to chambur con he ches,
In that worthely won.   450   *the world*
On tho morne cum a messengere
Fro tho Sawdyn with store chere,   *fierce countenance*
To tho emperowr sone he come;
He seyd, "Syr, Y bryng yow a lettur:
My lord is commun, wyll take hym bettur.   455   *coming*
Yesturdey ye slogh his men;
Todey he is commun into tho feyld
With knyghtys that beyrus speyr and schyld,   *bear*
Thowsandus mo then ten."
God sende Syr Gowther thro is myghth   460
A reyd hors and armur bryghth,
He fo[lw]yd thro frythe and fen.   *followed; woods*
When bothe batels wer areyd,
Truly, as tho romandys seyd,
Syr Gwother rode betwene.   465
Mony a sturdy gard he stombull,
Toppe over teyle hor horssus to tombull,
For to wytte withowt wene;
He hewde insondur helme and schelde,
He feld tho baner in tho feld   470
That schon so bryght and schene.
He leyd apon tho Sarsyns blake
And gard hor basnettus in too crake;   *helmets*
He kyd that he was kene.
    "A, lord God!" seyd tho emperowre,   475
"What knyght is yondur so styffe in stowr   *battle*
And all areyd in red,
Bothe his armur and his steyd,
Mony a hethon he gars to bled
And dynggus hom to tho deyd,   480
And hedur come to helpe me;

Anodur in blacke yesturdey had we
That styrd hym wyll in this styd,
Dyscomfytt the Sawden and mony a Sarsyn.
So wyll yondur do, as Y wene,   485
His dyntys ar heyve as leyde;
   His fochon is full styffe of stele—
Loke, he warus his dyntus full wele,
And wastus of hom neuer won."
Tho emperowr pryckus into tho pres,   490
Tho doghtty knyght with hym he ches,
And byrkons hom flesche and bonn.   *beat*
Tho Sawdyn to a forest fled,
And his ost with hym he led
That laft wer onslon.   495
Syr Gwother turnyd is brydyll bryght,
And rode befor is lorde full ryght,
To chambur then he [is gon.]
   When his armur of wer don,
His hors and hit awey wer son,   500
That he wyst not whare.
When he come into tho hall,
He fond tho emperour and is men all
To meyt was gwon full yare;
Among tho howndus down he hym seytt,   510
Tho meydon forthe tho greyhondus feytt,
And leytt as noghtt ware,
Fedde Hob tho fole, for sothe to sey,
Lyke as sche dyd tho forme dey.
To chambur sython con fare.   515
   Tho emperour thonkud God of heuun
That schope tho nyght and tho deyus seyvun,   *made*
That he had soo sped;
Dyscomfyd tho Sawdyn thwys,   *twice*
And slen is men most of prys,   520
Save thos that with hym fled.
"Anturus knyghtus come vs too,   *adventurous*
Aydur dey won of thoo,
Y ne wyst wher thei wer bred;
Tho ton in reyd, tho todur in blacke—   525
Had eydur of hom byn to lacke,   *been absent*
Full evyll we had benn steyd."
   They pypud and trompud in tho hall,   *piped and danced*
Knyghtus and ladys dancyd all

Befor that mynstralsy.   530
Syr Gwother in his chambur ley;
He lyst nowdur dance ne pley,
For he was full wery,
Bryssud for strokus that he had laghtth   *bruised; suffered*
When he in tho batell faghtth,   535
Amonghe that carefull cry.
He had no thoght bot of is syn,
And how he myght is soule wyn
To tho blys that God con hym by.
    Thes lordys to bed con hom bown,   540
And knyghttys and ladys of renown,
Thus this romans told.   *romance*
On tho morne come a messynger
And seyd to tho emperovr, "Now is wer,
Thi care mey be full cold;   545
My lord is comun with his powyr.
Bot yf thu gyff hym thi doghttur dere,   *Except*
He wyll hampur the in hold   *confine*
And byrkon the bothe blod and bon,
And leyve on lyfe noght won   550
Off all thi barons bold."
    "Y covnt hym noght," quod tho emperour;
"Y schall gare sembull as styff in stour,
And meyt hym yf Y mey."
Tho doghtty men that to hym dyd long   555   *belong*
Anon wer armyd, old and yong,
Be vndur of tho dey;   *about nine* A.M.
Thei leype on hors, toke schyld and speyr.
Then tho gud knyght Gwotheyr
To God in hart con prey,   560
Schulde sende hym hors and armur tyte;   *quickly*
Sone he had bothe, mylke whyte,
And rod aftur in gud arey.
    Hys to commyngus tho dompe meydon
        had sene,
And to tho thryd went with wene;   565
No mon hit knew bot God,
For he fard nodur with brag ne bost,
Bot preystely pryckys aftur the ost,
And foloud on hor trowd.   *track*
Tho emperovr was in tho voward,   570   *vanguard*
And Gowther rode befor is lord,

Of kynghttys was he odde.   *outstanding*
Tho berons wer to tho dethe dongon
And barons bryght in sladus slongon,   *valleys*
With strokus greyt and lowd.   575
   Tho Sawdyn bare a sabull blacke,
Three lyons rampand, withowt lacke,
That all of siluer sch[ene];   *shone*
Won was corvon with golys redde,   *gules*
Anodur with gold in that steyd,   580
Tho thryde with aser, I wene.   *blue*
And his helmyt full rychely frett,
With charbuckolus stonus suryly sett,   *carbuncle, firmly*
And dyamondus betwene;
And his batell wele areyd,   585
And his baner brodly dyspleyd;
Sone aftur tyde hom tene.
   Tho gud knyght Syr Gowtheyr,
He styrd hym styfly in his geyr,
Ther levyd non doghttear, Y wene;   590
Ylke a dyntte that he smotte
Thro owt steyll helmus it boott,   *cut*
He felld bothe hors and mon,
And made hom tombull to tho gronde;
Tho fote men on tho feld con stonde   595   *infantry*
And then ward radly ranne.
Tho Sawdyn for tho emperovrus doghttur
Gard Cryston and hethon to dye in slaghttur;
That tyme hym burd wele bann.   *He was compelled to*
                                        endure ruin

[The] whyle Syr Gwother freschely faghtte,   600
Many a doghtte hors is deythe ther kaghtte,
That he myghtte ouer reche;
All that he with his fawchon hytte
Thei fell to tho ground and ross not yette   605   *rose*
Nor lokyd aftur no leyche.
Bot he wold not for yre ne tene
No worde speyke, withowt wene,
For dowtte of Godus wreke.
Yf all he hongurt, noght he dyd eytte   610
Bot what he myght fro tho howndus geyt;
He dyd as tho pwope con hym teche.
   Syr Gwother, that stythe in stowre,
Rydys ey with tho emperovr

And weyrus hym fro wothe;	615	*protects; danger*
Ther was no Sarsyn so mykull of strenthe		
That durst come within is speyre lenthe,		
So doghttely wer thei bothe.		
With his fachon large and long		
Syche dyntus on them he dong	620	
Hor lyfus myghtte the lothe;		
All that euer abode that becur		*fight*
Of hor deythus meghtt be secur,		*certain*
He styrd his hondus so rathe.		
That dey he tent noght bot is fyght;	625	*heeded*
Tho emperour faght with all his myght,		
Bot radly was he takon,		
And with tho Sawdyn awey was led.		
Tho dompe duke gard hym ley a wed,		*made him hostage*
Stroke of his hed anon,	630	
Rescowyd is lord, broght hym ageyn,		
Lovyd [h]e God, in hart was ful feyn,		
That formod bothe blod and bonn.		
Ther come a Sarsyn with a speyre,		
Thro tho scholdur smott Gotheyr,	635	
Then made the dompe meydon mon.		*moan*
For sorro fell owt of hur tovre,		*tower*
Tho doghtur of tho emperovr		
To whyte withowt wene.		
A doghtty sqwyer in hur bare;	640	
Of all too deyus hoo styrd no mare		
Then ho deyd had ben.		
Tho lord come hom, to meyt was seytt,		
And tho doghtty knyght, withowt leytt,	645	
That had in tho batell byn,		
To chambur he went, dyd of is geyre,		
This gud knyght Syr Gwothere,		
Then myssyd he that meydon schene.		
Emong tho howndus is meyt he wann.	650	
Tho emperovr was a drvry man		
For his doghttur gent;		
He gard erlys and barons go to Rome		
Aftur tho pope, and he come sone		
To hur enterment,	655	*burial*
And cardynals to tho beryng		
To assoyle that swett thyng.		
Syche grace God hur sentt		

That scho raxeld hur and rase,   *stretched*
And spake wordus that wyse was   660
To Syr Gwother, varement.   *truly*
   Ho seyd, "My lord of heyvon gretys the well,
And forgyffeus the thi synn yche a dell,
And grantys the tho blys;
And byddus the speyke on hardely,   665
Eyte and drynke and make mery;
Thu schallt be won of his."
Scho seyd to hur fadur, "This is he
That faght for yow deys thre
In strong batell, ywys."   670
Tho pope had schryvon Syr Gother—
He louyd God and Mare ther—
And radly hym con kys,
And seyd, "Now art thu Goddus chyld;
The thar not dowt tho warlocke wyld,   675   *need; fear*
Ther waryd mot he bee."   *cursed*
Thro tho pope and tho emperovr asent
Ther he weyd that meydyn gent,   *wed*
That curtesse was and fre,
And scho a lady gud and ffeyr,   680
Of all hur fadur londus eyr;
Beyttur thurte non bee.   *need*
   Tho pope toke his leyfe to weynde;   *leave; travel*
With tham he laft his blessyng [hende],
Ageyn to Rome went hee.   685
   When this mangeyre was broght to ende,   *feast*
Syr Gwother con to Estryke wende
And gaffe tho old erle all;
Made [h]ym duke of that cuntre,
And lett hym wed his modur fre,   690
That lade gent and small;
And ther he made an abbey
And gaff therto rent for ey,
"And here lye Y schall";
And putte therin monkus blake   695
To rede and syng for Godys sake,
And closyd hit with gud wall.
All yf tho pope had hym schryvyn   *Although*
And God is synnus clene forgeuon,
Yett was his hart full sare   700
That euer he schuld so yll wyrke

To bren tho nvnnus in hor kyrke,
And made hor plasse so bare.
For hom gard he make thatt abbey
And a covent therin for ey   705
That mekull cowde of lare,   *knew of learning*
For them vnto tho wordus end   *world's end*
For hor sovlus that he had brend
And all that Cryston ware.
   And then he went hym hom ageyn,   710
And be that he come in Allmeyn   *Germany*
His fadur tho emperovr was deyd,
And he lord and emperowr
Of all Cryston knyghttus tho flowre,
And with tho Sarsyns dredde.   715
What mon so bydus hym for Godys loffe doo   *asks*
He was ey redy bown thertoo,   *prepared*
And stod pore folke in styd,
And ryche men in hor ryght,
And halpe holy kyrke in all is myght;   720
Thus toke he bettur reyd.
   Furst he reynod mony a yere,
An emperovr of greyt power,
And whysyle con he wake;   *wisely*
And when he dyed, tho sothe to sey,   725
Was beryd at tho same abbey
That hymselfe gart make;
And he is a varre corsent parfett,   *saint*
And with Cryston pepull wele belovyd;
God hase done for his sake   730
Myrrakull, for he has hym hold.
Ther he lyse in schryne of gold   *shrine*
That suffurd for Goddus sake.
Who so sechys hym with hart fre,
Of hor bale bote mey bee,   735   *trouble; helped*
For so God hase hym hight;
Thes wordus of hym thar no mon wast,
For he is inspyryd with tho Holy Gost,
That was tho cursod knyght.
For he garus tho blynd to see   740
And tho dompe to speyke parde,
And makus tho crokyd ryght,
And gyffus to tho mad hor wytte,
And mony odur meracullus yette,

Thoro tho grace of God allmyght.	745	
Thus Syr Gwother couerys is care,		*cures*
That fyrst was ryche and sython bare,		
And effte was ryche ageyn,		
And geyton with a felteryd feynd;		
Grace he had to make that eynd	750	
That God was of hym feyn		
This is wreton in parchemeyn,		
A story bothe gud and fyn		
Owt off a law of Breytyn;		*lay; Brittany*
Ihesu Cryst, Goddys son,	755	
Gyff vs myght with hym to won,		
That lord that is most of meyn. Amen.		
Explicit Syr Gother		

Notes

1. Editor's Note: Emendations are enclosed in square brackets and are mostly based upon Royal MS. 17.B.XLIII. The Anglo-Saxon rune thorn is transliterated to *th*. The rune yogh is transliterated to *g*, *gh*, or *z*.

Bibliography

Primary Sources

Aristotle. "Nichomachean Ethics." In *The Complete Works of Aristotle: Revised Oxford Translation*. 2 vols. Ed. Jonathan Barnes. Princeton: Princeton University Press, 1984. 2: 1729–1867.

———. *The Greek Commentaries on the* Nichomachean Ethics *of Aristotle*. Trans. Robert Grosseteste. Ed. H. Paul F. Mercken. Leiden: Brill, 1973.

Ashby, George. *George Ashby's Poems*. Ed. Mary Bateson. EETS e.s. 76. Oxford: Oxford University Press, 1899.

Banks, Mary Macleod, ed. *An Alphabet of Tales: An English 15th Century Translation of the* Alphabetum Narrationum *of Etienne de Besançon*. EETS o.s. 126–127. London: Kegan Paul, Trench, Trübner, 1904–05.

Bede. *Ecclesiastical History of the English People*. Ed. Betram Colgrave and R.A.B. Mynors. Oxford: Clarendon, 1969.

Bennett, William J, ed. *The Book of Virtues: A Treasury of Great Moral Stories*. New York: Simon and Schuster, 1993.

———. *Moral Compass: Stories for a Life's Journey*. New York: Simon and Schuster, 1995.

Bernard of Clairvaux. *De consideratione libri quinque ad Eugenium tertium*. Ed. J. P. Migne. *Patrologia Latina* 182, cols. 727–808.

———. *Flores sue sententia ex S. Bernardi operibus depromptae*. Ed. J. P. Migne. 1854. *Patrologia Latina* 183, cols. 1197–1204.

Blake, N. F., ed. *The Lay Folks' Catechism: Middle English Religious Prose*. London: Arnold, 1972. 73–87.

Boyd, Beverly. *The Middle English Miracles of the Virgin*. San Marino, CA: Huntington Library, 1964.

———, ed. *The Prioress's Tale. A Variorum Edition of the Works of Geoffrey Chaucer, II: The Canterbury Tales, 20*. Norman: University of Oklahoma Press, 1983.

Breul, Karl, ed. *Sir Gowther*. Oppeln: Eugen Franck, 1886.

Brunner, Karl. "Me. Disticha (aus Hs. Add. 37049)." *Archiv für das Studium der neueren Sprachen und Literaturen* 159 (1931): 86–92.

Burgh, Benet, trans. *Parvus Cato Magnus Cato.* Ed. Fumio Kuriyagawa. Seijo English Monographs 13. Tokyo: Seijo University Press, 1974.

Caxton, William. *Caxton's Book of Curtesye.* Ed. Frederick J. Furnivall. EETS o.s. 3. London: Oxford University Press, 1868.

————. *Vocabulary in French and English: A Facsimile of Caxton's Edition c. 1480.* With introductions by J.C.T. Oates and L. C. Harmer. Cambridge: Cambridge University Press, 1964.

Chaucer, Geoffrey. *The Riverside Chaucer.* Gen. ed. Larry D. Benson. Boston: Houghton-Mifflin, 1987.

Clark, Andrew, ed. *The English Register of Godstowe Nunnery near Oxford.* EETS o.s. 129. London: Kegan Paul, Trench, Trübner, 1905.

Conlee, John W. *Middle English Debate Poetry: A Critical Anthology.* East Lansing, MI: Colleagues Press, 1991.

Crow, Martin M., and Clair C. Olson, eds. *Chaucer Life Records.* Oxford: Clarendon, 1963.

Curley, Michael, trans. *Physiologus.* Austin: University of Texas Press, 1979.

Davis, Norman, ed. *Non-Cycle Plays and the Winchester Dialogues: Facsimiles of Plays and Fragments in Various Manuscripts and the Dialogues in Winchester College MS 33.* Leeds Texts and Monographs, Medieval Drama Facsimiles V. Gen. Ed. A. C. Cawley and Stanley Ellis. Leeds: University of Leeds Press, 1979.

————. "Two Unprinted Dialogues in Late Middle English and Their Language." *Revue des Langues Vivantes* 35 (1969): 461–72.

Doyle, I. A., ed. *The Vernon Manuscript: A Facsimile of Bodleian Library, Oxford, MS. Eng. Poet. a. I.* Cambridge: D. S. Brewer, 1987.

Duemmler, Ernst, ed. *Poetae Latini Aevi Carolini. Monumenta Germaniae Historica: Poetarum Latinorum Medii Aevi,* 1–2. Berlin: Weidmann, 1881–1884. Munich: Monumenta Germaniae Historica, 1978.

Duemmler, Ernst, ed. *Monumenta Germaniae Historica: Epistolae.* Vol. 4. Berlin: Weidman, 1895.

Duff, J. Wight, and Arnold M. Duff, ed. and trans. *Minor Latin Poets: Vol. 2.* Loeb Classical Library 434. Cambridge: Harvard University Press, 1935.

Dyboski, R., ed. *Songs, Carols and Other Miscellaneous Poems from Balliol 354.* EETS e.s. 101. London: Kegan Paul, 1907.

Early English Versions of the Gesta Romanorum. Ed. Sidney J. H. Herrtage. EETS e.s. 33. London: N. Trubner, 1879.

Eccles, Mark, ed. *The Macro Plays.* EETS o.s. 262. London: Oxford University Press, 1969.

Eisner, Sigmund, ed. *A Variorum Edition of the Works of Geoffrey Chaucer, Volume VI, The Prose Treatises, Part One, A Treatise on the Astrolabe.* Norman, OK: University of Oklahoma Press, 2002.

Evelyn-White, Hugh Gerard, ed. and trans. *Hesiod, the Homeric Hymns, and Homerica.* Loeb Classical Library 57. Cambridge: Harvard University Press, 1936.

Ford, Patrick K. *The Mabinogi and Other Medieval Welsh Tales.* Berkeley: University of California Press, 1977.

————, ed. *Math uab Mathonwy.* Belmont: Ford and Bailie, 1999.

Furnivall, Frederick J., ed. *Early English Meals and Manners*. EETS o.s. 32. London, 1868. New York: Kraus, 1990.

———, ed. *Hymns to the Virgin and Christ, the Parliament of Devils, and Other Religious Poems*. EETS o.s. 24. London: Trübner, 1867.

———, ed. *Political, Religious, and Love Poems*. 2nd ed. EETS o.s. 15. London: Kegan Paul, 1903.

———, ed. *Queene Elizabeth's Achademy*. London, 1869. EETS o.s. 8. New York: Kraus, 1981.

Gaide, Françoise, ed. and trans. *Avianus: Fables*. Paris: Les Belles Lettres, 1980.

Gantz, Jeffrey, trans. *The Mabinogion*. New York: Penguin, 1976.

Garmonsway, G. N. *Ælfric's Colloquy*. New York: Appleton-Century-Crofts, 1966.

Geoffrey of Vinsauf. *Poetria Nova*. Trans. Margaret F. Nims. Medieval Sources in Translation 6. Toronto: Pontifical Institute of Mediaeval Studies, 1967.

Giles, J. A., trans. *Roger of Wendover's Flowers of History*. 2 vols. London: Henry G. Bohn, 1849.

Goodich, Michael, ed. *Other Middle Ages: Witnesses at the Margins of Medieval Society*. Philadelphia: University of Pennsylvania Press, 1998.

Gower, John. Confessio Amantis. *The English Works of John Gower*. 2 vols. Ed. G. C. Macaulay. EETS e.s. 81–82. London: Oxford University Press, 1900–1901.

———. *Mirour de l'Omme*. The French Works. Vol. 1 of *The Complete Works of John Gower*. Ed. G. C. Macaulay. Oxford: Clarendon Press, 1899.

———. *Vox Clamantis*. The Latin Works. Vol. 4 of *The Complete Works of John Gower*. Ed. G. C. Macaulay. Oxford: Clarendon Press, 1902.

Guest, Charlotte, trans. *The Mabinogion*. Mineola, NY: Dover, 1997.

Gwara, Scott. *Latin Colloquies from Pre-Conquest Britain*. Toronto: Pontifical Institute of Medieval Studies, 1996.

———, and David Porter. *Anglo-Saxon Conversations: The Colloquies of Ælfric Bata*. Woodbridge, Suffolk: Boydell, 1997.

Halsall, Maureen. *The Old English Rune Poem: A Critical Edition*. Toronto: Toronto University Press 1981.

Handford, S. A., trans. *Fables of Aesop*. New York: Penguin, 1954.

Happé, Peter, ed. *Tudor Interludes*. Harmondsworth: Penguin, 1972.

Hazlitt, W. Carew, ed. *Early Popular Poetry of England*. London: John Russell Smith, 1864.

Hervieux, Leopold. *Les fabulistes latins depuis le siecle D'Auguste jusqu'a la fin du moyen age*. 5 volumes. Paris, 1893–99.

Hesiod. *Works and Days and Theogony*. Trans. Stanley Lombardo. Indianapolis: Hackett, 1993.

Hogg, James. *An Illustrated Yorkshire Carthusian Religious Miscellany London, Additional MS. 37049*. Salzburg: Institut fur Anglistik und Amerikanistik Universitat Salzburg, 1981.

Horace. *Satires, Epistles, and Ars Poetica*. Ed. and trans. H. Rushton Fairclough. Loeb Classical Library 194. Cambridge: Harvard University Press, 1929.

Horstmann, Carl, ed. *Altenglische Legenden (Neue Folge)*. 2 vols. Heilbronn: Gebr. Henninger, 1881.

———. *Englische Studien*. Vol. VIII. Heilbronn: Gebr. Henninger, 1885.

————, ed. *The Minor Poems of the Vernon MS.* London: Kegan Paul, Trench, Trübner, 1892.

James, M. R., ed. *The Apocryphal New Testament.* London: Oxford University Press, 1924.

Jones, Gwyn. *Welsh Legends and Folk-Tales.* London: Oxford University Press, 1955.

Jones, Thomas, ed. *Brut y Tywysogyon.* Cardiff: Wales University Press, 1941.

Laird, Edgar, and Robert Fischer, eds. *Pèlerin de Prusse on the Astrolabe: Text and Translation of His* Practique de astralabe. Binghamton, NY: Medieval and Renaissance Texts and Studies, 1995.

Langland, William. *The Vision of Piers Plowman: A Complete Edition of the B-Text.* Ed. A. V. C. Schmidt. London: Dent, 1987.

Latini, Brunetto. *The Book of the Treasure (Li Livres dou Tresor).* Trans. Paul Barrette and Spurgeon Baldwin. New York: Garland, 1993.

Longchamp, Nigel. *A Mirror for Fools: The Book of Burnel the Ass.* Trans. J. H. Mozley. Notre Dame: University of Notre Dame Press, 1963.

Lutz, Cora. "A Medieval Textbook." *The Yale University Library Gazette* 49 (1974): 212–16.

Lydgate, John. *The Fall of Princes.* 4 vols. Ed. Henry Bergen, Washington: Carnegie Institute, 1923.

Macrobius. *Commentary on the Dream of Scipio.* Trans. William Harris Stahl. 1952. New York: Columbia University Press, 1990.

Mannyng, Robert of Brunne. *Handlyng Synne.* Ed. Idelle Sullens. Binghamton, NY: Center for Medieval & Early Renaissance Studies, 1983.

Martin, Clarence Anthony. "Edinburgh University Library Manuscript 93. An Annotated Edition of Selected Devotional Treatises with a Survey of Parallel Versions." Dissertation, University of Edinburgh, 1977.

Martianus Capella. *Martianus Capella and the Seven Liberal Arts, Volume II: The Marriage of Philology and Mercury.* Trans. William Harris Stahl and Richard Johnson, with E. L. Burge. New York: Columbia University Press, 1977.

McKenzie, Kenneth, and William A. Oldfather. *Ysopet-Avionnet: The Latin and French Texts.* Urbana: University of Illinois Press, 1919.

Middle English Dictionary. Ed. Hans Kurath. Ann Arbor: University of Michigan Press, 1956–.

Mills, Maldwyn, ed. *Sir Gowther in Six Middle English Romances.* London: Dent, 1992.

Moffat, Douglas, trans. *The Complaint of Nature.* 1908. Hamden, CT: Archon, 1972.

Montaiglon, Anatole de. *Le Livre du Chevalier de La Tour Landry pour l'enseignement de ses filles.* Paris, 1854. Millwood, NY: Kraus, 1982.

Mooney, Linne R., ed. *The Kalendarium of John Somer.* Athens: University of Georgia Press, 1998.

Nicholas of Lynn. *The Kalendarium of Nicholas of Lynn.* Ed. Sigmund Eisner. Trans. G. MacEoian. Athens: University of Georgia Press, 1980.

Offord, M. W., ed. *The Book of the Knight of the Tower.* Trans. William Caxton. New York: Oxford University Press, 1971.

Ovid. *Metamorphoses.* 2nd ed. Ed. G. P. Goold. Trans. Frank Justus Miller. 2 vols. Cambridge: Harvard University Press, 1984.

Oxford English Dictionary. Rev. ed. Oxford: Oxford University Press, 1989.

Patrologia Latina. Ed. J.–P. Migne. 221 vols. Paris, 1844–1891.

Perry, Aaron Jenkins, ed. *John Trevisa: Dialogus inter militem et clericum.* EETS o.s. 167. London: Oxford University Press, 1925.

"Pierce the Ploughman's Crede." In *The Piers Plowman Tradition: A Critical Edition of Pierce the Ploughman's Crede, Richard the Redeless, Mum and the Sothsegger, and the Crowned King.* Ed. Helen Barr. London: Dent, 1993. 61–97.

The Pilgrimage of the Lyfe of the Manhode. 2 vols. Ed. Avril Henry. EETS o.s. 288 and 292. London: Oxford University Press, 1985–88.

Plato. *The Collected Dialogues.* Eds. Edith Hamilton and Huntington Cairns. Bollingen Series LXXI. Princeton: Princeton University Press, 1961.

Poole, Reginald Lane, and Mary Bateson, eds. Index Britanniae Scriptorium: *John Bale's Index of British and Other Writers.* 1902. Introduction by Caroline Brett and James P. Carley. Cambridge: D. S. Brewer, 1990.

Power, Eileen, ed. *Miracles of the Blessed Virgin Mary.* By Johannes Herolt. Trans. C. C. Swinton Bland. New York: Harcourt, Brace, 1928.

Quinn, Betty Nye. "ps. Theodolus." In *Catalogus Translationum et Commentariorum: Medieval and Renaissance Latin Translations and Commentaries.* Ed. Paul Oskar Kristeller. Vol. 2. Washington: Catholic University of America Press, 1971. 383–408.

Quintillian. *On the Teaching of Speaking and Writing: Translations from Books One, Two, and Ten of the* Institutio Oratoria. Ed. James J. Murphy. Carbondale: Southern Illinois University Press, 1987.

Reidy, John, ed. "A Treatise on the Astrolabe." *The Riverside Chaucer.* Gen ed. Larry D. Benson. Boston: Houghton-Mifflin, 1987. 661–683.

Rickert, Edith, ed. The Babees' Book: *Medieval Manners for the Young.* 1923. New York: Coopers Square, 1966.

Rothwell, William, ed. *Walter de Bibbesworth: Le Tretiz.* London: Anglo-Norman Text Society, 1990.

———. *The Anglo-Norman Dictionary.* London: Modern Humanities Research Association, 1977–1992.

Rudolfus Trudonis. *Gesta Abbatum Trudonensium. Patrologia Latina* 173, col. 188a.

Ryder, Arthur W., trans. *The Panchatantra.* Chicago: University of Chicago Press, 1925.

Seymour, M. C., ed. *On the Properties of Things: John of Trevisa's Translation of Bartholmaeus Anglicus* De Proprietatibus Rerum. 3 vols. Oxford: Oxford UP, 1975–88.

Skeat, W. W, ed. *The Complete Works of Geoffrey Chaucer.* 6 vols. Oxford: Clarendon, 1894–97.

———, ed. *A Treatise on the Astrolabe Addressed to His Son Lowys by Geoffrey Chaucer.* London: N. Trübner, 1872.

Slavitt, David R., trans. *The Fables of Avianus.* Baltimore: Johns Hopkins University Press, 1993.

Smith, Lucy Toulmin, ed. *A Common-Place Book of the Fifteenth Century.* London: Trübner, 1886.

Steele, Robert, ed. *Lydgate and Burgh's Secrees of Old Philisoffres.* 1894. EETS e.s. 66. New York: Kraus, 1973.

———. *Three Prose Versions of the* Secreta Secretorum. EETS e.s. 74. London: Kegan Paul, 1898.

Stockton, Eric, trans. *The Major Latin Works of John Gower: The* Voice of One Crying *and the* Tripartite Chronicle. Seattle: University of Washington Press, 1962.

Strecker, Karl. *Poetae Latini Aevi Carolini. Monumenta Germaniae Historica Poetarum Latinorum Medii Aevi*, 4.2–3. Berlin: Weidmann, 1914–23. Munich: Monumenta Germaniae Historica, 1978.

Swan, Charles, trans. *Gesta Romanorum*. London: Routledge, 1924.

Thoresby, John, ed. *Lay Folks' Catechism*. EETS o.s. 118. London: Kegan Paul, 1901.

"*Versus cuiusdam Scoti de alphabeto*." In *Poetae Latini Minores*. 6 vols. Ed. Amilius Baehrens. Vol. 5. Leipzig: Teubner, 1883. 5: 375–78.

Whiteford, Peter, ed. *The Myracles of Oure Lady*. Heidelberg: Carl Winter, 1990.

Wilson, Evelyn Faye. *The* Stella Maris *of John of Garland*. Cambridge: Medieval Academy of America, 1946.

The Winchester Anthology: A Facsimile of British Library Additional Manuscript 60577 with an Introduction and List of Contents by Edward Wilson and an Account of the Music by Iain Fenlon. Cambridge: D. S. Brewer, 1981.

Wright, Aaron E., ed. *The Fables of "Walter of England."* Toronto Medieval Latin Texts 25. Toronto: Pontifical Institute of Mediaeval Studies, 1997.

Wright, Thomas. *The Book of the Knight of La Tour-Landry*. EETS o.s. 33. London, 1868.

Zipes, Jack, trans. *The Complete Fairy Tales of the Brothers Grimm*. New York: Bantam Books, 1992.

Secondary Sources

Adams, Gillian. "Medieval Children's Literature: Its Possibility and Actuality." *Children's Literature* 26 (1998): 1–24.

Acker, Paul. "The *Crafte of Nombrynge* in Columbia University Library, Plimpton MS 259." *Manuscripta* 37 (1993): 71–83.

Allen, Elizabeth. "Chaucer Answers Gower: Constance and the Trouble with Philosophy." *English Literary History* 63 (1997): 627–55.

Allen and Greenough's New Latin Grammar. Ed. J. B. Greenough, G. L. Kittredge, A. A. Howard, and B. L. D'Ooge. New Rochelle, NY: Aristide D. Caratzas, 1931.

Anderson, J. J. "Gawain and the Hornbook." *Notes & Queries* n.s. 37 (1990): 160–63.

Archer, Rowena E. " 'How ladies . . . who live on their manors ought to manage their households and estates': Women as Landholders and Administrators in the Later Middle Ages." In *Woman Is a Worthy Wight: Women in English Society c. 1200–1500*. Ed. P. J. P Goldberg. Wolfeboro Falls, NH: Alan Sutton, 1992. 149–81.

Ariès, Philippe. *Centuries of Childhood: A Social History of Family Life*. Trans. Robert Baldick. New York: Knopf, 1962.

Avery, Catherine B. *The New Century Handbook of Classical Geography*. New York: Appleton-Century-Crofts, 1972.

Axton, Richard. "Gower—Chaucer's Heir?" In *Chaucer Traditions: Studies in Honour of Derek Brewer*. Ed. Ruth Mosse and Barry Windeatt. Cambridge: Cambridge University Press, 1990. 21–38.

Baltzell, Jane. "Rhetorical 'Amplification' and 'Abbreviation' and the Structure of Medieval Narrative." *Pacific Coast Philology* 2 (1967): 32–39.

Baron, F. Xavier. "Children and Violence in Chaucer's *Canterbury Tales*." *Journal of Psychohistory* 6 (1978–79): 77–103.

Barratt, Alexandra. "Works of Religious Instruction." In *Middle English Prose: A Critical Guide to Major Authors and Genres*. Ed. A. S. G. Edwards. New Brunswick, NJ: Rutgers University Press, 1984. 413–32.

Baugh, Albert C. "The Date of Walter of Bibbesworth's *Traite*." In *Festschrift fur Walther Fischer*. Ed. H. Opal. Heidelberg: Carl Winter, 1959.

Bell, Alexander. "Notes on Walter de Bibbesworth's *Treatise*." *Philological Quarterly* 41 (1962): 361–72.

Bennett, Michael J. "Education and Advancement." In *Fifteenth-Century Attitudes: Perceptions of Society in Late-Medieval England*. Cambridge: Cambridge University Press, 1994. 79–96.

Bennett, William J, ed. *The Book of Virtues: A Treasury of Great Moral Stories*. New York: Simon and Schuster, 1993.

———. *Moral Compass: Stories for a Life's Journey*. New York: Simon and Schuster, 1995.

Berndt, Rolf. "French and English in 13th Century England," *Sitzungsberichte der Akademie der Wissenschaften der DDR, Gesellschaftswissenschaften* (1976): 129–150.

Bestul, Thomas H. "Gower's *Mirour de l'Omme* and the Meditative Tradition." *Mediaevalia* 16 (1993): 307–28.

Biller, Peter, and Anne Hudson, eds. *Heresy and Literacy, 1000–1530*. Cambridge: Cambridge University Press, 1994.

Bingham, Jane, and Grayce Scholt. *Fifteen Centuries of Children's Literature: An Annotated Chronology of British and American Works in Historical Context*. Westport, CT: Greenwood, 1980.

Birch, Walter De Gray. "On Two Anglo-Saxon Manuscripts in the British Museum." *Transactions of the Royal Society of Literature*. 2nd ser. 11 (1878): 463–512.

Blackham, H. J. *The Fable as Literature*. London: Athlone, 1985.

Blair, Peter Hunter. *The World of Bede*. Cambridge: Cambridge University Press, 1970.

———. *Anglo-Saxon England: An Introduction*. 1959. New York: Barnes and Noble, 1996.

Blake, N. F. *William Caxton and English Literary Culture*. London: Hambledon, 1991.

Bliss, A. J. "Two Hilton Manuscripts in Columbia University Library." *Medium Ævum* 38 (1969): 157–63.

Bollard, J. K. "The Structure of the Four Branches of the Mabinogi." *Transactions of the Honourable Society of Cymmrodorion* (1974–1975): 250–76. Rpt. in Sullivan, *The Mabinogi*, 165–96.

Boisard, Pierre. "La Vie intellectuelle de la noblesse angevine a la fin du XIVe siècle d'apres le chevalier de La Tour Landry: Actes du Colloque du samedi 22 mars 1980." In *La Littérature angevine médiévale*. Angers: Université d'Angers, 1981. 135–54.

Boswell, John. *The Kindness of Strangers: The Abandonment of Children in Western Europe from Late Antiquity to the Renaissance*. New York: Pantheon, 1988.

Braddy, Haldeen. "Chaucer, Alice Perrers, and Cecily Chaumpaigne." *Speculum* 52 (1977): 906–11.

Breeze, Andrew. *Medieval Welsh Literature*. Portland, OR: Four Courts, 1997.

Brentano, Mary Theresa. *Relationship of the Latin* Facetus *Literature to the Medieval English Courtesy Poems*. Lawrence: University of Kansas Press, 1935.

Briggs, Julia. "Critical Opinion: Reading Children's Books." In *Only Connect: Readings on Children's Literature*. Ed. Sheila Egoff, Gordon Stubbs, Ralph Ashley, and Wendy Sutton. Toronto: Oxford University Press, 1996. 18–31.

Brockman, Bennett. "Children and Literature in Late Medieval England." *Children's Literature* 4 (1974): 58–63.

———. "Medieval Songs of Innocence and Experience: The Adult Writer and Literature for Children." *Children's Literature* 2 (1973): 40–49.

Bromwich, Rachel. "The Mabinogion and Lady Charlotte Guest." *Transactions of the Honourable Society of Cymmrodorion* (1986): 127–141. Rpt. in Sullivan, *The Mabinogi*, 3–18.

Brown, Carleton Fairchild. *A Register of Middle English Religious and Didactic Verse*. 2 vols. Oxford: Oxford University Press, 1916–1920.

Brown, Carleton. *Study of the Miracle of Our Lady Told by Chaucer's Prioress*. 2nd ser., no. 45. London: Chaucer Society, 1910.

———, and Rossell Hope Robbins. *The Index of Middle English Verse*. New York: Columbia University Press, 1943.

Bullough, Vern L. "On Being a Male in the Middle Ages." In *Medieval Masculinities: Regarding Men in the Middle Ages*. Ed. Clare A. Lees. Minneapolis: University of Minnesota Press, 1994. 31–45.

Bunt, Gerrit H. V. *Alexander the Great in the Literature of Medieval Britain*. Groningen: Egbert Forsten, 1994.

Burgess, Glyn. "Fables, French." In *Dictionary of the Middle Ages*. Ed. Joseph R. Strayer. Vol. 4. New York: Charles Scribner's Sons, 1989.

Burne, Glenn S. "Andrew Lang's *The Blue Fairy Book*: Changing the Course of History." *Fairy Tales, Fables, Myths, Legends, and Poetry*. Vol. 2 of *Touchstones: Reflections on the Best in Children's Literature*. Ed. Perry Nodelman. West Lafayette, IN: Children's Literature Association, 1987. 140–50.

Burrow, J. A. *The Ages of Man: A Study in Medieval Writing and Thought*. Oxford: Clarendon, 1986.

———. "Chaucer and Gower." In *An Outline of English Literature*. Ed. Pat Rogers. Oxford: Oxford University Press, 1992. 38–50.

———. Explanatory notes to "The Prologue and Tale of Sir Thopas." Chaucer, 917–23.

Bynum, Caroline Walker. *Jesus as Mother: Studies in the Spirituality of the High Middle Ages*. Berkeley: University of California Press, 1982.

Calin, William. "Gower." In *The French Tradition and the Literature of Medieval England*. Toronto: University of Toronto Press, 1994. 371–98.

Carr, A. D. *Medieval Wales*. New York: St. Martin's, 1995.

Carruthers, Mary J. *The Book of Memory: A Study of Memory in Medieval Culture*. Cambridge: Cambridge University Press, 1990.

Cary, George. *The Medieval Alexander*. Ed. D. J. A. Ross. Cambridge: Cambridge University Press, 1956.

Charles-Edwards, T. M. "The Date of the Four Branches of the *Mabinogi.*" *Transactions of the Honourable Society of Cymmrodorion* (1970): 263–98. Rpt. in Sullivan, *The Mabinogi*, 19–58.

Coffman, George R. "John Gower, Mentor for Royalty: Richard II." *Publications of the Modern Language Association* 69 (1954): 953–64.

Cohen, Jeffrey Jerome. *Of Giants: Sex, Monsters, and the Middle Ages.* Medieval Cultures 17. Minneapolis: University of Minnesota Press, 1999.

Comparetti, Domenico. *Vergil in the Middle Ages.* Trans. E. F. M. Benecke. New York: G. E. Stechert, 1929.

Conté, Gian Biagio. *Latin Literature: A History.* Trans. Joseph B. Solodow, Don Fowler, and Glenn W. Moot. Baltimore: Johns Hopkins University Press, 1994.

Copeland, Rita. *Rhetoric, Hermeneutics, and Translation in the Middle Ages: Academic Traditions and Vernacular Texts.* Cambridge Studies in Medieval Literature 11. Cambridge: Cambridge University Press, 1991.

Correll, Barbara. *The End of Conduct: Grobianus and the Renaissance Text of the Subject.* Ithaca, NY: Cornell University Press, 1996.

Couch, Julie Nelson. "Childe Hood: The Infantilization of Medieval Legend." *In Parentheses: Papers in Medieval Studies* (1999): 128–44.

Cowling, George H. *Chaucer.* London: Methuen, 1927.

Crampton, Georgia Ronan. "Chaucer's Singular Prayer." *Medium Ævum* 59 (1990): 191–213.

Cross, J. E. "Teaching Method, 1391: Notes on Chaucer's *Astrolabe.*" *English* 10 (1955): 172–75.

Curtius, Ernst Robert. *European Literature and the Latin Middle Ages.* Trans. Willard R. Trask. Bollingen Series 36. 1953. Princeton: Princeton University Press, 1990.

D'Arcussia, Charles. *La Conférence des fauconniers.* 1644. Paris: E. Jullien at Paul Lacroix, 1883.

Daly, Lloyd W. *Contributions to a History of Alphabetization in Antiquity and the Middle Ages.* Collection Latomus 90. Bruxelles: Latomus Revue D'Etudes Latines, 1967.

———, and Walther Suchier. *Altercatio Hadriani Augusti et Epicteti Philosophi.* Illinois Studies in Language and Literature XXIV. Urbana: University of Illinois Press, 1939.

Darton, F. J. Harvey. *Children's Books in England: Five Centuries of Social Life.* 3rd ed. Rev. Brian Anderson. Cambridge: Cambridge University Press, 1982.

Davenport, W. A. *Fifteenth-Century English Drama: The Early Moral Plays and Their Literary Relations.* Cambridge: D. S. Brewer, 1982.

Davies, Sioned. *The Four Branches of the Mabinogi: Pedair Keinc y Mabinogi.* Llandysul: Gomer, 1995.

———. "Storytelling in Medieval Wales." *Oral Tradition* 7, no. 2 (October 1992): 231–57.

Delany, Sheila. "Slaying Python: Marriage and Misogyny in a Chaucerian Text." In *Writing Women: Women Writers and Women in Literature, Medieval to Modern.* New York: Schocken, 1983. 57–59.

Demause, Lloyd. "The Evolution of Childhood." In *The History of Childhood.* New York: Psychohistory Press, 1974. 1–74.

Demers, Patricia, and Gordon Moyles, eds. *From Instruction to Delight: An Anthology of Children's Literature to 1850*. Oxford: Oxford University Press, 1982.

Dictionary of National Biography. London: Oxford University Press, 1939.

Digital Scriptorium. ‹http://sunsite.berkeley.edu/scriptorium/›

Diller, Hans-Jürgen. " 'For Engelondes sake': Richard II and Henry of Lancaster as Intended Readers of Gower's *Confessio Amantis*." In *Functions of Literature: Essays Presented to Erwin Wolff on His Sixtieth Birthday*. Ed. Ulrich Broich, Theo Stemmler, and Gerd Stratmann. Tübingen: Niemayer, 1984. 39–53.

Donaldson, E. Talbot. "Chaucer the Pilgrim." In *Speaking of Chaucer*. London: Athlone, 1970. 1–12.

Dove, Mary. *The Perfect Age of Man's Life*. Cambridge: Cambridge University Press, 1986.

Doyle, I. A. "Books Connected with the Vere Family and Barking Abbey." *Transactions of the Essex Archæological Society* n.s. 25 (1958): 222–43.

———. "The Shaping of the Vernon and Simeon Manuscript." In *Studies in the Vernon Manuscript*. Ed. Derek Pearsall. Cambridge: D. S. Brewer, 1990. 1–13.

Echard, Siân. "With Carmen's Help: Latin Authorities in the *Confessio Amantis*." *Studies in Philology* 95 (1998): 1–40.

Eisner, Sigmund. "Chaucer as a Technical Writer." *Chaucer Review* 19, no. 3 (1985): 179–201.

Elliott, Ralph W. V. *Chaucer's English*. London: Deutsch, 1974.

Evans, Cheryl, and Anne Millard. *Greek Myths and Legends*. London: Usborne, 1985.

Evans, D. Simon. *A Grammar of Middle Welsh*. Oxford: Dublin Institute for Advanced Studies, 1976.

Evans, G. R. *The Language and Logic of the Bible: The Earlier Middle Ages*. Cambridge: Cambridge University Press, 1984.

Everett, Dorothy. "A Note on 'Ypotis.' " *Review of English Sudies* 6 (1930): 446–48.

Farnham, Anthony. "Statement and Search in the *Confessio Amantis*." *Mediaevalia* 16 (1993): 141–58.

Fasold, Ralph. *The Sociolinguistics of Society*. New York: Basil Blackwell, 1984.

Fetterley, Judith. *The Resisting Reader: A Feminist Approach to American Fiction*. Bloomington: Indiana University Press, 1978.

Field, E. M. *The Child and His Book: Some Account of the History and Progress of Children's Literature in England*. 2nd ed. London: Wells Gardner, Darnton, 1892.

Finucane, Ronald C. *The Rescue of the Innocents: Endangered Children in Medieval Miracles*. New York: St. Martin's, 1997.

Fisher, John H. *John Gower: Moral Philosopher and Friend of Chaucer*. New York: New York University Press, 1964.

———, R. Wayne Hamm, Peter G. Beidler, and Robert F. Yeager. "John Gower." Hartung 7: 2195–210, 2398–418.

Fleckenstein, Joseph. "Karl der Grosse und sein Hof." In *Karl der Grosse: Lebenswerke und Nachleben*. Vol. 1 Ed. W. Braunfels. Dusseldorf: 1965. 25–50.

Fletcher, Alan J. "The Faith of a Simple Man: Carpenter John's Creed in the *Miller's Tale*." *Medium Ævum* 61 (1992): 96–105.

Ford, Patrick K. "The Poet as Cyfarwydd in Early Welsh Tradition." *Studia Celtica* 10/11 (1975–76): 152–62.

Förster, Max. "Das stabreimende ABC des Aristoteles." *Archiv für das Studium der neueren Sprachen und Literaturen* 117 (1906): 301–3.

————. "Die mittelenglische Sprichwörtersammlung in Douce 52." In *Festschrift zum XII. Allgemeinen Deutschen Neuphilologentage in München, Pfingsten 1906*. Ed. E. Stollreither. Erlangen: Verlag von Fr. Junge, 1906. 40–60.

————. "Zu dem mittelenglischen *ABC of Aristotle*." *Archiv für das Studium der neueren Sprachen und Literaturen* 117 (1906): 371–75.

Fowler, Alastair. *Triumphal Forms: Structural Patterns in Elizabethan Poetry*. Cambridge: Cambridge University Press, 1970.

Gardiner-Scott, Tanya. "The Missing Link: An Edition of the Middle English 'Ypotis' from York Minster MS XVI.L.12." *Traditio* 46 (1991): 235–59.

Garmonsway, G. N. "The Development of the Colloquy." In *The Anglo-Saxons*. Ed. Peter Clemoes. London: Bowes & Bowes, 1959. 248–61.

Gaylord, Alan T. " 'After the Forme of My Writynge': Gower's Bookish Prosody." *Mediaevalia* 16 (1993): 257–88.

Gieben, Servus. "Robert Grossetest and Medieval Courtesy-Books." *Vivarium* 5 (1967): 47–74.

Gillespie, Vincent. "Vernacular Books of Religion." In *Book Production and Publishing in Britain 1375–1475*. Ed. Jeremy Griffiths and Derek Pearsall. Cambridge: Cambridge University Press 1989. 317–44.

Gneuss, Helmut. "Anglo-Saxon Libraries from the Conversion to the Benedictine Reform." *Settimane di studio del Centro italiano di studi sull'alto medioevo* 32 (1986): 643–99.

Godwin, William. *Life of Geoffrey Chaucer*. 2 vols. London: T. Davison for R. Phillips, 1803.

Goodich, Michael. "Bartholomaeus Angelicus on Child-Rearing." *Journal of Psychohistory* 3 (1975): 75–84.

————. "Childhood and Adolescence among the Thirteenth Century Saints." *History of Childhood Quarterly* 1 (1973): 285–309.

Grady, Frank. "The Lancastrian Gower and the Limits of Exemplarity." *Speculum* 70 (1995): 552–75.

Grayzel, Solomon. *The Church and the Jews in the XIIIth Century*. Vol. 2, 1254–1314. Ed. Kenneth R. Stow. Detroit: Wayne State University Press, 1989.

Green, R. P. H. *Seven Versions of Carolingian Pastoral*. Reading, PA: Department of Classics, Reading University, 1980.

————. "The Genesis of a Medieval Textbook: The Models and Sources of the *Ecloga Theoduli*." *Viator* 13 (1982): 49–106.

Green, Richard Firth. *Poets and Princepleasers: Literature and the English Court in the Late Middle Ages*. Toronto: University of Toronto Press, 1980.

Grigsby, John. "A New Source of the *Livre du Chevalier de la Tour Landry*." *Romania* 84 (1963): 171–208.

Gruber, H. "Beitraege zu dem Mittelenglischen Dialoge 'Ipotis.' " *Anglia* 18 (1896): 56–82.

Gruffydd, William John. *Folklore and Myth in the Mabinogion*. Cardiff: University of Wales Press, 1958.

————. *Math vab Mathonwy: An Inquiry into the Origins and Development of the Fourth Branch of the Mabinogi with the Text and a Translation*. Cardiff: University of Wales Press Board, 1928.

Guddat-Figge, Gisela. *Catalogue of Manuscripts Containing Middle English Romances*. Munich: Wilhelm Fink Verlag, 1976.

Gunther, R. T. *Chaucer and Messahala on the Astrolabe. Early Science in Oxford*. 15 vols. Vol. 5. Oxford: Oxford University Press, 1929.

Hamilton, George L. "Theodulus: A Mediaeval Textbook." *Modern Philology* 7 (1909–10): 169–85.

———. "Theodulus in France." *Modern Philology* 8 (1910–11): 611–12.

———. "Les Sources du *Tiaudelet*." *Romania* 48 (1922): 124–27.

Hanawalt, Barbara. "Childrearing among the Lower Classes of Late Medieval England." *Journal of Interdisciplinary History* 8 (1972): 1–22.

———. "Conception through Infancy in Medieval English Historical and Folklore Sources." *Folklore Forum* 13 (1980): 127–57.

———. *Growing Up in Medieval London: The Experience of Childhood in History*. London: Oxford University Press, 1993.

———. *The Ties That Bound: Peasant Families in Medieval England*. London: Oxford University Press, 1986.

Hanford, James Holly. "Classical Eclogue and Mediaeval Debate." *Romanic Review* 2 (1911): 16–31 and 129–43.

Hardman, Phillipa. "A Medieval 'Library in Parvo.' " *Medium Aevum* 47 (1978): 268–73.

Harris, Leslie A. "Instructional Poetry for Medieval Children." *English Studies* 74, no. 2 (1993): 124–33.

Hartung, Albert, ed. *A Manual of Writings in Middle English, 1050–1500*. 9 vols. Hamden, CT: Shoe String Press, 1967–1993.

Henry, Robert. *History of Great Britain, from the First Invasion of It by the Romans under Julius Caesar*. 6 vols. London: 1781.

Herlihy, David. "Domestic Roles and Family Sentiments in the Later Middle Ages." In *Medieval Households*. Harvard: Harvard University Press, 1985. 112–30.

———. "The Family and Religious Ideologies in Medieval Europe." *Journal of Family History* 12 (1987): 3–17.

———. "The Making of the Medieval Family." *Journal of Family History* 8 (1983): 116–30.

———. "Medieval Children." In *Essays on Medieval Civilization: The Walter Prescott Webb Lectures*. Ed. B. K. Lackner and K. R. Philip. Austin: University of Texas Press, 1978. 109–42.

Herrtage, Sidney J. H. Introduction. In *Early English Versions of the* Gesta Romanorum. Ed. Sidney J. H. Herrtage. EETS e.s. 33. London: N. Trübner, 1879.

Hexter, Ralph J. *Ovid and Medieval Schooling*. Munich: Arbeo-Gesellschaft, 1986.

Hill, J. W. F. *Medieval Lincoln*. Cambridge: Cambridge University Press, 1948.

Hiscoe, David W. "Heavenly Sign and Comic Design in Gower's *Confessio Amantis*." In *Sign, Sentence, Discourse: Language in Medieval Thought and Literature*. Ed. Julian N. Wasserman and Lois Roney. Syracuse, NY: Syracuse University Press, 1989. 228–44.

Ho, Cynthia. "As Good as Her Word: Women's Language in *The Knight of the Tour d'Landry*." In *The Rusted Hauberk: Feudal Ideals of Order and Their Decline*.

Ed. Liam O. Purdon and Cindy L. Vitto. Gainesville: University Press of Florida, 1994. 99–120.

Hollingdale, Peter. "Ideology and the Children's Book." In *Literature for Children*. Ed. Peter Hunt. London: Routledge, 1992. 19–40.

Howatson, M. C., ed. *The Oxford Companion to Classical Literature*. Oxford: Oxford University Press, 1989.

Hunt, Peter. "Defining Children's Literature." In *Only Connect: Readings on Children's Literature*. 3rd ed. Ed. Sheila Egoff, Gordon Stubbs, Ralph Ashley, and Wendy Sutton. Oxford: Oxford University Press, 1996. 2–17.

———. Introduction. *Literature for Children: Contemporary Criticism*. Ed. Peter Hunt. London: Routledge, 1992. 1–17.

Hurt, James. *Ælfric*. New York: Twayne, 1972.

Irvine, Martin. *The Making of Textual Culture: "Grammatica" and Literary Theory, 350–1100*. Cambridge University Press, 1994.

Jambeck, Thomas J., and Karen K. Jambeck. "Chaucer's *Treatise on the Astrolabe*: A Handbook for the Medieval Child." *Children's Literature* 3 (1974): 116–22.

James, M. R. *A Descriptive Catalogue of the Manuscripts in the Library of Lambeth Palace*. Cambridge: Cambridge University Press, 1932.

Janson, H. W. *Apes and Ape Lore in the Middle Ages and the Renaissance*. London: University of London, 1952.

Johnston, Mark D. "The Treatment of Speech in Medieval Ethical and Courtesy Literature." *Rhetorica* 4 (1986): 21–46.

Jolliffe, P. S. *A Check-List of Middle English Prose Writings of Spiritual Guidance*. Toronto: Pontifical Institute of Mediaeval Studies, 1974.

Jones, Edgar. "Ancient Myths and Modern Children." *Use of English* 37, no. 1 (1985): 25–34.

Jones, Glyn E. "Early Prose: The *Mabinogi*." In *A Guide to Welsh Literature. Vol. 1*. Rev. ed. Ed. A. O. H. Jarman and Gwilym Rees Hughes. Cardiff: University of Wales Press, 1992. 189–202.

Jones, Gwyn, and Thomas Jones, trans. *The Mabinogion*. London: Everyman, 1974.

Jones, J. Gwynfor. "Government and the Welsh Community: The North-East Borderland in the Fifteenth Century." In *British Government and Administration: Studies Presented to S. B. Chrimes*. Eds. H. Hearder and H. R. Loyn. Cardiff: University of Wales Press, 1974. 55–68.

Jones, R. M. "Narrative Structure in Medieval Welsh Prose Tales." In *Proceedings of the Seventh International Congress of Celtic Studies*. Ed. D. Ellis Evans. Oxford: Oxbow, 1986. 171–198. Rpt. in Sullivan, *The Mabinogi*, 217–62.

Justice, Steven. *Writing and Rebellion: England in 1381*. Berkeley: University of California Press, 1994.

Kalinke, Marianne E. "Rev. of '*Gesta Romanorum*, Teil 1, Untersuchungen zu Konzeption und Uberlieferung, vol. 2, Texte, Verzeichnisse,' by Brigitte Weiske." *Journal of English and Germanic Philology* 93 (1994): 611–13.

Kelley, Douglas. "The *Fidus interpres*: Aid or Impediment to Medieval Translation and *Translatio*?" In *Translation Theory and Practice in the Middle Ages*. Ed. Jeanette Beer. Studies in Medieval Culture 38. Kalamazoo, MI: Medieval Institute, 1997. 47–58.

Kellogg, A. L., and Ernest W. Talbert. "The Wyclifite *Pater Noster* and *Ten Commandments*, with Special Reference to English MSS. 85 and 90 in the John Rylands Library." *Bulletin of the John Rylands Library* 42 (1959–60): 345–77.

Ker, Neil R. *Catalogue of Manuscripts Containing Anglo-Saxon.* Oxford: Clarendon, 1957.

Kittredge, George Lyman. "Lewis Chaucer or Lewis Clifford." *Modern Philology* 14, no. 9 (1917): 513–18.

Knoepflmacher, U. C., and Mitzi Myers. "From the Editors: 'Cross-Writing' and the Reconceptualizing of Children's Literary Studies." *Children's Literature* 25 (1997): vii–xvii.

Kristol, Andres Max. "L'enseignement du français en angleterre (XIIIe–XVe siecles) les sources manuscrites." *Romania* (1990): 289–330.

———. *Manières de langage (1396, 1399, 1415).* London: Anglo-Norman Text Society, 1995.

Krueger, Roberta. "Intergeneric Combination and the Anxiety of Gender in *Le Livre du Chevalier de la Tour Landry pour l'enseignement de ses filles.*" *L'Esprit Créateur* 33 (1993): 61–72.

Laistner, M. L. W. *Thought and Letters in Western Europe.* Ithaca, NY: Cornell University Press, 1931.

Landau, G. *Beiträge zur Geschichte der Jagd und der Falknerei in Deutschland.* Kaffel: Theodor Fischer, 1849.

Langmuir, Gavin I. "The Knight's Tale of Young Hugh of Lincoln." *Speculum* 47 (1972): 459–82.

Lapidge, Michael. "Æthelwold as Scholar and Teacher." In *Bishop Æthelwold: His Career and Influence.* Ed. Barbara Yorke. Woodbridge, Suffolk: Boydell, 1988. 89–118.

Leach, Arthur Francis. *The Schools of Medieval England.* London: Methuen, 1915.

Lee, B. S. "Seen and Sometimes Heard: Piteous and Pert Children in Medieval English Literature." *Children's Literature Association Quarterly* 23 (1998): 40–48.

Lerer, Seth. *Chaucer and His Readers: Imagining the Author in Late-Medieval England.* Princeton, NJ: Princeton University Press, 1993.

Lesnik-Oberstein, Karín. *Children's Literature: Criticism and the Fictional Child.* Oxford: Clarendon, 1994.

Lester, G. A. *The Index of Middle English Prose. Handlist 2: John Rylands University Library of Manchester and Chetham's Library, Manchester.* Cambridge: D. S. Brewer, 1985.

Lewis, C. S. "Gower." In *The Allegory of Love: A Study in Medieval Tradition.* New York: Galaxy, 1936. 198–222.

Lewis, R. E., N. F. Blake, and A. S. G. Edwards. *Index of Printed Middle English Prose.* New York: Garland, 1985.

Louis, Cameron. "Proverbs, Precepts, and Monitory Pieces." *Hartung* 9: 2957–3048, 3349–3404.

Lounsbury, Thomas R. *Studies in Chaucer.* 3 vols. New York: Harper & Bros., 1892.

Mac Cana, Proinsias. *The Mabinogi.* 2nd ed. Cardiff: University of Wales Press, 1992.

Macaulay, G. C. "John Gower." In *The End of the Middle Ages*. Vol. 2 of *The Cambridge History of English Literature*. Ed. A. W. Ward and A. R. Waller. 2nd ed. Cambridge: Cambridge University Press, 1932. 133–55.

Madeleva, M. "A Child's Book of Stars." In *A Lost Language and Other Essays on Chaucer*. New York: Sheed and Ward, 1951. 89–99.

Manly, J. M. "Litel Lewis My Sone." *Times Literary Supplement*, June 1, 1928, 430.

Mann, Jill. *Chaucer and Medieval Estates Satire: The Literature of Social Classes and the General Prologue to the Canterbury Tales*. Cambridge: Cambridge University Press, 1973.

———. "Beast Epic and Fable." In *Medieval Latin: A Bibliographical Guide*. Ed. F. A. C. Mantello and A. G. Rigg. Washington, DC: Catholic University Press, 1996. 556–61.

Marchalonis, Shirley. "Medieval Symbols and the *Gesta Romanorum*." *Chaucer Review* 8 (1974): 311–19.

Marcus, Ralph. "Alphabetic Acrostics in the Hellenistic and Roman Periods." *Journal of Near Eastern Studies* 6 (1947): 109–15.

Markus, R. A., ed. *Gregory the Great and His World*. Cambridge: Cambridge University Press, 1997.

Márkus, Gilbert. "What Were Patrick's Alphabets?" *Cambrian Medieval Celtic Studies* 31 (1996): 1–15.

Martin, Anthony. "The Middle English Versions of *The Ten Commandments*, with Special Reference to Rylands MS 85." *Bulletin of the John Rylands Library* 64 (1981): 191–217.

Martin, C. A. "Middle English Manuals of Religious Instruction." In *So Meny People Longages and Tonges: Philological Essays in Scots and Mediaeval English Presented to Angus McIntosh*. Ed. Michael Benskin and M. L. Samuels. Edinburgh: Middle English Dialect Project, 1981. 283–98.

Mason, John. *Gentlefolk in the Making: Studies in the History of English Courtesy Literature and Related Topics from 1531 to 1774*. Philadelphia: University of Pennsylvania Press, 1935.

May, Jill P. *Children's Literature and Critical Theory: Reading and Writing for Understanding*. New York: Oxford University Press, 1995.

McDowell, Myles. "Fiction for Children and Adults: Some Essential Differences." *Children's Literature in Education* 10 (1973): 551–63.

McGregor, J. H. "Ovid at School: From the Ninth to the Fifteenth Century." *Classical Folia* 32 (1976): 29–51.

Meale, Carol M. "The Miracles of Our Lady: Context and Interpretation." In *Studies in the Vernon Manuscript*. Ed. Derek Pearsall. Cambridge: D. S. Brewer, 1990. 115–136.

Mearns, Rodney, ed. *The Vision of Tundale*. Heidelberg: Carl Winter, 1985.

Mehl, Dieter. *The Middle English Romances of the Thirteenth and Fourteenth Centuries*. London: Routledge and Kegan Paul, 1969.

Meigs, Cornelia, Anne Thaxter Eaton, Elizabeth Nesbitt, and Ruth Hill Viguers. *A Critical History of Children's Literature*. New York: Macmillan, 1953.

Merrilees, Brian. "Donatus and the Teaching of French in Medieval England." In *Anglo-Norman Anniversary Essays*. Ed. Ian Short. London: Anglo-Norman Text Society, 1993. 273–91.

Millett, Fred B. *English Courtesy Literature before 1557*. Kingston, Ont.: Jackson, 1919.

Moran, Jo Ann Hoeppner. *The Growth of English Schooling 1340–1548*. Princeton: Princeton University Press, 1985.

Mosher, Joseph Albert. *The Exemplum in the Early Religious and Didactic Literature of England*. New York: AMS, 1966.

Murray's Small Classical Atlas. Ed. G. B. Grundy. 2nd ed. London: John Murray, 1917.

Mussafia, Adolf. "Studien zu den mittelalterlichen Marienlegenden." *Sitzungsberichte der kaiserlichen Akademie der Wissenschaften in Wien (phil.-hist. Klasse)*. 113 (Vienna, 1886) 917–94; 115 (Vienna, 1887) 5–93; 119. ix (Vienna, 1889) 1–66; 123. viii (Vienna, 1890) 1–85; 139. viii (Vienna, 1898) 1–74.

Nicholls, Jonathan. *The Matter of Courtesy: Medieval Courtesy Books and the Gawain-Poet*. Woodbridge, Suffolk: D. S. Brewer, 1985.

Nicholson, Peter. "The 'Confession' in Gower's *Confessio Amantis*." *Studia Neophilologica* 58, no. 2 (1986): 193–204.

Nodelman, Perry. *The Pleasures of Children's Literature*. 2nd ed. White Plains, NY: Longman, 1996.

North, J. D. *Chaucer's Universe*. Oxford: Oxford University Press, 1987.

———. *The Norton History of Astronomy and Cosmology*. New York: Norton, 1995.

Opie, Iona, and Peter Opie. *Children's Games in Street and Playground*. Oxford: Oxford University Press, 1969.

———. *The Lore and Language of School Children*. Oxford: Oxford University Press, 1959.

———, eds. *The Oxford Dictionary of Nursery Rhymes*. Oxford: Oxford University Press, 1951.

Orme, Nicholas. "Children and Literature in Medieval England." *Medium Aevum* 68 (1999): 218–46.

———. "The Culture of Children in Medieval England." *Past and Present* 146 (February 1995): 48–88.

———. *English Schools in the Middle Ages*. London: Methuen, 1973.

———. *Medieval Children*. New Haven: Yale UP, 2001.

Osborn, Marijane. "Chaucer's Dantean Presentation of Time in *The Canterbury Tales*: Libra and the Moon." *Vistas in Astronomy* 39 (1995): 605–14.

———. "The Squire's 'Steed of Brass' as Astrolabe: Some Implications for the *Canterbury Tales*." In *Hermeneutics and Medieval Culture*. Ed. Patrick Gallacher and Helen Damico. Albany: SUNY, 1989: 121–31.

Osternacher, Johannes. *Fünfter Jahresbericht des bischöflichen Privat-Gymnasiums am Kollegium Petrinum in Urfahr für das Schuljahr 1901/02*. Urfahr: Kollegium Petrinum, 1902.

———. *Quos auctores Latinos et sacrorum Bibliorum locos Theodolus imitatus esse videatur*. Urfahr: propre Lentium, 1907.

———. "Die ueberlieferung der *Ecloga Theoduli*. *Neues Archiv der Gesellschaft fuer aeltere deutsche Geschichtskundei* 40 (1915–16): 331–76.

Owen, Charles A., Jr., ed. *Discussions of the Canterbury Tales*. 1961. Westport, CT: Greenwood, 1978.

Owens-Crocker, Gale R. "Hawks and Horse-Trappings: The Insignia of Rank." In *The Battle of Maldon A.D. 991*. Ed. Donald Scragg. Oxford: Basil Blackwell, 1991. 220–238.

Parkes, M. B. *English Cursive Book Hands 1250–1500*. 1969. Rpt. Berkeley: University of California Press, 1980.

———. *Pause and Effect*: *An Introduction to the History of Punctuation in the West*. Berkeley: University of California Press, 1993.

Pearsall, Derek. *The Canterbury Tales*. London: George Allen & Unwin, 1985.

———, ed. *Studies in the Vernon Manuscript*. Cambridge: D. S. Brewer, 1990.

———. "Rev. of *The Winchester Anthology*: *A Facsimile of Additional Manuscript 60577 with an Introduction and List of Contents by Edward Wilson and an Account of the Music by Iain Fenlon*." *Notes & Queries* 228 (1983): 162–65.

Peck, Russell A. *Kingship and Common Profit in Gower's* Confessio Amantis. Carbondale: Southern Illinois University Press, 1978.

Plimpton, George A. *The Education of Chaucer. Illustrated from the Schoolbooks in Use in His Time*. London: Oxford University Press, 1935.

———. *The Education of Shakespeare. Illustrated from the Schoolbooks in Use in His Time*. Oxford: Oxford University Press, 1933.

Plunkett, T. F. T. "Chaucer's Escapade." *Law Quarterly Review* 64 (1948): 33–36.

Porter, David. "Anglo-Saxon Colloquies: Ælfric, Ælfric Bata and *De Raris Fabulis Retractata*." *Neophilologus* 81 (1997): 467–80.

———. *Anglo-Saxon Conversations*: *The Colloquies of Ælfric Bata*. Woodbridge, Suffolk: Boydell, 1997.

———. "The Latin Syllabus in Anglo-Saxon Monastic Schools." *Neophilologus* 78 (1994): 463–82.

Potter, Robert. *The English Morality Play*: *Origins, History, and Influence of a Dramatic Tradition*. London: Routledge, 1975.

Power, Eileen. "The Ménagier's Wife." In *Medieval People*. New York: Doubleday, 1924. 99–124.

Raby, F. J. E. "*Turris Alethie* and the *Ecloga Theoduli*." *Medium Aevum* 34 (1964): 226–29.

Raymo, Robert R. "Works of Religious and Philosophical Instruction." Hartung 7: 2255–2378; bibl. 2467–2582.

Rex, Richard. "Chaucer and the Jews." In "*The Sins of Madame Eglentyne*" *and Other Essays on Chaucer*. Newark: University of Delaware Press, 1995. 13–26.

Riché, Pierre. *Education and Culture in the Barbarian West*: *From the Sixth through the Eighth Century*. Trans. John J. Contreni. Columbia: University of South Carolina Press, 1976.

———, Guy Devailly, André Mussat, and Léon Fleuriot. "De L'Amorique a la Bretagne." In *Documents de L'Histoire de la Bretagne*. Ed. Jean Delumeau. Toulouse: Privat, 1971. 69–104.

Rigg, A. G. *A History of Anglo-Latin Literature, 1066–1422*. Cambridge: Cambridge University Press, 1992.

Robbins, Rossell Hope. "The Poems of Humfrey Newton, Esquire, 1466–1536." *Publications of the Modern Language Association* 65 (1950): 259–60.

———, and John Levi Cutler. *Supplement to the Index of Middle English Verse*. Lexington: University Kentucky Press, 1965.

Roberts, Brynley F. *Studies on Middle Welsh Literature*. Lewiston: Edwin Mellon, 1992.

Robinson, P. R. "The Vernon Manuscript as a 'Coucher Book.' " In *Studies in the Vernon Manuscript*. Ed. Derek Pearsall. Cambridge: D. S. Brewer, 1990. 15–28.

Robson, Margaret. "Animal Magic: Moral Regeneration in *Sir Gowther*." *Yearbook of English Studies* 22 (1992): 140–153.

Rothwell, William. "A Mis-Judged Author and a Mis-Used Text: Walter de Bibbesworth and His 'Tretiz.' " *Modern Language Review* 77 (1982): 282–93.

Rubin, David Lee, and A. Lytton Sells. "Fable." In *The New Princeton Encyclopedia of Poetry and Poetics*. Ed. Alex Preminger and T. V. F. Brogan. Princeton, NJ: Princeton University Press, 1993. 400–1.

Saccio, Peter. *Shakespeare's English Kings: History, Chronicle, and Drama*. New York: Oxford University Press, 1977.

Saunders, Corinne. " 'Symtyme the fende': Questions of Rape in *Sir Gowther*." In *Doubt Wisely: Papers in Honour of E. G. Stanley*. London: Routledge and Kegan Paul, 1996. 286–303.

Schultz James A. *The Knowledge of Childhood in the German Middle Ages, 1100–1350*. Philadelphia: University of Pennsylvania Press, 1995.

Shahar, Shulamith. *Childhood in the Middle Ages*. London: Routledge, 1990.

Shaner, Mary. "Instruction and Delight: Medieval Romances as Children's Literature." *Poetics Today* 13 (1992): 1–15.

Shavit, Zohar. *The Poetics of Children's Literature*. Athens: University of Georgia Press, 1986.

Skeat, W. W. "An Anglo-Saxon Enigma." *Athenaeum* 24 (April 1897): 543.

Smith, David Eugene. Rara Arithmetica: *A Catalogue of the Arithmetics Written before the Year MDCI, with a Description of Those in the Library of George Arthur Plimpton of New York*. Boston: Ginn, 1908.

———. *Addenda*. 1939. New York: Chelsea, 1970.

Smith, Elva S. *The History of Children's Literature: A Syllabus with Selected Bibliographies*. Rev. ed. by Margaret Hodges and Susan Steinfirst. Chicago: American Library Association, 1980.

Southern, Richard. *The Staging of Plays before Shakespeare*. London: Faber, 1973.

Southern, R. W. "The English Origins of the 'Miracles of the Virgin,' " *Mediaeval and Renaissance Studies* 4 (1958): 176–216.

Spivack, Bernard. *Shakespeare and the Allegory of Evil*. New York: Columbia University Press, 1958.

Steadman, John M. "The *Ecloga Theoduli*, the *General Estoria*, and the Perseus-Bellerophon Myth. *Mediaeval Studies* 24 (1962): 384–87.

Stephens, John, and Robyn McCallum. *Retelling Stories: Traditional Story and Metanarrative in Children's Literature*. New York: Garland, 1998.

Stevens, Martin. "The Royal Stanza in Early English Literature." *Publications of the Modern Language Association* 94 (1979): 62–76.

Stock, Brian. *Myth and Science in the Twelfth Century: A Study of Bernard Silvester*. Princeton, N.J.: Princeton UP, 1972.

Stow, George B. "Richard II in John Gower's *Confessio Amantis*: Some Historical Perspectives." *Mediaevalia* 16 (1993): 3–31.

Strecker, Karl. "Ist Gottschalk der Dichter der *Ecloga Theoduli?*" *Neues Archiv der Gesellschaft fur altere deutsche Geschichtskunde* 45 (1923–24): 18–23.

Strohm, Paul. *Social Chaucer*. Cambridge: Harvard University Press, 1989.

Suchier, Walther. *L'Enfant Sage*. Dresden: Max Niemeyer, 1910.

———. *Das Mittellateinische Gespräch Adrian und Epictitus: nebst verwandten Texten (Joca Monachorum)*. Tubingen: Max Niemeyer, 1955.

Sullivan, C. W., III. "Inheritance and Lordship in Math." *Transactions of the Honourable Society of Cymmrodorion* (1990): 45–63. Rpt. in Sullivan, *The Mabinogi,* 347–66.

———, ed. *The Mabinogi: A Book of Essays*. New York: Garland, 1996.

Sutherland, Robert D. "Hidden Persuaders: Political Ideologies in Literature for Children." *Children's Literature in Education* 16, no. 3 (1985): 143–57.

Sutton, Josephine D. "Hitherto Unprinted Manuscripts of the Middle English *Ipotis*." *Publications of the Modern Language Association* 31 (1916): 114–60.

Tarvers, Josephine Koster. "The Abesse's *ABC*." *Yearbook of Langland Studies* 2 (1988): 137–41.

Tatar, Maria. *Off with Their Heads! Fairy Tales and the Culture of Childhood*. Princeton, NJ: Princeton University Press, 1997.

Teskey, Gordon. *Allegory and Violence*. Ithaca, NY: Cornell University Press, 1996.

Thomas, Joyce. "The Tales of the Brothers Grimm: In the Black Forest." In *Fairy Tales, Fables, Myths, Legends, and Poetry*. Vol. 2 of *Touchstones: Reflections on the Best in Children's Literature*. Ed. Perry Nodelman. West Lafayette, IN: Children's Literature Association, 1987. 104–17.

Tryon, Ruth W. "Miracles of Our Lady in Middle English Verse." *Publications of the Modern Language Association* 38 (1923): 308–88.

Tucker, Nicholas. *The Child and the Book: A Psychological and Literary Exploration*. Cambridge: Cambridge University Press, 1981.

Tuer, Andrew W. *History of the Horn-Book*. 1897. New York: Benjamin Blom, 1968.

Turville-Petre, Thorlac. *The Alliterative Revival*. Cambridge: D. S. Brewer, 1977.

Utley, Francis Lee. "Dialogues, Debates, and Catechisms." Hartung 3: 669–745.

———. *A Manual of the Writings in Middle English 1050–1500*. Ed. A. Hartung. 1972. 742–3 and 900.

Valente, Roberta L. "Gwydion and Aranrhod: Crossing the Borders of Gender in Math." *Bulletin of the Board of Celtic Studies* 35 (1988): 1–9. Rpt. in Sullivan, *The Mabinogi,* 331–45.

Vandelinde, Henry. "*Sir Gowther*: Saintly Knight and Knightly Saint." *Neophilologus* 80 (1996): 139–47.

Vitto, Cindy L. "*Sir Gawain and the Green Knight* as Adolescent Literature: Essential Lessons." *Children's Literature Association Quarterly* 23, no. 1 (1998): 22–28.

Walker, Sue Sheridan. "The Feudal Family and the Common Law Courts: The Pleas Protecting Rights of Wardship and Marriage, c. 1225–1375." *Journal of Medieval History* 14 (1988): 13–31.

———. "Widow and Ward: The Feudal Law of Child Custody in Medieval England." In *Women in Medieval Society*. Ed. Susan Mosher Stuard. Philadelphia: University of Pennsylvania Press, 1976. 159–72.

———. "Wrongdoing and Compensation: The Pleas of Wardship in Thirteenth and Fourteenth Century." *Journal of Legal History* 9 (1988): 267–307.

Wall, Barbara. *The Narrator's Voice: The Dilemma of Children's Fiction*. New York: St. Martin's, 1991.

Wallace-Hadrill, J. M. *Bede's Ecclesiastical History of the English People*: *A Historical Commentary*. Oxford: Clarendon, 1988.

Walter, Jean Thiébaut. *L'Exemplum dans la littérature religieuse et didactique du moyen âge*. Paris: Occitania, 1927. New York: AMS, 1973.

Ward, A. W., and A. R. Waller. *The Cambridge History of English Literature*. 15 vols. New York: Putnam, 1907–33.

Ward, Benedicta. *Miracles and the Medieval Mind: Theory, Record and Event*. Ed. Edward Peters. Philadelphia: University of Pennsylvania Press, 1982.

Ward, H. L. D. *Catalogue of Romances*. Department of Manuscripts in the British Museum. Vols. I and II. London, 1883.

Warton, Thomas. "On the *Gesta Romanorum*." In *The History of English Poetry from the Close of the Eleventh Century to the Commencement of the Eighteenth Century to Which Are Prefixed Three Dissertations*. Vol. 1 of 3. 1824. London: Richard and John E. Taylor, 1840.

Wasserman, Julian. Afterword. In *Allegoresis: The Craft of Allegory in Medieval Literature*. Ed. J. Stephen Russell. New York: Garland, 1988. 215–27.

Waugh, Evelyn. *Brideshead Revisited*. Boston: Little, Brown, 1945.

Welsh, Andrew. "The Traditional Narrative Motifs of the Four Branches of the *Mabinogi*." *Cambridge Medieval Celtic Studies* 15 (Summer 1988): 51–62.

———. "Doubling and Incest in the *Mabinogi*." *Speculum* 65, no. 2 (April 1990): 344–62.

West, Andrew Fleming. *Alcuin and the Rise of the Christian Schools*. New York: Scribners, 1901.

Wetherbee, Winthrop. "Genius and Interpretation in the *Confessio Amantis*." In *Magister Regis: Studies in Honor of Robert Earl Kaske*. Ed. Arthur Groos with Emerson Brown, Jr., Thomas D. Hill, Giuseppe Mazzotta, and Joseph S. Wittig. New York: Fordham University Press, 1986. 241–60.

———. "John Gower." *The Cambridge History of Medieval English Literature*. Ed. David Wallace. Cambridge: Cambridge University Press, 1999.

Whiting, Bartlett Jere. *Proverbs, Sentences, and Proverbial Phrases from English Writings Mainly before 1500*. Cambridge: Harvard University Press, 1968.

Wickert, Maria. *Studies in John Gower*. Trans. Robert J. Meindl. 1953. Washington, D.C.: University Press of America, 1981.

Wolpe, Berthold. "*Florilegium Alphabeticum*: Alphabets in Medieval Manuscripts." In *Calligraphy and Palaeography: Essays Presented to Alfred Fairbank on his 70th birthday*. Ed. A. S. Osley. New York: October House, 1966. 69–74 & plates.

Wolter, Eugen. "Der Judenknabe. 5 Griechische, 14 Lateinische und 8 Französische Texte." In *Bibliotheca Normannica*. Ed. Hermann Suchier. Halle: Max Niemeyer, 1879. 2: 1–128.

Wright, Roger, ed. *Latin and the Romance Languages in the Early Middle Ages*. University Park: Pennsylvania State University Press, 1996.

Wülcker, R. P. *Altenglisches lesebuch*. Vol. 2. Halle: Max Niemeyer, 1879.

Yeager, R. F. "John Gower and the Exemplum Form: Tale Models in the *Confessio Amantis*." *Mediaevalia* 8 (1982): 307–35.

———. *John Gower's Poetic: The Search for a New Arion*. Cambridge: Boydell and Brewer, 1990.

Index